Leveraging Lean in Surgical Services

Creating a Cost Effective, Standardized, High Quality, Patient-Focused Operation

Leveraging Lean in Surgical Services

Creating a Cost Effective, Standardized, High Quality, Patient-Focused Operation

Joyce Kerpchar • Charles Protzman • George Mayzell, MD

CRC Press
Taylor & Francis Group
Boca Raton   London   New York

CRC Press is an imprint of the
Taylor & Francis Group, an **informa** business
A PRODUCTIVITY PRESS BOOK

CRC Press
Taylor & Francis Group
6000 Broken Sound Parkway NW, Suite 300
Boca Raton, FL 33487-2742

© 2015 by Charles Protzman, Joyce Kerpchar, and George Mayzell
CRC Press is an imprint of Taylor & Francis Group, an Informa business

No claim to original U.S. Government works

Printed on acid-free paper
Version Date: 20141110

International Standard Book Number-13: 978-1-4822-3449-7 (Paperback)

Visit the Taylor & Francis Web site at
http://www.taylorandfrancis.com

and the CRC Press Web site at
http://www.crcpress.com

Contents

SECTION I

SECTION II

Preface: Leveraging Lean in the Surgical Services

This book is intended as guide for healthcare executives and leaders, managers, process improvement team members, and inquisitive frontline workers who want to implement and leverage Lean in the Perioperative Service Area. Its foundation is based upon the Shingo prize winning book, *Leveraging Lean in Healthcare: Transforming Your Enterprise into a High Quality Patient-Care Delivery System*.[1] The core chapters provide detailed information on the concepts, principles and implementation of Lean in the healthcare environment. We felt it was critical to provide the reader with a broad foundation on the application of Lean in healthcare so one can see the how Lean can be applied throughout the continuum of care from the emergency room, to surgery and other support services. Lean concepts and tools can begin in any clinical or non-clinical support area within an integrated delivery system and universally applied.

High-Quality Patient Care is imperative in healthcare. We strive for the highest quality care systems, in the pursuit of the triple aim:

1. improving health of the population,
2. enhancing the experience of care (quality and satisfaction i.e., value), and
3. reducing the per capita cost.

Organizations must find effective ways to maximize value. The Lean Business Delivery System is one way to accomplish this.

Lean is a different way to think. It begins with understanding the voice of the customer and focusing on delivering value. Lean provides the foundational concepts and tools to identify and eliminate waste. We do not encourage working faster or harder, as "haste makes wastes," just more efficiently.

Business means that Lean applies to anything that is a process, whether it is part of the physical patient care, information systems, or business systems (i.e., accounting, billing, marketing, etc.). All business processes should flow in order to reduce through the whole system.

Delivery refers to what it takes to deliver your product or service to the customer. The focus is on what value is added to the customer. The delivery of Surgical Services has both internal and external customers. External customers can be employer groups, ACOs (accountable care organizations), or entities that are paying for services and seeking value. They may have a broader vested interest as new payment models evolve as they may be engaging in risk sharing arrangements. Additionally, with the changing healthcare environment and patients becoming more "value" savvy related to pricing, due to increasing copays and coinsurance. Patients and "payors" who may be employer groups or ACOs (Accountable Care Organizations) as well as CMS (through bundled payment models) may be engaging in cost comparisons of procedures, episodes of care, evaluating HCAHPS/patient experience and outcomes. There is a shift in the perspective payment system as hospitals begin to be reimbursed for outcomes and a continued movement to value based care. The internal customers are the surgeons and anesthesia providers who directly render services to the patient as well as physicians who refer patients and healthcare staff who are dependent on efficient, effective processes. Thus there are more customer perspectives than ever to consider.

---

[1] *Leveraging Lean in Healthcare: Transforming Your Enterprise into a High Quality Patient-Care Delivery System*, Proztman, Mayzell, Kerpchar.

System means the surgical or procedural event is part of a larger integrated delivery network or system and is included as part of the supporting infrastructure. There needs to be an effective transition of care as patients move from the medical management to the surgical episode and back, in care delivery. It is more critical than ever to look across the overall hospital or clinical *System* and understanding that every process we try to improve is linked or integrated with other processes. For example, the surgical department relies on effective processes and staff in radiology, laboratory and pharmacy resources in order to produce a surgical stay that is efficient, cost effective, of high quality. It is difficult to change one process without impacting several others, one must continually assess for potential "unintended" consequences.

When you put all these words together, it leads to a culture change that is powerful for any organization. The culture change is such that if you really apply Lean concepts and tools, you can become a world-class leader. If you have started or are considering Baldrige, or the Shingo Prize, Lean positively impacts virtually all the criteria. Baldrige and Lean are about never-ending, continuous iterations of improvement.

The book is divided into two sections by design.

- Section I is a broad overview of the application of Lean in healthcare.
- Section II focuses on Implementing Lean in the Surgical Services.

The chapters are designed, in most cases, to stand alone. Therefore, you will find some repetition throughout the book. Section I defines Lean, the concepts, tools and principles, and key components of implementing Lean. It begins with descriptions of each of the Lean tools and concepts and how to apply them. They are organized in typical order of use and hierarchical priority; however, it should be noted that not all the tools are used all the time or necessarily in the same order. We use the tools when appropriate to solve the problems at hand. We have spent many years studying and implementing Lean in small, medium, and large healthcare systems and organizations, and have found sharing lessons learned can be extremely valuable.

Section II, focuses on the application of Lean in the Surgery Department. The format begins with an overview of the normal operation of each area from a traditional standpoint and where typical problems occur. Then we walk through various Lean initiatives and show how we have used value stream mapping, following the patient and staff, along with other Lean tools for process improvement. We introduce actionable blueprints so results can be duplicated or modified for use at other institutions. We also include examples, stories, case study/results, and lessons learned.

Between the authors, we have read more than 500 books on Lean, Six Sigma, and total quality, many of them from Productivity Press, to which we owe a debt to Norman Bodek, a pioneer in this field. We have been a customer of Productivity Press (now CRC Press) for many years and leveraging their expertise. We use many of these books during our 1, 3 and 5 day Lean training sessions where we have taught students from all over the world.

This book focuses primarily on Lean. It is our experience that the majority of initial productivity improvements in healthcare come from implementing Lean. We recommend using Lean concepts and tools first to streamline processes and eliminate waste, then applying Six Sigma tools to reduce variation in process. It is difficult to utilize the Six Sigma toolset on non-stable or standardized processes.

This book promotes a philosophy based on acting on fact based on measurable results and clear improvements in quality and efficiency. We also point out the tangible and intangible challenges around measuring return on investment (ROI).

Lean is not just an operations initiative. If implemented properly, the Lean philosophy will encourage changes in all aspects and areas of your organization. There are too few pages here to contain all the knowledge and techniques of implementing a Lean business delivery system. Instead, this book strives to include the most basic information that will be common to most processes.

Adopting a Lean culture is discussed, which includes implementing continuous improvement through both scientific management and a respect for people to enable one to make decisions based on data vs. subjective opinions. The tools and implementation tips in this guide are designed to take you out of your comfort zone and provide you with facts to base decisions on who and what is ultimately value-added to your customer.

A journey of a thousand miles begins by taking the initial step.[2]

The pursuit of continuous improvement has no end. The book drives home the importance of viewing your transformation as a Lean journey. After the process has had its first Lean implementation where we change the systems, it is then followed up with ongoing small improvements. Everyone has to make these improvements everyday. It is this ongoing focus on the process which yields significant results over time. Some of these small improvements will turn into large improvements. The good news is we are always searching for the "One Best Way," yet always knowing there more waste to be found and eliminated.

The reader should find encouragement and excitement with each success. We hope you will create your own lessons learned whether by success or setback and share them with us. Your joy must be found in the quest to becoming Lean, because there is no end to what you and your organization can accomplish. We wish you all Good Luck on your Lean journey!

[2] Laozi, http://acc6.its.brooklyn.cuny.edu/~phalsall/texts/taote v3.html, http://www.religiousworlds.com/taoism/ttcstan3.html Lao Tzu, Tao Tc Ching ch. 64.

Acknowledgments

This book includes many of our own firsthand experiences over the years and also references the work and experiences of many other reputable individuals who have worked in the world of Lean. We have been influenced by a great many who have chronicled their own Lean experiences, some of which we have incorporated into this work. We would like to thank all of those, too numerous to mention here, who have worked with us on Lean teams in the past and the senior leadership whose support made them successful. This book would not have been possible without your hard work, perseverance, and courage during our Lean journey together. Again, it would be impossible to cite all of them and, if we overlooked anyone, we truly apologize, but we hope each recognizes that this book wouldn't have come to fruition without their influence and expertise.

We would like to thank the following for their contributions to voluntarily co-author or contribute to the original Shingo prize winning book *Leveraging Lean in Healthcare* as well as the addition of others who made the breakout of the book series possible as listed by type of contributing content:

1. History of Lean—Kenneth Hopper, international consultant and writer on management and industrial management history; co-author of book, *The Puritan Gift*
2. Finance, Marketing, and Our Hospitals—Brian Maskell, president of BMA Associates, who read several drafts of this chapter and provided content, editing advice, and text on the "Lean accounting" part of the chapter
3. Nutritional Services—Shawn Noseworthy, RD, LD, MSA, director of Food and Nutrition Services, Florida Hospital Memorial Medical System
4. Emergency Department
   a. Jody Lazarus, RN, CMAS, CCTC, MBA, BS, manager Nurse Auditing, Patient Financial Services, Adventist Health Systems
   b. Jacob L. Kriedermann, Lake Erie College of Osteopathic Medicine at Seton Hill University
   c. John Lewis, President and CEO, AMCH Hospital
   d. Joyce Wright MS, Executive Director Operational Excellence, AMCH Hospital
5. Inpatient Floors—Douglas C. Johnson, RN, Lean Six Sigma Black Belt and Susan Sanches, RN, MA Lean Sigma Black Belt
6. Laboratory—Mauren Harte, Lean Six Sigma Master Black Belt, HartePro Consulting Primary Care Clinics and Pharmacy—Steve Stenberg, president, Continuous Progress
7. Michael Hogan of Progressive Business Solutions, LLC, whose partnership on many of these hospital projects has been invaluable. Mike's project work and resulting ideas have indirectly contributed to many parts of this book.
8. Special thanks to Rick Malik, Audrey Knable, and JoAnn Hegarty of ValuMetrix® Services for their help and guidance. Business Improvement Group has had a very successful and long-standing strategic partnership with ValuMetrix® Services, the division of Ortho-Clinical Diagnostics that provides expert Lean consulting to hospitals. Working together, we have been able to help healthcare organizations take the first steps along the path of their Lean journeys as we work toward improving healthcare for all. Without ValuMetrix® Services, this book would not have been possible.
9. Presbyterian Hospital in Albuquerque for their help and support: Alison B. Stanley, Director of Process Excellence, Beth Smith, MBA, Director, Perioperative Services for CNM, and Steve Griego, Master Black Belt.
10. Russ Scaffede for his insight into the Toyota System and for his contributions through numerous e-mail correspondence and edits with various parts of the book. He is owner

of Lean Manufacturing Systems Group, LLC and Management Consulting Consultant, vice president of manufacturing at Toyota Boshoku America, past general manager/vice president of Toyota Motor Manufacturing Power Train, and past senior vice president, senior vice president of Global Manufacturing at Donnelly Corporation. Russ is co-author of the book, *The Leadership Roadmap: People, Lean & Innovation*, along with Dwane Baumgardner.

11. Many thanks to Kenneth Hopper and William Hopper for their assistance and input into this book. Kenneth and William are the authors of *The Puritan Gift: Reclaiming the American Dream amidst Global Financial Chaos*; their bios can be found at www.puritangift.com. It was Kenneth who brought the Civil Communications Section's (CCS) existence, mission, and contributions to light. Kenneth interviewed Charles Protzman Sr. in the early 1970s, which resulted in several articles on the CCS.

12. Joel Barker for his permission in referencing the paradigm material so important and integral to Lean implementations.

13. Thanks to Amy Evers, PhD, vice president of Type Resources, Myers-Briggs Type Indicator® certified, for her help and editing suggestions on the MBTI section

14. Thanks to our Productivity Press editor, Kris Mednansky, who has been terrific at guiding us through our first writing project.

15. Many thanks to Cheryl Fenske, Fenske Communications, LLC, for the initial professional edit of the original book.

16. Tim Schindele, Lewis Lefteroff and Brigit Zamora for taking valuable time out of their schedules to provide insightful thoughts, edits, and critiques of the initial drafts.

17. MaryBeth Protzman for her help in typing, editing, and reading over the many drafts of this text. We could not have done this project without the many hours she has devoted to this project. We are a good team.

18. Allison Waldmann for the hours of editing and formatting of the chapters.

19. MaryBeth Protzman, Lauren Protzman, and J.C. Protzman for their transcription support.

20. Daniel Protzman, Tim Schindele, Donna Fox, Jack Protzman, and Jon Banks for their editing assistance.

21. The AlliedSignal Bendix Communications Division "Hats" team for all their assistance and support, which resulted in our initial successful Lean culture changes in manufacturing.

22. The families of all the authors for their support and contributions throughout the process of this project.

23. There are many more individuals who contributed to this book, both directly and indirectly. We have worked with a great many dedicated individuals—too many to list here—who have shared their knowledge and experiences with us. While it is impossible to cite them all, we hope they see this book as the culmination of our respect and appreciation for all they have done.

24. William M. Tsutsui, associate dean for International Studies, professor of History, College of Liberal Arts & Sciences, University of Kansas, for his assistance in Japanese Kanji translation.

Authors

Charles W. Protzman, III, MBA, CPM, is a Shingo Prize Winning Author and internationally renown Lean consultant with over 31 years experience in Materials and Operations Management. He spent 13½ years with AlliedSignal, now Honeywell, where he was an Aerospace Strategic Operations Manager and the first AlliedSignal Lean Master. He has received numerous special-recognition and cost-reduction awards. Charles was an external consultant for DBED's World Class Maryland Consortium while he was with AlliedSignal. He had input into the resulting World Class Criteria document and assisted in the first three initial DBED World Class Company Assessments. Charles has taught students in Lean Principles and Total Quality from all over the world.

In November of 1997, Charles Protzman formed Business Improvement Group, LLC (B.I.G.). B.I.G. is located in Baltimore, Maryland and specializes in implementing Lean thinking. Charles has spent the last 18 years implementing successful lean product line conversions, kaizen events, and administrative business system improvements (transactional lean) across the globe.

Charles participated in numerous Benchmarking and Site visits including a two-week trip to Japan in June 1996, where he worked with Hitachi in a kaizen event. He is a Master facilitator and trainer in TQM, Total Quality Speed, Facilitation, Career Development, Change Management, Benchmarking, Leadership, Systems Thinking, High Performance Work Teams, Team Building, Myers Briggs Styles Indicator, Lean Thinking and Supply Chain Management. He also participated in Baldridge Examiner and Six Sigma Management Courses. He was an Assistant Program Manager during "Desert Storm" for the Patriot missile-to-missile fuse development and production program.

Joyce Kerpchar, PA, is a Shingo Prize Winning Author and health care expert, with over 30 years of healthcare industry experience and currently serves as a Director at Florida Hospital Orlando, which is part of the Adventist Health System, an acute-care, tertiary hospital caring for more than 1.5 million patients a year. She joined Florida Hospital in 2001 and has held a variety of roles as Interim Director of Strategic for Surgical Services, Director of the Institute for Surgical Advancement, and a Senior Consultant implementing Lean across the eight campuses in a variety of clinical departments. She is a Six Sigma Black Belt and is a certified MBTI instructor, Product and Project Manager, with roles developing and implementing software applications.

She began her career as a board certified physician's assistant in cardiovascular and thoracic surgery and primary care medicine. Prior to joining Florida Hospital, she held a variety of administrative positions in healthcare-related industries, which included managed care operations and contracting for a PruCare/Prudential Healthcare who served 200,000 members in nine counties in Central Florida, Product Management for Avio Corporation, a provider of information technology for ambulatory healthcare organization, and was a partner in a consulting firm which specialized in business and market entry strategy for high tech start-ups.

Ms. Kerpchar is passionate about leveraging Lean in healthcare processes to eliminate waste and reduce errors, to improve the overall quality, and to reduce the cost of providing healthcare

Dr. George Mayzell, MD, MBA, FACP, is the senior chief medical officer and chief clinical integration officer for Adventist Midwest Health. He joined the organization in January 2013 after serving as CEO of Health Choice and Senior Vice President of Methodist Le Bonheur Healthcare in Memphis, Tenn.

Dr. Mayzell has more than 30 years of experience in medicine and is a board certified internist and geriatrician. He received his medical degree from the University of Medicine and Dentistry of New Jersey and his MBA from Jacksonville University.

He previously served as senior medical director of managed care for University of Florida and Shands Hospital. He spent more than 10 years with Blue Cross Blue Shield of Florida, working as regional medical director for care and quality and corporate managing medical director for pharmacy and care. Additionally, he has more than 10 years of practice experience.

Mayzell has co-authored two books, *Leveraging Lean in Healthcare* and *Physician Alignment: Constructing Viable Roadmaps for the Future.*

Mayzell and his wife have three children. In his spare time, he enjoys reading and writing.

Section I

1 Introduction to Lean

THE NEED FOR CHANGE

Perform an Internet search on Lean healthcare and within 0.29 sec there are 9,403,000 hits.[1] A recent ASQ study shows

> 53 percent of hospitals report some level (minor, moderate, or full) of Lean deployment, and 42 percent of hospitals report some level of Six Sigma deployment. Few hospitals participating in the study report "full deployment" of either Lean (four percent of hospitals) or Six Sigma (eight percent). The reasons that neither method has been deployed in hospitals include: the need for resources (59 percent of hospitals), lack of information (41 percent), and leadership buy-in (30 percent). Eleven percent of hospitals surveyed were not familiar with either method.[2]

Healthcare organizations have seen their customers shop for services, with access to information at their fingertips. Customers today seek out treatment and provider options and soon will be able to seek out services that offer the most value. Quality information is also starting to be available and understandable. Pay for performance (perceived customer value) and healthcare reform will reinforce the need for healthcare organizations to offer customer value, yielding high quality and a high service at low cost. Every Healthcare entity is working to achieve the Triple Aim goals adopted by the Centers for Medicare and Medicaid (CMS), to improve the patient experience of care (including quality and satisfaction), improve the health of populations and reduce the per capita cost of healthcare.

Today, we live in a competitive global economy. The global market drives the selling price as customers seek to find the best value at the lowest cost. The value of our healthcare in service, quality, and cost is being compared to healthcare around the world; therefore, the global market, in turn, will impact the customer's (patient's) value proposition. The worldwide system impacts our ability to increase or maintain our profits; we can no longer just raise our prices! Global competition today is as close as your Internet screen. Today, if companies want to raise their profit, their only option is to *reduce* costs. This means that companies have to be able to manufacture or provide the best and most services they can, in as little space as possible, with the least amount of inventory, with the fewest number of people, and the least number of errors. This is a challenge. Companies that can delight their customers with the lowest cost will survive in the upcoming decade of increased competition. Nowhere is this truer than in healthcare. Hospitals have experienced this with the current Medicare reimbursement model and have been shifting the cost of providing services for Medicare patients and the uninsured to the insured. (Cost shifting) Hospital reimbursements have always had a "fixed" component with contracted payments. They often manage profits by cutting costs and employees (FTEs). This is not a sustainable strategy. Eventually they will have to move to a more efficient care delivery model to be successful. With healthcare reform and increasing healthcare costs always on the horizon, it appears that the only way to survive will be for organizations to become Lean.

Healthcare organizations must reduce costs and set predictable delivery systems (outcomes) in place that can meet or exceed customer expectations, to grow their businesses. As they better understand the customer value stream, they will identify opportunities to streamline or expand services and grow both horizontally and vertically through partnering or the acquisition of other companies.

---

[1] Internet Google search on February 2014.
[2] "Hospitals See Benefits of Lean and Six Sigma," *ASQ Releases Benchmark Study Results*, March 17, 2009.

They will be able to gain market share by providing improved customer value and satisfaction, expand service lines and product offerings, i.e., add outpatient radiology services or set up urgent care or outpatient clinics adjacent or aligned to their facilities.

In summary, implementing Lean principles provides a foundation for healthcare-related businesses and the opportunity for hospitals to eliminate waste. The waste is then converted into value-added services that lower labor costs while increasing the output. This makes the organization more efficient and provides a firm foundation for growth.

NATIONAL AND GLOBAL COMPETITION

In this world of global competition, there is an ever-changing landscape in the world of healthcare. Not so long ago, very few hospitals were adopting Lean principles as a way to eliminate waste, improve processes, and become more competitive. Today, there are an increasing number of healthcare systems showing interest in learning about and deploying Lean. It is no longer used solely to provide a competitive edge; it is practiced to help these organizations grow and stay in business. With yearly reductions in reimbursement, hospitals must determine how they will stay in business and what practices they will adopt to survive.

Emerging entities are trying to drive healthcare services to the global marketplace, offering high-end surgeries in Bangkok, Dubai, and other foreign nations (see Figure 1.1). American insurance companies are also beginning to include some foreign healthcare facilities in their networks. Although the real value in moving healthcare services out of the United States is controversial, it further demonstrates the importance to identify ways to provide high quality, affordable options. The emergence of healthcare alliances between Boeing and Cleveland Clinic[3] where patients are

Medical Tourism or Healthcare travel to India

Medical tourism—also know as medical outsourcing, **medical travel**, health value travel, health tourism or healthcare tourism—is the concept of traveling abroad to a particular destination to avail the opportunity of the world-class **Healthcare services** offered by the best experienced Healthcare professionals at the technologically most advanced **medical facilities overseas** at **affordable** costs. The low-cost offshore healthcare procedure is usually combined with family holidays so the concept is also called medical vacation travel, health vacation travel, medical value travel, healthcare value travel abroad, health value tour etc. Medical tourism to India means availing world-class Healthcare services in India at just a small fraction of the cost of the same Healthcare procedure in the home country thereby managing a big saving on health care costs. The medical surgery treatments in India facilitated by Life Smile healthcare is an easy access to advanced Health Care Technology, world-class medical healthcare services, **board certified surgeons / doctors**, JCI (JCAHO) / ISO accredited hospitals, affordable low-cost medicare and immediate treatment—no wait list.

Affordable, Low-Cost Health Services, Medical Treatments& Patient Care with Life Smile

World-class, advanced, **high quality** healthcare in India is 60% to 90% cheaper in comparison to developed economies due to: extremely favorable currency exchange rates with USD, GBP, EURO and other major currencies, lowest medical malpractice insurance coverage cost for medical professionals, India is a developing economy so services sector costs are low, India is also one of the world's largest producer and exporter of bulk drugs so high quality medicines are cheap.

Treatment costs in India more...

FIGURE 1.1   Medical tourism example. Source: From http://www.healthoursindia.com/. With permission.

[3] Boeing to send some insured workers to Cleveland for cardiac care, Seattle Times, October 18, 2012.

sent from across the nation to receive Cardiac Care and the arrangement between Walmart and six center of excellences where 1.1 million patients can receive no cost (to the patient) cardiac and spinal surgery[4] will force healthcare entities to re-look at how they are providing care across the value stream to compete in the bundles payment market.

Lesson Learned

As the price of healthcare continues to climb and reimbursement continues to decline, the only way hospitals will survive in the future is to reduce costs. Lean thinking is all about reducing costs through a culture of ongoing continuous improvement.

CHALLENGES FOR THE HEALTHCARE WORKER

Hospitals and healthcare organizations are not the only ones facing competition. U.S. workers are faced with and have been losing their jobs to offshore labor at an alarmingly increasing fashion. With the exception of companies like Toyota, it seems the days of employee loyalty or even companies that encourage employee loyalty are virtually gone. Companies should value, respect, and listen to their employees.

LEAN AND LAYOFFS

Most workers feel Lean is designed to eliminate their jobs. When we ask staff who are exposed to Lean what they think of when they hear the word, we get feedback that the word "Lean" or "becoming Lean" conjures up ideas related to cutting costs and eliminating staff. This is not the impression we would like to make as we embark on a cultural revolution. This is not an unfounded concern. Implementing Lean principles will free up people from their jobs because we can now get more output or productivity with less labor. Attrition and hiring freezes on new staff or positions can normally mitigate this risk, especially if the hospital is proactive. There is generally a shortage of qualified nursing personnel and technical staff in hospitals; therefore, layoffs tend to be less of an issue. Most hospitals do not go into Lean with the desire to lay off people, and it has been our experience that layoffs are rarely related to process improvements; however, businesses engaging in Lean generally do so because they have a "compelling need to change" and, at times, this may be related to a business condition that forces a reduction in growth or loss of a service line. Lean was not the driving force that caused the need to reduce their workforce.

Lesson Learned

To truly make Lean successful there must be a management commitment not to lay anyone off as a result of continuous improvement. People will not work to eliminate their jobs.

TRADITIONAL HEALTHCARE MODEL

The traditional hospital (since the 1970s or so) and healthcare business model would never work in the manufacturing world. In the current healthcare model:

1. The hospital provides the staff, materials, equipment, and billing.
2. Depending on the healthcare system, physicians may be part of an employed physician group, a contracted group by the hospital, a private community-based physician group, or

---

[4] HOW WAL-MART MAY HAVE JUST CHANGED THE GAME ON HEALTH CARE, by Dan Diamond, California Healthline, October 17, 2012.

solo practitioners. In most instances, hospitals are composed of components of each, with a large component often being volunteer independent medical staff.

3. Private insurance companies and government-funded Medicare and Medicaid pay the bills. There are few "self-pays." Most of the time this is a nice way of saying "no pays."

4. Government and other state and industry bodies regulate it.

While some may argue that the U.S. healthcare system is the best in the world, many would argue the contrary. There is still much room for improvement and that there may be other countries' healthcare systems from which we can learn.

The British National Health Service provides free universal coverage for all citizens. The principal hospitals are nationalized, with managers, doctors, and nurses effectively being public servants. The standard of care varies from exceptionally high, particularly in the great teaching hospitals, to mediocre, with occasional complaints of poor care.[5]

In the French system, 65% of the medical cost is paid for by the government, with the balance picked up by private insurers. French Emergency Department (ED) doctors are paid one-third to two-thirds of their U.S. counterparts ($50K to $100K per year).[6] The French have a unique approach to Emergency Care. Emergency calls are screened by a physician who decides whether to respond and what type of team to respond, or to tell the patient to come into the emergency room. Ten percent of calls to which they respond are handled by a full team, including a physician to diagnose the problem and stabilize the patient on the scene, then take the patient to the hospital that specializes in their needed care. The French system costs approximately $3400 per capita (person) with no uninsured vs. almost double per capita in the United States with millions uninsured.

In the Canadian model, the government appoints the CEO who is responsible to run the hospital and meet budget. The business model is different, yet the hospitals run similarly to U.S. hospitals. The main difference we have witnessed is that, while operational challenges are similar, there are different incentives to improve government-run health systems. This is in large part because the systems tend to work on budgets that do not always reimburse the hospitals by the number of patients treated. Where this is the case, continuous improvement may provide more capacity but no financial incentive to physicians to see those patients and, in fact, increased patient volume can actually hurt compliance to a fixed budget. In the Canadian system, we have witnessed surgeons who left at 4.00 p.m. with patients waiting. These patients were told there was no time to get them in, and they need to be rescheduled. This is simply explained: it was time for the surgeon to go home. Since they are not paid by the patient operation, there is no financial incentive to stay. The system wants increased capacity (shorter wait lists), the hospital must minimize costs, and adding capacity may only increase costs for consumables or other fixed per-patient expenses, and the physicians' only incentive may be their compassion for the patient. Of course, much of this same struggle can be similar in inner-city U.S. hospitals that primarily treat Medicaid patients and, in fact, may lose money for each patient they treat. Despite the funding model, we can all come back to the common need to decrease costs while simultaneously improving quality and access to care.

---

[5] Kenneth Hopper and William Hopper, *The Puritan Gift: Reclaiming the American Dream amidst Global Financial Chaos* (New York: I.B. Tauris) 2009.

[6] CBS video, *Sunday Morning, A Votre Santé, CBS Sunday Morning: Why The French Can Afford To Get Sick*, Paris, October 26, 2008 (CBS). 8 years ago, the World Health Organization released a study ranking France as having the best healthcare system in the world. Yet the study's methodology is questionable. From Euro Health 2006, previously ranked by WHO as the best performer, the French health system is not without problems. It has traditionally operated with little regard for efficiency or cost containment. It has the highest rate of pharmaceutical use in the EU, while, until recently at least, there has been little attempt to incorporate cost effectiveness into policy making. The health workforce is aging; geographical inequalities in access to services exist, moreover, promotion and prevention have not been high priorities. http://www.euro.who.int/observatory/publications/20020324_26.

Once the United States instituted EMTALA[7] in 1986, U.S. national healthcare was launched. EMTALA mandated hospitals treat anyone who arrives at the ED the same, regardless of their ability to pay. This was an unfunded mandate; however, for those who can't be turned away from an ED, presenting to the emergency room for a minor sore throat or earache is an expensive national solution.

INTRODUCTION – SO WHAT IS LEAN?

No one has more trouble than the person who claims to have no trouble.

—Taiichi Ohno
Father of the Toyota Production System

There are hundreds of books that address Lean thinking and the Toyota Production System (TPS). Lean is a term that originated in manufacturing to describe a way of running companies as an enterprise. Becoming Lean requires the continual pursuit to identify and eliminate waste and establish efficient flow within the overall organization. The term "value stream" is used today to describe what is involved in producing a product or service from raw material, manufacturing, distributing, wholesaling, and retailing to recycling. Even though healthcare and service organizations may not begin with raw material or even manufacture a product, they still have value streams related to providing healthcare services to their customers.

Lean concepts were originally developed around manufacturing, so we have used some manufacturing terms and examples throughout the book in order to best explain the underlying meanings to the reader. Lean principles have been adapted to healthcare, and as such, the reader needs to be able to stretch and convert referenced manufacturing examples to apply them in their healthcare environment.

"Lean" is a term used to describe a philosophy and way of thinking. Lean has its roots in the United States, but what we know today as Lean was taken to another level and expanded company-wide by Toyota. Lean, if implemented properly, is an enterprise-wide initiative that requires a cultural change. It will not be successful if it is directed only at the frontline staff. This means if Lean or Lean/Sigma (the combination of Lean and Six Sigma) is to be truly successful it must include all functional areas (i.e., finance, marketing, information systems, etc.), all levels, from the board of directors to the patient, and all value streams within the enterprise. Lean principles are based on what is known today as the Toyota Production System. Toyota Motor Company has been working on implementing and improving the application of Lean principles since Taiichi Ohno started in their machine shop in Japan in 1945.[8]

Typical Lean results, when given sufficient time to work, can result in:

- 20–80% productivity improvement
- 50–90% reduction in inventory
- 50–99% throughput time reduction
- 30–50% reduction in space requirements
- 10–30% reduction in overheads

---

[7] http://www.cms.hhs.gov/emtala/. In 1986, Congress enacted the Emergency Medical Treatment & Labor Act (EMTALA) to ensure public access to emergency services regardless of ability to pay. Section 1867 of the Social Security Act.

[8] Art Smalley, "A Brief History of Setup Reduction," www.artoflean.com; also Taiichi Ohno, *Toyota Production System* (New York: Productivity Press) 1988.

LEAN IS NOT A QUICK-FIX SOLUTION; IT TAKES TIME. WE MUST BE PATIENT WITH THE PROCESS, BUT IMPATIENT WITH THE RESULTS.[9] IT IS CRITICAL TO GET EVERYONE TRAINED IN LEAN AND INVOLVED IN THE PROJECTS, WHETHER THEY ARE POINT KAIZEN EVENTS OR LEAN IMPLEMENTATIONS

LEAN AND HOSPITALS

First of all, we can all agree that hospitals are not factories. Factories deal with products while hospitals deal with people. While our products in factories cannot talk to us, patients do talk to us before, during, and after they go through our processes.

We have found that organizations and processes within the healthcare environment are not all that different from organizations within factories. Most departments are organized in silos, while executive leadership is located sometimes on the top floor or even in another building miles away, and they spend the majority of their time in meetings. They have no time left to get out to the floor (*Gemba*) "actual place" to see what is happening first hand. Most healthcare leadership teams do not have a clear understanding of their value streams or interconnectivity of their processes. In today's literature, this is referred to as "big company disease." It is ironic that this manufacturing terminology has the healthcare connotation "disease."

Listed below are the worst symptoms of this disease.[10]

1. People can't get anything done because they are always at a meeting. Meetings are not run effectively, people show up late, don't come to any conclusions, actions aren't recorded, and there is no follow up.
2. Your employees do not think of the customer as the number one priority and are more concerned with internal politics.
3. The company has more than five layers from the frontline to the president and is slow to respond to any type of challenge, leadership initiative, or customer feedback. It takes more than an hour to make a decision.
4. The company hires consultants to do their strategic planning.
5. The company tends to emphasize consensus at the expense of professional insight.
6. The budgeting process takes over a week and, in some cases, 3–6 months, and then finance dictates the budget.
7. The company reacts to people's opinions and makes "knee-jerk" decisions vs. discovering and acting on data and facts.
8. Talk about past glories increases at the expense of future dreams, resulting in general complacency and stagnation.
9. Authority, loyalty, and respect are replaced by the desire for power at the expense of your employees.
10. You pay a service to water your plants.

We hypothesize that "big company disease" starts at the point where leaders switch from wearing many hats to when they are assigned one hat for a specific department and are not responsible for the entire value stream. This begins the "that's not our job" discussions. Breaking down the barriers of silo thinking and understanding the value stream is critical to the transformation that needs to occur when deploying lean. The goal with Lean is to get back to fundamentals in management. We need to restore the ideals of company loyalty, gain domain knowledge of the business, have supervisors

---

[9] *Speed is Life*, Tom Peters, a co-production of Video Publishing House and KERA, 1991.
[10] Influenced by Tsuyoshi Kawanishi, legendary former CEO of Toshiba Semiconductor, *Chip Management, Ten Symptoms of Big Company Disease*, as compiled by Professor Yoshiya Teramoto of Meiji Gakuin University, and influenced by Bob Norton, "Big Company Disease is Most Often Fatal for Startup Companies. The Top Ten Signs a Company has 'Big Company Disease'," http://www.clevelenterprises.com/articles/big_company disease.html.

able to train employees in the job, develop our leaders by promoting from within, and insourcing our products and services.

Prior to Lean, we literally sat in meetings and listened while managers lied outright to executives about how things were going on the factory floor. If the manager never leaves his/her office, how will he/she ever know about actual problems, lack of progress being made, or if what is reported is the truth? How reliable is the information transferred from layer to layer up to the CFO, CEO or Board of Directors?

This is the case for hospitals as well. When we initially tour hospitals, we see materials everywhere, from the stash the nurses keep in pockets or desk drawers, to closets, shelves, and rooms full of inventory. Much of this is what we call "just-in-case" inventory. We constantly hear, "we need more space," "we don't have enough room," "our workstations are too small," or "our area layouts are poorly designed." We see lots of batching everywhere in the hospital. Why should we change when "we have always done it this way for the last 20 years?" We fail to see opportunities for improvement, and when we do finally see them, our expensive equipment and inventory-based batched systems, finance, and cultures get in our way of moving forward. When you do make the decision to embark on a Lean journey, you must realize and admit how little you know about your processes or how to improve those processes. Remember, all the problems you have today are the result of changes you or someone prior to you made in the past. You must abandon the old way of doing things, along with the brute force results-based management style (i.e., telling your managers that they must improve customer satisfaction within a month), which drives "wild and crazy" behaviors. This reactive management approach creates a "shoot-from-the-hip" mentality, adds variation, and results in endless workarounds, ultimately creating metrics telling you what you want to hear vs. what you need to know.

Once we start to understand Lean tools and that Lean is a philosophy and a different way of thinking, we can start to see applications to remove waste, create flow, and increase velocity in the healthcare world.

In manufacturing, most factories make things, while other factories repair things. If you think about it, hospitals are more in the repair business. Whether we work in a hospital, stand-alone emergency room, urgent care center, or any type of clinic, we tend to be in the business of diagnosing what is wrong with someone, developing a treatment plan of care, and then implementing the plan and monitoring the results. If we are in the rehab business, hospice, nursing home, or long term care facility, we are generally involved in some portion of carrying out the plan of care and monitoring the patient. Healthcare businesses, just like factories, have "systems" based on and designed with many processes. We all have government and outside regulatory bodies to deal with that create an uncertain political and economic future. We all have formal and informal SYSTEMS at work, and anything that is a Process can be improved and thus Leaned out.

Some areas of hospitals and healthcare institutions function almost exactly like factories. Nutritional services, engineering/maintenance, laundry service, laboratory, and pharmacy are very similar to their counterparts in manufacturing. Factories and hospitals, while very different and unique, share many of the same issues around implementing continuous improvement. The acceptance of Lean principles, concepts, and tools is often easier to implement in these areas, but remember, waste elimination and Lean tools can be applied across the continuum of healthcare.

What Results Can You Expect?

We have been implementing Lean in hospitals for many years now. Reductions in labor of 50% or more have been experienced in nutritional areas. We have increased productivity in most areas, from 30% to 50% or more. We have reduced length of stay (LOS), which we also call throughput time, by up to 80%. We have reduced emergency room waits to see a doctor from 14 hrs down to less than 30 min, resulting in declines in "left without seeing doctor" (LWSD) and have seen dramatic increases in physician productivity. Laboratory turnaround times have been reduced by 50%

and inventory in surgery and pharmacy reduced by millions of dollars. We have also been able to increase the number of surgeries performed within the current scheduled time frames by up to 20% or more per surgeon. The results one receives from implementing Lean strategies are directly proportional to the investment the business puts into them. If you have a CEO and Board that are knowledgeable in Lean principles and the best people are dedicated and supported to implementing the initial improvements, that business will see excellent results. If you have a CEO and Board that support Lean and put some of their best people into the effort, they will see good results but may not sustain them.

THE CEO AND LEAN

Lean is a journey. Some hospitals and clinics have tried Lean or Six Sigma and had bad experiences. This is unfortunate as it tends to hurt their overall improvement efforts. Many hospitals have started with Six Sigma tools and while getting good results they have had difficulty reducing variation in a complex system with few standardized processes. Our experience in the United States is that:

- 40% of companies are either not exposed to Lean, dabble with it, or choose not to try it
- 40% will make ongoing attempts and struggle with it and may have pockets of excellence where several projects have improved and some have sustained
- 20% will try it with some level of success (and of these, 5% will take Lean further)

Although these statistics may leave some asking why even attempt the Lean journey, we have found that organizations who engage in Lean achieve results that exceed traditional process improvement initiatives. Providing an advanced discussion as to what organizations encounter as they engage in a Lean journey, sharing lessons learned, and helping organizations to understand what can help make a Lean implementation successful will improve the success and sustain the rate of Lean. The bottom line is that implementing Lean is not easy; however, if implemented correctly, it has worked extremely well. The proliferation of Lean in healthcare will help achieve a customer-focused, high-quality, cost-effective healthcare system.

Over the first few years of implementing Lean we generally start with implementing Lean and following up with a Six Sigma effort. Generally, the CEOs "support" the Lean initiative rather than lead it until they see the outcomes for themselves. So the initial part of the journey generally results in "pockets of excellence" from various events or implementations throughout the organization.

If the CEO gets on board and drives Lean as part of the strategic plan and then incorporates "Hoshin" (goal setting by top management followed by bottom-up planning to meet those goals), they will see excellent results in bottom-line improvement. Results will be direct cost savings and significant cost avoidance. We define cost savings as those that directly hit the bottom line, whereas cost avoidance refers to items that would have increased costs had we not alleviated the need for them. In addition, the elimination of waste in a process will decrease the process steps and reduce the opportunities for errors, thereby improving customer satisfaction and, quality.

We have had hospital clients that, over the first 5 years, have saved millions of dollars, avoided hiring significantly more labor, and avoided major new construction projects. Notice that we quantified these results over the first 5 years. Many times, hospitals don't see huge bottom-line improvements immediately, as it takes time to Lean out the overall system: however, some projects can quickly result in large gains. Quality and service can be improved substantially. Customer satisfaction as well as physician, surgeon, and staff satisfaction improve as well.

Lean is not a venture that should be entered into lightly. It takes a tremendous amount of training and perseverance and sometimes brute force to implement.

Unfortunately, there will be "casualties," as not everyone will buy in; therefore, there may be a need to place people on a different "seat on the bus" (or a different bus altogether); however, the benefits are extremely rewarding. With all the uncertainty in healthcare today, if healthcare institutions are to survive, they will *have* to implement Lean. The auto industry is a good example. You can see what has happened to the companies that did not or were late to adopt Lean. Very early adopting hospitals started implementing Lean Six Sigma back in the late 1990s. The healthcare business is way behind the curve but can still catch up. With the ongoing pressure from insurance companies and government to cut costs, the decision to implement continuous improvement will eventually not be a choice but a necessity for a hospital's survival.

TYPICAL LEAN METRICS AND OUTCOMES

Results are highly dependent on the culture, equipment, layout, training, and ability to sustain all Lean system implementation guidelines. Results may vary depending on the department and data required for sustaining the new Lean processing methods. In all areas, cycle time of key individual operations and processes need to be measured and monitored; normally these data types are not available or currently measured. It is developed through the Lean implementation.

There are typical results we see in Lean implementations, but they don't happen without dedication, monitoring, and buy-in. Lean is a culture change and should be part of your business strategic plan. It is not unusual to take 2–3 years to see results start to impact the bottom line, even though you will see the results immediately in the areas you are improving. Lean is not a quick-fix solution. Lean should be considered a commitment that once started, never ends.

Hospitals that truly embrace this culture change will overtake their competition and will improve their patients' experiences. Hospitals that don't embrace this eventually, may not survive. The Joint Commission on Accreditation of Healthcare (JCAHO), the Agency for Healthcare Administration (ACHA), and other regulatory bodies are starting to embrace Lean. Truly Lean institutions don't fear audits, but embrace them as opportunities. If our processes were really all standardized, would we ever fear an audit?

POTENTIAL LEAN RETURNS BY DEPARTMENT

The following section describes the results one can expect by hospital department; there can be both tangible ("hard") and intangible ("soft") benefits defined for a Lean initiative. We have put these in terms of ROI for those readers who deem it necessary (Table 1.1).

TYPICAL RESULTS/RETURN ON INVESTMENTS (ROI) AND IMPLEMENTING LEAN

ROI is very important and can be an important metric to gauge the success of your Lean implementation; however, ROI in and of itself can be a very misleading metric and is not the true goal of any Lean practitioner.

In today's manufacturing and healthcare organizations, the ROI tends to equate to only one thing—eliminating full-time employees (FTEs). No one wants to admit it, but in many organizations quality, safety, and inventory all take a back seat. Many times Lean consultants are asked up front by CEOs and CFOs to stipulate how many FTEs they are going to take out, even before the first meeting.

Executives must understand ROI can come in the form of clinical improvements, financial performance, increase in market share, and/or improved service. Generally, most Lean initiatives provide benefits in more than one area. ROI comes in the form of hard dollar savings such as FTE savings (decrease in the use of contract or travelers), operational savings such as a reduction in LOS, waste of medications, reductions in over processing patients, and supply savings. Soft dollar savings such as cost avoidance (avoiding new construction, doing more in the same or less space, capital dollars) and revenue increases (backfill or capacity opportunity) are only recognized if the organization has a plan in conjunction with Lean to grow their business. Improvement in first case starts and turnover reduction enable an increase in capacity with the same or less staff in the same number of

TABLE 1.1
ROI Summary by Area

Tangible ROI

Emergency Department (Outpatient)	Surgery	Laboratory	Pharmacy	Radiology/Ultrasound	Inpatient Throughput	Nutritional
Increase volume due directly to Lean initiative not just LWSD. (May require some layout changes. Lean gives ability to predict capacity)	Pre-admitting test improvements—ability to handle more patients with same staff. (May require some layout changes. Lean gives ability to predict capacity—point of use testing laboratory)	Ability to do more testing during the same amount of time (increase in volume opportunity)	Ability to fill more requests in less time and with less space	Ability to increase volumes (capacity) with same staffing	Ability to expand capacity but does not necessarily reduce headcount	Reduced headcount
Cycle time improvement door to MD (critical productivity metric) resulting in lower LWSD%	The ability to do more cases in the same amount of time with improved outcomes	Potential for reduced headcount	Potential headcount reduction (FTEs) in pharmacy	Reduced backlog in some areas (time request to appointment availability)	Can free space in ED and other areas (decrease patients holding for beds)	Reduced inventory
Increased volume (with same staffing) and less over time	Potential for reduced staffing in Sterile Processing Department, staffing scheduling changes in OR (staff to demand)	Space savings	Savings of waste from over-producing and wasting IV solutions	Possible reductions in staff or staff over time or ability to expand hours with same staff	Increased staff satisfaction and retention	Reduced space
Inventory reduction in material supplies	Potential large returns in inventory and reduced need for instrument sets and reduction in excess and obsolete materials	Reduced inventory	Reductions in inventory		Reduction in LOS	Potential to eliminate need for cook chill process
Increase in physician productivity	Turnaround time reduction with reductions in case cancellations and delays	Reduced excess and obsolete materials	Quicker turnaround of stat and regular orders		Can free space in ED, PACU, and other areas	
Outpatient LOS reduction	Increase in surgical volumes (if marketing plan is a component of Lean initiative)	Typically better quality and tracking of specimens	Increased capacity		Reduce or eliminate diversions	

Potential for reduction of inpatient LOS	Increased capacity	Significantly reduce or eliminate expired materials			
Improvement in patient readiness resulting in higher percentage of first cases that start on time	Quicker turnaround of results—patient safety				
Increased physician and staff satisfaction and morale resulting in potential staff retention benefits	Improved staff and physician retention				
Quicker case build times, decrease in equipment replacement and sharpening, with resulting decrease in defects by count (overall)	**Non-Tangible ROIs**				
Increased physician and staff satisfaction and morale resulting in potential staff retention benefits	Increased patient and staff satisfaction	Increased patient and staff satisfaction	Increased patient and staff satisfaction	Increased patient and staff satisfaction	Increased patient and staff satisfaction
Less searching by staff		Less stat orders			
Level loading scheduling models					
Standard work leads to compliance in universal protocols resulting in improved third party audit results					
Quicker patient throughput and resulting reduced need for Pre-Op and PACU beds	**Challenges**				
Initial high resistance to change based on implementation of new system model	Major layout changes normally required	Potential for more frequent deliveries	May require changes to registration	May require staff scheduling changes (staff to demand)	May require renegotiation of supplier contracts
May require physician scheduling changes and investment in scheduling software and patient contact software for appointment reminders	Can save investments in new automated type equipment	May have ability to use third shift tech and or nursing resources for re-stocking	May require changes to scheduling process	Cultural shift (patients accepted to units during shift change)	May require capital for layout changes and removal of or different equipment
When selecting metrics or Big "Y"s such as patient satisfaction, or LOS, these may require programs (or sequential Lean initiatives) as there are many "x"s that drive patient satisfaction to obtain the desired results					
Level loading may result in block time policy changes—standardization of drop off times and release of blocks, add on emergency cases review. May require changes in surgery service line room assignments, introduction of day of surgery scheduling rules					

continued

TABLE 1.1 (continued)
RO Summary by Area

Challenges

Emergency Department (Outpatient)	Surgery	Laboratory	Pharmacy	Radiology/ Ultrasound	Inpatient Throughput	Nutritional
Data gathering to support ROI	Will require physician collaboration on standard order sets and agreement on common definitions for cycle and turnover times, surgeons council creation or participation and development of enforcement rules, i.e., cancel case, lose block time, etc., and escalation process, and standardizing of instruments sets and equipment	Will require staff scheduling changes for Phlebotomy laboratory	Resistance to point of use pharmacy floor locations	May require marketing efforts to backfill excess capacity to show additional revenue	Needs support from physicians and/or hospitalists to break batch "rounding" habits and changes to discharge process	May require changes to menu offerings
	May require labor expense to revise preference cards and real-time updating of preference cards, and ongoing (after the project) par level adjustments	May require changes to skill sets and job descriptions	Data gathering to support ROI	Data gathering to support ROI	Hospitalists will resist move to "unit-based" care	Data gathering to support ROI
	May require investment in some inventory tracking (RFID) and may require negotiation of supply chain contracts	Requires stand up vs. sit down operations			Decentralizing some departments and realignment of some departments in the organization	
	Changes to flip rooms or readiness rooms—determination and communication related to use of flip rooms, induction rooms, and priority of "rules" surrounding use of flip rooms if indicated					
	May require changes to anesthesia contract, will require review and standardization of anesthesia guidelines. Standardization of floor preparation of patients. Mandatory pre-testing by acuity level 72 hrs prior or case canceled/future loss of block time with anesthesia review 24 hrs prior to surgery					

hours. If ROI is going to be your main objective, it is recommended that all projects engage a financial analyst (at least part-time) to assist in calculating the financial ROI that will be accepted by the organization. If the initiative is anticipated to provide the opportunity to increase capacity, marketing must be engaged to develop and execute a plan to drive more business to backfill the time that has been "freed up" because of the elimination of waste, otherwise real value will not be achieved.

One of the most challenging facets is coming to an agreement on what the ROI should be. Generally, the Financial Department of the organization is only interested in the "bottom line," in other words, "when can they adjust the department's budget and show the reductions?" Executives must keep an open mind and be willing to challenge those who believe each initiative must yield hard dollar savings. Hard dollar savings can and will be achieved, but may not be an immediate return on every project and may have a longer time horizon.

As organizational proponents begin to engage in Lean deployments, all "eyes" will be on the Lean initiative. One reason ROI is emphasized is because everyone has heard of the potential improvements and successes in other industries and other healthcare organizations. Executives want to make sure the initiatives they are sponsoring yield success. If they are hiring consultants, they want to justify the price they are paying for their services. Organizations must realize that there will and should be successes on each Lean initiative; however, the correct infrastructure must be in place to train, implement, and sustain the gains. The most successful ROIs are recognized when there is a cultural shift and the entire organization, both vertically and horizontally, "buys" into Lean. Seeing and eliminating waste is how the organization does business, leveraging tools, such as *Gemba* walks (go to the place and see) and top (leader) to bottom (frontline) standard work, are implemented. We are often asked how long it takes to see results. There should be immediate results in flow and productivity, while financial results may lag behind. Sustainability will need to be proven.

Lesson Learned

You will know you are further down the Lean culture path when building a culture of ongoing continuous improvement every day outweighs the insistence on implementing only those perceived large ROI projects first!

Most companies are driven by a "short-term focus." We are always worried about the next quarter results. While the short term is important, we must convert our decision making to a long-term focus if we are going to survive. ROIs tend to be short-term focused. Paybacks within one to two years are normally prescribed. Toyota has a long-term focus; some companies, among them Toyota, SC Johnson, Medtronic, and Unigen Pharmaceuticals, are rumored to have 100-year business plans.[11]

Lesson Learned

The solution to this sole ROI focus is simple yet takes great patience to achieve. Ultimately, it is the efficiency of the "process" and layout that dictate how many FTEs are required. Once waste is removed, the process and the layout, designed for "flexing," spell out what one needs to effectively run that particular operation. If one focuses on improving the process, the ROI will take care of itself.

At Hospital X, we applied Lean in one operation with only 11 employees in a batch nutritional environment. The Lean tools proved we only needed six people to run the process in half the time, with 100% better quality in order to support the current demand. Freeing up five people is a great ROI. Still, management didn't believe it and kept eight to nine employees there, just to make sure. In their eyes, this gave them a two-person buffer. In essence, the area ran worse because they kept the extra people in place. This meant there was two to three people's worth of idle time across the

---

[11] Brian Gongol, "100-Year Business Plans," http://www.gongol.com/research/economics/100yearplans/, http://www.nutraingredients-usa.com/Industry/Unigen-pens-100-year-plan.

eight to nine left. Six months later, we were told the area wasn't running well, and we didn't meet the ROI target for the area. So what good was putting the ROI together when management wasn't going to listen or be held accountable to follow through on freeing up and finding homes for the additional people?

Lesson Learned

Once reductions are identified, management must have the fortitude to act on facts and make the changes without laying people off.

In Hospital X, food production Lean lines went from eight people, 8 hrs per day to three people for 4 hrs per day of running time. In this case, management was accountable and worked hard to continuously improve the system after it was installed. It took more than a year to get there and became more productive than even Lean predicted.

Patience and perseverance is the key. What is really required is upper level "executive" leadership to drive culture change, adoption, and deployment. Toyota did not get there in a month. It took decades to implement the TPS system, and they are still working on perfecting it today. As healthcare organizations embark on their multiyear Lean journey, they will need to determine what they will accept as their ROI strategy and how to articulate the benefits of Lean across the enterprise in order to sustain ongoing cycles of continuous improvement.

Lesson Learned

Companies that are truly Lean no longer keep track of ROIs. They implement Lean because focusing on continuous process improvement is the right thing to do for their patients and their organization's survival.

LEAN AND SYSTEMS THINKING

BOILED FROG SYNDROME

If a frog is thrown into a pot of boiling water, it will jump out. If the frog is placed into a pot of water and you slowly turn up the heat to a boil, we will have "frog legs" for dinner.

The point of this story is that after several months to a year of being in the same job most of us no longer recognize all the waste that surrounds us. After all, it has become part of the familiar landscape. Sometimes this waste can only be seen by "outsiders" unless we train ourselves to see it again. When we identify waste and ask why it is there, we often encounter answers like, "I don't know" and "because we have always done it that way" or "this is the way I do it but everyone else does it differently" or "I thought it was stupid to do it that way when I arrived, but no one would listen to my suggestion, and told me just do it, so I just gave up."

Think back to your first day at your current job. Was there something you were shown or told and you said to yourself, "Wow! I can't believe they do it this way!" Then ask yourself, "Are you still doing it that way today?" If the answer is "yes" then you are a boiled frog.

SYSTEMS THINKING PRINCIPLES

Lean fosters systems thinking. Lean tools are designed to help one see the value stream from the beginning or starting point of the service or product to the end of the service or product delivery to the customer, thereby making the system more transparent. Most inherent inefficiencies are caused by flaws within the overall hospital system. Because most organizations are segmented into silos, people may not be trained, organized, or incentivized to see how the system as a whole is working.

This creates challenges in identifying the true root cause of problems. In our experience, we have found that hospitals and all healthcare integrated delivery systems have similar challenges. It is generally not the individual or worker who causes the problem or waste, but the wastes inherent within the system that drive the staff person to work inefficiently. We have found that your staff will do the best job they can with the tools you give them. Therefore, the only way to fix problems is to change the systems. We have found[12]:

- The system controls us more than we control it.
- The world works through systems, but we are not trained to understand or manage them.
- The inventory contained in the system is directly proportional to the amount of inherent risk that is in the system.
- System structure determines managerial behavior and organizational performance.
- Most of us make decisions in a vacuum; we only look at our piece of the system, our department, not the larger whole.
- To change the system you must change the structure, not the symptoms.
- Small events trigger large reactions creating chaos.
- Today's problems come from yesterday's solutions.
- The easier it is to see the whole system, the easier it is to fix the elements of the system.
- Small changes in the system structure can yield great change in behavior.
- Assigning blame results in a failure to see any systemic implications.

The statements above represent the challenges inherent in non-systems thinking. As we gain a better understanding of Lean systems and learn more about why and how to implement Lean in healthcare, we will begin to understand how Lean helps break down barriers found in most systems. As the barriers are broken, we create better workflow and communication and we better understand the value stream or the service we are delivering to our customer. In summary, implementing Lean principles within the context of "systems thinking" provides a foundation for businesses to eliminate waste and ultimately survive. Lean can provide extraordinary results if implemented properly, given time, and if the method of accounting for Lean savings is revised.

Lesson Learned

The Lean business delivery system is an ongoing journey in the pursuit of waste elimination and error reduction. By understanding and utilizing "systems thinking," it should enable more healthcare organizations to provide affordable healthcare and ultimately facilitate true healthcare reform in the form of coverage, quality, and cost in the future.

Viewing the Hospital with Systems Thinking

The TPS System, sometimes also called the "Thinking Production System," is an integrated system developed by Toyota that combines its management philosophy and standard operations into the optimal production of products that sell with a high-value-added proposition for the customer.

Providing healthcare products and services also requires an integrated delivery model that starts with the customer requiring a service, which sets off a series of integrated activities to produce the desired results (Figure 1.2). Healthcare institutions need a management philosophy, standardized operations and processes, supplier participation, and refined logistics to deliver the highest quality product to their customers.

When viewing the hospital as a system, we identify inputs and outputs, but the system as a whole is very interdependent on all of its parts. If one part fails, it impacts the entire system. For example,

---

[12] Peter Senge, *The Fifth Discipline* (New York: Doubleday) 1994.

Patient Throughput Process

ED Time - 3hr 20mn Mar, May, Oct 07 data	Bed Req to Dispo 5hr 23 min (6 hr 6 min SD) 50% of IP Input	Unit Caring / Treatment Time		Patient Leaves → Housekeeping Arrives	Housekeeping arrives → Bed cleaned	Bed cleaned → Pt Occupies
Preop (2hrs early) Surgery time (162 min +9 avg. delay min) and 23 Hour Obs May and Oct 07 data	PACU > 2hr LOS 14% of patients held for avg of 2hr 8mn (5.8mn/pt) SD 1hr 14mn (5.5% of 13.5 pts = .75 pts)	LOS Estimate - 4.4 days for treatment and recovery time Notes: •Avg 6.06 days Medicare LOS (30%) •Estimate (from DRG LOS report) without L&D = 5.1 days LOS	Discharge order written → pt leaving			
DA Bed req → assigned	Bed assigned → pt arrival NO DATA AVAILABLE	•90% or more of Surgery patient treatment is predictable	Varies by D/C Location	Varies By Time of Day	Room Clean Full Clean	Potential Overlap?
Cath Lab NO DATA AVAILABLE		•Blocks below apply more to ED and Direct Admit patients				

ED : 8 hr 43 min
Surg : 6 hr 56 min
DA : TBD

Front End

Decision to admit until treatment started | Treatment Started until recovery or meets criteria | Meets Criteria to D/C order written

Estimate 8 Hours (.25 LOS)
2 hr 45 min Best Time
(STAT) until Bed Ready

Back End

FIGURE 1.2 Patient throughput process. Notice where it is labeled "no data available". Lean projects often require data which does not currently exist and must be manually captured via reports, employee handwritten notes, or direct observation. Chart was first created by Kia Loo, Lean practitioner, Business Excellence Consulting.

if the ED is over capacity and waiting on inpatient beds, the post-operative recovery unit may also be competing for the same beds, both vying for the same support resources, such as transportation or maybe even a CT slot (Figure 1.3). In addition, we find floor units waiting for pharmacy to complete medication orders, while all areas of the hospital await laboratory results.

For instance, a physician needs a laboratory result in order to discharge a patient. If the phlebotomist does not draw the patient's blood in time or there is a delay in the laboratory getting the result to the physician, the physician may not be able to discharge the patient at the time he/she is rounding. This could result in further delays, up to another day in some cases, for the patient, as it

Systems Overview – Patient Flow

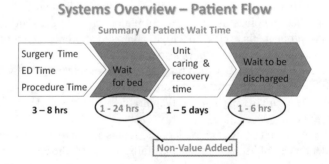

FIGURE 1.3 Hospital System Patient Flow originally created by Kia Loo, Lean Practitioner. Source: B.I.G Files.

is more difficult to reach the physician once he/she is out of the hospital or occupied performing a procedure. The delay also impacts the hospital's ability to clean the bed and change over the room for the next patient, which, in turn, may impede overall flow and create bottlenecks in the ED or surgery. These delays are mostly hidden within their LOS (length of stay) and are very costly to the hospital.

Lesson Learned

The hospital is a complex system generating systemic-type problems. Each part is dependent on the others. These problems need to be approached with systems thinking tools; yet, most of us are never trained in systems thinking.

To further highlight the inter-relationships within the hospital at a system level, we can look at the suppliers to the system in relation to bed availability (Figure 1.4). Hospital primary feeders (inputs) or suppliers consist of patients who enter through the ED, surgery, both in and outpatients, and scheduled admissions for inpatients. Minor feeders or suppliers include procedural areas such as the Cardiac Catheterization Laboratory, Electrophysiology Laboratory (EP), Radiology, and transfers from other hospitals, nursing homes, etc. Outputs occur in the system when patients leave the hospital or clinic (Figure 1.5). They leave the system as outpatients or through the discharge process from inpatient units to home, skilled nursing facilities (SNFs), or other extended care facilities (rehabilitation, etc.). Outpatients can be sent home on the same day from the ED or surgery. Constraints on the overall process include:

- Improper match of bed demand to the supply beds available (includes SNFs, etc.)
- Lack of understanding of supply (patients coming in) and demand needed (timing issue)
- Long turnover times throughout the hospital - (surgery, bed cleaning, etc.)
- Midnight census
- Mismatch of staffing and demand (created by -staffing to demand, traditional shift assignments and lack of monitoring)

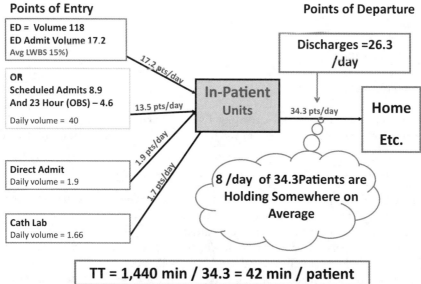

FIGURE 1.4   Hospital systems current state view inflows vs. outflows. First created by Kia Loo, Lean practitioner, Business Excellence Consulting.

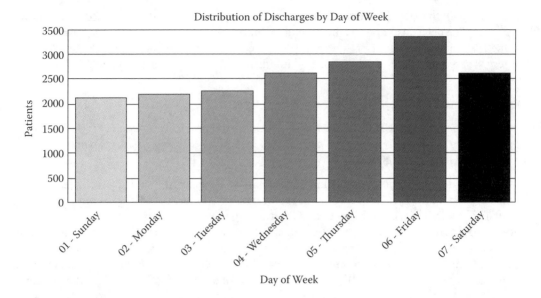

FIGURE 1.5   Hospital discharges by Day of Week.

- Support processes, many often centralized, can also impede flow:
  - Transportation
  - Registration
  - Scheduling
  - Pharmacy
  - Core and non-core laboratory
  - Nutritional services
  - Catering
  - Housekeeping
  - Radiology
  - Billing
  - Insurance verification
  - Central scheduling
  - Pre-admission testing
  - Engineering/maintenance

Then there are other departments like marketing, finance, and information systems. All these areas play a role in the integrated delivery system and have processes that can be improved significantly.

WHAT IS A LEAN BUSINESS DELIVERY SYSTEM?

The goal of the Lean Enterprise is to supply the best value to the customer, at the right time, with the highest quality at the lowest cost. This means creating a culture of continuous improvement and an environment where everyone in the organization participates in eliminating waste and streamlining processes in order to supply the best value to the customer. Best value means meeting or exceeding the customer's expectations for delivery and service for both product quality and customer-desired quality before and after their encounter. A company's primary mission is not solely to satisfy its customer, but exceed customer's expectation and promote customer loyalty, while making a profit to stay in business.

Lean Business Delivery System Vision

The vision for a Lean Business Delivery system is to have an organization with no waste. Imagine any business process today with zero waste. Lean initially started as a process improvement method for manufacturing, but a Lean Business Delivery system is not only a manufacturing shop floor initiative. Lean is now used for all business models and, if Lean principles are implemented properly, they will prompt changes from all parts of the organization, including finance, accounting, marketing, sales, HR, engineering, etc. Eliminating waste, also known as *Muda,* can be applied to any business process, including information systems, bed management administration, registration, transport, laboratory, pharmacy, ED, radiology, surgery, clinic, general physician offices, or other service areas.

A true Lean system, sometimes referred to as operational excellence, integrates or is simply an extension of past initiatives, including: Total Quality, Deming's 14 principles, Just in Time, Six Sigma, Kanbans, and Kaizen, to name a few. The tools in this book are designed to help you find waste in your organization. We have seen the Lean tools applied from shop floors to offices, hospitals to home builders, and even PTA volunteers to Moms and Dads at home.

If utilized properly, Lean tools will expose waste but do not guarantee the elimination of waste. That job will be up to each organization. When your organization becomes literally obsessed with the total elimination of waste in everything it does and is never satisfied with the current state, then your organization will be well on its way into its Lean journey. Lean should be viewed as a competitive business strategy and must be implemented in combination with a strategy to grow the business.

Understanding the Value of the Lean Business Delivery System

The Lean Business Delivery model begins with understanding customer expectations. Let's start with a basic example of going out to a restaurant. What kind of demands or expectations do you have when you walk into a restaurant? Most of us expect good service. We expect the waiter or waitress to be attentive to our needs, recognize us if we go there frequently, and address us by our name. We expect the food to be delivered on time, to our order specifications in the quantity promised on the menu, and served at the appropriate temperature. We expect the meal to be manufactured in a clean and orderly environment and prepared correctly or in essence "done right the first time."

Related to speed, the restaurant would need to understand if the customers who frequent their restaurant view speed of service as value, or is the expectation of food delivery an even-paced, slower atmosphere. It is critical to understand what your customers want and value. Most of us just expect good value for our money. Sometimes we are willing to pay a little more if we know we are getting superior service. Examples of superior service might be the 1 hr dry cleaner, or overnight delivery.

It is difficult, if not impossible, to achieve or exceed customer expectations if we don't have a good understanding of what the customer views as value-added. If there is waste in the process then there will always be opportunities for variability and inconsistency thus leading to opportunities for customer dissatisfaction. We find healthcare organizations don't routinely survey "customer value." Today's healthcare customer does not necessarily pay fully or directly for the majority of care received. At a minimum, the customer would expect a positive outcome (high quality, error or mistake-free), in a courteous (caring) environment, and in a timely manner. This is rapidly changing as the consumer is becoming more attuned to healthcare reform and may be directly paying for a higher percentage of his or her healthcare costs to one that is more value-based. One of the challenges is that, until recently, patients assumed quality and wanted service. Now they demand both.

We describe the Lean system at a high level in the model pictured in Figure 1.6. On the left side are the Lean tools. Lean tools can be applied to anything that is a process. On the right is the marketing and growth piece. The goal is to grow the business at the same rate that we are improving the business. The model works as follows: Lean is an enabler for growth but does not guarantee

Business System from a Leadership Perspective

We must look at the overall business as a system!

FIGURE 1.6 Business systems overview model.

growth. Growth must be part of the overall Lean initiative in order to succeed. When a company can produce its products with less waste than its competition, it has a distinct advantage. The increased profits can be invested in research and development, capital equipment, higher wages, or passed on to customers to undercut the competitor's price. Organizations must understand that *waste threatens all our jobs*[13] and the health of the business.

JUST IN TIME: THE FIRST PILLAR OF THE TOYOTA PRODUCTION SYSTEM MODEL

Companies need to be more responsive to customers, provide what the customer orders, in the quantity and quality the customer orders, at just the right time that the customer wants it. This is called Just in Time. JIT is one of the two pillars of the Toyota system (Figure 1.7). The goal behind JIT is to use the minimum amount of inventory, equipment, time, labor, and space necessary to deliver JUST IN TIME TO THE CUSTOMER!

Our healthcare definition of JIT developed by nurses is: "Giving the Right patient, the Right care, the Right way, while providing a Great Patient Experience." It includes providing the staff with the necessary and proper tools and supplies in the right locations, when they need them, and in the right amount with shortest nurse travel distances within efficient layouts.

The goal is to create an efficient system with the same or better quality and safety than exists today. It doesn't do any good to create the most efficient or quickest system if we don't have the same or better patient and staff safety, ergonomics, and quality.

Excess inventory and idle time are always signs of problems.

Excess inventory hides problems. The analogy for this is to think of water rushing down the river. When the water level is high, the rocks are invisible. If you are white water rafting, kayaking, or canoeing, you look for the open "Vs" in order to traverse the rocks, but mostly you move swiftly over the rocks. As you lower the water level of the river, the rapids appear and the rocks rise to the surface. This is the same with inventory. When we have lots of inventory (high water), we never see all the waste (rocks) because we are too busy navigating it, rushing around and over it. Waste hides

---

[13] Mark Jamrog, principal, The SMC Group LLC.

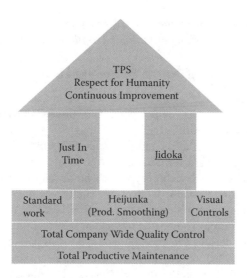

FIGURE 1.7   Toyota House. Source: B.I.G Files.

other waste. The rocks represent waste that was "hidden" by either inventory or other wastes or "work arounds" created within a process, otherwise known as "hidden wastes." As one lowers the water (inventory), which in healthcare can be reducing patients waiting times, overflowing charts, or excess operating room (OR) or hall supplies and instrument sets surface, one starts to expose the problems or rocks (other hidden wastes) underneath along with all the variations that exist in the system. One must make sure there is a continual pursuit to drive down waste.

JIT does not mean zero inventories. All systems need some inventory to function. JIT means there is a small amount of inventory available at point of use before it is needed. It means that the nurses don't have to go to the supply area or closet to get what they need; it should be right there where they need it. We call this at "point of use" inventory. The goal is to work with the minimum amount of inventory necessary but still be safe for the patient.

An Example of One of the Rocks—Short-Staffed

Restaurants can provide another analogy for hospitals. Have you ever walked into a restaurant and had to wait, even though you could see several open tables? This can create a frustrating feeling. Normally, this means the restaurant did not schedule enough staff or is short-staffed, perhaps due to someone calling in sick, so they don't want to seat the customer without being able to provide quality customer service.

Hospitals face a similar problem. Many hospitals today run "short-staffed" in order to try to save money or they simply can't find enough nurses. If the hospital is short-staffed, even though they may have beds available, they will not be able to open the beds for use as there is not enough staff to care for patients. Therefore, the hospital cannot accommodate the total patient demand. As a result, patients incur waits and delays, and other departments (i.e., ED and OR) dependent on the floors may back up.

In Hospital X's post-anesthesia care unit (PACU), the administration chose to staff to average demand. This resulted in closing four to six beds in PACU (22 to 16). This meant, on average, there were enough nurses but whenever they exceeded the average surgery demand per day or per hour or had an influx of pediatric patients (which require one-to-one care), the PACU would back up the OR rooms and pre-operative area (Pre-Op). This would delay surgeries, present safety issues for any emergency cases that may arise, and frustrate staff and physicians, resulting in extending the workday, overtime pay for many nurses, technicians, and housekeepers, and low morale. The ability to extend the workday and pay overtime hid the initial problem of the conscious decision to run short-staffed in PACU. Did the money saved by cutting two or three PACU nurses justify the cost of the overtime and frustration and eventual loss of the surgeons?

JIDOKA—THE SECOND PILLAR OF THE TOYOTA PRODUCTION SYSTEM

The closest Engish translation of *Jidoka* 自働化[14] is autonomation or automating with a human touch. The Japanese term "is ji-do-ka," which consists of three Chinese characters. The first character, ji—"自" means the worker him or her "self," do—"動" means "movement," and ka—"化" means "to change." In the TPS, the second character was replaced by 働—which translates to "work or to labor." It added a character (radical) in the front representing "human" to the original 動.[15] This idea is credited to Sakichi Toyoda,[16] who developed a spinning loom that would automatically shut off if a thread snapped. Creating "smart machines" or machines that can stop themselves if they make a mistake is a central principle to the Lean system. This links to the idea of mistake proofing at the source. The goal is to prevent the error so that a defect does not result. With *Jidoka*, machines are designed to detect a defect prior to passing it on to the next process. Machines should check items before they work on them and after they work on them. An example of a *Jidoka* machine in healthcare is the smart IV pump. The pump uses bar codes on the drug to make sure the right drug is delivered to the right patient, at the correct rate. Another example would be an IV pump that stops and signals when it is empty vs. letting air enter the patient when the solution runs out. This same idea transcends to safety with the philosophy that the machine should protect the human. Many times in the laboratory setting, one laboratory specimen can be used for more than one test. "Splitting" a laboratory sample in two is called aliquoting. This used to be a manual process that posed a safety risk to laboratory technicians who had to perform this task. With the new automated technology, this can now be performed by a machine, eliminating the "human" intervention.

The second idea of *Jidoka* is that machines and equipment should be designed so that humans do not need safety glasses or protective gear. Protected cages and laser curtains should prevent injuries to workers. One of the principles of Lean is to be able to separate man from machine. Machines should do heavy, repetitive, or dangerous work. This concept translates to the worker in kanji with "ji" added to "do" or self-work. This idea of self-work means that if the worker feels that "this is not right" or "I am creating a defective product," he/she must immediately stop the conveyor.[17] Stopping the line or the process is a difficult concept to get across in manufacturing and can also be difficult in healthcare. In the United States, our short term "make the quarterly numbers" strategically conflicts with this concept.

The third idea associated with **Jidoka** is mistake proofing or "poka yoke," meaning never pass on a bad part. A few examples of **Jidoka** or mistake-proofing techniques in healthcare include the Broselow® Tape for Pediatric Trauma. The tape measure is color-coded according to height, and appropriately sized medical devices and doses of medications are contained in packets of the same color to facilitate rapid treatment and reduce calculations and dosing errors; orange-colored oral syringes are designed so they will not fit onto any IV tubing, providing a visual alert and design, so oral medication cannot be accidentally administered intravenously, and the sponge-counter basket, visi-sponge, automatically assists in keeping track of sponges removed from a patient and doing all the paperwork for the nurses. Another example is Sani-track which Sani-Track Hand Hygiene Compliance System has monitored over 2.5 million hand hygiene events. Another is Endoclear® which manufactures a wiper device for the cleaning and visualization of endotracheal tubes,

---

[14] Translation provided by Professor William Tsutsui, Associate Dean for International Studies, Professor of History, College of Liberal Arts & Sciences, The University of Kansas.

[15] Video, *A Passion for Manufacturing, the Essence of the Toyota Production System*, www.saiga-jp.com, kanji to English dictionary, http://dict.regex.info Japanese to English dictionary.

[16] Taiichi Ōhno, *Toyota Production System* (New York: Productivity Press) 1988.

[17] Japanese Management Association, *Kanban Just in Time at Toyota* (New York: Productivity Press) 1986.

manufactured by EndOclear LLC (San Ramon, CA). The EndOclear device is a sterile single-use wiper that clears away secretions and biofilm from the inside of the endotracheal tube (ETT) and provides visualization inside the ETT.[18]

JIDOKA MEANS: NEVER PASS ON A BAD PART OR PATIENT

In the book, *The Nun and the Bureaucrat*,[19] the authors cite several hospitals that encouraged their nurses to admit mistakes. This is an application of *Jidoka* in healthcare and is one of the keys to Lean systems. Mistake-proofing examples in hospitals are numerous. But errors and mistakes cost all of us money and, more important, lives. Humans are at best three Sigma. Consider that three Sigma (with a 1 1/2 sigma shift) is approximately 66,000 mistakes per million opportunities. As long as the process depends on a human, the system will probably never get better than two or three Sigma because humans make mistakes. In order to mistake proof or foolproof processes, we need a way to take the humans out of the equation. Mistakes and errors not only cause human tragedy, but also add expense to an already overburdened healthcare system.

APPLYING JIDOKA TO HEALTHCARE

We have machines and equipment all over the hospital. They are in the laboratory, radiology, the ORs, and in the patient rooms on the floors. How do we know the equipment is working correctly, measuring correctly, or notifying us when it should? If you expand the concept to mistake proofing, how do we eliminate errors in hospitals? We constantly encounter articles, news reports, and journals highlighting all the errors made in hospitals. In many cases, patients' lives are put on the line because our processes and machines are not mistake proofed. In the book, *The Nun and the Bureaucrat: How They Found an Unlikely Cure for America's Sick Hospitals* and the subsequent video, *Good News: How Hospitals Heal Themselves,* these preventable mistakes are exposed with, in some cases, simple solutions.[20] At the end of the documentary the following interim results were reported at various hospitals after the implementation of the continual improvement philosophy, elimination of blame, and the creation of a management vision and the application of Lean:

- An 85% reduction in hospital-acquired infections that were often fatal and cost $30,000–$90,000 each
- A 63% reduction in central line infections since 2001, half of which are fatal and each cost $30,000 to treat
- Lowering of staph infections from 26 per 1000 patients to 8 per 1000
- Decreasing intensive care unit mortality from 5.5% to 3.3%
- Lowering acute diabetic complications from 13.5% to 5%

---

[18] www.t/-sgrp.com/healthcare/sponge-track, TSG's low cost, passive RFID based Soap/Alcohol dispenser wall mount, provides a Passive UHF RFID platform, for dumb dispensers, which provides time stamped enter/exit/sanitize event data, to assist in quantifying and monitoring hand hygiene compliance. MDEA FINALIST: endOclear wiper device for the cleaning and visualization of endotracheal tubes, manufactured by EndOclear LLC (San Ramon, CA). Entry submitted by Innovative Design LLC (Danvill, CA). The endOclear device is a sterile single-use wiper that clears away secretions and biofilm from the inside of the endotracheal tube (ETT) and provides visualization inside the ETT. Supply and design credit to JG Plastics Group LLC (Costa Mesa, CA), and Hiemstra Product Development LLC (San Francisco, CA). http://www.canontradeshows.com/expo/awards/awards/index.php?catId=-1&year=2012&view=View

[19] Louis M. Savary and Clare Crawford-Mason, *The Nun and The Bureaucrat* (Washington, D. C.: CC-M Productions) 2006, 40–41.

[20] Louis M. Savary and Clare Crawford-Mason, *The Nun and The Bureaucrat* (Washington, D. C.: CC-M Productions) 2006.

THE TOP OF THE TOYOTA HOUSE—RESPECT FOR HUMANITY

Companies that are successful in Lean grow their businesses and provide jobs for people. Over time (typically, a couple of years), as hospitals improve their bottom line, we encourage them to share a portion of the extra profits with their employees. Some companies increase employee benefits, set up gain sharing plans, provide cash bonuses or incentive reward programs to help drive results and desired behaviors. After several years of implementing Lean, our goal should be to share bonuses monthly up to 20%–30% or more of an employee's annual pay in monthly, quarterly, or yearly payments. Companies can attract and keep the best because reducing their costs makes them not only more flexible with their customers' pricing, but also more flexible with employees' paychecks.

Lesson Learned

Lean works best with a clearly stated policy, up front, which ensures no one will be laid off as a result of Lean or continuous improvement activities. Most people will not contribute to a team if they think they will be laid off as a result. Tying Lean to layoffs or FTE cutbacks won't prevent you from getting results, but it will keep you from getting the additional results that evolve from creating a Lean culture where employees contribute ideas every day. Many companies unknowingly have limited their improvements because this communication was not handled properly. The improvements they get are only those that the management dictates to their employees. This is not a Lean culture.

A good Lean system implementation, or what some may term System Kaizen, provides staff with the opportunity to suggest improvements within their work areas, which improves the flow of communication and ideas. Listening to staff and implementing their suggestions always yields an improvement in morale and is part of the "Respect for Humanity" concept. Everyone works together as a team and has the opportunity to learn additional jobs and skills; this is referred to as cross-training. The more skills learned, the more marketable and valuable the employee becomes to any company. The opportunity will also exist for you to lead your team in daily production activities and coach others in the skills you have learned. This provides the foundation to build leadership skills.

Implementing Lean does not only impact each person on the unit or clinical area, but everyone in the hospital or clinic will also be affected in some way. Eliminating waste in administrative processes will free up people, and the need for middle management personnel will also be reduced over time. Moving to value streams or service line organizations will provide better "line of sight" to the patient. Overhead should be reduced by 30% or more after several years. This means staff positions are converted into line positions. Those in administrative positions or middle management positions need to constantly expand their skill sets and stay current with training if they are to continue to add value to the company.

As organizations embark on their Lean journey, they need to understand that every department within the enterprise can benefit from becoming "Lean." If every area is not actively engaged in the "pursuit of waste elimination" (or becoming "Lean"), then you have not crossed the cultural chasm of "Lean thinking." One main reason why so many companies fail in this cultural transformation is that organizations implement pieces of the Lean system but not the whole system. Lean thinking is a cultural change. If it stays in the realm of multiple projects, then it will run out of steam when resources and budgets get tight. That is why it must be leadership-driven, but staff-level-implemented.

It is a very challenging and difficult journey that ultimately requires understanding and commitment to be successful. The book, *The Leadership Road Map*,[21] explains in detail what is necessary to create a Lean culture and how to begin and sustain the Lean journey from a CEO's point of view.

---

[21] Dwane Baumgardner, former CEO of Donnelly Corporation, and Russ Scafede, senior vice president of Global Manufacturing, Donnelly Corporation, past general manager/vice president of Toyota Motor Manufacturing Power Train, and consultant.

It starts with the culture piece, i.e., creating your vision and values and provides templates or blueprints to create your Lean road map.

Lesson Learned

It is imperative that everyone be relentless in the elimination of waste by analyzing all components affecting the value stream. A culture of continuous improvement must be created from the top down and from the bottom up. We must create and nurture a learning organization that will cause us to un-learn some of the things we currently practice. The organization must be willing to expand the tool-kit to be able to address any challenge by utilizing Lean Tools, Six Sigma Tools, and other innovative techniques. By constantly lowering operating costs, we increase the opportunity to reward and improve our processes.

LEAN IS A JOURNEY

Depending on the improvement needed and waste identified, a multi-year program may need to be established to determine sequential initiatives that will drive the desired results. Remember, the healthcare delivery system is comprised of many interrelated parts; many "x's" (or causes) will impact a Big "Y" (goal). For example, there are many little x's which drive an OR room turnover time (BIG Y). It may start with the staff understanding what it means to have a room ready, and when is the room ready to bring the patient in, anesthesia must be ready for the patient, the room must be cleaned, supplies and instruments readied for the case as well as "picked" accurately. The staff must be available, and each must understand what his/her role is, or what we call their "standard work." If you have the patient ready at the time the OR calls, and yet the supplies or anesthesia are not available, turnover will take longer. Therefore, there may need to be several Lean initiatives in order to effectively tackle room turnover. The overarching goal of Lean thinking is to get everyone in your organization focused on improving the process. The difference between Toyota and other companies is that Toyota makes thousands of improvements every month as a result of every employee working with his/her group leaders and managers. Every once in a while, one might get a big (ROI) improvement, but that is not the main focus. Most companies worldwide tend to only focus on the largest ROI projects first and miss the opportunity to get everyone involved in the improvement process.

Lesson Learned

You will know you are further down the Lean culture path when building a culture of ongoing continuous improvement every day outweighs the insistence on implementing only those perceived large ROI projects first. Thousands of small improvements turn into large overall returns. Sometimes, a project with a lower ROI can lead to a project with a higher ROI. Many times, jumping to the highest ROI project is not the best strategy.

In summary, although there may be some differences between manufacturing and providing patient care, the Lean Business Delivery system has been shown to have application within healthcare organizations, such as hospitals, clinics, surgery centers, free-standing laboratories as well as other support areas and will continue to grow as more organizations realize the benefits gained through the Integrated Delivery System/Network (IDS/IDN).

2 Batching vs. Lean Thinking and Flow

BATCHING VS. LEAN THINKING AND FLOW

"The current cost and quality pressures hospitals are facing provide a natural burning platform for Lean introduction. 10 years ago, I had to convince the leadership teams change was necessary, and those opportunities existed. This is no longer the case... the 'pull' for Lean is evident"[1]

—Tom Chickerella Corporate VP & Program Management Officer
Vanguard Health Systems, Nashville, Tennessee

Lean thinking is the continual and relentless pursuit of eliminating waste in our systems and processes. To think Lean is to think of how we can eliminate waste in every activity we do. The term Lean was coined by John Krafcik in is his paper "Triumph of the Lean Production System" for his Master's thesis at MIT Sloan School of Management in 1988[2]. Lean is described as: the five-step thought process for guiding the implementation of Lean techniques as easy to remember, but difficult to achieve:

1. Specify value from the standpoint of the customer.
2. Identify all the steps in the value stream for each product family, eliminating those steps which do not create value.
3. Make the value-creating steps occur in tight sequence so the product will flow smoothly for the customer.
4. As flow is introduced, let customers pull value from the next activity.
5. As value is specified, value streams are identified, wasted steps are removed, and flow and pull are introduced. Begin the process again and continue it until a state of perfection is reached in which value is created with no waste.

Learning to develop how to "think Lean" is more difficult than it sounds. One must learn to recognize waste in order to clearly see it. In order to see it we must first understand how waste is defined.[3]

As you walk around the workplace, do you see any waste? Waste surrounds us every day and results in lost time and frustration. But lost time is very difficult to see or track. Once trained in Lean, we are actually able to see the lost time and the lost output as it occurs. Lean is a different way of thinking and philosophically approaching how we work and manage our organizations. By

---

[1] Personal correspondence from Tom Chickerella, Corporate VP & Program Management Officer, Vanguard Health Systems, Nashville, TN.

[2] http://rk2blog.com/2010/03/08/the-etymological-origin-of-Lean/ "In fact, it is well known that LEAN was coined by John Krafcik in his 1988 SLOAN MANAGEMENT REVIEW article "Triumph of the Lean production system." that It is less well known that Krafcik adopted the term late in his academic career. In his early academic papers, including "Learning from NUMMI" (1986), an internal working paper of MIT's International Motor Vehicle Program, through his 1988 MIT masters thesis, he didn't call it LEAN. He called the production system used by Toyota and a small number of other Japanese automakers FRAGILE".

[3] Influenced by Mark Jamrog, principal, The SMC Group.

eliminating waste, we increase the percentage of added valued to our processes. To be value-added,[4] an item must:

- Be desired by the customer
- Physically or mentally change the patient for the better
- Be done correctly the first time

If it does not meet all three criteria, the item is not considered value-added. Some items may be required by the customer but do not physically change the product. (Such as a physical exam by a doctor.)

Lesson Learned

Our analysis shows that we typically spend only 5%–30% of time doing value-added steps for our patients/customers.

BATCHING VS. FLOW IN A HEALTHCARE ENVIRONMENT

What is batching? The word batch[5] comes from Old English and originally meant "to bake" or "something that is baked." Even today we tend to bake things which are made in batches (i.e., batch of cookies or making a triple batch of cupcakes). A batch system is where one step of a process is done to multiple items or things at a time before the next step or process is started. This process is repeated until all steps are completed for the lot. One doesn't see the first finished piece until the entire batch is completed.

Batching includes things you may not realize. When we go to the copy machine we normally collect all the things we want to copy first. If we are getting drinks for several people, we will put the ice in all the glasses first. If we are making several sandwiches (Figure 2.1), we will layout the bread first, put the ham on each one, then the cheese, the final piece of bread, cut them all, and finally on to plates.

BATCHING EXAMPLES

- Traffic lights are batch
- Traffic circles are flow
- Traffic lights that are timed to allow flow are somewhere between batch and flow
- Highways (with no traffic lights) are examples of flow with parallel lanes (unless you get too many cars)
- Elevators are batch
- Escalators are flow

Process Definition

A process is anything with an input which is transformed in to something else representing an output. An input starts with raw material (or information). It is then converted during the process to the output desired (or sometimes not desired, i.e., defect). It can be physical or mental; it can be a manufacturing step for a product or a series of transactional steps to arrive at a result or report. It can be cocoa turned into hot chocolate or milk and marshmallows are added to it to make it more creamy and delicious.

---

[4] As defined in the AMA video, *Time: The Next Dimension of Quality*, by the American Management Association.
[5] From Middle English *bache* (or *bacche*) ⸝Old English *bæcce* ("something baked") <*bacan* ("to bake"). Compare German *Gebäck* and Dutch *baksel*.

FIGURE 2.1   Nutritional Services Batching Sandwiches. Source: BIG Files.

A process can be information which is transformed into a different output by a particular input. When we take a patient's history in an ED, we have an input of information from the patient which produces an output which is the medical chart. Writing an email or text is a process. Writing this book is a process.

Batching Systems

Batching systems and processes and the resulting variations are the hidden enemy of Lean Thinking. It is this "batching" mindset which makes sustaining the one-piece flow philosophy difficult. This mindset is always present in all of us and unconsciously lurking in the background ready to disrupt Lean Practitioners.

Why People Love to Batch?

We have found eight major forces which drive us to batch. These are

1. **Our Minds and Predispositions**
2. **Set-ups/Changeovers**
3. **Travel Distances**
4. **Equipment**
5. **Processes**
6. **Idle time**
7. **Space**
8. **Variation**

1. **Our Minds Predisposition – "It's the way we think"**
   The single biggest incentive to batch comes from us… humans. For some reason we seem to be "programmed to batch" from birth. Could it be in our DNA? We have never run into

people that objected to batching; but after many years of objections to one-piece flow one can assuredly deduce batching must be an innate quality we all possess, and for some reason we all seem to be hardwired to think batching is the most efficient system.

If it was not for this paradigm, we think most companies would naturally already be one-piece flow. Have you ever had a discussion with someone not exposed to Lean where you did not have to "DEFEND" one-piece flow and work very hard to explain why it is better than batching?

So, what is it about batching? We believe we are all just like a dog who instinctively buried his bone. None of us were taught to batch, we just naturally believe it is the right way to get things done. Most people believe it is more efficient and more productive to repeat the same operation on all pieces at the same time. This is why we believe achieving single piece flow in Lean implementations often fail and why it is so easy to undo once it's implemented.

For example, a new CEO who knows nothing about Lean or Flow can easily kill the Lean program many times without realizing. It only takes one person at the top to reverse years of progress. If Lean is not somehow interwoven into the culture, it will not sustain because all of us are constantly trying to undo it with our conscious or subconscious minds!

Lesson Learned: Our experience is 99% of people are not born to think Lean nor do they just figure this stuff out on their own. Many times, if they do figure it out they don't realize it and go back to batching, i.e., the way it was always done before.

2. **Setup or Changeovers**

The second reason for batching is setups or changeovers. This is the amount of time it takes to set up or change-over an area or piece of equipment. An example would be changing an OR room over for the next surgery case. The longer the setup the more we tend to batch. Therefore, we must reduce setup times before going to one-piece flow.

Lean Results: At hospital X, reducing changeover times for OR rooms increased the units capacity by 27%, allowing the surgeon to perform two more cases each day and leave earlier.

3. **Transportation**

Transportation is how long it takes or the distance required to travel from one area to another. The longer the travel distance, the more we batch. For example, we all will tend to carry as much as we can at one time to a distant room or medical unit. It might be medicine, supplies, paperwork, towels, etc. How often would you go to the supermarket and purchase only one day's worth of groceries at a time? In order to implement Lean, we must work to reduce these travel distances.

Lean Results: In a hospital ED (Emergency Department) process by cutting down travel time for the Provider, we reduced the wait time to see the Provider by 80% and reduced the waiting room from 10 hours to zero. In the winter, 18% of people left before seeing the doctor; now it is less than 1%.

4. **Equipment**

Equipment can force us to batch. If you have a centrifuge that holds fifty tubes of blood, would it make sense to load it with only one test tube?

Lean Results: Hospital X – Core Lab Daily Tube Volume increased from 2,399 to 3,079 or 28% by going to small 4 tube centrifuges (Figure 2.2).

5. **Processes**

Some systems are composed of batch type processes. Making slides from a specimen in Histology, mixing IV medicines (for multiple patients), and making cookies are all examples of batch processing. This would also include centralization of processes like transport or registration

FIGURE 2.2   Lab Mini Centrifuges located at the machine point of use (POU). Source: BIG Archives.

6. **Idle time**

   If someone is idle, they will find things to do (batch) to try and keep busy. We see idle time everywhere in hospitals. It is not necessarily the person's fault but generally the system's fault in which they are working. Most of the time this is driven by poor layouts. For example a person is placed at a desk and is only busy when someone comes to the desk to ask them a question or to register a patient.

   Lean Results: By changing the layout and streamlining the processes in pre-testing, we were able to obtain the following results in Table 2.1.

7. **Space (Too little or too much)**

   When we don't have enough space, we tend to batch in the space we have simply because we don't have room to flow the process. When we have too much space, we tend to batch because we have plenty of room to store the extra inventory.

8. **Variation**

   Variation in processes drive batch production and often lead to centralization. Hospitals, in particular, are faced with high levels of variation (patient volumes). In order to implement Lean, we must work to stabilize and standardize our processes.

   Lean Results: *At hospital X by standardizing processes in the ED, we were able to virtually eliminate the waiting room. We also experienced similar results in other surgical pre-testing areas.*

One-Piece/Patient Flow

One of the key concepts in Lean is "one-piece flow" or small-lot processing. One-piece flow or single-piece flow refers to the processing or servicing of each patient, one at a time. When we have overcome the things which force us to batch and move to flow we find it is always faster and results in a decreased errors.

Lesson Learned: *In order to flow we must eliminate the reason for batching. You have to believe in your heart one-piece flow is always better than batching to be successful in Lean Thinking and then continue to work to achieve it despite the obstacles. This is easy to say but very difficult to do.*

TABLE 2.1
Pre-Testing Clinic Results From Three Different Hospitals Implementing Lean Pre-Testing Departments

	Hall Patients	Phone Calls	Total Patients and Calls	# Nurses	# Clerical	# Techs	Total Persons	Working Days'	Working Hours (assumes 40 hrs per week)	Nursing Hours Per Patient Visit	Total Labor Hours Per Patient	Patients Seen Per Person Per Day	# Total FTEs	Hours Per FTE	Notes
Hospital #1	UK	UK	13,000	22	2	6	30	250	45,760	3.52	4.80	1.73	UK	UK	No data on change nurses
Hospital #2	10,534	3962	14,496	11	3	2	16	250	22,880	1.58	2.30	3.62	UK	UK	Secretaries also do scheduling
Hospital #3	12,314	6376	18,690	9.9	3	2	14.9	250	20,592	1.10	1.66	5.02	14.80	1.65	Does not include change nurse. 11 nurses but 9.9 FTEs. Actual productivity running 1.39 or less

Note: Hospital #1 was profiled in a paper as having streamlined their care compared to hospital #2 and #3, which conducted Lean system implementations. UK = unknown.

Converting from batch to one-piece flow reduces cycle times by reducing delays in the process, hence reducing the inventory needed within that process.

Authors Note: As we implement one-piece flow, waste and variation immediately surface, showing clearly opportunities to improve each step in the process. The by product is all the problems you have ever had come to the surface and then get blamed on implementing Lean!

By reducing the steps in the process, we also reduce the opportunity for defects in the process. Consider the common example of folding and stuffing one hundred envelopes in a batch mode:

Step 1: Fold the letters. The first letter is picked up off the stack of copies and folded. Once it is folded, it needs to be stored or placed somewhere, which requires space... and space costs money! The next letter is then picked up, folded, and placed on top of the first folded letter. In the process of folding the letters, some may fall off the pile or off the table, requiring the process to stop. We may have to recount the stack of letters to validate how many we folded. The process continues until all one hundred letters are folded.

Individual tasks for Step 1 are: reach for letter, grasp and pick up letter, fold letter, move letter to table, put down letter, recount if necessary.

Step 2: Stuff the envelopes. The first folded letter is picked up and stuffed into the envelope. Remove the adhesive strip and seal the envelope. The envelope is now placed in a new location, which requires even more space! Once again, space costs money. (When this concept is expanded to consider the entire inventory in an area or system, it results in the need for some type of computerized inventory tracking system.)

Individual tasks for Step 2 are: reach for letter, grasp and pick up letter, move letter, reach for envelope, grasp and pick up envelope, move envelope into position, stuff letter in envelope, seal envelope, move envelope back to table, put down envelope.

Step 3: Placing stamps and mailing labels. Each of the envelopes is picked up again and a stamp and mailing label is placed on the front of the envelope. Once again, they are placed on the table in a third location, requiring additional space!

Individual tasks for Step 3 are: reach for envelope, grasp and pick up envelope, move envelope, reach for labels, grasp and pick up labels, move labels into position, apply labels to envelope, move to table, put down envelope.

There were a total of twenty-four individual tasks across all three steps. If we considered the need to complete a batch of 100 envelopes and each of the three major steps (i.e., fold, stuff, place labels) took 1 min for each piece, the entire batch would be completed in 300 min (100 envelopes x 3 tasks x 1 min each = 300 min); however, the first envelope would be completed and ready to be mailed in 201 min, but we wouldn't normally see it until the entire batch of three hundred were completed. This does not include the time it took to pick up and put down the envelopes each time.

Now let's explore defects and errors. First, with batching, when do we find the defect? The answer is normally once the batch is completed or in the last step. In Lean and Six Sigma, we learn that each step in a process is an opportunity for a defect. There were twenty-four total steps in this process. It can be postulated that each of these steps, particularly in the hospital world, is an opportunity for defects to occur. For example: Can something or someone get damaged during transportation? Patient falls are one of the number one problems in most hospitals. Can things get damaged in storage? Have you ever seen equipment get damaged in storage in an operating room, hallways, or equipment storage area?

Lesson Learned: *If we can eliminate the steps, we also eliminate the opportunity for the defect, thus improving quality.*

ONE-PIECE FLOW EXAMPLE

Let's revisit the envelope example (Figure 2.3). If we revise our process to one-piece flow, it would look like this:

1. Reach for the letter.
2. Grasp and pick up the letter.
3. Move the letter.
4. Fold the letter.
5. Reach for and grasp the envelope.
6. Pick up the envelope.
7. While holding the envelope, stuff with the letter already in your other hand.
8. Seal the envelope.
9. Reach for and grasp the stamp and mailing labels.
10. Put stamp and address labels on envelope.
11. Move the envelope.
12. Put the envelope down.

When do we get our first piece? The answer should be 3 min, i.e., fold, stuff, and label. Using single-piece or one-piece flow, the process went from twenty-four steps to twelve steps or a 50% reduction in individual tasks! So, in retrospect, batching doesn't really save us anything; in fact, it only costs us more in the long run. Therefore, batching is not truly the most efficient system. We just think it is!

With one-piece flow, the first envelope was completed in 3 mins compared to 201 min when batching. The entire process was completed in 300 minutes, which is equal to the batch processing but not including the extra time to pick up and put down each envelope throughout the process. However, we don't see the first piece in the batch model until the entire batch is completed.

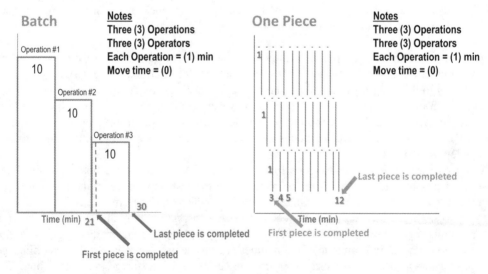

FIGURE 2.3 Batch versus one-piece flow example. When processing 10 pieces, we get our first piece in batch at 21 min versus 3 min in flow and our last piece at 30 min in batch versus 12 min in flow. With one-piece flow, we average a part a minute off the line or office process. Source: From The effect of Lot Delay Reductions, Shingo, S., The Shingo Production Management System, Productivity Press, pp. 17, 116. Copyright 1990 used with permission from Taylor & Francis.

In our one-piece flow scenario, if the number of resources performing the work was increased to three staff members, then all the work would have been completed in 102 min (3 + 99 min), with the remaining envelopes being completed with a cycle time of every minute vs. the 300 min in the batching environment.

In addition, twelve steps were reduced, thus reducing twelve opportunities for defects times 100 pieces, for a total reduction of twelve hundred defect opportunities. While Lean may not always yield an increase in quality, it will certainly not cause a degradation. It is not unusual to get an increase in quality, and many times, it is unexpected. In addition, if a defect occurs in our one-piece flow scenario, we find it right away, and our rework is minimal and limited to one piece, instead of at the end of a batch where the entire batch may be defective.

We have a Lean saying:

> **"When you work on something you don't need, you can't work on something you do need!"**
> - Charlie Protzman

This is extremely important. This is the premise behind the waste of overproduction, and while this saying sounds simple, it is violated all the time. Toyota differentiates this by highlighting the difference between apparent vs. true efficiency. True efficiency occurs only when we increase efficiency without overproducing. A common example of overproduction in the hospital is the Pre-Op area. The Pre-operative (Pre-Op) area typically has all outpatients arrive at 5:00 a.m. for their 7:30 a.m. cases. Think of the behavior this batching drives. The practice of bringing patients in "batches" at the same time of the morning ultimately requires that we have more staff and more space to handle all the patients throughout the system, i.e., registration, surgery waiting or admitting, Pre-Op, etc.

Since all patients are arriving at the same time:

- They are often processed prior to the time they would be required to be ready for their surgical procedure, due to the fact patients are all arriving at the same time regardless of their surgical time.
- They are processed in the wrong order (loss of FIFO) and the OR finds they still wait for patients to be ready.
- Larger Pre-Op area with more beds are required to hold the patients.

This batching results in excess labor not only to process the patients, monitor the patients, but in installing systems to keep track of all the patients. This creates challenges in being able to "pull" inpatients from the floors to the Pre-Op area in time for surgery. The end result is a Pre-Op area jammed full of patients waiting for surgery, but the surgery area is not ready for them. Then, all of a sudden, we have an emergency patient who needs to go to surgery, but there is no room in Pre-Op to process the ED patient.

Lesson Learned - *A product or patient in a batch process spends most of its time (greater than 80% or more) waiting (storage) and typically less than 10% in value-added processes. Queues in the process result in longer throughput times, requiring more inventory, rooms, staff, and larger waiting rooms to fill the demand. This also creates very unhappy patients.*

Another example of batching in hospitals is the "morning run" in the laboratory. Physicians order tests to be drawn, analyzed and resulted in time for their morning rounds. In a given unit one might have thirty blood specimens in tubes collected at one time and then sent to the laboratory for processing. All specimens are received in the laboratory at the same time and then moved to the centrifuge area. The centrifuge (or several large centrifuges) can hold the entire batch. Once the specimens are spun, they are moved to a rack in the chemistry department. They are all logged into the system together and then placed into a batch processor. In essence, they move through the overall system as a large batch from machine to machine or station to station.

GROUP TECHNOLOGY[6]

Group technology is a tool used to divide up categories of patients or products into families or like "groups" or service lines and then working on them using one-piece flow or small lots. It is like having traffic lights which are timed to allow a batch of cars at a time to flow down the street. Group technology falls somewhere between batching and one-piece flow. An example would be having cardiac surgery and vascular surgery—"like or similar services"—share the same surgical suites or patient care areas, as they use similar supplies and surgical instruments.

Lesson Learned

We need to establish level loaded (balanced flow) pull systems and advanced planning in order to better manage the day-to-day flow through surgery.

PRODUCTIVITY - DEFINITION

What is productivity? What does it mean to be more efficient? Efficiency or being more productive is doing more output with the same or fewer resources and more efficiently by utilizing all resources—man (labor), method (process), machine (equipment), and materials (supplies)—in the best way possible.

BATCHING THE DOMINO EFFECT

How does a physician conduct patient rounds? Typically, physicians round first thing in the morning, and there may be several physicians rounding on a large unit within a short period of time. Historically, depending on the layout of the unit, the physician would have taken several patient charts and head off to see their patients. This is the beginning of "domino effect batching." The batching occurs in large part because of the travel distance that would be incurred if the doctor had to walk back to get a chart each time he/she needed to see the next patient. In essence, the waste of excess travel distance is forcing the batch process.

This has changed with the adoption of Computerized Order Entry; now physicians can write orders that are directly transmitted to the pharmacy, laboratory or radiology. There are still "waves" of orders being received as many physicians round at the same time in the morning. However, technology has helped "level load" the transmission of orders as charts are no longer "stacked" at the unit secretary's desk waiting for processing, which historically were not processed in FIFO (first in first out order).

PEAK DEMAND

Let's look at one of these departments. Laboratory receives a large batch of orders that need to be drawn, processed and resulted by 06:00 in preparation for physician early morning rounding (from several units in the same time period). When this occurs, we refer to this as "peak demand." Peak demand is the point where demand spikes in the process due to the "domino effect."

Since one person can't handle the workload during peak demand, more staff is allocated during these periods. But in the off-peak demand times, the remaining staff are left with little or nothing to do (idle). In some cases, it is difficult to staff for peak demand, so it is handled with less people. As demand fluctuates, the system is stressed, bottlenecks are created, and staff members become frustrated. Because the orders bottleneck, the pharmacy inevitably gets behind, which further inhibits orders being processed in first in, first out (FIFO) order. What is interesting is if you ask the staff how their day went, they don't think about their idle times, but they dwell on the times they were over-stressed!

---

[6] John L. Burbidge, *Group Technology* (London: Mechanical Engineering Publications) 1975.

The nursing staff typically has little or no visibility into the status of their patient's orders in the laboratory queue. This creates the need for many phone calls by the frustrated clerical and nursing staff to follow up on their patient's results. Because these queues develop as a result of the batching, we have to design *STAT* processes to handle those orders that are critical in order to ensure these orders are processed first during peak demand periods. We thus create *STATS* not for patient needs, but for staff and process needs. This further bottlenecks the system and leads to more *STATS*, further adding to the problem.

Peak demand is a phenomenon that also happens outside healthcare. For example, restaurants refer to this as being "slammed." In non-Lean manufacturing companies it is referred to as "end of the month."

What is the problem here? The problem statement would be, "there are numerous spikes in demand throughout the hospital, creating bottlenecks, staff frustration, and customer dissatisfaction," impacting timely order or service fulfillment. In order to begin to identify the root cause of the problem, we would chart the demand and map the process. Then, with further probing, we would go to the actual place (*Gemba*) on the unit and use the five why's to determine the causes or what we call Xs in the Six Sigma equation: $Y = f(x)$, which are driving the problem(s).

We would find physician rounding is filled with activities that contributed to the batch process. We would also find that the doctor rounding system is the root cause of the spikes in demand and the need for *STAT* orders in not just the pharmacy but throughout the entire hospital.

Underlying factors that play a role in physician rounding might be the travel distance to the central location where the charts are stored vs. at the bedside, manual ordering and charting, missing charts, and "this is the way we have always done rounding," as well as how the unit clerk has always processed the orders.

All this occurs with little understanding or a lack of awareness by the doctors as to how their activities might be impacting the process downstream. What could be done to fix root causes? In essence, one needs to consider changing the entire system.

Improvements could include level loading and eliminating batch processing, where possible. If the systems were level loaded, this would require less staffing, since peak demands would diminish and the need for *STAT* orders would be minimized if not eliminated as bottlenecks shrink or disappear. Additionally staff would feel less frustrated and stressed at the end of the day. What if there was an orderly way to process the orders in FIFO by the unit clerk? What if the charts could be accessed through a computer or PDA? What if the doctor could enter the orders at the time of the patient visit, i.e., computerized physician order entry (CPOE), similar to a restaurant touch screen? CPOE drives one-piece flow. This example is just a simple representation of batching and some of the causes and potential solutions, which may impact the healthcare system in the near future.

Examples of Batching in Healthcare

Chart Preparation

Hospital X had a process called "chart preparation." Charts were prepared in advance for patients who were scheduled for surgery. As faxes and other paperwork were received from doctors' offices and elsewhere, the information was placed into a large folder and then separated into patient named manila folders and put in what the secretary believed was the proper order. Two or three days prior to surgery, each secretary would go through and organize the papers in the patient manila folders again and again, placing the information contained in the large folders to the patient folders in order. The manila folders were scattered everywhere in the department. The day prior to surgery, the secretary would search for the manila folders, pull out the hard charts and stack them up. She would take the manila patient named folders and place each one into a hard chart. Then she would go back and reorganize what was in the manila chart again and place it into the hard chart, occasionally having to punch holes in the paperwork. They were always behind when they were supposed to be two weeks ahead.

The Chart Problem

There was the perception among the workers that they didn't have enough clerical staff to keep up with all the paperwork. The unit was considering hiring another full-time secretary to assist in the chart preparation process. To determine whether or not this was actually a problem, a series of questions related to the process were asked (ask "why" five times) to determine if the root cause of the problem was the need for additional staff.

During video analysis, the first question put to the clerk was if she had placed the contents of the chart (in the manila folder) in the correct order the previous day and, "if so, why was the second clerk putting it into a different order in the hard chart today?" The response was, "Because that is the way we have always done it." What was observed was that these charts were handled over and over and over again, adding no value.

Lean Result:

A staff member, department manager and the acting supervisor were engaged during the Lean implementation to help analyze and change the process. Several process changes occurred.

- First, the manila folders were eliminated and the paperwork was placed in the proper order, directly into the hard charts. Each chart was now only handled once and the ongoing batching and handling of every manila folder every day was eliminated.
- An assembly line model for the charts was constructed utilizing one-piece flow. This resulted in freeing up space where batch processing of charts used to occur. If new paperwork came in, the chart was pulled and the paperwork put into the right spot in the hard chart.

Prior to the improvement, the secretaries had trouble keeping up with the charts required for the day of surgery. After the improvement, the chart completion rate increased from 40% to more than 80% the day prior to surgery. In addition, 50% of the charts were completed three or more days prior to surgery, which had never been accomplished before. One final improvement was to add EFAX[7] to eliminate all the lost orders faxed in from the doctors' offices. This improved surgeon satisfaction and eliminated many phone calls back and forth to the doctor's offices.

APPLICATION OF ONE-PIECE FLOW TO HEALTHCARE

How can the concept of single-piece flow apply in the healthcare setting? Let's look at how routine blood tests are drawn and completed in time for physicians to round on their patients. Generally, laboratory tests are drawn between 2 a.m. and 5 a.m. each morning. This is normally a batch process in which the phlebotomists go from room to room to collect blood. Each patient may have one or several test tubes of blood drawn, depending on the number and type of tests ordered by the physician. In most cases, phlebotomists draw half of the patients on the unit, depending on the location of the "tube" system station (which is utilized to transport specimens to the laboratory). The specimens are sent in batch mode via a tube system to the laboratory, where they all drop in the bottom of the tube station at once. Sending multiple patients specimens down to the laboratory in large batches can create difficulties for laboratories that are trying to meet turnaround time metrics, e.g., lab tests draw to result times in Table 2.2.

The phlebotomist arrived on the unit and began the first patient at 2:58 a.m. and was able to complete a routine patient's blood draw within a 4–6 min time period. She then proceeded and had 2 patients that were difficult to draw, taking 9 and 12 min. The phlebotomist took 59 min to complete 7 patients, and all the blood was then sent to the laboratory at the same time.

What if the laboratory was trying to achieve an average turnaround time of 60 min? Table 2.3 shows the actual time by patient in minutes from the time the first patient was drawn to the time the

TABLE 2.2

Phlebotomist Times of the Patient Draw Process

Patient	#1	#2	#3	#4	#5	#6	#7	At Tube Station
In room	2:58	3:03	3:08	3:21	3:28		3:38	3:46	
Out room	3:01	3:07	3:20	3:26	3:32		3:44	3:55	3:57
Travel (min)		2	1	1	2	6	2	2	
Draw time	0:03	0:04	0:12	0:05	0:04		0:06	0:09	
Delays			Difficult blood draw		Delayed by RN			Difficult blood draw	

Total process time from drawing first patient to tube station on unit — 0:59

phlebotomist reached the tube system. If we assume (for this example) that it would take a minimum of 20 min for each specimen to reach the laboratory by tube, be received, checked in, and have the test performed (result) in the laboratory, then the first two specimens could not possibly meet the target of 60 min (patient blood draw to result). The next two specimens would more than likely be at risk of not meeting the goal as well. Therefore, it would be a challenge for the laboratory to meet the 60 min turnaround time.

Let's apply the concepts of single-piece flow to the scenario above. If all specimens were drawn one at a time and then immediately sent to the laboratory, the goal of a 60 min turnaround would be achieved; however, it probably does not make sense to expect a phlebotomist to perform a blood draw on a single patient and then travel to the tube station after each blood draw. Remember, travel distance forces us to batch! One can still apply the concept of single-piece or small-lot batching to this scenario and have the phlebotomist only draw 2–4 patients as shown in Table 2.4.

This would not only make the probability of achieving the turnaround time goal, but it would also level load the work in the laboratory as shown in Table 2.5.

We can conclude that one-piece or one-patient flow is "true efficiency" vs. "apparent efficiency." Productivity equals paid hours per unit (both direct and indirect). It is only efficient if we do it better than or within the standard without overproducing. If we raise only the output without looking at our true demand, then this is considered apparent efficiency. If we add workers or machines to raise the output but the demand is not there, then we overproduce, which is the number one Lean waste.

TABLE 2.3

Morning Run Blood Draw Process—7 Patients

Patient	Draw Complete to Tube*		Tube to Result (est)		Estimated TAT
1	0:56	+	20	=	76
2	0:50	+	20	=	70
3	0:37	+	20	=	57
4	0:31	+	20	=	51
5	0:25	+	20	=	45
6	0:13	+	20	=	33
7	0:02	+	20	=	22

Drawing all 7 patients in one "batch" impacts the ability to meet 60 min TAT.

*Note may vary slightly pending travel distances to tube.

TABLE 2.4
Morning Blood Draw—4 Patients

Patient	#1	#2	#3	#4		At Tube Station
In room	2:58	3:03	3:08	3:21		
Out room	3:01	3:07	3:20	3:26		3:32
Travel (min)		2	1		1	6
Draw time	0:03	0:04	0:12	0:05		
Delays			Difficult blood draw	Delayed by RN		

Total process time from drawing first patient to tube station on unit   0:39

TABLE 2.5
Morning Run Blood Draw Process—4 Patients

Patient	Draw Complete to Tube*		Tube to Result (est)		Estimated TAT
1	0:31	+	20	=	51
2	0:25	+	20	=	45
3	0:12	+	20	=	32
4	0:06	+	20	=	26

Sending to lab after drawing 4 patients will enable the process targets
of 60 min to be achieved.
*Note may vary slightly pending travel distances to tube.

One-piece flow (or small-lot production) results in shorter throughput times, reduced inventories, increased responsiveness to customers, reduced cost, and reduced opportunities for defects. Other examples of batching in hospitals are surgery or catheterization laboratory start times, all at 7:00 or 7:30 a.m. (all the cases beginning at the same time), requiring all the resources to prepare and transport at the same time, creating an artificial peak demand instead of potentially staggering or level loading the work at intervals; this also creates the domino effect throughout the hospital to support services.

We have never run into a process that we could not improve by applying the Lean principles of flow and waste elimination. As Joel Barker states in the video, *The Business of Paradigms*,[8] "Those who say it cannot be done should get out of the way of those who are doing it."[9]

FLOW—ONE-PIECE FLOW OR SMALL LOT[10]

One-piece flow will always get the first piece completed significantly quicker than batching. One-piece flow reduces cycle times, inventory and storage time, as well as highlighting waste in the process.

We were staying in a hotel in Columbia, SC, when a bellhop saw me waiting for the elevators at around 11 a.m.—check-out *time. Much to the chagrin of his front desk supervisor, he said to me,*

---

[8] Joel Barker, *The Business of Paradigms* video.
[9] Joel Barker, *The Business of Paradigms* video.
[10] For more information read Leveraging Lean in Healthcare, Protzman, Mayzell, Kerpchar ©2011, CRC Press.

"You know, if they would just stagger the checkout, the waits for the elevator wouldn't be so long."
I told the person he was absolutely correct.

Many hospitals have the same challenges and flaws with their overall hospital throughput. We find the majority of patients tend to be discharged around the same time of the day. In fact, many hospitals are trying to create model similar to hotels and discharge their patients all at the same time. We think this approach is fundamentally flawed. When discharges from the hospital are batched, all the problems that go with batch-type systems are created, leading to more chaos and requiring more staff to transport patients out of the hospital (or delays in discharges). This is because all the resources are being pulled at the same time. In addition, just like the hotel, everyone is trying to use the elevators at the same time. The idea should to level load your discharges as they occur throughout the day. Demand for rooms is not all at the same time. In fact, post-operative care units will start needing beds around 9 a.m., and demand diminishes by mid-afternoon as surgeons complete the peak case demand for the day. The goal should be to match availability to demand. In addition, when all the patients are all made ready for discharge at the same time it creates challenges for room cleaning and changing over beds.

3 Lean and Change Management

All progress comes from change, but not all change is progress.

—Unknown

If you want to go fast... go alone, if you want to go far... go together

—Unknown

Change management is not only a large part of Lean, it also occurs before, during, and after any Lean implementation. One should not underestimate the importance of this component to successfully disseminate, deploy, and sustain Lean.

IMPLEMENTING LEAN IS ABOUT BALANCE

We have a saying that Lean is 50/50 task vs. people. Fifty percent of Lean is implementing Lean tools. This is the scientific management part of Lean. The other 50% of Lean is the "people" or "culture" piece which requires significant change management. There must be a balance between these two pieces. If the Lean balance scale swings too much to the scientific management side, we can end up with low morale and discontent with the ultimate result being unionization. If we swing too far on the people side, then we end up with no discipline on the floor and no chain of command. People do whatever they want to do, are not accountable, hoard their knowledge (to protect their job), and are out of control. That is why striking this balance before, during, and after the ongoing improvement phase of Lean is so important.

LEAN CULTURE CHANGE

While learning and implementing Lean tools is not easy, implementing the people piece or what Toyota calls "Respect for Humanity" is much more difficult. The people piece includes encouraging people not only to buy-in and accept Lean, but also to embrace and sustain the changes. The real goal of Lean is to create a continuous improvement culture where employees are contributing ideas every day and supervisors or team leaders have budgeted 50% or more time to implement these improvements on a daily basis.

Lean is a very difficult culture to create. In discussing this with Jerry Solomon, multiple Shingo Prize winner,[1] Jerry said, "Why would you want to embark on the Lean journey when over 90% of companies fail in their quest to truly become Lean? What will your company do differently to be successful?"

Lesson Learned

It is extremely important if you are starting a Lean journey that you contemplate and truthfully answer the question above. We ask this of any healthcare institution or department even thinking about going down the Lean path. Think through it, plan and map it out, get the right people on board, don't waiver, and never look back. Hopefully, we can reverse this to 90% of companies being successful in implementing Lean and Six Sigma.

---

[1] Jerrold Solomon, *Accounting for World Class Operation* (Fort Wayne, IN: WCM Associates) 2007, *Who's Counting* (Fort Wayne, IN: WCM Associates) 2003. Both books won the Shingo Prize.

Homework

Answer the following question: What are you going to do differently that will make you one of the 10% of healthcare companies in the world that is successful in implementing Lean?

This chapter explores various change models and topics to consider in your Lean quest. Since every company is different, it is difficult to throw out a "cookie cutter" solution for implementing culture change. Suffice it to say, that to be successful and truly sustain, the change must start and be driven from the top level which must create a pull (and at times "pushed") from the line leadership. There are many tools out there to choose from[2] and we have selected a few that we use across all implementations. The first concept of change management we explore is paradigms.

PARADIGMS

How many times have you had a great idea for improving a process? How many of you had trouble implementing your new idea? This is the concept Joel Barker explores in his video series, *Business of Paradigms*. He describes paradigms as "a set of rules or regulations we use to filter data." Data that meet our expectations passes through our filters easily. Data that doesn't meet our expectations is sometimes rejected out of hand or is very difficult for us to see. "Sometimes we simply ignore the data that doesn't fit our paradigms." We all have paradigms and they are easy to slip into without realizing it. Barker goes on to say that paradigms are good because they help us filter out unneeded data, but they can be bad when our paradigm becomes "the" paradigm, or the only way to see things. The real challenge lies in recognizing and dealing with them.

We are all full of great ideas on how to improve, and all great ideas tend to meet resistance. Many times, those great ideas come from outsiders because they are not vested in your internal paradigms. The first step we take in change management is to educate those participating in the change about the trap of paradigms. This serves two purposes:

1. It helps to open up their minds to the changes we will be making.
2. It lets them know that people are not so open-minded to the changes we will be making. There will be resistance.

CHANGE EQUATION

Understanding the change equation (Figure 3.1).

The Change Equation is a critical concept that we use with every company. It was originally developed by Gleicher, Beckard, and Harris. Their equation was $D \times V \times F > R_{\text{change}}$,[3] which stood for Dissatisfaction x Vision x Next Steps > Resistance to Change.[4]

Our modified equation is $C \times V \times N \times S > R_{\text{change}}$. Over many years of implementing Lean, we have found we always come back to this equation with every Lean implementation or Point Kaizen.

$$\textbf{C x V x N x S > R}_{\text{Change}}$$

FIGURE 3.1 Change Equation. Source: BIG.

---

[2] www.12manage.com and many books on change management—see suggested reading list in the Appendix.

[3] Richard Beckhard and Reuben T. Harris (1987) and by Coopers and Lybrand as part of the AlliedSignal TQ training.

[4] http://ezinearticles.com/?Change-Guided-By-A-Mathematical-Formula&id=260182, April 21, 2009. Gleicher, Beckhard, and Harris have found an equation that shows the relation to overcome resistance to change. The formula is modeled in the following way: D x V x F > R.

C · COMPELLING NEED TO CHANGE

We have traded the *D* for dissatisfaction with the *C* which is having or creating a COMPELLING need to change (Figure 3.2). While we agree that dissatisfaction is important and as Shingo said, "Dissatisfaction is the Mother (relationship) of all improvement,"[5] we feel dissatisfaction, by itself, is not a strong enough word. People can be dissatisfied but never change. Change is hard. People constantly complain about how dissatisfied they are but because they are so used to the old way of doing things, they don't want to change or feel they can't change. If we don't have a compelling need to change, then all efforts are futile as, ultimately, nothing will change. If change does occur and it is not driven or supported, it will have no chance of sustaining the process.

To be successful with Lean, we have to literally have so much passion for continuous improvement, no matter how successful you currently are, that we need to eat, live, and breathe waste reduction. Successful companies struggle the most to implement lean. This is because success so easily and unkowingly breeds complacency and complacency is the enemy of Lean. The Chinese have a saying… Only the one who knows he can swim dies in the river[6].

In one of my training classes a CEO told us that he was told when he took over as President, "Not to kill the golden goose." The company had always been very profitable. Therefore, he was afraid to make any changes for fear that somehow he would kill the cash cow. During the class he spoke to all of us and said that now he sees he was wrong and how much cash was being wasted. He now began to see how much more profitable they could all be.

There are two ways to incentivize change.

- One is to have an actual "crisis" or business case that, without change, the organization will not survive. The crisis dictates a true compelling need to change.
- The other way is to invent a crisis or to set very high goals for the organization that can't be achieved by doing it the way it has always been done before. This creates a healthy "fear" or paranoia that keeps the organization constantly changing/improving. While this can be done at a department level, it will only sustain when championed at the senior executive level. This is how to create the "pull for Lean."

WHY CHANGE?

When faced with this question, our answer is "What is the option?"

- Can we afford to continue to work with the level of waste in our current processes?
- Have past improvements really worked? Remember, all of the solutions we have put in place over the years have gotten us to where we are today!
- Do you want to be world class?
- Is your department or company world class? (Figure 3.3)
- Are other departments you impact, your internal customers, really satisfied with your performance?
- How many of you are satisfied with your current processes and results?
- Can your company or department survive in the future if it does not change?

$$C \times V \times N \times S > R_{Change}$$

FIGURE 3.2 Change Equation. Source: BIG.

---

[5] Shigeo Shingo, *Non Stock Production* (New York: Productivity Press) 1988.
[6] Chinese proverb shared with me by Snow Jiang.

FIGURE 3.3 OR Room Used as Storage B.I.G. Archives.

- Are your customer's satisfied with your performance, in quality, delivery and cost? Patient consumer's and "Purchasers" (Insurance, ACOs and Employer Groups)

Healthcare is a dynamic industry; not to change is the equivalent of moving backwards.

Lesson Learned

Did you create that process? Remember, most of us tend to be most resistant to change what we have previously implemented.

The cost of all waste goes to your bottom line. For example, if you are idle, who is paying for that waste? If you have to search for something, who is paying for that waste? The answer is: the patient who is our customer, and in healthcare, if it is not the patient, it is you, the taxpayer, as the customer who is ultimately paying for the waste in the form of higher healthcare costs. The waste adds cost to the bottom line because the hospital is paying you while you are idle or searching. This cost makes organizations less profitable, and when organizations we work for become less profitable, financial managers start looking for bodies to layoff. Hence, the cost of the waste threatens all our jobs.[7]

Dr. Berwick, previous president and CEO of IHI,[8] said he recognizes the central irony of U.S. healthcare: "While a great many Americans don't receive the care they need, another large segment of the population receives unnecessary care in a system that is bloated by its emphasis on growth and profit—rather than on better health." Berwick has estimated that "up to half of the more than $2 trillion that the U.S. spends on healthcare does nothing to relieve suffering." To the contrary, "much of it adds to suffering."[9]

The same study estimated that another $210 billion is wasted each year on medical paperwork. At the [Cleveland] clinic's patients' accounts office, rows of cubicles are piled high with file folders and printouts, testimony to its dealings with thousands of different health plans from hundreds of insurance companies all over the country. Thousands of times a day, clerks pick up the phone and get put on hold like anyone else who calls an insurance company. Industry estimates put the average cost of handling a phone call at $3, to each party… in which the clinic's 2,000 doctors require 1,400 clerks to handle their billing.[10]

---

[7] Mark Jamrog, principal, The SMC Group—original quote "Waste threatens all our jobs."

[8] http://www.ihi.org/ihi/aboutus/people.aspx, Donald M. Berwick, MD, MPP, FRCP, president and chief executive officer.

[9] http://www.healthbeatblog.org/2008/02/how-do-we-fund.html, February 1, 2008, "How Do We Fund National Health Reform?" Health Beat Blog, Maggie Mahar.

[10] Jerry Adler and Jeneen Interlandi, "The Hospital That Could Cure Health Care," *Newsweek*, Published November 27, 2009. From the magazine issued December 7, 2009, The evidence was in the 2008 *Dartmouth Atlas of Health Care*.

An estimated 40% of U.S. healthcare spending is wasted on inefficiency, duplicative or unnecessary tests and treatment, error and complications that result from lapses of quality.[11]

Cindy Jimmerson,[12] a nurse who has also been pursuing Lean healthcare methods, states, "The national numbers for waste in healthcare are between 30–40%, but the reality of what we have observed by doing minute-by-minute observation over the last 3 years is closer to *60%!* That's waste of time, waste of money, and a waste of material resources. It's nasty! The waste is not limited to administrative costs, which most research on healthcare has documented. It's everywhere: patient care and non-patient care alike."

V · Vision

The next letter in the change equation is *V* for vision (Figure 3.4). A good example of a vision statement comes from the Civil Communications Section (CCS) Management Training Course[13] for Newport News Ship Building Company, whose vision statement went like this:

- We will build good ships here
- At a profit if we can—at a loss if we must—
- But; always build good ships!

"This is the guiding principle of this company. And it is a good one, too, because it's concise, but it tells the whole reason for the existence of the enterprise. And yet inherent in these few words there is a wealth of meaning:

- The determination to put quality ahead of profit,
- A promise to stay in business in spite of adversity, and
- A determination to find the best production methods.

Every business enterprise should have as its very basic policy a simple clear statement, something of this nature, which will set forth its reason for being. In fact, it is imperative that it should have such a fundamental pronouncement because there are some very definite and important uses to which it can be put. The most important use of basic policy is to aim the entire resources and efforts of the company toward a well-defined target. In a general way, it charts the course that the activity of the company will follow.[14]

Vision is important in the change equation because if people understand the vision and the change that is required supports the vision, then the change will be easier to "sell" and become accepted/adopted, reducing the resistance to change.

$$C \times \textcircled{V} \times N \times S > R_{Change}$$

FIGURE 3.4   Change Equation. Source: BIG.

---

[11] http://www.prhi.org/docs/ROOT Celebrating 10 Years of the Pittsburgh Regional Health Initiative.pdf.

[12] Cindy Jimmerson, *A3 Problem Solving For Healthcare* (New York: Productivity Press) 2007.

[13] *CCS Training Manual*, Charles Protzman Sr. and Homer Sarasohn, 1949–1950. An e-book transcription of the version presented at the 1949 Tokyo seminar has been prepared by *Nick Fisher* and Suzanne Lavery of ValueMetrics, Australia, and is widely available on the Internet. The documents that formed the final English version, which was translated by Bunzaemon Inoue and others and published in 1952 in Japanese by Diamond Press, are in the Civil Communications Section Archive, Hackettstown, NJ.

[14] Jim Collins, *Good to Great* (New York: Harper Business Press) 2001validate.

$$C \times V \times N \times S > R_{\text{Change}}$$

FIGURE 3.5 Change Equation. Source: BIG.

$$C \times V \times N \times S > R_{\text{Change}}$$

FIGURE 3.6 Change Equation. Source: BIG.

N · NEXT STEPS

N stands for next steps (Figure 3.5). Once we know we have a compelling need to change and know and understand the vision, we need to determine the next steps (not just the first) to get to the vision. These steps come from assessing where we currently are relative to the vision. If the "Lean road-map" of how we are going to achieve the vision is communicated and people gain an understanding of it, this will help diminish the resistance to change.

S · SUSTAIN

The final letter, *S*, stands for sustain, which we have added to the original equation (Figure 3.6). Once we have implemented our next steps, we must sustain ongoing improvement. This is the most difficult step of all. Sustaining is the true test of whether there was a compelling enough reason to change and a sign if the other letters were implemented properly. Once again, the only way to truly sustain is with top management leadership and drive (not just support). The leadership must be unwavering and totally committed to sustain and continually to foster a compelling need to change and improve.

Notice there is a multiplication sign between each letter. This is because if any of the letters are zero or are not addressed, we will not overcome the R_{change}, which stands for resistance to change. In addition, each step needs to be followed in order. When you stop and think about it, this is really a problem-solving model for change.

CHANGE AND WHAT'S IN IT FOR ME

It is critical to recognize that with the introduction of change each employee is going to ask, "What's In It For Me" (WIIFM) when challenged with a new initiative. It is important that when we begin to answer this question, it is addressed from multiple perspectives. For example, an Operating Room director is in the middle of a Lean initiative that will reduce turnover times between cases and, if successfully implemented, can shorten the surgery day by 1 hr. This means that employees will no longer have to stay past their normal working hours to finish routine surgical cases.

Let's look at this from different perspectives:

- Employee #1 is silently concerned that she will no longer receive the five to ten overtime hours per week she is accustomed to; therefore, the project will potentially impact her current lifestyle.
- Employee #2 is a working parent who has struggled over the past year to pick up her children at daycare; from her perspective, the project is a positive one. We find the WIIFM question applies to changes even in our personal lives.

Management has to be ready with the answers that will address both positive and negative impacts from the employees' perspective. If we do not answer this question, employees are left in the dark, and they will mentally fill in the gaps or blanks of information which is not clearly communicated. They will naturally think the worst, and rumors will run rampant.

Think about the proverbial call from the school nurse. The nurse leaves a message on your voice mail asking you to call her back. What starts going through your mind? You start to think the worst things that could possibly happen.

LEAN AND CHANGE MANAGEMENT

Think about it. People only fear changes they perceive as negative in some way. After all, none of us resist changes we perceive as positive. Would any of you object to the change of increasing your pay by 10%? Even if I made the change without telling you ahead of time, it would probably be viewed as positive. Positive changes or changes that fit our paradigms pass through our filters easily. It is the negative changes that meet resistance. It is crucial not only to know the answers to the six change questions below, but also to be able to frame them in a positive fashion. This should not be difficult if there is a truly compelling need to change. The key to WIIFM is to answer the questions below from the point of view of the employee. What do they really want to know and why? These questions will help you communicate to the organization the compelling need to change.

We generally suggest scripting answers to the following questions prior to starting the Lean journey to show that all of the organization is aligned:

1. What is the change we are making?
2. Why are we making the change?
3. How will it affect the employee? Now and in the future?
4. How will it affect the company? Now and in the future?
5. What's in it for the employee if we make the change?
6. What's in it for the company if we make the change?

Once scripted, it is important to communicate the answers with the staff in each department prior to rolling out the Lean implementation. This tool forces the leadership to think through each of these questions. The answers must be compelling enough to support the big *C* in the change equation.

LEAN AND ORGANIZATIONAL CHANGE - "RIGHT SEAT ON THE RIGHT BUS"[15]

The next tool we call "the right seat on the right bus." This concept from the book, *Good To Great*,[16] is part of our change management toolset. The goal is to find out if your employees are on the right bus or, in other words, supporting our change initiative and then assess if they are in the right seat on the bus (i e , in the right place in our organization chart) to help us get to the next level of change. To implement this tool, we take the organization chart and review the persons in each position. This is a very difficult process and should be taken very seriously from a critical and realistic point of view.

The other dimension in this tool is time. It is possible for a person to be in the right seat on the right bus during one time frame but maybe not for the next. One may not have the necessary skills required to implement the next phase. Do not underestimate the importance of having the right people in the right seat on the bus as it will impact the success of your organization as you go through a Lean journey.

*We had a director at Clinic X that supported the necessary Lean changes during our implementation phase and we got great results. But the director did not have the willingness and drive to sustain and continue improving the area. Two of the director's staff members were fighting the Lean changes at every opportunity but covertly, behind the scenes. The director, after much coaching and counseling, refused to confront these individuals and make the necessary changes to coach and mentor them. Therefore, the director was not in the right seat or even **on** the right bus after the implementation. The director eventually left the company.*

---

[15] Jim Collins, *Good to Great* (New York: Harper Business Press) 2001.
[16] Ibid.

One has to decide what time frame to use, but generally it pays to review the organization every 6 months to a year. If we determine someone is not going to be in the right seat but is on the right bus, there are a couple of options. This means either the person needs to be moved to another area of the organization where they can be successful or they need a clear plan to receive coaching, mentoring and skills to stay in the same seat. Sometimes, they're just not the right fit for where the organization is going.

The goal of the evaluation is to determine the development needs required to keep the person in the same role. This should be a collaborative process. The persons being evaluated should also be given the opportunity to determine if they have the skills to take them to the next level. They should be asked to write down what they think are their strengths and weaknesses. These should be compared with the evaluator's perception of their strengths and weaknesses. Differences should be discussed. The end result should be either to agree on a move or on what steps should be taken to raise the level of skills for the individuals to stay in the same roles.

Lesson Learned

During any culture change there are some individuals (sometimes at the highest levels) that after coaching and mentoring honestly believe the changes will never work. The longer you hold on to these individuals, the more difficult it will become to implement and sustain the change.

RESISTANCE TO CHANGE

We all fall into the guilty category when it comes to our resistance to change, some of us more than others; however, it is important to realize that we can view change not only as a threat, but also as an opportunity. Staff members who look at it as a threat resist the change and focus only on the negative. Many times, it results in a self-fulfilling prophecy, where the person ends up being moved, or let go, because they couldn't adjust to the change. Everything that happened fit their paradigm, making them believe, "the change would not succeed; therefore, I will not succeed."

Those who embrace change and see it as a positive not only succeed but also have fun doing it. They also tend to advance in their organizations. Some people are just naturally early adopters for change while others wait and sit back to see what will happen. We need to remember that, in any given area of the organization, you will find all types of people, at all levels, who respond to change differently, and we must be prepared and have a plan in place to deal with each of them.

How often do you say:

- *"It can't be done"*
- *"Management won't let me…"*
- *"They won't give me a larger budget…."*
- *"More labor or staff is the ONLY solution…"*
- *"We tried that before…"*
- *"I can't make changes because…"*
- *"My department's metrics look great… What does it matter that we impacted the other department… That's their problem!"*
- *"I'm tired of hearing about customer satisfaction issues. We know we have problems… we will fix them when we get that new facility with more beds and space."*
- *"We can wait on that improvement… the new software we are installing will solve all our problems!"*

CHANGES… HIGHS AND LOWS

As we implement the recommended changes, the teams as well as individuals and process owners tend to go through highs and lows. This is normal. It is important to try to manage people's expectations and to minimize the highs and lows they experience. If the team cannot recover from the low, then the implementation can fail. If expectations get too high, the team cannot meet them and will feel like they failed.

RULE OF UNINTENDED CONSEQUENCES AND BUMPS IN THE ROAD

Part of systems thinking is the rule of unintended consequences. No matter how much we plan, we still run into unexpected problems or situations. This is not unusual and is, in fact, normal. As long as there is not a safety-related issue, it is very important not to overreact to these unintended consequences or how people initially react to change. Change is difficult and people react in different ways and say things that sometimes might be out of character. If we overreact and make "on the fly" adjustments, without a fact-based problem-solving approach, it can have disastrous effects and even kill the implementation. In addition, if we keep changing things, people get confused and frustrated. So we need to analyze these situations as they occur as opposed to reacting to them and see what we can learn going forward. We need to look at these as "bumps in the road" and move on and persevere with the change. When communicating expectations for change everyone should recognize process changes will not roll-out "perfectly." Team members and staff should realize that most changes in process will require adjustment initially as they become fully operationalized. These revisions should be expected and not viewed as failures. In addition, the processes that are implemented today will NOT remain the same for months or years. A continuous improvement plan should be in place so processes are revised based upon changes to the business over time.

CHANGE IS A FUNNY THING

Change is part of the very fabric of our everyday lives. It is ironic that, in some respects, the only constant in our lives is change. Everyday something or someone we know has changed. Each day we get one day older!

There are different parts to this equation. We have to deal with the change itself, the rate of change, and the repercussions of the change. In order to be successful, we need to give people as much control over the change as possible. We need to over-communicate "why change," train people in the "changes," and show how the changes will help them and the organization. We need to be sensitive to the fact that change is uncomfortable for most of us and deploying Lean can literally turn people's worlds upside down. We may not necessarily change what they do, but we may change when or how they do it, with the added expectation that everyone does it the same way. We need to create an environment that is "change friendly" and train and coach people on how to deal with change.

WE ARE ALL INTERCONNECTED BUT NOT TYPICALLY MEASURED THAT WAY

We are all interconnected, so it is important that if we change a process, we ascertain its impact on other inter-related processes. This is especially true and critical in healthcare. It does no good to make our area better at the expense of another area. How can we work together to improve the overall system? It is critical that changes are not made in silos and that the cross-departmental views and/or value streams are evaluated and the appropriate stakeholders are engaged in process changes. Any proposed changes should be performed through collaboration and then communicated to all staff involved.

HORSE ANALOGY

During our Lean system implementations, we find people at all levels who resist change. Some people just seem physically incapable of changing their paradigms. As stated in Thomas Kuhn's

The Structure of Scientific Revolutions,[17] "It is as though some scientists, particularly the older and more experienced ones, may resist indefinitely, most of them (eventually) can be reached in one way or another." Our analogy is: We lead the horse to water. The horse drinks the water. The horse likes the water... But then refuses to drink it again. We find it odd that we implement the new process and people like it! They get great results; but, if allowed, will go back to the old way of doing it. How can this be? How often have you experienced this in your organization?

COMPARISON TO WHERE WE ARE TODAY

Many times, as we introduce new Lean concepts, people will dismiss them out of hand. This is because they are comparing what we are saying to the current work environment. In most cases, the transition to Lean thinking and Lean practices is so different that it is impossible to imagine what is possible.

At Hospital X we were discussing creating a level-loaded schedule for a clinic. The nurse manager told us it wasn't possible. We agreed with her and analyzed together the current way they were scheduling. We found the root cause was how the scheduling software was being utilized. Once we changed their scheduling paradigm and made some minor modifications to the software they were able to level load the schedule.

Lesson Learned

Even though we try to help people see the vision, sometimes it is difficult for them to see it or "get it" until we actually implement the changes and they experience it. There are two types of people... those who will believe it when they see it and those who will see it when they believe it.

EMPLOYEE SUGGESTION SYSTEMS

It is estimated that

- 80% of Toyota's improvements suggestions come from line personnel and are implemented by team leaders and managers.[18]
- 10% come from Point Kaizen events.
- 10% come from the GI (good idea) club,[19] an elite chartered invitation-only Toyota group.

This estimate was confirmed by Russ Scaffede,[20] who stated, "I would certainly state without question 80% is low. You must understand and deal with resistance from key stakeholders (leverage Stakeholders Analysis tools), build an effective influence strategy and communication plan for the change, and determine its effectiveness. Again, the relationship in the equation is multiplicative, which suggests if any of the components are zero, the change will not be effective. For example, if you have a great process in quality "10" but cannot articulate the message and have it accepted the result is "0" that the change will occur.

---

[17] Thomas Kuhn, *The Structure of Scientific Revolutions* (Chicago, IL: University of Chicago Press) 1996 p.162.

[18] Toyota Kata, Mike Rother, McGraw Hill, 2009, 40 million ideas in 20 years book, Yasuda, Productivity Press, ©1990, www.artoflean.com, Understanding A3 Thinking: A Critical Component of Toyota's PDCA Management System, Sobek, Productivity Press ©2008, Managing to Learn, John Shook, ©2008.

[19] Yuzo Yasuda, *40 Years, 20 Million Ideas: The Toyota Suggestion System* (New York: Productivity Press) 1990.

[20] Russ Scaffede, owner, Lean Manufacturing Systems Group, LLC and Management Consulting Consultant, vice president of manufacturing at Toyota Boshoku America. Past general manager/vice President of Toyota Motor Manufacturing Power Train, Past senior vice president, senior vice president of Global Manufacturing at Donnelly Corporation, co-author with Dwane Baumgardner and Russ Scaffede, *The Leadership Roadmap, People, Lean & Innovation* (Great Barrington, MA: North River Press) 2008.

TABLE 3.1
Toyota Suggestion System

Year	Number of Suggestions	Number of Suggestions/Person	Participation Rate (%)	Adoption Rate (%)
1976	463,442	10.6	83	83
1977	454,552	10.6	86	86
1978	527,718	12.2	89	88
1979	575,861	13.3	91	92
1980	859,039	19.2	92	93
1981	1,412,565	31.2	93	93
1982	1,905,642	38.8	94	95
1983	1,655,868	31.5	94	95
1984	2,149,744	40.2	95	96
1985	2,453,105	45.6	95	96
1986	2,648,710	47.7	95	96
1987	1,831,560	–	–	96
1988	1,903,858	–	–	96

Source: Yasuda, Y., *40 Years, 20 Million Ideas: The Toyota Suggestion System*, Productivity Press, Cambridge, MA, 1990. With permission.

In 1988, the Toyota suggestion rate was four suggestions per month per employee with a 96% implementation rate, and a 95% participation rate resulting in 20 million ideas over a 40-year period (Table 3.1). In comparison, the typical U.S. company averages about one-sixth of a suggestion per month per employee.[21] Toyota's is not a normal type of suggestion system. There is no "suggestion box" that gets reviewed by management prior to implementation. Suggestion box systems normally use up significant amounts of time in the review, return on investment (ROI) analysis, and approval cycles. The employee may or may not hear back on their suggestion, which can negatively impact the employee's perception of the solicitation. Toyota, on the other hand, budgets 50% of the team leader's time to implementing and encouraging employee suggestions. They try out the suggestion prior to submitting it for approval. This is why their implementation rate is so high. The Toyota system is explained in detail in the book, *40 Years, 20 Million Ideas: The Toyota Suggestion System*[22].

BARRIERS TO CHANGE

The biggest barrier to change is YOUR MIND! Words like *I can't... It won't work... I already know... It won't work here... I tried that before... I don't want to run it that way... It's not our way... We need more data... How do you know it will work?*

These words should raise a big red flag. We have a saying, "When you say 'I can't' you admit your own ignorance!"[23] Our other saying is "if you tell me you CAN'T, I will agree with you that you CAN'T and then I will go find someone who can!"

---

[21] Yuzo Yasuda, *40 Years, 20 Million Ideas: The Toyota Suggestion System* (New York: Productivity Press) 1990.
[22] From Yasuda, Y, *40 Years, 20 Million Ideas: The Toyota Suggestion System*, Productivity Press, Cambridge, MA, 1990. With permission.
[23] Source: Kanban/JIT at *Toyota/Management Begins at The Workplace*, Japan Management Association.

Most Loved Words

A favorite story growing up was *The Little Engine That Could*.[24] The Little Engine kept saying, "I think I can, I think I can." The most loved words with Lean are: *What if we could... What if we tried... How can we... I know we can... I saw someone else doing it...Why didn't it work the last time... When was the last time we tried... Maybe the manufacturer can help us... Let's benchmark a company that is doing it that way... Let's take the best from YOUR WAY and MY WAY and make it OUR WAY...*

Top Ten Signs That People Don't Get It (Concrete Heads)

You will find that a subset of individuals will resist change and, in fact, may not be able to make the transition to work within a Lean environment. "Concrete Heads" is the Japanese term for someone who does not accept that the organization must be focused on the elimination of waste.[25]

1. Just wait until it breaks, then we can replace it.
2. We are too busy to implement Lean now. We have to make the end of the month.
3. We need to cut indirect labor!
4. We need more inventory and more space.
5. Tell me what I need to do. When will you get to us?
6. We have improved enough already. Why should we improve anymore? Is there any return (ROI)?
7. We don't want to invest in teams or training; we would rather lay them off as soon as we eliminate jobs!
8. We don't need to benchmark other companies; besides, the travel budget has been cut again.
9. We have to make double-digit return on sales. We can't get there with Lean!
10. What does "get-it" mean? Do I have it?

Does Your Organization Have Sacred Cows?[26]

As organizations begin to implement change, they often encounter "Sacred Cows" (Figure 3.7). Sacred Cows are an outmoded belief, assumption, practice, system, or strategy, generally invisible,

FIGURE 3.7   Sacred Cow. Source: Clip Art Unknown.

---

[24] Watty Piper and Loren Long, *The Little Engine That Could* (New York: Philomel Books) 2005.

[25] www.gembutsu.com/articles/leanmanufacturingglossary.html.

[26] Robert Kriegel, *Sacred Cows Make the Best Burgers* (New York: Warner Books) 1996.

that inhibit change and prevent responsiveness to new opportunities. If not recognized and addressed, the transition to a Lean organization may be challenging.

Homework

List four Sacred Cows at your company.
- *How would you change them? Complete the following sentences:*

- *This job would be great if I didn't have to…*
- *What a pain it is to…*
- *It's a waste of time to….*
- *I could be more productive if I didn't have to…*
- *We could save a lot of money if we stopped…*

LEADERSHIP AND ORGANIZATIONAL CHANGES

When considering the area of change management, we need to consider how effective we are as leaders and how we roll out the change to our team members. As we implement Lean changes, consider the following.

If Lean is implemented properly, it impacts the entire organization (Figure 3.8). Organizational changes occur in three ways. They are manifested in structural changes, personnel changes, or a combination of both. Many concepts are discussed in the books, *Good to Great*, *Lean Thinking*, *Toyota Culture*, and *Inside the Mind of Toyota*.

When we start to discuss organizational changes, many middle managers become concerned with their jobs and start to view Lean as a threat to their future. This concern needs to be recognized and addressed prior and throughout the Lean journey.

As structural changes occur, roles and responsibilities may change as well. As roles change throughout the organization, it is very important that we communicate these changes and how they will impact the individuals involved and the organization. We use a tool for this called a roles and responsibilities matrix. This tool is described in Jay Galbraith's book, *Designing Organizations*,[27]

Organizational System Design

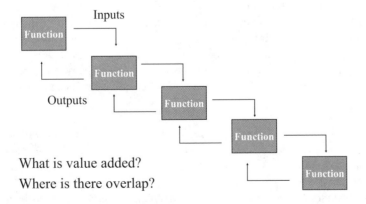

FIGURE 3.8   Organizational Design Tool. Source: BIG Archives - Original Source Unknown.

---

[27] Jay Gailbraith, *Designing Organizations* (San Francisco, CA: Jossey-Bass) 1995.

TABLE 3.2

Roles and Responsibilities Matrix

Roles Decisions	Sales	Segment Marketing	Insurance	Mutual Funds	Marketing Council	CEO	Finance	Human Resources	Regional Team
Product price									
Package design									
Package price									
Forecast	A	R	C	C	C	I	I	X	X
Product design									

R = Responsible; A = Approve; C = Consult; I = Inform; X = No Formal Role.
Source: Designing Organizations, Jay Gailbraith, Jossey-Bass Inc, 1995.

although there are other models out there (Table 3.2). When using this model, each person is assigned a level of ownership (role) to the responsibility. The level of ownership can be responsible, approve, consult, inform, or none. There should only be one person responsible for ownership/responsibility. Co-owners can cause confusion, redundancy, and excuses as to why a responsibility was not carried out. People can share ownership, but there should still be only one overall owner.

It is important to have clarity in roles and yet not have people become so myopic that things don't get done because they weren't assigned. Sometimes people will just stop doing parts of their job and say it was because of Lean. This is not the case. Initially Lean doesn't normally change what you do, although it may change how you do it (sequence of the steps) or expand what you do, i.e., cross training. Everyone in the organization should be able to clean up their areas and sweep the floor, as we all take pride in our workplace and jobs.

We have and recommend using this model during a Lean initiative so there is a clear understanding of the key stakeholders and what each persons role is related to initiative decisions and participation, i.e., responsible, approval, consultive, inform, or no role.

COMMUNICATION, CHANGE AND LEAN

There is a well-known model study from UCLA[28] that discusses the components of communication (Figure 3.9). It states that communication is made up of 7% words, 38% tone of voice, and 55% body language. We have found this model extremely important with change and Lean. Since the introduction of e-mail, texting, and Twittering into society, think of the implications of the communication basis itself. Have you ever had someone misinterpret an e-mail or text message? E-mails and text messages are only 7% of communication. Sometimes we can introduce a little more by adding a smiley face. What percent is telephone? The answer is 45% because we still can't see the body language.

Lesson Learned

When you need to communicate with someone, consider the best way to communicate. Consider communicating in several different media (visual, verbal, e-mail, etc.) in order to effectively communicate the message. Sometimes there is no substitute for face-to-face communication. Consider having a trusted friend review your e-mails prior to sending (preferably someone with an opposite MBTI (C) style to yours). The communication and mechanism should be multi-faceted and outlined in a communication plan which should be monitored and tracked with the implementation. Right or

---

[28] Based on a 1971 study by Dr. Albert Mehrabian, UCLA, referenced by J. Griffin, *How to Say it at Work* (Paramus. Prentice Hall Press) 1998.

What's Missing in E-Mail?

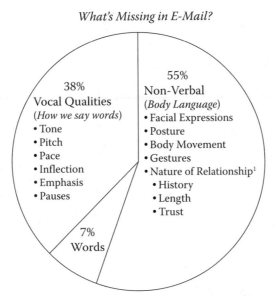

38%
Vocal Qualities
(*How we say words*)
• Tone
• Pitch
• Pace
• Inflection
• Emphasis
• Pauses

55%
Non-Verbal
(*Body Language*)
• Facial Expressions
• Posture
• Body Movement
• Gestures
• Nature of Relationship[1]
  • History
  • Length
  • Trust

7%
Words

From a 1971 study by Dr. Albert Mehrabian, UCLA.
Referenced in Griffin, J (1998); How to Say It at Work;
Paramus, NJ; Prentice Hall Press.

[1] Not from Mehrabian study.

FIGURE 3.9 Communication Model. Source: See info above.

wrong, we have seen in many organizations communication is placed last on the priority list when in fact many obstacles or challenges could have been eliminated if communication had taken place prior to the event. Reflect back on changes or events that had occurred in past few years in your organizations; could you think of a few in which improved communication could have improve the outcome or acceptance?

SUMMARY

Change management, or the "people" component, can and will determine the overall success of any Lean initiative and, in turn, impact overall Lean transformation of an organization. There are many facets to a successful change management effort. It begins with a compelling need to change, a clear vision, communicating the next steps, and then leveraging change management tools to monitor and address resistance to change. Identifying pockets of resistance and managing with appropriate actions will require continual effort throughout the Lean initiative and will continue as Lean is disseminated throughout the organization. The most difficult part of Lean is establishing the culture of continuous improvement. The underpinnings of this lay in change management and leadership.

4 Lean Foundation

In God we trust. All others bring data.

—W. Edwards Deming

LEAN FOUNDATION - THE BASICS MODEL - BASELINE

THINK—SEE—ACT LEAN

The Lean journey begins with becoming familiar with the Lean concepts, potential Lean results, and successes and lessons learned from other organizations. One must realize that, in order to become Lean, the organization will need to undergo a cultural transformation.

We discussed earlier that Lean is a new way of thinking, seeing, and acting.

- To THINK LEAN one must think about eliminating waste in every aspect of what is done every day.
- To SEE LEAN is to be able to see and learn what waste is and how to identify waste in all activities that we do.
- To ACT LEAN by taking action to remove the waste.

We must enable and empower each employee so they can help in the daily process of eradicating waste.

Rolling out your Lean journey can begin in several ways. It can start with a Point Kaizen event, identifying a small sub-process or activity, a Five S event, or a Lean system pilot implementation, which is a larger transformation initiative.

SYSTEM LEAN IMPLEMENTATION APPROACH UTILIZING THE BASICS MODEL

For organizations serious about converting from their old batch-driven systems to Lean, which in healthcare could represent processes which would have significant throughput challenges due to batch type processing such as laboratory, surgical throughput, etc., we recommend the larger transformation approach or what we call the Lean system implementation approach (Kaikaku). This approach looks at the overall process from beginning to end and has proved sustainable across many hospital systems.

To perform a larger transformational Lean initiative, we have outlined a model that can be used as a guide when applying Lean concepts and tools. There are six phases that follow the simple acronym "BASICS" (Figure 4.1). Each letter stands for the main theme for the activities that occur in its phase: *B*aseline, *A*ssess, *S*uggest solutions, *I*mprove, *C*heck results, and *S*ustain. In reality, the activities that occur in any Lean initiative can be mapped to most traditional methodologies, i.e., PDSA (plan, do, study, act), PDCA (plan, do, check, act), or DMAIC (define, measure, analyze, improve, control), etc. The P in PDSA or PDCA, which stands for Plan, really doesn't provide all the activities intuitively required, as one needs to do more than just plan in the first phase of PDCA when initially converting from batch to Lean systems.

Many organizations that are deploying both Lean and Six Sigma have standardized their improvement roadmap to the acronym DMAIC. It works well for organizations implementing Six

Phases

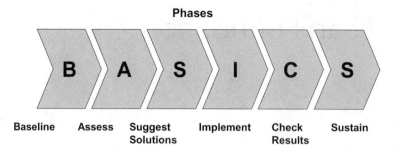

| Baseline | Assess | Suggest Solutions | Implement | Check Results | Sustain |

FIGURE 4.1 BASICS Model. Source: BIG.

Sigma tools. While Lean activities have been and can be mapped to each phase; it can be confusing because the Lean tools can be applied across many of the DMAIC phases. We have found that remembering the acronym DMAIC and what each letter stands for can be challenging.

We have opted for a more simplistic model, hoping that it may be easier for staff to follow and remember as they go through the problem solving activities and steps. Within each of the six phases, we have highlighted, by category, what one may have to do, communicate, and deliver while moving from phase to phase.

The BASICS model contains Total Quality (TQ), Lean and Six Sigma tools (Figure 4.2). We will refer to this model throughout the book. The categories under each BASICS phase are:

Deliverables: provide an idea of what should be completed at the end of the phase
People tools/activities: activities and tasks related to facilitating change and culture
Task tools: activities geared to the application of tools
Implementation steps: outline critical tasks and activities that should be considered for implementation and moving to the next phase
Communication: activities related to communication throughout the initiative
Timeline: provides an estimated duration spent in each phase

The BASICS Lean system implementation approach is based 50% on the principles of scientific management, developed primarily by Frank Gilbreth, implemented by Taiichi Ohno and taught to thousands of students by Shigeo Shingo. The other 50% is based on change management (the people piece) discussed throughout the book. This approach is utilized to convert processes from batch to one-piece flow. Listed below is a summary of the BASICS steps to a Lean implementation.

Baseline (B)
1. Charter the team and scope the project
2. Baseline metrics, voice of the customer (VOC)
3. Value stream map (VSM) the process
4. Determine the customer demand and Takt time (TT)

Assess/analyze (A)
5. Product Process Flow analysis (PFA)—become the patient or product
6. Group tech analysis
7. Work flow analysis (WFA) of the operator
8. Changeover analysis

Suggest solutions (S)
9. Make and approve recommendations
10. Create the optimal layout for the process

Follow the BASICS to Implement Lean

		Baseline Pre-Implementation	Assess	Suggest Solutions	Implement	Check Results	Sustain
Deliverables	Objectives	Company Vision, Values and Purpose					
		Principles	Code of Conduct/Contract for Change				
		Company Goals & Objectives	Department Goals and Objectives				
		Lean Vision & Values					Lean Advisory Committee
		Team Charter Document	Project Expected Results				
	Resources	Assign Executive Sponsor					
		Select Leadership Steering Committee					
		Dedicated Lean Resources					
	Analysis	Customer Feedback (VOC)	Customer Value Added Proposition				
		Stakeholder's Analysis	Agreed ROI with Executive Leadership				
		Supplier Analysis	Supplier Data (# of, # certified etc.)				
	Plans	Hoshin Plan					
		High Level Implementation Plan	Executive Review Schedule				
		Project Plan	Phase Gate Review Plan	Phase Gate Review		Draft Control/Sustain Plan	Final Control Plans/Sustain Plans
		Change Management Plan	Opportunities for Improvement	Standard Work	Quick Win Results and Celebration	Five S Audit Sheet/TPM Checklist	Plan for Continuous Process Improvement
		Resource Plan	Dedicated CI resources	Roles and Responsibilities Matrix		Pilot Results	Employee Idea System/Employee Satisfaction Program
		Communication Plan	Quick Hits List				
		Training Plan	Cross Training Plan	Cross Training Matrix			
		Materials Plan	Layout / Master Layout	Group Tech Matrix - Identify Product / Process Families	Material Flow Plan/PFEP		
		Measurement Plan	Baseline Metrics: Customer Demand/Takt time/+QDIP plan/ Industrial Eng., quality, delivery	Lean Metrics	Visual Displays/Visual Controls	+QDIP Data	
People Tools	Analysis	Employee Satisfaction	Succession planning				
		Customer Satisfaction					
	Psychology	Myers-Briggs (MBTI)					
		Learning Organization	Knowledge Management	Lessons Learned	Capture Lessons Learned	Capture Lessons Learned	
		Team Dynamics (Forming)	Team Dynamics (Storming)	Team Dynamics (Norming)	Team Dynamics (Performing)	Quick Response Team	
		Psychology of Change	Change Equation (Management)	Change Equation (Departments)	Change Management		
	Lean Training	BASICS Process					
		Lean Overview Training	Gemba Walks	Cross Training Matrix			
		Lean Champion Training				Leader Standard Work	
		Lean Topic Training					Quality Circles
		Project Leader Training					
	Skills Training	Effective Meeting Techniques	Location Meeting Review Cadence	Huddles			
		Communication Skills	Crucial Conversations				
		Problem Solving					
		Creative Thinking	Brainstorming				

		Baseline Pre-Implementation	Assess	Suggest Solutions	Implement	Check Results	Sustain
BASICS Process	Customer Analysis	Customer data: Sales,warranty, quality, demand		Block Diagram		Lean Advisory Committee	
Task Tools	Location Analysis	Location Lean Audit	Collect Current Data	Create Metric Plan	Define Panel Charts	Ongoing Data Collection Plan	Balanced Scorecards
		Area Readiness Assessment	Current Work Procedures	Five S	Position and Label Tool Locations	Five S Audit Plan	
		People Assessment	Full Work Analysis	Staffing Analysis and Plan			
		Project Control Matrix	Assess Roles and Responsibilities	Ten Most Wanted List of Improvements		Action Plans	
		Interviews, SME, KANO, etc	Feedback from process participants	Fit Up List			
	Material Flow	Plant Layout Analysis	Group Tech Matrix, Product Process Flow	Layouts - master and area			
		Material Flow Analysis	Water Spider Process	Material Warehouse/Routes/ Inside bins/Kanbans - production and withdrawal			
		Level Loading (Heijunka)	Materials Strategy, Inventory Turns, Thruput	Plan for Every Part that will...			
		Process Flow Mapping	Value Stream Mapping/Value Add Percentages	Line Balance - bumping			
	Process Capability	Process Capability Analysis	Workstation Analysis	Part Production Capacity Sheet			
		Video and Photo Documentation	Ten Cycle Analysis/Waste Diagnosis	Standard Work Combination Sheet/Job Breakdown/Standard Work/Work Breakdown/Workflow analysis			
		SMED - Setup Reduction		SMED / Setup Reduction			
		QFD House of Quality	Quality Tools -SFMEA, DFMEA, PFMEA, Control Plans	Workstation Design improvements	Control Plans/Sustain Plans		Six Sigma Tools
		Critical To Quality Matrix					
		Operational Equipment Effectiveness (OEE)					
	Product Design & Accounting	Equipment Reliability (TPM)		TPM		TPM Checklist	
		DFM Analysis	Cost Benefit Analysis				
		Lean Accounting					

		Baseline Pre-Implementation	Assess	Suggest Solutions	Implement	Check Results	Sustain
Implementation	Resources	Select Pilot Executive Champion	Gemba Walks with Executives	Project recommendations and approvals		Gemba Walks	Gemba Walks
		Select Pilot Area and Leader				I.D. Gaps	Transition to Value Stream Manager
		Select PI Consultant	Initial Walk Through with PI Consultant	Identify quick wins	Implement quick wins	Develop Actions to address gaps	
		Choose Pilot Team/Area	Begin Overview Lean Training	Layout recommendations and approvals	Implement Layout Design		
		Identify dedicated CI resources	Analyze the Product Flow	Develop Kanban and Heijunka	Implement Kanbans		Continuous Process Improvement
	Objectives	Charter the Pilot Team	Develop Group Tech Matrix	Develop Andon Plan			Implement Sustain and Follow up Plans
		Set Pilot objectives and goals	Conduct Work Flow analysis	Recommendations and materials strategies	Implement materials strategies	Process Capability	
		Identify Potential Risks	Setup / Changeover Analysis	5s, Visual Mgmt	Tool Location and Labeling		
	Plan/Roadmap	Develop implementation plan	Solicit feedback from process participants	Develop new work procedures, guidelines	Implement new workstation design		
		Develop training plan for Pilot team	Implement change management plan	or standard work procedures	Implement Standard Work		Implement new idea system
		Develop change management plan	Build Ahead or Work Arounds in Place prior to implementation phase			Update Metrics	
		Develop communication plan			New Performance Metrics, Day by Hour and Month by Day Charts	Review Metrics vs. Targets	Implement new Reward System
		Develop budget for Pilot				Update ROI	Lean Projects Budgeted in Annual
						Share Pilot results and revisions	Create Plan for Area Tours/Presentations
							Reducing labor/lead time with PDCA
							Implement TPM

		Baseline Pre-Implementation	Assess	Suggest Solutions	Implement	Check Results	Sustain
Communication		Leadership / Executive Briefings	Leadership updates	Leadership Updates	Board Level Report Out		
		PI Consultant meetings					
		Daily Leadership Meeting					
	Plan	Location Rollout Meeting	Weekly or Bi Monthly Mgmt updates				
		Implementation Schedule	Milestone Posting	Milestone Posting	Milestone Posting	Milestone Posting	Milestone Posting
		Visual Implementation Schedule	Visual Communication Postings	Visual Communication Postings	Visual Communication Postings	Visual Communication Postings	Visual Communication Postings
		Visual Measures	Assess current metrics	Define Lean metrics	Post Metrics/Visual Displays	Visual Scorecard	Visual Scorecard
		60 second Elevator Speech		Recognize Successes	Recognize Successes	Recognize Successes	Recognize Successes
Timeline		Up to 3 months	Up to 2 Months	Up to 2 Months	Up to 2 Months	Up to 2 Months	Ongoing

FIGURE 4.2 Basics Model. Source: Authors Visio File.

11. Design the work stations
12. Create standard work
13. Determine the capacity and labor requirements
14. Train staff in the new process

Implement (I)

15. Implement the new process—use pilots
16. Implement Lean metrics
17. Incorporate Five S and visual controls
18. Mistake proof and TPM the process

Check (C)

19. Lean Audits, Huddles, and Sustainability Boards

Sustain (S)
20. Kaizen, Kaizen, Kaizen
21. Suggestions implemented from the floor are part of the culture
22. Plan do check act—over and over and over again

A Customer Service Story

The foundation of Lean starts with the customer. This sign was posted on the wall in a fast food restaurant in Madera, California (Figure 4.3). *We actually witnessed an employee kick a customer out of the store who had complained about how his sandwich was made. The other customers were shocked and baffled as to what could have caused this behavior, knowing it could have just as easily been one of them booted out! What could possibly lead to these behaviors and a sign like this being posted for everyone to see?*

We start with this story as it underpins many of the problems in many establishments today—the lack of customer service.

In the hospital, we often lose sight of our primary customer, which is the patient. We have other customers both internal customers such as physicians and fellow staff members that are recipients of services to provide patient care. We also have external customers, insurance companies or (payors/contractors of service) and now Accountable Care Organizations (ACOs) who also have service expectations. We must never lose sight when we design our processes to ensure that we are focused on our patients. There are instances in healthcare where, in order to design the most efficient patient process, we actually have to design the process around the surgeon or emergency department (ED) physician. This is a paradox with Lean. In order to focus on the patients and get them seen as quickly as possible or, in the case of surgery or the ED, to make sure the surgery is performed on time, we need to focus on making our physician providers as efficient as possible.. This is not a bad thing as we can only get patients through the process as quickly as our physicians can see, examine or operate on them.

We have a variety of customer-focused tools in our Lean process improvement BASICS toolbox. The tools are not listed in any particular order, and it should not be construed that every tool must be used during an implementation. We have worked in many hospital environments where they insisted we use every Six Sigma and/or Lean tool. We always challenge this type of thinking. If the thinking is to train someone in a particular tool, that would make sense; but, otherwise, it is a waste of time to implement a tool just for the sake of implementing the tool! Only the necessary tools should be utilized to solve the existing problem. If we were working on repairing a bicycle tire tube, we wouldn't take off the pedals.

FIGURE 4.3 Customer Service? Source: BIG Archives.

Lesson Learned

BASICS tools should be used as needed to secure the necessary customer and stakeholder feedback, solve the particular problem at hand or to expose the waste necessary to identify the root cause to solve the problem that has been identified. In other words, use the tools that are needed to solve the problem—no more or no less.

We have found many hospitals engaged in Six Sigma prior to learning about Lean. This can lead to difficulties when trying to implement Lean. In some organizations a "competition" between Green/Black Belts and so called Lean specialists/Masters develops when, in fact, a synergy of the tools and concepts should be leveraged to gain a better result.

At Hospital X a Master Black Belt took over the Six Sigma and Lean efforts but, over the course of 2 years of restructuring, he was the recipient of a succession of leaders in an organization that had little or no Lean knowledge. They admonished the outside consultants for poor return on investments (ROIs) (which were the result of finance fighting the new Lean systems) and implemented a rigorous project tracking *system designed to select only projects with the highest "finance-approved" ROIs.*

This true story, while in healthcare, is remarkably similar to that referenced in *Toyota Culture*[1] and is important to understand that Lean tools are a different toolset and should be considered complementary to Six Sigma tools. Both Lean and Six Sigma begin with the voice of the customer (VOC). Although both Lean and Six Sigma work toward quality improvement, through decreasing process variation, error, and defect reduction, frontline staff often have a greater challenge with Six Sigma tools. Lean concepts and tools are better suited toward driving a cultural transformation. Lean encourages a different way of thinking, focusing on waste elimination, value-added activities, and process flow.

In healthcare, because there are unstable processes with significant variation, most organizations find it more prudent to begin with Lean tools to identify and eliminate waste and streamline processes. As waste is taken out of a process and the process becomes more predictable, variation rises to the surface. We recommend following up with Six Sigma tools to refine and strive toward perfection. It can be a challenge to utilize the Six Sigma tools on widely variable processes; however, there are many Six Sigma tools related to measurement systems that augment the Lean tools in relation to data collection, interpretation, and change management. It is interesting to note Toyota does not have a Six Sigma program.[2] In an article by Mike Micklewright, he claims, "Six Sigma training is wasteful… It has watered down Lean efforts, it has watered down variation reduction efforts, it has created bureaucracies, it has isolated people," so he is putting his Black Belt up for sale![3]

We must keep in mind that all problem-solving models stem from Shewhart's plan-do-study-act. The Japanese changed it to plan do check act[4] (PDCA) and called it the Deming Wheel. BASICS aligns with the PDCA model with baseline, analyze, and suggest improvements corresponding with the plan phase, implement is the do phase, C is the check phase, and the last S is the act phase. The Lean tools can be made to fit in just about any problem-solving model. BASICS fits the DMAIC model with Baseline aligning with Design and Measure, Assess aligning with Analyze, Suggest Solutions and Implement aligning with Improve and Check Results and Sustain aligning with Control.

[1] Jeffrey Liker, *Toyota Culture* (New York: McGraw-Hill) 2008, 29–30.
[2] Jeffrey Liker, *The Toyota Way* (New York: McGraw Hill) 2004. This book does not use complex statistical tools to explain the principles behind Toyota's success. On page 253, author Jeffrey K. Liker writes, "…Toyota does not have a Six Sigma program. Six Sigma is based on complex statistical analysis tools. People want to know how Toyota achieves such high levels of quality without the quality tools of Six Sigma. You can find an example of every Six Sigma tool somewhere in Toyota at some time. Yet most problems do not call for complex statistical analysis, but instead require painstaking, detailed problem solving. This requires a level of detailed thinking and analysis that is all too absent from most companies in day."
[3] "Black Belt for Sale," *Quality Digest*, www.qualitydigest.com/print/4366, October 18, 2009.
[4] Matthew May, *The Elegant Solution* (New York: Free Press) 2007.

It should also be noted that Lean/Sigma tools include all the Total Quality (TQ) tools. While we suggest the BASICS model as a way to convert batch to Lean flow, we still support use of the PDCA or PDSA model or the DMAIC model for ongoing improvement cycles once the initial Lean system implementation is completed. The choice of model is not as critical as long as there is a consistent, logical, organized approach to ongoing problem solving in which every employee has been trained.

BASELINE METRICS

The first letter of our BASICS Lean foundation model "B" stands for a baseline, driven by customer value (Figure 4.4). If you don't know what your customer finds valuable or is willing to pay for, then you can't have a vision of what to improve. If you don't have process related metrics that show where you are, you can't possibly measure if you have improved.

This doesn't mean you can't improve, but how will you know if you did and by how much? During the baseline phase, the Lean roadmap is set up by determining the business problem(s) that needs to be solved as defined by the customer and capturing the "current state" of the process. Capturing the current state includes observing, mapping, and videotaping the process, understanding current metrics, potentially developing new or revising existing "process" metrics, and outlining the initial goals and objectives of the proposed initiative. During the baseline phase, a project charter should be created that outlines the Lean initiative, and both the executive sponsor and team should be selected.

Gathering baseline data is a key component in this phase, and any subsequent recommendations for improvements must be driven by "managing by fact." We have found collecting data to be extremely challenging in hospitals and, when one does get data, one has to really question if it is reliable. We find when healthcare organizations collect data, accuracy is assumed. As data is scrutinized during Lean/Sigma projects, data inaccuracies surface, challenging the very data that everyone in the organization has been utilizing for years to make decisions.

DATA, REVENUE, AND HOSPITALS

Let's discuss what we normally find with the data at hospitals.

At Hospital X, we met with a Vice President of finance to work out our cost per case. Prior to the VP's arrival, we were provided with three different financial reports. After reviewing the reports, we found each report contained conflicting data. During our meeting, we confronted the Vice President with the problem. We thought we had stumbled on this great revelation only to learn she already knew of the problem. The reports came from three different hospital information systems that didn't talk to each other. We asked how she decided which report to use. She told us honestly that they just picked whichever report best fitted the need at the time!

We found that this is not an isolated case. Many hospitals have lots of data, but it is difficult to access because it is spread across many disparate systems and databases, and the validity of much of the data is in question. Many hospitals do not have standard definitions for their "data touch points,"

Phases

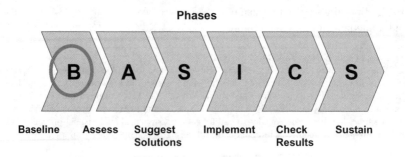

FIGURE 4.4   BASICS Model – Baseline Phase. Source: BIG.

such as 'surgery start', or 'patient in', and, if they exist, staff generally doesn't follow them because they either don't understand the definitions or they are too busy to capture the data in real time. Data collection becomes an estimate instead of a "true value."

THE IMPACT OF DATA ON LEAN – PROCESS FOCUSED METRICS

Therefore, most hospitals have little valid information when it comes to how long processes take, what their products or services cost or what they should be charging for their delivery of care. Hospitals do not normally know how much revenue they are losing because of poorly constructed policies and processes. Another problem hospitals fight is the simple fact that staff generally only care about the patient and are not concerned with the financial health of the organization or "money." We hear them say, "We weren't trained about collecting charges or money in nursing school." They do not feel it is part of their job to know, and when it is brought up we often hear, "now you want us to only focus on finance and charge capture instead of taking care of patients."

Lesson Learned

First, we must recognize that the hospital is, in fact, a business and normally a large employer in the area and a benefit to the community. Without revenue and profit, a business cannot survive, which puts every job in the organization along with the community benefit in jeopardy.

If there is not enough revenue, everyone will lose. Cost cutting and layoffs take place and new "cutting-edge" equipment cannot be purchased.

While it is important that the first and foremost priority is taking quality care of the patient, there are two problems with the nursing attitude of "we are only concerned about the patient." In the current state of healthcare, it is imperative that healthcare workers understand how their actions impact the "care" business.

- First, if charges are not accurately captured and billed for services rendered, in the age of diminishing reimbursement, hospitals may be unable to survive. Nurses are more frequently required to assist in coding as part of their documentation "near real-time" in order to more accurately reflect services provided. In addition, if we choose to consistently use the most expensive supplies, then we will not be able to offer affordable healthcare.
- Second, in the event that a staff member is ever called to court, medical legal questions could arise from having conflicting information in the medical record.

Lesson Learned

While we empathize with the clinical staff that the patient is the number one priority, we do ourselves and the patient, the ultimate customer, an injustice if we do not properly document and bill for services provided for all medical supplies used during the course of their treatment. We put the hospital and patients at risk from an employment, legal, community, and affordability perspective.

CUSTOMER SATISFACTION

Do You Know What Your Customer Really Wants? The Patient: "It's Really All About Me!"

Our ultimate goal should be to provide the customer with the highest quality care, the right care, at the right time, in the shortest amount of time to do it safely, while giving the patient a great hospital experience. All Lean and TQ tools should be implemented with the customer/patient in mind. Without the customer, we have no business. The tools we are going to cover are in the baseline phase of the model and are not necessarily in any type of prioritized order. The task and people tools are designed to extract the VOC; however, it is imperative that we begin each initiative by understanding what the customer values and desires. Too often when we go into hospitals we are told the customer expectations by the staff. When we probe a bit, we find that the expectations communicated were, in fact, not those of the customer but what the staff *thought* the customer wanted. We need to understand what makes a good customer/patient experience through the *customer's* lens, not the lens of the staff.

At Hospital X, during our process of improving their ED, we were told that patients (customers) did not want to move through the process. We were also told patients wanted to have one room and the same nurse throughout their stay. When we asked the patients what they thought, we were told that they did not mind moving as long as progress was being made and they did in fact, not need the same nurse throughout their visit as long as they received good consistent care. What was important to the customer was that they were seen quickly by the physician and that the nurse treated them nicely, professionally, and in a timely manner. They wanted the staff to continually communicate with them as they progressed through their visit.

It is surprising how many nurses and clinical staff forget or don't think it is important to communicate to their patients as they move through the process.

Lesson Learned

Find out what is really important to your patients. Don't be afraid to ask them. Ongoing patient communication is the real key to increasing customer satisfaction. Lack of communication creates voids and leads to anxiety as patients do not know what to expect and fear the unknown.

VOICE OF THE CUSTOMER SURVEYS

The only way to truly find out what the customer wants is to solicit feedback directly from the customer. There are many ways to obtain the VOC, such as holding focus groups, leveraging subject matter experts, and customer surveys. The customer survey can be done face-to-face, via e-mail, via Internet (i.e., Survey Monkey[5]), by phone, etc. The goal is to understand the "Big Y" or desired outcome of your customer and understand what is required (the 'x's' or little 'y's necessary) to meet the Big Y. It is also important to feel the pain your customer feels and understand your customer's ultimate expectations or what they deem "valuable." There is nothing like experiencing the process yourself to feel what the customer goes through. In 2002, CMS partnered with the Agency for Healthcare Research and Quality (AHRQ), another agency in the federal Department of Health and Human Services, to develop and test the HCAHPS Survey. The HCAHPS (*Hospital Consumer Assessment of Healthcare Providers and Systems*) Survey, was the first national, standardized, publicly reported survey. The 32-item survey instrument and data collection methodology measures patients' perceptions of their hospital experience. The HCAHPS Survey asks recently discharged patients about aspects of their hospital experience that they are uniquely suited to address. The core of the survey contains 21 items that ask "how often" or whether patients experienced a critical aspect of hospital care, rather than whether they were "satisfied" with their care. HCAHPS scores are based on four consecutive quarters of patient surveys and are publicly reported on the *Hospital Compare* Web site, www.medicare.gov/hospitalcompare. In FY 2014, the Hospital Value-Based Purchasing (Hospital VBP) program links a portion of Inpatient Prospective Payment System (IPPS) hospitals' payment from CMS to performance on a set of quality measures, which include the Clinical Process of Care Domain, the Patient Experience of Care Domain, and the new Outcome Domain. The HCAHPS Survey is the basis of the Patient Experience of Care Domain[6]. This has placed a greater emphasis on hospitals understanding their customer. It is important when developing surveys to establish some type of objective, measurable criteria, and solicit open-ended feedback. The measurable feedback of customer satisfaction will allow us to see if we are improving. The answers we get to subjective questions provide significant value and insight into what customers are really thinking.

---

[5] http://www.surveymonkey.com/.

[6] Internet citation: HCAHPS Fact Sheet. August 2013. Centers for Medicare & Medicaid Services (CMS), Baltimore, MD USA, www.hcahpsonline.org. * CAHPS® is a registered trademark of the Agency for Healthcare Research and Quality, a U.S. Government agency

It is important not to violate the survey rules, generally a 5- to 7-point scale[7] with questions not written in such a way that they could lead to biased answers.

It is important to develop ongoing customer feedback processes to make sure the changes we make as a result of continuous improvement are not negatively impacting our customers.

THE VIP VISIT

At many hospitals, we have witnessed the all-important phone call from the president or one of the senior leadership team to notify the department director that one of their own is coming to the hospital. It may be for the ED or surgery, but this sets up "the all-important VIP visit" status for that patient. Everyone in the process scrambles to make sure everyone knows who the VIP is and when they are coming. It is not unusual for the referring leader to visit or accompany the VIP through the process. Often, this is the president's or senior leader's only exposure to how the processes really run. It is also the only time the staff may ever see them.

But, in actuality, the senior leader does not see how the normal process runs; they only see how the "VIP process" is run. So the leader gets a "warped," unrealistic view of the process.

Lesson Learned

If you are the executive in a hospital organization and you have to call to set up a VIP visit, then your processes need much improvement. Otherwise, why would you call ahead to arrange the VIP visit? Shouldn't all patients get "the VIP" treatment?

EASY TO DO BUSINESS WITH[8]

The term ETDBW means that an organization is "easy to do business with." This discussion is inspired by the book, *The Agenda*.

Homework

Call the company you work for, pretending you are a disgruntled customer or a patient with a problem or ask to speak with the CEO, then note how difficult it is to get hold of the person you are searching for and how long it takes. How many menus do you have to go through? How often did the computer not recognize your verbal response? How long are you put on hold? How many people do you have contact with? Did you get disconnected? Did you try to press 0 to speak to a person only to be sent back to the main menu?

Being ETDBW means that the business accepts orders or requests for service when and by whatever means it is most convenient for the customer. It means the orders or services are provided in the customer's terminology. It means the organization makes it painless for a customer to check the status of an order or result. Businesses need to eliminate the endless series of futile phone calls to uninterested and uninformed functionaries, who have been trained only to refer the caller to someone else equally uninformed or hang up because they exceeded their response time metrics.

It means the hospital or business sends a simple bill that is expressed in comprehensible terms—in other words, a bill that someone other than a cryptanalyst can decipher. In addition, hospitals have a greater responsibility that their customers understand, in terms of "simplistic language," what services are provided (tests) and instructions surrounding their care.

Homework: Walk around, place a call….Is your hospital or healthcare enterprise ETDBW?

---

[7] http://www.surveygizmo.com/survey-blog/question-scale-length/ need a 5- to 7-point scale.
[8] Michael Hammer, *The Agenda* (New York: Crown Business) 2001.

CENTRALIZED = BATCHING

Some systems come with inherent and predictable waste. The models used by non-Southwest carriers represent a "centralized," sometimes called "center of excellence," business model. Southwest uses a decentralized point-to-point model. Centralized models are characteristic of "batch" thinking.

By changing the paradigm and eliminating seat assignments, Southwest does away with all that waste. Boarding with no seat assignments seems to be as efficient, if not more efficient, for the business traveler than other carriers. It is also easier for the customer who now just grabs any seat and families with small children who now board after the "A" group, allowing them to sit together.

What Does All This Have to Do with Hospitals?

Our experience with most hospitals is that their processes probably worked well at one time; however, over time, just about every hospital has added and built new rooms, operating rooms (ORs), towers, and in addition, may have added services and service lines. As they have grown and expanded, the old systems have been unable to keep up; new pieces of equipment in departments are placed wherever there is "room" rather than where they should have gone from a process flow perspective, thus creating numerous workarounds for the staff. The result is that, in many instances, nurse managers, directors, and other support staff have become very high paid "firefighters" and expediters, having to create work arounds in layouts and systems to get their day to day tasks accomplished. We then tend to promote those who are good with "get it done in any way possible (hero-like) behaviors."

Hospitals over the years have migrated more and more to centralization. Within most hospitals, transportation, registration, the laboratory, sterile processing, and scheduling are all centralized.

Homework

Sit in any of your lobbies and listen to your patients. Ask them: How do they feel? How long have they been waiting? What do they need? What could have made their experience better?

Lesson Learned

Hospitals can learn a lot from manufacturing and other service business models. Yes, the Lean Production System is applicable to healthcare and, if given time and support from the top, can reap great rewards.

CUSTOMER VALUE-ADDED PROPOSITION

As we have stated several times, we need to know our customers' expectations. Another tool for this is to develop a model of the customer's value-added proposition. This concept is covered in depth in a book entitled *The Agenda* (Figure 4.5). The organization needs to understand all the components that affect the customer's desired expectation and then decide how the organization wishes to position itself when compared to the competition. This proposition explores which attributes are considered key to the market being served and can graphically depict how the organization serves that market vs. the competition.[9] The example here is for a hotel. Based on our study of the VOC and the marketplace, we are offering a continental breakfast, decent room, and great business offerings at a low price. This tool can be leveraged to help understand what is critical to their customer's and/or physician's quality expectations and how they compare to local or regional competitors.

---

[9] Harvard Business Review; Michael Hammer, *The Agenda* (Crown Business Publishing) 2001.

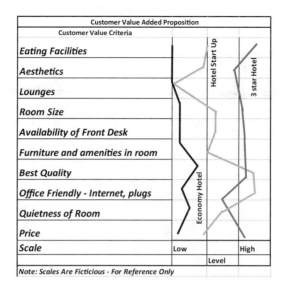

FIGURE 4.5 Customer Value Proposition. Source: BIG File (Inspired by *The Agenda* by Michael Hammer, Crown Business Publishing, ©2001).

CUSTOMER QUALITY INDEX

As you begin to appreciate what the customer sees as value, the Customer Quality Index may be beneficial. The Customer Quality Index will help determine where one desires to be positioned in the marketplace by visually allowing one to plot services, products, etc., related to price vs. quality.

KANO MODEL

We recommend that everyone becomes familiar with the Kano[10] model of customer satisfaction (Figure 4.6). As we go through our Lean initiatives and make improvements, we must not lose sight of the fact that, as customers of healthcare products and services, all patients and purchasers expect a "basic level" of customer satisfaction (basic vs. delighter as described by Dr. Noriaki Kano). They expect high quality and outcomes that meet the standard of care for services rendered, with zero defects or errors. Remember that waste, unnecessary steps, and lack of process standardization provide opportunities for errors and defects. This principle is also explained in the book, *Total Company Wide Quality Control*.[11]

As processes are designed, it is critical that basic customer needs are met and feedback loops designed so that further work can continue to move toward "delighting" the customers. Remember, if basic needs are not met, customers will look elsewhere, you will lose market share and may not understand why. In addition, as you add "improvements," make sure you understand these new improved activities and services that have increased customer satisfaction today will become tomorrow's expectations. Once the "delighter" is delivered and customers return, they will grow to "expect" the services that were used to delight and they will be disappointed if they do not receive the same level of service or care. In healthcare, quality and customer satisfaction often get blurred

---

[10] http://en.wikipedia.org/wiki/Kano_model, Kano, Noriaki; Nobuhiku Seraku, Fumio Takahashi, Shinichi Tsuji (April 1984). "Attractive quality and must-be quality" (in Japanese) *Journal of the Japanese Society for Quality Control* 14 (2): 39–48. http://ci.nii.ac.jp/Detail/detail.do?LOCALID=ART0003570680&lang=en.

[11] Yoshio Kondo, *Company Wide Quality Control (Zenshateki Hinshitsu Kanri)* (translated by J. H. Loftus) (Japan: JUSE Press) 1993.

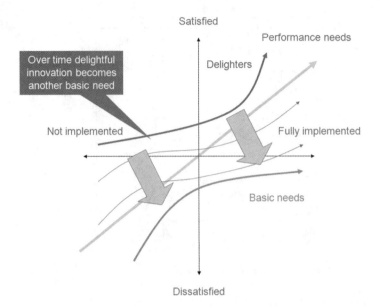

FIGURE 4.6   Kano model of customer satisfaction.

in the patients' minds. They often assume quality, and relate poor customer satisfaction to poor quality care.

BASELINE THE PROCESS

As we move through the B phase of the BASICS model, we need to gain an understanding of the current process. This includes understanding the process by going to the place where the process occurs and walking the process with the frontline staff, managers, and team. It is at this point that you need to "put your Lean glasses on," noting how the product and patient move from beginning to end, or for a service, what it takes from request to delivery. In addition, this allows you the opportunity to start asking why five times as you search for root causes and begin to identify waste and opportunities for improvement.

VALUE STREAM MAP (VSM) THE PROCESS

Value stream mapping is part of our baselining toolset. VSM techniques are explained in two books, *Learning to See*[12] and *Seeing the Whole*.[13] Since the introduction of these books, many subsequent books utilize VSMs as part of their instruction. This book is no exception.

This tool has been used successfully in laboratories, pharmacy, radiology, ED, OR, catheterization laboratory, clinics, etc. (Figure 4.7). While a VSM is a good tool for virtually any type of process, it is one of the best tools for mapping administrative processes like scheduling, HR, revenue cycle, purchasing, sales, marketing, engineering, finance, and new business development. It can even be used to capture a physician or surgeon's office processes.

The VSM allows one to see the overall systems and subsystems and inter-related dependencies at work in healthcare inpatient and outpatient clinical or non-clinical areas as it follows the value stream that crosses departmental silos.

---

[12] Rother and Shook, *Learning to See* (Cambridge, MA: Lean Enterprise Institute) 1999.
[13] Jim Womack and Dan Jones, *Seeing the Whole* (Cambridge, MA : Lean Enterprise Institute) 2003.

Value Stream Map - Surgical Department

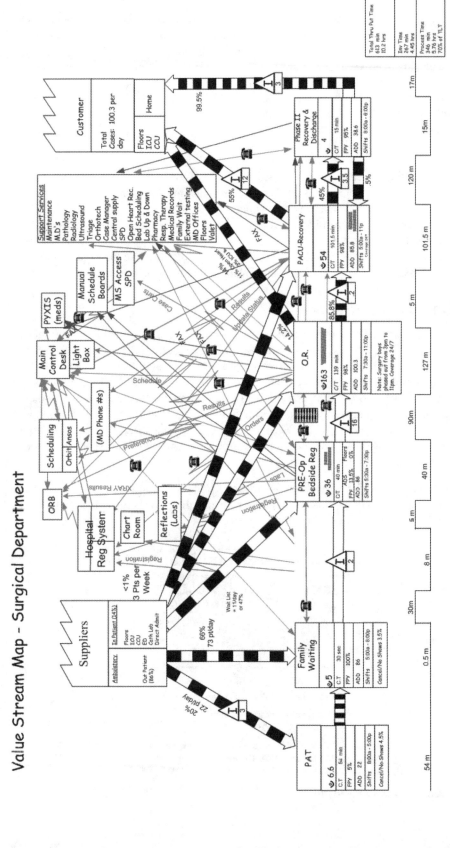

FIGURE 4.7 Surgical System Value Stream Map. Source: BIG Files.

VALUE STREAM DISCUSSION

The VSM is like a process map on steroids. It looks at how the product, or patient, physically flows through the process, as well as the flow and inter-relatedness of the information necessary to process the patient. It combines traditional process flow mapping, focusing on the longitudinal view of the process, with data to create a "roadmap" to help you identify opportunities for improvement. The VSM also has all the elements of the SIPOC tool built in. The VSM:

- Visualizes the flow
- Forces one to look at the big picture/system(s)
- Identifies the current state of the process
- Helps highlight the waste in the process
- Helps determine the sources (causes) of waste
- Provides a common language for discussing problems and improvements
- Makes necessary decisions about flow very apparent
- Enables innovation—brainstorm ideal and future states that leave out wasted steps while introducing smooth flow and leveled pull
- Provides a visual roadmap of prioritized opportunities to the strategic plan (i.e., projects and tasks) necessary for improvement (management tool to track progress)

VALUE STREAM MAPPING AND HEALTHCARE

There are hundreds of "processes" in the healthcare environment. There are high-level steps/activities, "process level" and "sub-process levels." A process box in a high-level VSM, if broken down, could end up being its own process, or sub-process VSM. The level and details depicted in VSM will depend on the business problem you are trying to solve. The VSM outlines the process and categorizes what is actually process time and storage (waiting) time for the healthcare customer as they go through the process. It also shows the information flow, materials flow, and a timeline with a results box that shows the overall process vs. storage time. The value stream lends clarity to the process, helping to reveal process steps that impede throughput and highlight where waste (non-value activity) are prevalent (Figure 4.8).

Authors' Note: A flaw of most VSMs is when one assumes that just because a step is classified as a process step, it must be value-added; this is not the case. In actuality, VSMs typically mix up value-added and non-value-added activities in the process steps.

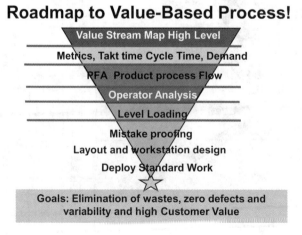

FIGURE 4.8 Roadmap to Value Based Processes.

Lesson Learned

We all want to think everything we do adds value, so some of us will play with the definitions of value-added to "make us feel better." This can do more harm than good. The goal of any process improvement tool is to highlight the waste in the process and expose variation. If we "end up deceiving ourselves" or work to make audit tool standards lower so that "we feel better," we are degrading the improvement process and lowering our standards.

The value stream is the first layer of the process, which will help provide focus on areas that have opportunities for process improvement. The elimination of waste or non-value-added steps in a process will decrease the chance to make errors, decrease variability and streamline the process. This will be financially advantageous and yield an improvement in the quality of outcomes. In healthcare, we can VSM both the patient and the information flow process independently. It is not unusual for the information flow, whether electronic or paper, to ultimately pace the progress of the patient.

VALUE STREAMS OBJECTIVES

- Visually identify process vs. storage steps
- Help to identify which steps can be eliminated, rearranged, combined, or simplified
- Facilitate opportunities to improve flow
- Enable opportunities to see where information systems need to be able to talk to each other
- Identify where we can create pull systems
- Provide a vehicle to manage the area and feed employee "objective" evaluations
- Enable one to strive for perfection
- Creates a management roadmap to track the elimination of waste and improvements
- Updating your value stream maps is a great way to keep track of your progress over time

VSMs can be used to track your progress with Lean improvements and are a great tool to teach staff to find more areas to improve within their processes. The tool is a great way to engage employees in understanding the overall process and helps to break-down silos across departmental value streams.

TRADITIONAL HOSPITAL SYSTEMS - SILOS

When an organization is divided up by function (i.e., transport, laboratory, Pre-Op, PACU, registration, etc.), each department is only concerned with the processes in their area. Most traditional hospital organizations are set up in these functional silos. Due to organizational design, each department supervisor or manager is doing the best job they can within their span of control and within the department they manage.

In Hospital X we were developing a high-level VSM of surgical patients from the time they were scheduled for surgery to the time they reached the Post-Op recovery unit, only to discover we could not find one person within the surgery department who could describe the entire process. In addition, there were different managers for pre-testing, Pre-Op surgery and Post-Op recovery.

Lesson Learned

Do not underestimate the silos in your organization. Even within the same service line there are silos that exist which need to be addressed so everyone is working toward the same goal.

LEAN GOALS

When patients or customers are in contact with the organization or enter the facility, they should not see silos. For example, their perception of the experience with the laboratory may begin with a phone call to a secretary or in the parking garage with cleanliness and signage.

Everyone in the organization should be aligned to the same goals with NO SILOS, where each patient is OUR patient, not THEIR patient. Some Lean ideas would be:

- Require that centralized departments become decentralized.
- Radiology (currently done with portable x-ray machines) and a mini laboratory co-located in the ED department, if possible.
- Each department responsible for its own transportation.
- Every department owns every patient and the patient's outcome.
- Put processes, materials and equipment in line and at point of use.
- Right size laboratory testing, i.e., implement tests at point of use like I-Stat[14] Troponin point of care testing in the ED triage area, surgical pre-testing and Pre-Op areas.
- Level load and smoothly flow, with transparent handoffs, for patients across departments. View all departments as part of one overall system.
- Consider replacing functional department heads with one overall process owner or value stream manager who is responsible for the entire process flow including functional departments. This may involve reassigning persons within functional departments to report to the value stream manager.

In the hospital setting, value streams start with a supplier to the process (i.e., a doctor's office or vendor). We eliminate the functional view of the department and look to create product families (service lines) or value streams defined as a cross-functional value stream.

PARTS OF A VALUE STREAM MAP

VSMs have four major parts (Figure 4.9). In the middle of the map is the first, which is how the patient or information flows. At the top of the map is the second, or all the information system boxes required to make each process work or to status the process box. The third part is the timeline at the bottom of the information required for the map. The timeline is a saw tooth that has the storage time on top and cycle times on the bottom of the saw tooth which is totaled in a results box showing the overall storage vs. process time. The fourth part is the materials flow from supplier to customer.

VALUE STREAM MAP ICONS

There are many references to VSM icons.[15] Figure 4.10 depicts some standard icons that we utilize, as well as lines to show manual information flows (i.e., someone hand-carrying information verbally or written and communication, such as fax, e-mail, snail mail, telephone, etc.).

We also utilize the balance of traditional Lean symbols (i.e., supermarkets, withdrawal, etc.); however, VSM could be as simple as hand-written sticky notes on a wall or as sophisticated as utilizing software packages to create VSM diagrams.

VALUE STREAM MAP DEFINITIONS

Our approach is to make the VSM as realistic as possible. The process box also includes a data box. So we try to get statistically accurate data to populate the boxes where we can as opposed to the entire map being a snapshot in time. While some maps can be done in a day, we find that when combined with teaching a value stream mapping team and collecting real data, it normally takes a week and sometimes 2 weeks for a large process (like an overall perioperative services VSM) in a large

---

[14]   http://www.abbottpointofcare.com/istat/www/products/Cartridge_Brochure.pdf.
[15]   Mike Rother and John Shook, *Learning to See*, Lean Enterprise Institute (LEI), 2003 www.lean.org; *Lean Lexicon*, by and published by the Lean Enterprise Institute (LEI), 2003 www.lean.org, Jim Womack and Dan Jones, *Seeing the Whole* (LEI) 2002.

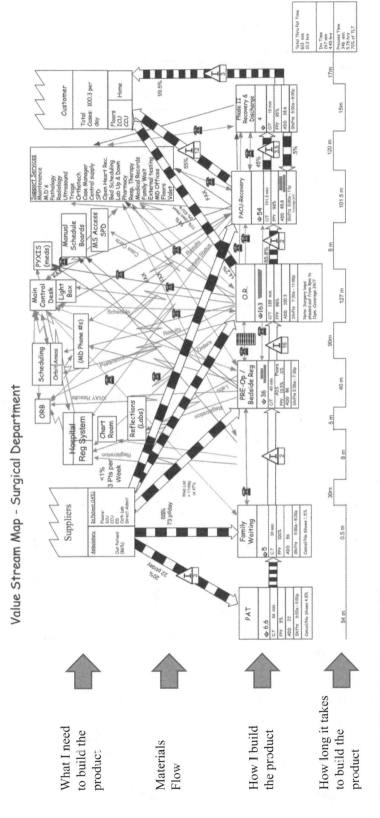

FIGURE 4.9 VSM Parts. Source: BIG File.

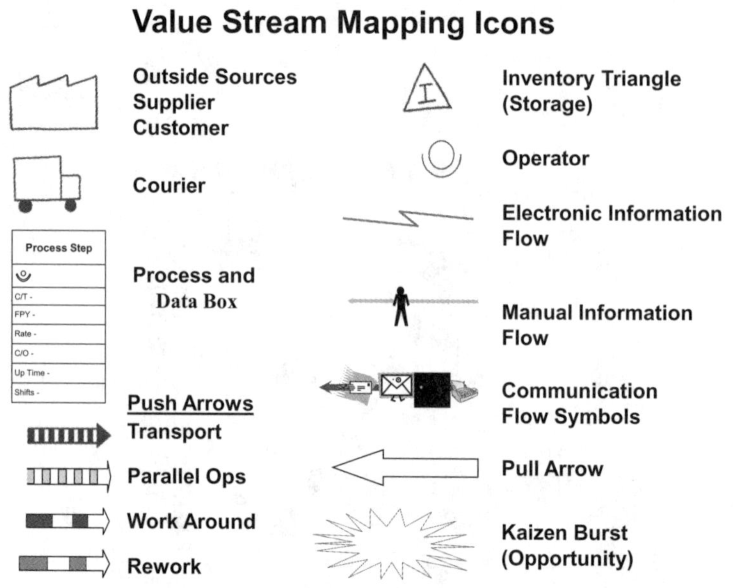

Value Stream Mapping Icons

Outside Sources
Supplier
Customer

Inventory Triangle
(Storage)

Operator

Courier

Electronic Information
Flow

Process Step
☺
C/T -
FPY -
Rate -
C/O -
Up Time -
Shifts -

Process and
Data Box

Manual Information
Flow

Communication
Flow Symbols

Push Arrows
Transport

Parallel Ops

Pull Arrow

Work Around

Rework

Kaizen Burst
(Opportunity)

FIGURE 4.10   VSM Icons. Source: *Learning to See* and BIG File.

hospital. We normally create the map with paper and pencil and post it® notes. We send the team out to walk the process and interview the staff in order to begin the outline of process and storage boxes. The basic current state map can be drawn in less than a day, sometimes less than an hour. We then send the team out to collect data for each process and storage box. The map undergoes constant changes as we invite stakeholders in to review the map. Getting accurate data for the process boxes can take from hours to several days depending on the VSM scope. The maps are reviewed by the major stakeholders along with the project prioritization schedule at the senior leadership debriefing. A normal schedule for a week long VSM event would be:

Day 1
- VSM training class
- Walk the process and interview staff
- Use yellow stickies and flip chart paper to outline the process and storage boxes

Day 2
- Collect data and fill in information flow system boxes

Day 3
- Collect data, finish arrows to communication boxes, draw in materials
- Brainstorm ideal state
- Create ideal state map
- Brainstorm project list and separate task vs. project
- Note which projects could be done within the year

Day 4
- Create future state map
- Complete project prioritization
- Complete data collection
- Develop final report out and convert VSM to Visio®

Day 5

- Leadership presentation and team celebration

The VSM deliverables include three maps:

1. Current state
2. Ideal state
3. Future state

in that order, and a prioritized project list.

CURRENT STATE VALUE STREAM MAPPING

The first step is to create the VSM based upon the current state. This provides the opportunity to fully walk through the current state or "reality" and then focus on what it will take to improve the clinical or administrative process. Many times we use Value Stream Maps in place of or as part of a hospital Lean assessment. It is a great way to figure out where to start a Lean project.

Mapping the current state requires walking the process, gathering a team of subject matter experts consisting of frontline staff and those familiar with the process. You cannot do this just sitting in a conference room.

The VSM must describe what actually occurs in the process, not what is written in policies or how supervisors or managers may believe the process is occurring. It is critical to capture reality in order to truly identify waste and non-value activity as described, as well as the supporting data. Once this is accomplished, the team moves on to define the ideal state. All of our VSMs are initially hand drawn. This is because it is easier for non-computer people to participate and make changes as the map is reviewed. For presentation purposes, we often convert these maps to Microsoft Visio® and print them out to flip chart size. This is because most healthcare executive cultures are not quite ready for hand-drawn VSM presentations.

Lesson Learned

You have to pick the hills you want to die on. It is not worth trying to change executives' perceptions at a first-time meeting to consider A3 charts or hand-drawn maps. It is sometimes better to compromise on the Lean principles than lose a client or not have the opportunity to expose or implement Lean in a department.

An example of a hand drawn PACU value stream is shown in Figure 4.11.

IDEAL STATE

Once the current state is constructed, a second VSM is performed, the ideal state map. It should be done as a brainstorming session in which the team determines what the process would be like if they were starting with a clean slate using a blank piece of paper, with all barriers removed. Mapping the ideal process is looking at the process with:

- All the money in the world
- All the technology available
- What it could look like 5 or 10 years from now

Teams should not spend more than an hour on this step. The purpose is to get teams to brainstorm, get them out of the box, and shift paradigms to vision the possibilities.

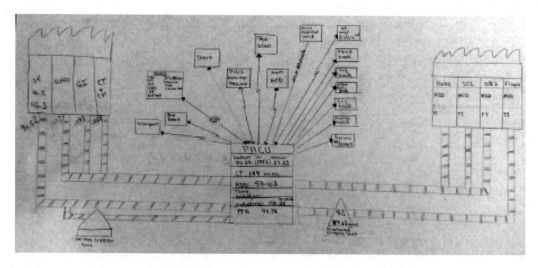

FIGURE 4.11   PACU VSM. Source: BIG File.

FUTURE STATE VALUE STREAM MAPPING

Once the ideal state VSM is completed, the final step is to construct a future state map (Figure 4.12). The future state map is created by the same team and normally looks at what could be accomplished from the ideal state map realistically over the next year out, but can look out 2 years. This is accomplished by reviewing the current state map to determine the following:

- Which activities can be eliminated, rearranged, simplified, or combined?[16]
- Which events can be done in parallel?
- What is the critical path?
- How many people touch it?
- Where are there handoffs between participants (mistakes, waits)?
- Are there activities that are duplicated by the same or another person or department?

VALUE STREAM MAP PROJECT LISTS, PRIORITIZATION MATRIX, AND TRACKING

The team creates "Kaizen bursts" or potential projects and identifies quick wins (changes that could be done immediately to improve the process, usually unnecessary waste activities) that can be implemented to get the process from its current state to future state (Figure 4.13). As the team reviews and designs the "future state" process, the opportunities are placed in a list to improve process speed. Each opportunity is ranked based on impact to the strategic planning goals (Figure 4.14) (which may include service, people, finance, clinical, operations etc.), ease of deployment, and cost. In addition, ranking should occur to understand the risk and impact to other departments for each solution that is proposed. The list of potential opportunities provides a roadmap of continuous improvement activities that the clinical area can work on and track progress over the next year.

The project prioritization matrix is prioritized to support the goals of overall strategic plan. It provides the necessary linkage aligning the department's projects and tasks to the company's goals. These tasks and projects become part of the process owners objective job goals for the year and are tied to their performance reviews and bonuses (if applicable).

---

[16] Junichi Ishiwata, *Productivity Through Process Analysis* (New York: Productivity Press) 1997.

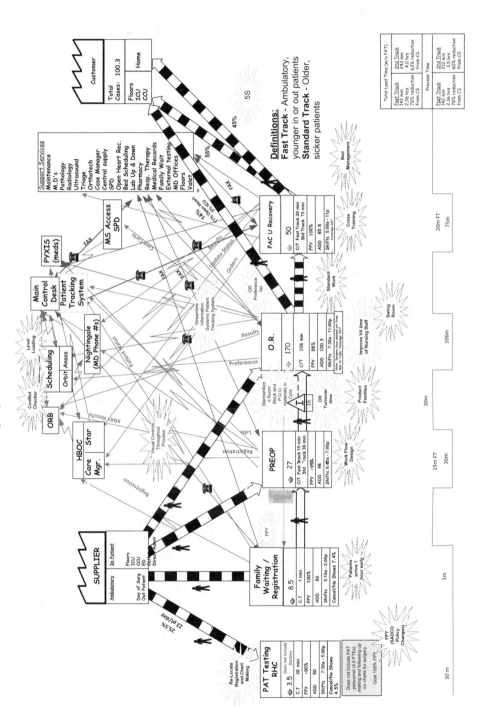

FIGURE 4.12 Surgery Future State Map with Kaizens.

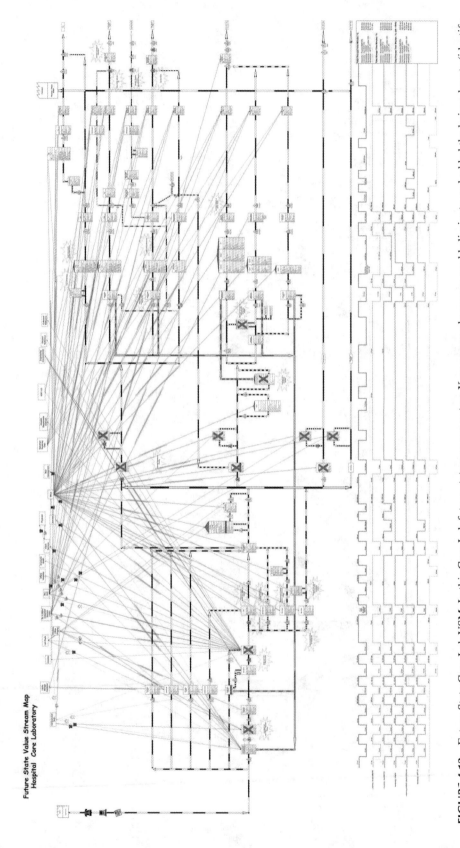

FIGURE 4.13 Future State Core Lab VSM. In this Core Lab future state map we put an X on process boxes we could eliminate and added the kaizen bursts (identifying possible smaller sub-projects). Some companies put the kaizen bursts on the current state map and others put them on the future state map. Notice there are several timelines to depict the flows of each of the processes, i.e., hematology, chemistry, etc.

Proposed Projects or Tasks Description	Project or Task	Financial Impact (Cost/Benefit)	Ease of implementation	Improved Customer / Patient / Stakeholder Perspective	Cycle time impact	Future Perspective (Growth, Quality, Safety, etc...)	Totals	Status
1. 5S OR equipment storage area	T						0	75% complete
2. 5S OR hallway	T						0	Open
3. Unclamp each instrument before sending to CS	T						0	100% complete
4. Eliminate instrument container washing process	T						0	100% complete
5. Improve pre-op patient information FFY	P	5	3	5	5	5	23	Open
6. Demand and supply matching for frequent used instrument sets	P	3	5	1	3	3	15	Open
7. OR scheduling process	P	3	1	3	3	3	13	Open
8. Improve 7:30 case start on-time	P	3	1	3	3	3	13	Open
9. Cross training for Pre-op, PACU and PreTesting staff	P	3	1	3	3	3	13	Open
10. Assess block time effectiveness	P	3	1	3	3	3	13	Open
11. Case cart assembly process standardization	P	1	5	1	3	3	13	90% complete
12. Level loading cases by : service line, instrument type, patient type	P	3	1	3	3	3	13	Open
13. Reassess PreTesting demand and staffing need	P	1	5	1	1	3	11	Open
14. Visual control for processes (KPIs)	P	1	5	1	1	3	11	Open
15. OR room stock standardization	P	1	5	1	3	1	11	100% complete
16. CS demand and staffing need study	P	3	3	1	1	3	11	100% complete
17. Reduce unnecessary flashing	P	3	3	3	1	1	11	In Process (new equip purchase)
18. Align supply area to resource map (preference card)	P	1	5	1	1	1	9	80% complete (bin locations ID'd but needs to be uploaded by Surgery IS)

Ranking: 1-low impact, 3-med impact, 5-high impact

FIGURE 4.14 Project Prioritization Matrix. Source: BIG Files.

VALUE STREAM LAYOUT MAPS (SOMETIMES REFERRED TO AS SKITUMI MAPS)

During our VSM teachings, we always use the phrase that the process boxes "are a process, not a place." However, the information in VSMs can help guide layout revisions to help optimize flow. "Value stream layout maps" leverage the value stream mapping data by overlaying the process boxes (data) on top of the existing master layout. This is an excellent way for leaders to help visualize how their overall layouts create bottlenecks and waste. This is also a good way to look at your overall master layouts or block diagrams of the hospital overall and develop high-level systemic approaches to improvement.

BASELINING THE PROCESS—DATA COLLECTION AND ANALYSIS—CURRENT STATE

Lean is about being able to "manage by fact" and understanding all the data related to the current process and what it can deliver. Next, we will go through the types of data needed to get a true picture of the best way to deliver customer value. The data captured in the baseline phase provides the foundation for the calculations and comparisons for the improvements as we methodically move through the phases. Although we will not be able to go through each and every item and tool mentioned in the baseline phase (B) of the BASICS model, we will introduce you to the key pieces of data and calculations in the baseline phase. We will begin to introduce demand, TT, cycle time, throughput time, staffing, peak demand, inventory, and work in process (WIP), and cover some key financial data points.

TAKT TIME/PRODUCTION SMOOTHING

Takt[17] time (German root means metre, tempo, or beat) is equal to the available time to produce a product or service divided by the customer demand required during the available time.

Most healthcare personnel are not familiar with the term Takt time (TT) or production smoothing. TT allows us to look at a process or a group of activities and determine, based on customer demand and available time, how a process needs to run related to time. When we take yearly or monthly demand and divide it by working days, it aids in production smoothing or leveling the activities within the process; this will be discussed in detail later in the book.

Takt time (TT) = available time ÷ customer demand

AVAILABLE TIME

Available time is equal to the total time per shift less uncovered breaks, meeting etc., where the workplace shuts down. In healthcare available time normally equals the total shift time as staff and managers cover breaks. However, in some vet offices, general practitioner offices or commercial pharmacies it's not unusual for the office to shut down over lunch or planned break. If a normal shift was 10 hrs with an hour for lunch then the available time would be equal to 9 hrs. So the available time is actually the "work" time available for the department or unit.

CUSTOMER DEMAND

In Lean, everything starts with the customer, and the first piece of data we need is to determine true customer demand. Understanding customer demand is critical since it impacts what hours

---

[17] http://www.answers.com/topic/takt –Takt – Metre or time, as in *Dreivierteltakt* (3/4 time), *im Takt* (in strict tempo) etc., or bar (measure), as in *Taktstrich* (bar-line). http://www.websters-online-dictionary.org/definition/takt – German rhythm, clock time, stroke.

we need to be open and the number of staff required. It is an integral part of many of our other calculations. In a hospital or clinical setting, the best or most accurate demand numbers are based on current (actual) and future (or projected) forecasted demand. If we cannot get actual and forecasted numbers, we often have to rely on historical data. As we all know, sometimes history is not a good predictor of the future, as case mix, new services, and business development may alter demand.

We capture demand yearly, monthly, daily, by day of week, etc., and it is important to understand demand at the lowest possible level, especially if there are wide swings in demand cycles, such as in the laboratory "morning run." One of our rules with Lean is to always convert calculations to represent a day's worth or sometimes an hour's worth of demand. This is because it is easier for people to understand a day's or hour's worth of something vs. a week's, a month's or a year's worth. This will also make it easier to calculate the rest of the formulas as we work through the implementation.

As we begin to relate demand to activities performed, we must be able to analyze demand in terms of how or when it is needed. For example, we would be inaccurate at scheduling nurses in the emergency room if we based how many nurses we need on a daily (24 hrs) basis instead of understanding trends in demand by shifts, or preferably, in hours. If we scheduled staff equally throughout the day, we would find that we are overstaffed on nights and understaffed on days. Managers must recognize the importance of understanding and monitoring demand. If not, they may fall victim to "staffing to desire," where they will often find that they do not have the staff they need at the times they are needed, thus creating an artificial appearance that more staff is needed overall when, in fact, it is just not being scheduled properly to "match" the customer demand.

Customer demand has to be analyzed in the same increment of time as available time to be compared with TT.

PEAK DEMAND

Hospitals and clinics incur a phenomenon we have termed peak demand. In many areas, such as in the emergency room, OR, laboratory, radiology, and pharmacy, it can be difficult to level load the schedule. Even though the ED demand is predictable, patients do not necessarily arrive evenly spaced. It doesn't mean it can't be level loaded, but it is much more challenging and may require "non-conventional shifts" to optimize resources to meet customer demand.

Lesson Learned

We have modeled ED arrivals across several hospitals by hour and have predicted patients waiting to see the doctor at any time during the day or evening, to within 1–2 patients.

Another area that has peak demand is surgery. The main driver is most surgeons want a 7:30 a.m. start or cut time and want to end their day by 4:00 p.m. or 5:00 p.m. This forces a large number of cases through first thing in the morning and drives when and how many resources (people, equipment, and facilities) are needed throughout the rest of the hospital to support it. Think about what impact this has on the entire organization and the staffing requirements for surgery. Thus, having all the cases start at the same time creates a domino effect of batching and drives when beds need to become available and when transport staff is needed. The number of Post-Op recovery staff and beds, as well as the need for critical care unit beds around the same time. Another driver is add-on or emergency cases. Imagine if we level loaded the demand each day. What differences would that make?

Peak demand can also occur during certain months of a year, such as seasonal (i.e., EDs in "snow bird" states during January to March). Peak demand can occur during weeks of a year, certain days (i.e., surgery Tuesday–Thursday) and during certain hours of the day (i.e., laboratory morning runs, ED after 5:00 p.m.). We have found that maybe with the exception of add-ons, surgery demand is as predictable as is ED demand (and even add-ons are somewhat predictable). Peak demand drives a tremendous amount of waste. Supporting peak demand requires extra staffing, extra rooms, and extra equipment. Once peak demand is over, what do we do with the extra staff, rooms, and equipment once the demand drops and rooms are left empty and staff turns idle? The goal is to level load demand, but until that can be done, we need to account for this peak demand or we will be unable to provide services.

Customer demand has to be analyzed in the same increment of time as available time to be compared with TT.

CYCLE TIME

Cycle time is collected as part of the baseline phase so we can again understand the current state. It is calculated in different ways, but each should have the same result. They are:

1. The amount of time each person actually spends completing their part of the operation if the work is evenly distributed.
2. The daily or hourly available time divided by the daily or hourly demand of the process. *(Note: This is different from TT, which is based on the demand of the customer.)*
3. Dividing the total labor time (TLT) by the number of people in the process, again assuming it is evenly distributed.
4. Timed to the actual individual output of the process, i.e., the length of time between the discharges of each individual patient.

The collection of cycle time early in the Lean initiative provides a baseline of the activity or process. It is a very important data point since it can be used as an in-process metric. Once all or part of the waste is eliminated, it will be monitored in the "C" or check phase (BASIC). The current cycle time data will be compared to the future state cycle time of the proposed new process during the "S" or sustain phase of the BASICS model. The goal would be to match cycle times to TT, but they are generally not the same in healthcare owing to all the variation that exists in the processes.

CYCLE TIME AND TAKT TIME—WHAT'S THE DIFFERENCE?

To begin to "put the puzzle together," we differentiate between (Takt time) TT and cycle time (CT). In order to optimize the process flow, we need a clear understanding of cycle time and TT. As we have previously discussed, cycle time is obtained through performing the product process and operator analysis. Cycle time is the actual working rhythm of the area or the amount of time each person must meet to complete their part of the operation.

Many use TT synonymously with cycle time, but we differentiate because we believe they are different. TT is a calculation that is based strictly on customer demand, where cycle time is based on the area's demand for that day or hour and/or the time it actually takes you to do a particular activity.

Our goal is to match cycle time to TT, but this may not always be possible. In a hospital, cycle time would be based on the demand at which we choose to "staff" or assign resources to perform activities in the area. Despite what is imagined, demand in hospitals is surprisingly predictable. In hospitals, due to scheduling limitations, based on hours one can work and jobs one can perform, it can be difficult to balance cycle times and TTs. Sometimes, we cannot always afford to staff to peak demand for all areas all the time, as this is not practical in all hospital settings.

Cycle time and TT can initially be confusing concepts. To illustrate, we will use the following example:

TT = available time ÷ customer demand

In an OR we schedule 12 hr shifts from 7:00am to 7:00pm. If the "demand" on a normal day for surgical cases is 45, then our Takt time (TT) calculation is:

- Available time = 12 hr or 720 min
- OR Room Time (patient out to patient in) = 3 hrs (180 min)
- Total demand = 45 surgical cases per day
- Takt time = 720 ÷ 45 = 16 min

The TT is based on the AVERAGES and assumes everything is LEVEL LOADED (or evenly distributed). In order to complete the surgical schedule of 45 patients, the OR would need to process a patient in and out of the OR every 16 min. It is important to note that this has nothing to do with how long it takes to do process someone (or perform a case), or how many people work in the department. If the surgical case load for the day is more or less, then the TT would need to be adjusted.

Takt time will also vary based upon the number of shifts. Assuming the demand stays constant at 45/day the Takt time would be:

- 16 min TT for 1 shift
- 32 min TT for 2 shifts

This is because the available time increases and the demand remains the same.

The same effect can be achieved by running 2 parallel clinical processes on 1 shift at a 32 min TT ("cells" or "tracks" or in the case of surgical ORs it would be rooms).

32 min TT ÷ 2 tracks = 16 min average cycle time overall, i.e., 2 patients completed every 32 min

We need to be able to balance the "line" or spread the work evenly across the area and flex resources to achieve maximum throughput. Sometimes, using these techniques helps to better balance work from shift to shift. Balancing the work has a corresponding effect on the number of people required in the OR. Based on the analysis, we need to be able to answer the following questions:

- What is the peak demand each OR should be able to meet?
- Are the ORs capable of performing each operation for each service line? In other words, are all OR room sizes and equipment standardized in hospitals?

DESIGNING CYCLE TIME TO TAKT TIME

Sometimes, we may choose to run at a faster or slower cycle time. This will cause us to over or under-produce to Takt time. To "design" a process leveraging cycle time information, we can alter the available time to run the process. We can do this by:

- Adding or taking away shifts (extending or decreasing the "work day")
- Adding or taking away rooms
- Running the rooms fewer days per week or fewer hours per day
- Combining or separating products/services in a work area or room

In the OR, for example, we may need to

- Open or close more ORs to meet the TT
- Add or balance the activities of the resources to a particular task to decrease the "rate limiting activity," thus reducing the "patient in" to "next patient in" cycle time

- Assess equipment cycle time such as the ability to clean/sterilize in a timely manner between cases
- Purchase additional or different equipment to facilitate flow
- Invoke work standards, standard work, and expectations
- Clarify roles and responsibilities among staff

Remember to assess everything that may impact the patient in and out of the OR. If we just looked at TT and cycle time and determined we had enough rooms to run a typical surgical day based on demand, we would be missing the opportunity to eliminate waste, optimize productivity, and grow our business within the current space.

Length of Stay (LOS)

LOS in healthcare is becoming more critical with the announcement of Centers for Medicare & Medicaid Services with the initiation of the bundle payment models as prescribed by the 2010 healthcare reform law. The Bundled payment models are intended to drive efficiency in the care of expensive Medicare patients. The models' designs vary in how they bundle episodes of care and may even vary with each hospital's negotiated contract. These demonstration projects require the collaboration between physicians and hospitals extending across the value stream coordinating care in many cases from preadmission to post discharge. "This effort necessitates hospitals and doctors "looking in depth at the current processes of care in the preadmission period, in admission period, in post-acute period in the primary care period and evaluating where there is waste, where's the inefficiency and where are the quality problems right now?" says Coleen Kivlahan, MD, the AAMC's Senior director of Health Care Affairs. "And where are we doing things that we don't really, have evidence base attached to those, and eliminate those." Additionally, St. Bernardine's Barron is certain that his hospitals should go forward now and learn what they can, and he believes those networks who figure out how to improve care and be more efficient, "who know how to manage populations and improve quality will deliver a value proposition, and they will be successful, and will be where the business is going. The future is not that far ahead."[18]

Since many organizations utilize Lean to tackle patient throughput issues, it is important that one gains an understanding of how LOS is calculated, as this is a key metric or key process indicator (KPI).

Throughput time is calculated by adding the total processing, inspection, transport, and storage time, or the sum of all the cycle times in a process. Once we have throughput time, we can divide it by the TT or necessary cycle time to determine the WIP (or work in progress) inventory required to meet the cycle time. Keep in mind that in hospitals, the products are patients and, hence, WIP in healthcare is synonymous with patients waiting for the next step.

The following is an example of the formula to determine the size of a waiting room.

If each patient spends 168 min of time waiting with a 12 min TT, then length of stay (LOS) divided by TT is equal to 14 rooms or 1 room that can house 14 patients to support the waiting area.

It is important to be aware that LOS includes value-added and non-value-added time. One of the primary goals every manager should have is to reduce the LOS without impacting another areas or department's LOS. Since LOS is such an important factor in all areas of the hospital and clinics, there may come a time when hospitals employ "value stream leaders" who would then oversee their overall LOS for a value stream or service line.

---

[18] http://www.nonprofithealthcare.com/news/newsview.asp?id=2195

LENGTH OF STAY IS DIRECTLY CORRELATED TO INVENTORY

Little's Law[19] states that the inventory in the system is equal to the throughput time divided by the cycle time.

The longer the LOS, the more inventory or "patients" exist in the system. Inventory in manufacturing is totally different from healthcare in that the product can't talk to you while it is moving through the factory. Yet, the concept that hospitals can learn from factories is not that farfetched when you consider both have demand, time in which the demand has to be completed, and the need to reduce costs to be profitable and stay in business.

Inventory is divided into 3 basic types:

1. Raw material
2. Work in Process or Progress (WIP)
3. Finished goods

Raw material is material (or people) that have had no direct labor added to them. WIP is any raw material that has had labor added but is not finished. Finished goods are any material that has had all the direct labor added to them.

A good WIP inventory analogy is a laundry example.

If we do our laundry every 2 weeks, how many days of clothes do we need? We need at least 14 days worth of clothes plus the time it takes to launder them. If it takes 3 days to launder them, then we need a total of 17 days. If we do our laundry once a week and it now takes a day to do the laundry, we can cut the inventory required from 17 days to 8 days. As we cut our throughput time and increase our first past yield (FPY, the total throughput yield of the system), our costs can't help but be reduced.

Tom Peters said, "In their book, Stalk and Hout say the consumption of time should become the primary business measurement performance variable,[20] i.e., ahead of the 'P' word profit. Sounds silly at first blush, sounds brilliant at second blush because if you get the 'T' word right then the 'P' word takes care of itself. There is no way in hell you can do a job in 4 hrs as expensively as you can do it in 9 months."[21] In addition, if we can reduce our throughput time we can now increase our capacity (assuming we have the demand).

LENGTH OF STAY—A KEY METRIC

We recommend LOS as a key Lean productivity metric along with other metrics on patient safety, quality and customer satisfaction. LOS can be used at the highest level to monitor patient-centered processes. Throughput time (LOS) as a metric used for laboratory, pharmacy or nutritional service areas is very similar to manufacturing processes. Why is the metric LOS so important? This metric is important because most other metrics ('x's') impact LOS, which would be our big "Y." The longer the LOS in a hospital:

- The greater the number of touchpoints and hand-offs leading to opportunities for "defects" or errors.
- The more it costs to house the patient.
- The more supplies required during their stay.
- The more labor required to take care of them.
- The need for more space and rooms.
- The longer the throughput time, the longer the patients are tying up a bed, which means we see fewer patients and our costs (fixed) and opportunities for defects increase.

---

[19] http://iew3.technion.ac.il/serveng/Lectures/Little.pdf
[20] George Stalk and Thomas Hout, *Competing Against Time* (New York: MacMillan) 1990.
[21] Tom Peters, "Speed is Life" video, Video Publishing House and KERA, 1991.

Every leader should understand that each extra minute of throughput time/LOS adds costs defined in a variety of ways, but most of that cost is hidden.

Understanding and managing LOS is critical to most hospitals as it impacts whether or not they can admit or treat that next patient in the ED or perform that next surgery. Managing LOS means the difference between whether we need to build that new hospital or doctor's office building, wing, add more surgical suites, add another MRI machine or build a larger facility. Managing LOS can impact the financial viability of a healthcare organization.

Homework

Work with your financial support team to determine what every minute or hour of LOS costs (in dollars) and how optimizing LOS can impact your hospital or clinic.

Safety, service, quality, delivery and cost all tie to the LOS metric. If we shorten LOS, our costs go down, our patient safety increases, our patient satisfaction increases, we deliver on time (meet the schedule), and we reduce our costs (and, in addition, we add capacity to potentially generate more revenue). The longer the LOS, the more complex our processes seem to become and the more frustrating it is for our staff members who are trying to move patients to keep the ED and ORs flowing. Longer throughput times drive holds in the OR and in the ED. In the OR, this results in inpatient/surgeons' cases being delayed, which extends the workday and costs additional labor time or overtime; this does not include the "human life quality" costs. In the ED, extended LOS results in delays in access to seeing the physician; after 2–3 hrs patients start to leave. This is a safety risk for the patient and a potential loss of revenue for the hospital. The impact of extended LOS within the EDs on patient experience and the ability to treat additional patients that many hospitals have adopted "hallway beds" at times of overcapacity. Additionally CMS has added Emergency Department throughput – median time from ED arrival to ED departure for admitted patients as a core measure to ensure organizations address the challenge of extended ED stays[22]. Nurses and doctors get frustrated dealing with patients angry about having to wait so long to see them. The greater the danger to the patient contracting a hospital or nosocomial[23] infection.

It is important to remember that LOS is related to patient mix and acuity, so LOS goals may be different at each facility. Comparing LOS over time at the same facility is best at the start, as long as patient mix does not change too much. While it is true that revenue will generally increase with shorter LOS, this assumes diagnosis-related group (DRG) payment (like Medicare) or case rate payments, there are still a few payers that pay on a per diem (daily rates), which pay more for longer LOS. The movement toward bundled payment models will drive organizations such as hospitals or ACOs to tightly manage LOS.

REDUCING LENGTH OF STAY

How do we reduce LOS? First, we have to understand what comprises LOS. LOS is made up of all the individual process cycle times that contribute to it. So we must look at total throughput time for a patient to get through our hospital, whether they enter through the OR, ED, catheterization laboratory, transfer, or direct admit until their exit by being discharged home.

Homework

One action you can immediately take is to have all your managers and supervisors define throughput time in their areas, then calculate and understand what their cycle times and

---

[22] 2011-2012 Eligible Hospital & Critical Access Hospital Clinical Quality Measures (CQMs), http://www.cms.gov/ Regulations-and-Guidance/Legislation/EHRIncentivePrograms/Downloads/CQM_Hospitals_2012_02_02.pdf

[23] Louis M. Savary, *The Nun and the Bureaucrat* (Washington, DC: CC-M Productions) 2006.

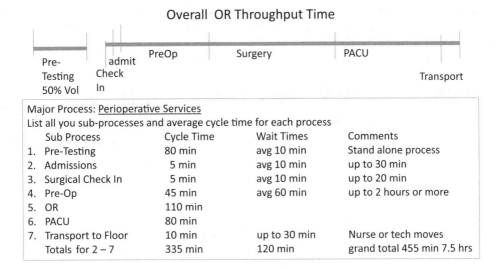

Overall OR Throughput Time

Major Process: Perioperative Services			
List all you sub-processes and average cycle time for each process			
Sub Process	Cycle Time	Wait Times	Comments
1. Pre-Testing	80 min	avg 10 min	Stand alone process
2. Admissions	5 min	avg 10 min	up to 30 min
3. Surgical Check In	5 min	avg 10 min	up to 20 min
4. Pre-Op	45 min	avg 60 min	up to 2 hours or more
5. OR	110 min		
6. PACU	80 min		
7. Transport to Floor	10 min	up to 30 min	Nurse or tech moves
Totals for 2 – 7	335 min	120 min	grand total 455 min 7.5 hrs

FIGURE 4.15   Overall Throughput Time. Source: Authors.

resulting throughput times are for the processes for which they are responsible. The more we reduce the cycle time for each process, the less inventory we need, the less rooms we need, etc. A format for that report is shown in Figure 4.15.

We place a cautionary note, however, on metrics such as customer satisfaction and LOS, as there are a substantial number of contributing factors ('x's') to both of these metrics. One isolated Lean initiative may not—and we have found through experience that it will not—be able to impact all the contributing factors to significantly "move" the needle on these metrics, and a series of initiatives is required. For example, in the ED, if we did a survey and identified that customer satisfaction was important, we may need to measure and improve cycle time from door-to-doctor examination, along with nurse touch point communication and ancillary services to improve the overall LOS. If the ED had an internal Lean initiative, they could have a significant impact and control on all the factors except LOS. This is because ED LOS depends on the LOS or turnaround time of other departments, such as radiology, laboratory and, ultimately, the inpatient units. Therefore, Lean initiatives require understanding the "value stream" and how to integrate the silos.

NUMBER OF STAFF REQUIRED

LOS also impacts the number of staff or labor required to run the organization. The longer a patient stays within the system, whether it is in processing a registration, having a procedure, or being evaluating in the ED, it is necessary to understand the number or (headcount) of staff, the number of hours worked per week and skill level of each staff member. In a Lean initiative, capturing this data should be done at the beginning of the project. This will yield the amount of labor hours currently used by skill set.

So LOS or throughput time has a big impact on the number of rooms required in addition to the labor required. The longer the patient is in the process, the more resources they consume and the more expensive their visit becomes.

Interestingly enough, the majority of hospitals do not have incentives built into their physician contracts or departments for LOS or for efficiency (i.e., door-to-doctor examination) times. In the ED, these two times are a dichotomy. Physicians in the ED, as a rule, don't handoff patients, so we end up trading LOS (i.e., disposition and discharge) with door-to-doctor examination time because there is only one physician and he can't examine 2 patients at the same time or examine and dispose/

discharge 2 patients at the same time. If physicians ever determined that they could handoff the disposition of patients (which, in some cases, may not be desirable), this would alleviate the problem.

TOTAL LABOR TIME

The definition of TLT is the sum of value-added labor plus non-value-added labor. The TLT comes from the operator analysis section described later. Once we have the TLT we can divide it by TT or cycle time to determine the number of staff required, the total staffing hours and convert it to dollars. Later, this will help us to calculate any labor savings and improvement in productivity through the Lean initiative.

QUIZ

Problem 1
If it takes on average 5 days to get an inpatient through the hospital and the TT is 10 min, how many rooms do we need? If level loaded, how many patients would arrive and leave each day?

Problem 1

5 days × 24 hrs × 60 min = 7200 min.

Number of rooms = LOS ÷ Takt time = 720 rooms.
Number of patients per hour = 60 min in an hour ÷ 10 min Takt time = 6 patients per hour.
Level loaded would equal 6 patients per hour every 24 hrs or 144 patients per day.

Problem 2
If it takes 2 hrs to get results in an ED after the patient has been seen, and TT is 10 min, how big a waiting room do we need?

120 min (waiting for results (LOS)) ÷ 10 min Takt time = 12 patients in waiting room.

WEIGHTED AVERAGE

Often, we do not open or utilize "rooms" 24 hrs per day, whether it is in a procedural area, surgical suite, or even in a post-procedural recovery unit. We may "open" or make the rooms available for use based on demand. Sometimes, we have to calculate weighted averages in order to use some of the formulas.

TABLE 4.1
Weighted Average Number of Rooms

Weighted Average Example					
1	2	3	4	5	6
			= col 1 * col 3	= col 4/188	c = col 5 * col 1
# of Rooms	Scheduled Hours	Hours	Total Hours	Weighted Avg Factor	Weighed Average Rooms
17	7 a.m. to 3 p.m.	8	136	72.3%	12.30
10	3 p.m. to 7 p.m.	4	40	21.3%	2.13
3	7 p.m. to 11 p.m.	4	12	6.4%	0.19
10	average		188	1	14.62

Let's say surgery suites are utilized in the following manner (Table 4.1):

17 rooms from 7:00 a.m. to 3:00 p.m. (8 hrs)
10 rooms from 3:00 p.m. to 7:00 p.m. (4 hrs)
3 rooms from 7:00 p.m. to 11:00 p.m. (4 hrs)

What is the average number of rooms we use? Number of rooms: 17 rooms + 10 rooms + 3 rooms = 30 rooms. The next step would be to take 17 rooms x 8 hrs = 136 hrs. We do this for each one and arrive at 188 for the total hours. We then divide the total hours for each room divided by the grand total of hours (188 hrs). This gives us the weighted average factor that we then multiple by the number of rooms, which gives us the weighted average number of rooms over the entire range of staffed hours 7:00 to 11:00 p.m.

Remember the goal is to manage by fact and understand your data. We need to discover what data is available in your organization and what confidence level of accuracy can be placed on data. The bottom line is that is great, but it is the human interpretation of this data that is critical. Sometimes it helps to have a couple of people looking at the data to make sure the formulas are correct. The team, which includes the executive sponsor and the Lean initiative owner, must understand the information and determine what is reasonable to accomplish in relation to the organizational goals. In addition, as situations change, the calculations must be redone to make sure that everyone continues to manage by fact or the system will breakdown.

FINANCIAL METRICS

Being able to articulate and quantify financial metrics can be important, especially in early Lean implementations when organizations are still trying to "prove the value" of adopting Lean. Outlined below highlights some of the data points one might consider gathering during the initial phases of the initiative to begin to construct the financial component of the ROI.

MEASURING INVENTORY AND CASH FLOW

Most hospitals don't seem to formally track inventory consistently and, if they do, it is typically not very accurate. In fact, unlike manufacturers, cash flow is not even tracked as a key metric at many hospitals. Some hospitals have even said that if our cost of capital is only 4%–5%, why should we care about how much inventory we have? In fact, reducing inventory may negatively impact our profitability.

As a result, most hospitals have little or no idea of their inventory costs, whether in the surgical suite or emergency room or other departments, especially at the frontline management level. The cost of surgical supplies in storage, "lost" or excess and obsolete (out of date) can be significant. The problem is that most healthcare organizations "think they know" what it is; however, we have found that in most hospitals the data are ripe with inaccuracies. In healthcare, inventory can refer to many things: supplies, number of rooms, or even number of patients waiting (in different situations when it pertains to Lean). Related to financial metrics, we generally consider it as it pertains to supplies. Inventory can be expressed in dollars or number of turns or what we call days of supply (DOS).

Traditional inventory turns are expressed by[24]:

Sales or COGS (Cost of Goods Sold) ÷ last 3 months average inventory.

---

[24]Erich Helfert, *Techniques of Financial Analysis* (Chicago, IL: Irwin Publishing) 1997, page 110; also www.inventoryturns.com.

In Lean, we look at "forward looking" DOS, which is expressed by:

Sales or COGS ÷ next projected 3 months of average inventory.

We calculate DOS by taking:

Inventory dollars on hand ÷ a day's worth of average inventory.

In order to figure out a day's worth of inventory, we need to calculate the inventory used over a specified period and divide it by the number of days in that period. For example, if a surgical services department has $6 million in supply inventory and they use $1.2 M per month, we would take $1.2 million per month and divide it by 30 calendar days per month:

$1,200,000 ÷ 30 days = $40,000 per calendar day.

If we take the $6,000,000 supply inventory on hand.

$6,000,000 ÷ $40,000/day = 150 calendar DOS.

Once we have DOS, we can calculate inventory turns: Inventory Turns = calendar or annual working days ÷ DOS.

For example: 365 days in the year ÷ 150 DOS = 2.43 turns per year

When figuring out par levels in surgery, however, the approach above would be misleading, as it averages the inventory over all 7 days of the week. When we figure par levels, (we need to figure it out for each part individually (we call this a plan for every part PFEP[25])) and look at weekdays only and, in some cases, peak demand on weekdays (i.e., if we do most of our heart cases on 1 or 2 days), unless you are routinely doing cases on the weekends.

Note

Most hospitals at the operational level prior to Lean initiatives do not look at inventory in this manner; however, the materials management area may track inventory *turns.*

WORK IN PROCESS INVENTORY

Throughput time ÷ CT (Cycle time) = amount of WIP inventory

Consider the following inventory example related to equipment needed for surgical cases. If it takes 3 hrs to get equipment though the cleaning/sterilization process and the CT is 60 min per surgical case, the number of equipment sets could be calculated. Knowing that it takes 3 hrs to perform the cleaning sterilization process (including transport and there are no other delays) or 180 min ÷ 60 min = 3 equipment sets, to run the system. It is important to be able to leverage the data and manage by fact to be able to know whether you have the right amount of equipment to do the work.

SALES OF REIMBURSEMENT PER EMPLOYEE

Sales or revenue by itself is a misleading metric for hospitals and clinics and is not generally used, as the price charged does not typically represent what the hospital gets reimbursed nor does it often relate

---

[25] Rick Harris, *Making Materials Flow* (Cambridge, MA. Lean Enterprise Institute (LEI) 2006.

to what it costs to deliver the service. Also, hospitals in the United States are required to take patients whether the patient can afford to pay or not.[26] This creates challenges for hospitals as they attempt to manage their costs without having control on what they can charge. For example, if the charge for "plasma" goes up, they cannot necessarily pass on the cost to their customers like many businesses can, as many of their payers' pay "fixed" reimbursements and many customers may not pay at all.

CONTRIBUTION MARGIN

Contribution margin, revenue, or reimbursements per employee are good overarching metrics for Lean. They are a high-level look at the contribution per employee, and we should have a set percentage goal to increase this each year.

COST PER CASE

Cost per case can be another misleading metric; however, it can also be a key metric if used correctly; but we have to be careful how it is used and calculated. It can be a deceptive metric if one does not account for the weighted average of case mix. For instance, orthopedic cases use very expensive implants. If the ratio of orthopedic cases increases, so will the overall average cost per case.

Our goal with Lean is not just to look at leading and lagging indicators but to focus on real-time process based metrics (Table 4.2).

DATA AND WHAT PEOPLE THINK

In the quest of gathering accurate data, over and over we ask people how long things take, with regard to performing activities within a given process. Most managers and staff provide an estimate; however, when we video or conduct a time study, they are almost never correct. In fact, they are generally surprised once they are given the "real" data. As soon as someone says, "I think" or "it was" or "it should be," then one knows the person is not really sure. If our goal is to act on fact, then this becomes a problem. Why go into all this with Lean?

In order to improve, we need to know our starting point. If we can't baseline our metrics, we can't know how much we improved. Remember the old saying, "Minutes count but seconds rule."[27]

TABLE 4.2
Short-Term Metrics—Results vs. Process Focused

Results Focused		Process Focused
Leading	**Lagging**	**Real Time**
On-time delivery	Inventory turns	Takt, cycle, and throughput time
Labor as a percentage of net sales	EBIDTA	Visual controls—delivery system by hour
Quality measures	Return on assets	Quality—immediate countermeasures and root cause
Cost of quality	Gross profit	Standard work audit
3 months forecasted DOS	Cash flow	Immediate patient feedback
Customer satisfaction	Contribution margin	Add on—unplanned stoppages number and hours
		Patient readiness

---

[26] http://www.cms.hhs.gov/emtala/. In 1986, Congress enacted the emergency Medical Treatment & Labour Act (EMTALA) to ensure public access to emergency services regardless of ability to pay.

[27] Shawn L Noseworthy, RD, LD, MSA, Director of Food and Nutrition Services, Florida Hospital Memorial Medical System, 301 Memorial Medical Parkway, Daytona Beach, FL 32117 USA, shawn.noseworthy@fhmmc.org.

It is very difficult, even with all the data and reports produced, to get good baseline data because the data are only as good as those entering the data. Having everyone working to the same data entry point definitions and capturing it in the same "reproducible and repeatable" manner in order to make sure it is accurate can be a difficult challenge.

For example, in one ED, we were told that the correct data was always entered and updated several times a day. Yet, when we dug deeper, we found it took at least 24 hours of reviewing every case from the prior day before the data was even 80% accurate. Think about it—these are legal documents! We found this not to be an isolated incident. Consider trying to meet a quality metric of door to EKG within 10 min and every staff member documents the time using unsynchronized clocks. Could this impact whether the metric was actually met? Other EDs take several days to calculate their actual arrivals and complete their charts. How can one manage the ED effectively without the critical information at the right time or in "real time or near real time" in order to make the adjustments needed to react to problems within a timely manner? After all, it is too late to fix the problem if the process has been completed and the customer has left.

The baselining phase sets the stage for the Lean initiative. The executive sponsor and operational managers should understand their KPIs and identify the key metrics that will be impacted.

SUSTAINABILITY AND ACCOUNTABILITY

A culture of organizational accountability is critical in order to sustain Lean. Once we implement Lean in an area, there is a need for it not only to be sustained, but also to be continuously improved. When implemented, most processes may be 80% defined, the remaining 20% need to be further refined as staff works the process and identifies more opportunities to eliminate variation and waste. Without accountability in place, too often we see the areas or organizations backsliding.

Lesson Learned

Once you implement Lean, any problem that shows up, even if you have had it for the last 30 years, will now get blamed on Lean.

One fundamental and extremely challenging problem that we often encounter early in most healthcare organizations is a lack of accountability throughout the organization. Most organizations truly believe they have accountability standards and measures in place; however, Lean initiatives will test the effectiveness of the organization's ability to impose top-to-bottom accountability.

As one engages in Lean, it will quickly become apparent that it is not all about the Lean tools. Lean consultants' roles within or outside our organizations are questioned repeatedly. What role do Lean consultants play?

We often respond that it is not unusual to spend more than 50% of our time in management consulting, teaching analytical skills, coaching, and acting as a catalyst for change; the other 50% of the time is spent teaching and applying the Lean tools. Often, we initially encounter basic "Management 101" type projects, i.e., determine how much inventory there is in surgery, baseline metrics, or develop basic reporting or productivity calculations for an area. There is nothing necessarily wrong with this; however, it shows the lack of resources or training programs in place to help the clinical talent that has been moved into management roles to get their basic analytical and managerial tasks completed. Managerial coaching is extremely important, as managing a Lean process is very different from that of a batch-type process. It is important to start this counseling and coaching immediately and help the manager build the infrastructure necessary to support the Lean culture.

PROCESS OWNERS DO NOT ALWAYS HAVE THE SKILL SETS NECESSARY TO MANAGE IN A LEAN ENVIRONMENT

Many companies and their leadership "talk Lean" but don't necessarily "walk Lean." If account-abilities are not in place and understood early in the initiative, then you will not change the culture and Lean will become a flavor of the month.

At Hospital X, we had an issue where, once the initial implementation was complete, the process excellence organization decided they were not responsible to ensure the brand new Lean implementations were sustained. Finance also stated that they did not have the responsibility to ensure the implementations were sustained. This really surprised us. We all agreed it was the process owner's job to sustain and improve; however, the process owners were not far enough along in understanding the Lean management system to handle it. We brought up the issue with the Lean steering committee. In their opinion, it was the responsibility of the process owner to sustain. Of course, we agreed, but our concern was whose responsibility it is to follow up on the process owner?

At Hospital X they have a unique approach to Lean. They use Lean Senseis to coach their leaders for six months to a year. This way the leader is held accountable to learn the Lean cutlure and tool sets and then use the Leader as Teacher principle to disseminate the learnings via ongoing point, system or 3P kaizens to their team.

This is always an issue because, at most hospitals, there is little accountability throughout the management chain for metrics. As a result, if we leave "sustain and accountability" to only the process owners to continuously improve their metrics and adhere to their control plans it can be a recipe for disaster. A cultural change must occur and process improvement must become the way the organization does business. As the Lean journey begins, there needs to be a mechanism to track, monitor, and report on Lean deployments on an ongoing basis.

Since Lean is about the continual pursuit of eliminating waste, there needs to be a way to ensure that there are continuing cycles of improvement and that management and frontline staff members are actively engaged in operationalizing Lean concepts.

Lesson Learned

It is critical to supply initial and ongoing training on how to manage in a Lean environment and provide opportunities to train new managers and employees in Lean thinking. Accountability and follow-up must be addressed if organizations are going to be successful. It should be part of the "High Level Lean Road Map." The senior leadership team must drive accountability to sustain Lean implementations through their line organization and continue to coach and develop the process owners.

5 Basic Lean Concepts and Tools – Assessment and Analyze

Time waste differs from material waste in that there can be no salvage. The easiest of all wastes and the hardest to correct is the waste of time, because wasted time does not litter the floor likewasted material…

—**Henry Ford, 1926**

The next letter in our BASICS model is *A*, which stands for *Assess/Analyze*. The main tools that make up this analysis are Product Process Flow analysis (PFA), full work/operator analysis (WFA), and changeover reduction. The goal of these tools is to uncover the obvious and less obvious waste. This process of finding waste theoretically never ends.

So let's talk about waste. The heart of the Toyota system is eliminating waste. This is the main premise of the entire system. First, we need to expose waste and then get rid of it. Most of you are familiar with the seven wastes at Toyota, but these wastes are just a starting point, as there are many more types out there.

LEVELS OF WASTE

1. The first level is obvious waste—low-hanging fruit (or walking on it).
2. The five S wastes—the easiest wastes to see.
3. The seven (eight) wastes—explained below.
4. Boiled frog waste—the waste that is hard to notice because it is old and we pass by it every day.
5. Tribal waste—sacred cows—waste in our culture and systems.
6. Hidden unseen waste—waste we don't typically see. You really have to hunt for it! The hardest waste to find, yet the most dangerous. Sometimes it is waste hiding behind other wastes.

Low-Hanging Fruit

This is the easiest waste because it is easy to see and very obvious to anyone looking at the area. It could be a long waiting line, things out of place, people walking to a printer, schedules not posted, charge nurse reviewing all the charts, etc.

Five S Wastes

We will discuss the five S wastes later in the book, but basically these wastes have to do with housekeeping. These wastes include things not labeled, trash not picked up, or areas that need to be cleaned.

The Seven (Eight) Wastes

Listed in Table 5.1 are the seven wastes, including an eighth waste that we've added, which is the waste of talent. We have found the biggest drivers of the eight wastes is "the batching mindset" and Layouts.

TABLE 5.1

Symptoms of the Seven (Eight) Wastes

The Seven/Eight Wastes

Over Production Symptoms	Waste Of Idle and Wait Time Symptoms	Waste Of Transporting Symptoms	Waste Of Too Much Processing Symptoms	Waste Of Excess Inventory Symptoms	Waste Of Wasted Motions Symptom	Waste Of Defects Symptoms	Waste Of Talent Symptoms
Unbalanced staff scheduling	Idly watching equipment operate	Having multiple information systems	Asking the patient the same questions multiple times	Complex tracking systems	Inconsistent work methods	Mistakes made in patient care	Staff not tapped for ideas
Unbalanced material flow	Idle people or machines	Inappropriate bed assignments on admission	Placing OR scheduling information in multiple systems	Multiple forms, multiple copies, multiple weeks' supplies	Long reach/walk distances	Patient returns (OR, readmit)	Staff not developed by their boss
Having more than we need of anything, supplies, beds etc.	Outpatient lab draw results take 1.5 hours	Placing multiples calls to transport	Excessive duplication in OR, SPD, pharmacy, nursing units	No standardization of supplies	Centralized Printers/Copiers/Fax locations	Frequent rescheduling of office appointments	Lack of Discipline
Not notifying food service of diet changes and discharges	Surgeons waiting in between surgeries	Excess patient transfer/movement	Multiple signature requirements	Long turnaround times on floor beds	Searching for anything, for example, equipment	Adverse drug events	Staff doesn't follow standard work
Extra floor space utilized	Unbalanced scheduling/workload	PACU or OR Backed Up	Performing services patient doesn't need, for example lab work	Unused appointment slots	Multiple patient handoffs	High infection rates and falls	Staff waits to be told what to do

Backups between departments, for example, ED to in-patient admit	Numerous & large waiting rooms	Temporary warehouses & multiple storage locations	Manual distribution of numerous report copies	Empty beds	Long lead-times	High incidence of bill rejects	Staff hired in from the outside
25% of surgical supplies picked and returned to the shelf	Reduced productivity (visible)	Walking intermittent samples to lab or going to get prescriptions multiple times	Sorting, testing, and inspection	Extra rework/hidden problems	Convoluted facility & workplace layouts	Utilization review, infection control, legal, and risk management inspections	Staff does repetitive same job over and over
Picking and opening OR instruments but not using them so they must be re-sterilized	Patients wait between multiple appointments	Staff copies patient chart for transfer between facilities	Duplicating physical assessment at triage & in treatment area	Duplication of supplies in temporary storage areas, patient rooms, closets, and so on	Prolonged pre-op testing times	Inappropriate communication of patient transfer mode with order entry	Poor morale
Scrap and wasted food	Techs move patients from PACU	Finished patient chart walked to financial counselor	Punching holes in paper to place in the patient chart	One surgical services cart alone had $250 k of sutures	Poor workplace layout for patient services	Pharmacy refilling "multiple dose" medications	Staff not included in decision making or financials

Source: Authors.

HOW DO YOU FIND WASTE?

The most difficult waste to see is the waste that occurs in processes that we ourselves have created. When these wastes are pointed out to us, we tend to be defensive. This is normal behavior and justified in that it shows ownership over the process. We should take pride in everything we do. But because we take pride in our areas, we should be willing to expose the waste. Being defensive gets in the way because it discourages others from telling us when they see a problem or when they find waste. In a Lean culture, we need to understand there is *always* a better way to do something. The best way to figure it out is to constantly ask "why?"

Lesson Learned

Never get too attached to your solutions and encourage anyone who tours your area to provide feedback—a list of good things and bad things they witnessed. Thank them when you receive it.

To find waste, you have to go out and look for it and then recognize it for what it is. Honda does this with an exercise they call the three A's,[1] which are to Go to the Actual Place and see the Actual Part in the Actual Situation (Figure 5.1).

In our Lean training classes, we ask our students to go out to the floor and write down waste wherever they see it. Many come back with 30–50 examples of waste. When we ask the supervisors what would have happened in the past if someone had come to them with a similar list, they tell us that they would have shut down, been defensive, and continued to do what they always did.

Examples, in addition to the eight wastes, include walking waste, watching waste, searching waste, large machine waste, conveyor waste, layout waste, meetings waste, and "picking up and setting down without using it" waste. Honda's three A's led to their Five P[2] program, which targets five strategic improvement areas:

1. Best **P**osition—improve global competitiveness
2. Best **P**roductivity—improve the process

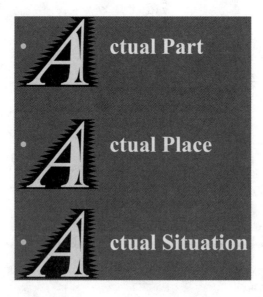

FIGURE 5.1   Honda's Three A's. Source: BIG.

---

[1] R. Dave Nelson, Patricia Moody, and Rick B. Mayo, *Powered by Honda* (Hoboken, NJ: John Wiley and Sons) 1998, 101.

[2] R. Dave Nelson, Patricia Moody, and Rick B. Mayo, *Powered by Honda* (Hoboken, NJ: John Wiley and Sons) 1998, 25.

3. Best **P**roduct—improve quality and delivery
4. Best **P**rice—decrease cost
5. Best **P**artners—improve Honda/supplier relationship

Homework

Can Honda's Five P's work for healthcare? Think about it and write down how it could work for you.

30-30-30 EXERCISE

Taiichi Ohno was known for drawing a chalk circle around managers and making them stand in the circle sometimes for an entire shift until they had seen and documented all of the problems he wanted them to see in a particular area (Figure 5.2). Today the "stand in a circle" exercise is known as a 30-30-30 and is a great way to train someone's eyes to see waste and to provide structure for the team leader to carry out daily improvement or for the busy executive with limited time to go to the *Gemba, "the real place"* and see what is really happening. The exercise entails telling the person to stand in a circle for 30 min or more and just watch and look around to capture at least 30 wastes and then spend 30 min fixing one of them. When one spends time in the *Gemba* (the area where the work is being done) standing in the Ohno circle, you will see the gap between the target condition, if it even exists, and the actual condition.

Homework: *Go out and walk through your area or someone else's area. Answer the following questions.*

PEOPLE

- *What are people doing (or not doing)?*
- *Are we tapping their brains? Is there an idea board in the area?*

EQUIPMENT

- *What is the equipment doing or not doing?*
- *How smart is the equipment?*

FIGURE 5.2   Ohno Circle. Source: Unknown.

- *Where is the high-volume equipment, like chemistry or hematology in a core laboratory, located? Closest to the tube system or furthest away?*
- *Is it batch or flow equipment?*

COMMUNICATION

- *How do we know if there is a problem?*
- *Is the area on plan or on schedule? The area should talk to you.*

VISUAL CONTROLS

- *Is the area Five S'd? Is the area neat and organized?*
- *Are there visual controls in place?*
- *Are there any metrics posted?*
- *Is standard work posted?*

LEADERSHIP

- *What behaviors do the leadership drive? Is it obvious in the area?*
- *Are there audits in place?*
- *Did you ask people what they are measured on?*
- *Are people afraid of their leaders?*

When we assess companies, we do this same exercise. We look to answer these questions and more. For example, do leaders role model the behaviors they desire? In a Lean environment, there is no place for egos and arrogance. Generally, when we do this exercise, we find that people are usually busy all the time. The next question we have to ask is, "What are they busy doing?"

Homework

30-30-30 (a good time for this exercise is at the end of the day or right after lunch). Go spend 30–60 min (depending on time available) standing in one place (Ohno circle) in the hospital and see how many of the eight wastes you can identify. Use Figure 5.3, shoot for 30 suggestions and then fix one that you find while you are there. It normally works best if you pick an area that is not your own.

Lessons Learned

Now that you have completed your homework, what did you find? Did you find some waste? What level was it? If you were to tell the process owner about the waste you found, how do you think it would be received? If someone were to come into your area and tell you what they saw, how would you receive it now? How would you have reacted prior to this exercise? The key is not to be defensive; instead, recognize the waste that exists and work to get rid of it. Generally, outsiders will see wastes that insiders do not see. Was it easier to identify wastes in an area that belonged to someone else? If that was your area to manage, supervise, or work, would you have found as many wasted activities? How would it have felt if you were the supervisor and the wastes were reported to you? How would you have reacted prior to this exercise? Are you a boiled frog?

Sometimes, outsiders help to show us the waste that we don't see or we intentionally or unintentionally refuse to see. We all tend to be "boiled frogs." The term boiled frog is used to symbolize the inability of people to recognize or react when things happen gradually. When they become immersed in their environment, they tend to become complacent. We should recognize the waste that exists, thank those who tell us, and work to eliminate it.

Key Observation Work Sheet - Fill in each observation - 1 per page and summarize findings on Key Waste Summary Sheet

Overview

Waste Observation Number	Process Owner	Person Assigned Task	Standard Work Updated (if applicable)	All Employees Trained if Applicable	Persons Involved in Solution	Supervisor Sign off

Detailed Findings

Waste Discovered - Enter Text Here	Waste Discovered - Enter Before drawing or picture here

Enter Causes and Highlight Root Cause	What is a temporary Fix You can implement

Enter Improvement Ideas (if applicable - fill in improvement idea cards and post on idea board)	What is the permanent Fix You can implement

HC / LB	HC / HB
LC / LB	LC / HB

Enter Action(s) to be taken, responsibilities, Due Date and Follow Up Date

Action To Be Taken	Responsibility	Due Date	Follow Up Date	Status	Reaudit Date	After Picture

FIGURE 5.3 Key Waste Observation Sheet. HC – high cost; LB – low benefit; HB – high benefit; LC – low cost. Source: BIG File.

COST OF WASTE

What is all this waste doing to your customer's experience? In factories, the products can't talk back; but, in hospitals and clinics they do, and often. Our customers can help us to identify waste we don't see. We need to listen to our patients, physicians, and co-staff members. Remember: Waste is like a virus; initially, it is hidden and incubates. If we don't treat it or get rid of it, it festers, mutates, and then grows and multiplies all around us. Waste creates workarounds to our processes. Waste creates poor staff and customer satisfaction because we are constantly searching for things and delaying patient care and treatment. Ultimately, waste decreases our ability to compete in the marketplace. Waste causes variation and imperfection in our processes. The big question is, do we have enough dissatisfaction with the waste to create a compelling need to change the system?

BASELINE ENTITLEMENT BENCHMARK

We explain this concept to help with the assessment step. Each process is in place to solve some type of problem. Wherever we start in solving a problem we call the Baseline phase, i.e., this is where we are today (measurement-wise).

The idea behind Entitlement is that it is the best you can get with the current process or paradigm for solving the problem. We find this is normally 3 times the value-added time. The only way to improve is to move to benchmarking.

Benchmark is implementing a totally new paradigm to solve the problem. The goal of considering the ideal state during any of our analysis is to ask yourself what is not being done or can't be done today, but if it could be done, it would fundamentally change what we do.[3]

Technology is a great place to see this concept play out. Joel Barker, in his video Paradigm Pioneers, uses the problem of how to record and play music. We started with reel to reel tape recorders - Baseline. These were then improved to 8 track players, VCRs, then much smaller cassette recorders and then mini cassette recorders. We now reached Entitlement. This was the furthest they could go with the "Tape based" paradigm. But this technology still had problems. If you wanted to play a song at the end, you had to fast forward the tape until it reached the song. Also the tape would sometimes break! To get better we needed a new paradigm (Benchmark) to solve the problems with. So we invented the digital paradigm with CD/DVD recorders, then the MP3 players, and now everything is electronic, downloadable and backed-up so it is replaceable. No more tape to break, CDs or VHS tapes to carry.

FIVE WHY'S

This familiar tool, which involves asking "why" up to five times, helps to get to the root cause of a problem.

EXAMPLE:

Urine analysis (UA) testing is taking too long (over an hour) to get results in the laboratory, and we just installed a new machine 2 months ago.

- *Why? The new UA machine is a problem.*
- *Why? The laboratory technicians don't believe the results.*
- *Why? They don't trust the new UA machine. They can't believe the machine is better than their old manual style of testing so they always run their manual tests to confirm it.*

---

[3] Joel Barker, *Business of Paradigms* video.

- *Why? How often does it agree with the new machine? All the time. The new machine has never been wrong! In fact, the new machine has proven some of their manual tests were wrong.*
- *Why do they continue to conduct the manual tests? No one has investigated this before and forced them to stop the manual test.*

Lesson Learned: *It is not unusual for people to react to the symptoms of the problem without getting the facts. We all love to just throw solutions at the problem without gathering any data. Sometimes, the problems are hidden. Sometimes, we believe we think we are experts only to find out we don't know what we don't know. As you reduce the waste in processes, you shrink the time it takes to get the patient or product through the process. If you get patients through the process faster, you then increase your capacity. We look at capacity as work plus waste.*

ANOTHER TOOL TO GET RID OF WASTE: THE FIVE W'S AND TWO H'S[4]

The goal of this tool is to work to find the root cause of a problem. How do you know when you have identified the root cause? The answer is: when you have fixed the problems so it never comes back. This is also called *Poka Yoke*.[5] Poka Yoke is a Japanese term that means "mistake-proofing." The aim would be to eliminate any opportunity to create a defect by preventing, correcting, or drawing attention to the problem at the time when it would occur, thus mistake "proof."

Author's Note: Even though our goal is to fix problems so they never come back, we always need to be on guard to make sure the fix for the problem sustains. We also have to guard against the thought process which says once I have mistake proofed the problem I don't need to continue to look for improvements.

The five W's are composed of asking why for each of the five W's (*when?, where?, what?, who?,* and *why?*). The two H's are *how?* and *how much?* This method is described in detail in Shingo's book, *Kaizen and the Art of Creative Thinking*.[6]

WHEN—When is the best time to do it? Does it have to be done then?
WHERE—Where is it being done? Does it have to be done here?
WHAT—What is being done? Can this work be eliminated?
WHO—Who is doing it? Would it be better to have someone else do it? Why am I doing it?
WHY—Why is that work necessary? Clarify its purpose.
HOW—How is it being done? Is this the best way to do it? Are there any other ways of doing it?
HOW MUCH—How much does it cost now? How much will it cost to improve?

ROOT CAUSE ANALYSIS—A3 STRATEGY

A great tool for root cause analysis is the tool Toyota uses called the A3 document (Figure 5.4). It is a way to get all your information in one place on one sheet of paper. A book that highlights this approach is *Understanding A3 Thinking: A Critical Component of Toyota's PDCA Management*.[7]

---

[4] Yuzo Yasuda, *40 Years, 20 Million Ideas* (New York: Productivity Press) 1991.
[5] Shigeo Shingo, *Poka Yoke, Zero Quality Control* (New York: Productivity Press) 1986.
[6] Shigeo Shingo, *Kaizen and the Art of Creative Thinking* (Hakuto-Shobo) 1959; English translation (Enna Products Corp. and PCS Inc.) 2007.
[7] Durward K. Sobek II and Art Smalley, *Understanding A3 Thinking: A Critical Component of Toyota's PDCA Management* (CRC Press) 2009, http://www.surveygizmo.com/survey-blog/question-scale-length/.

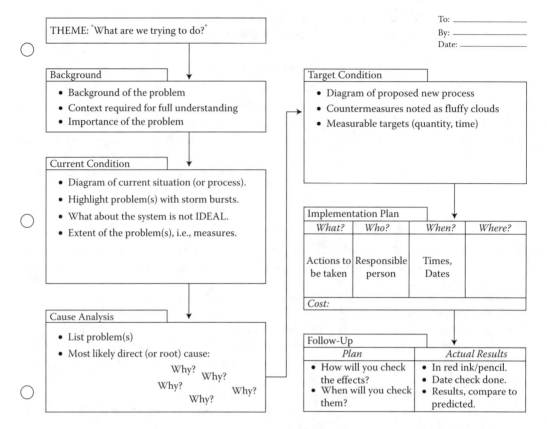

FIGURE 5.4   A3 Problem-solving model. Source: From Durward K. The A3 Report, http://coe.montana.edu/ie/faculty/sobek/a3/report.htm, with permission.

FISHBONES AND LEAN

Kaoru Ishikawa (Figure 5.5) is credited with developing the fishbone tool. Today, this is known as one of the basic Total Quality (TQ) tools. These tools are very applicable in hospitals. The fishbone is a tool to help identify root cause. It works by putting the problem at the head of the fishbone, then brainstorming and categorizing all the reasons for the problems (Figure 5.6). The first layer of problems, which are placed on the main branches of the fish, is normally only the symptoms of the problems that we see. We then ask "why?" for each major branch, which creates sub-branches. We ask "why?" until we get to the bottom branch or root cause. This tool provides a way to see all the problems in an area at a glance. Fishbones are a great tool for collecting, categorizing, and root-causing feedback from staff.

It is important to leverage tools to gain an understanding of the root cause of the problem. Identifying root causes allows for the correction of defects and is essential in preventing problems from reoccurring, which ultimately improves the overall process and quality of the result.

If you don't know where you are going, any path will take you there.

PROBLEM-SOLVING MODEL

Every company should standardize on a problem-solving model (see Table 5.2) and teach it to every employee. Lean is continuous problem solving, so we need all our employees to have a common language when they get together to work in teams to fix problems.

FIGURE 5.5   Mr. and Mrs. Ishikawa, October 1974. Source: Courtesy of Proztman Family Archives.

Many companies/hospitals have standardized on a model most commonly, Shewhart's Plan Do Study Act (PDSA), or the PDCA Deming model. Regardless of the model used, it is important that everyone be trained in the model so they speak the same language. Most problem-solving models follow this format:

- What is the problem?
- Develop counter-measures.
- What is the baseline or point from which we are starting and developing the key measures around the process that will ultimately determine if you improved the process?
- What is the vision for where we want to be?
- What are the gaps between the baseline and the vision?
- What is the root cause? List all the gaps that exist. Filter the gaps into those you can control vs. those that have to be given to a higher level of management to solve.
- Brainstorm solutions to how we can overcome the gaps between the baseline and the vision.
- Implement the solutions one at a time.
- Check to see if they solved the problem.
- Start over again.

At Toyota, the word *problem* is not a bad word, contrary to most U.S. companies. If we don't admit we have a problem or develop systems to expose problems, then we will never reach world class. If we continue to bury problems, they just get worse. A good analogy for this is our patients themselves. If we have a problem, what do we do? We go to the doctor. What happens if we put off going to the doctor? In most cases, the problem will become more acute. By the time we go to the doctor, the condition may be much more complex and difficult to treat. This is true for organizations as well.

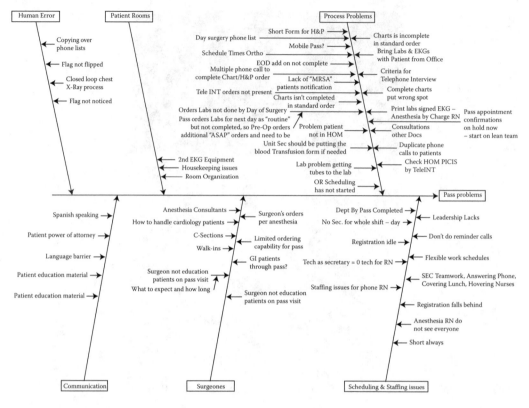

FIGURE 5.6 Fishbone Example. Source: BIG Files.

Lesson Learned

Make "problem" a good word. Find them, identify them, don't be afraid to call them what they are, and fix them so they don't come back.

PROBLEM STATEMENTS

Go to the floor or department and discover first-hand what the real problem is. Test (ask why) to see if the answer is a symptom of the problem or a true root cause. It is important to provide the

---

TABLE 5.2

8D Problem-Solving Model

The Global 8 Disciplines Are:

1. Form the Team
2. Describe the Problem
3. Contain the Problem
4. I.D. the Root Cause
5. Formulate and Verify Corrective Actions
6. Correct the Problem and Confirm the Effects
7. Prevent the Problem
8. Congratulate the Team

Source: Rambaud, *8D Problem Solving*, PHRED Solutions, 2007. With permission.

---

necessary training to identify a good statement of the problem. A good problem statement should be an objective statement of the problem with any relevant data. It should not include a solution. It should be verifiable. A bad problem statement would be:

- 7:30 a.m. first case start times are 32% on time due to surgeons being late.

This is missing verifiable data and assumes the physician is the problem.

- 7:30 a.m. case start times are late, resulting in poor physician satisfaction.

This is missing verifiable data and assumes it results in poor physician satisfaction.

- 7:30 a.m. first case starts are 32% on time because we need to improve pretesting.

While the solution may be true, it might not be the root cause. Thus, it sets the problem solvers with a paradigm of what the solution should be.
An example of a good problem statement:

- Based on our start times report dated: _____, 7:30 a.m. first case start times are 32% on time vs. our goal of 90% on time.

Clearly stating the scope and objectives of the project will help the team achieve the objectives.

- Where does the process start?
- Where does the process end?
- What is the customer demand for the product?
- What is the peak demand the cell should be able to meet?
- What models/options are included or excluded?
- What sub-processes exist?
- How many shifts are used vs. how many should be used?
- Has new equipment been developed or bought that needs to be installed?
- What other objectives must be met (i.e., housekeeping, inventory, quality, space, others)?

LEAN TOOLS - ANALYZE/ASSESSMENT

We have to grasp not only the Know-How but also 'Know-Why.'

—**Shingo**

The tools in the assessment phase help break down the process layer by layer, as if you were peeling back an onion, to reveal the waste. The application of each tool enables us to drill deeper into what is really occurring in the process or "value stream" (Figure 5.7).

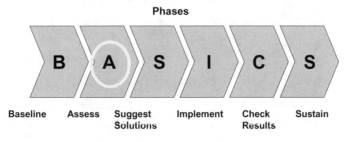

FIGURE 5.7   BASICS Model - Baseline. Source: BIG.

Utilizing Lean tools provides the opportunity to analyze a process from several facets.

1. The first analysis tool is to follow the product. In healthcare, this can be a thing, like a drug, blood tube, x-ray, or chart, but more commonly, it is the patient going through the process.
2. The second analysis tool is to follow the operator. The operator is the person performing the activities that transform the product or service into what is desired by the customer. This can be any person in the healthcare service delivery system, e.g., a physician, administrator, manager, unit secretary, nurse, or laboratory technician.
3. The third analysis tool looks at changeovers that may occur in the process. In healthcare, changeovers can be loading and unloading a patient from an magnetic resonance imaging (MRI) machine or turning over an operating room (OR) suite from one patient to another.

When we talk about the overall process flow, we are looking at the inter-relationship between process steps and the activities that staff perform. In Lean, the flow of the product/patient and the work of the operator/staff person are on two different axis (Figure 5.8). Applying the tools methodically will enable you to deconstruct a process into its individual sequence of steps and then transform and reconstruct the process into one that improves customer value. The transformation within a process occurs through analyzing and eliminating waste, creating the right work flow, developing standard work, understanding working to customer demand, level loading the activity or demand, layout and design, and providing the right tools and quantity of supplies (inventory) at the right time and in the right place. The application of Lean tools results in a reduction of errors, decreased variability, improvement in throughput, increased productivity, and improvement in overall quality. Ultimately, these are financially rewarding to the supplier of the services or product.

When you initially expose people to the terms and tools, there is a language "conversion" that needs to occur from manufacturing to healthcare as the terminology and the manufacturing references can be foreign to healthcare workers. Examples include "operators" = staff or worker, "products" = patients or test tubes etc., "in storage" = waiting i.e., patient or product (specimen, medication etc.) in the process. This is extremely important in order to ease the transition and help in the adoption.

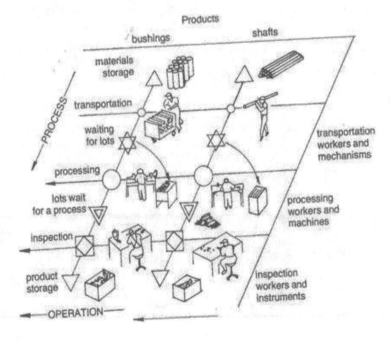

FIGURE 5.8 Shingo network of process vs. operations. Source: Shingo Books, Productivity Press.

Lesson Learned: *Be mindful as you expose healthcare personnel to the Lean concepts and tools that manufacturing terminology can become a barrier to acceptance, as we often hear, "We do not work in a factory… we take care of patients."*

BASICS—ASSESS THE PROCESS

Step One: Understand and Assess the Overall Process

A process is "a series of actions or operations conducing to an end; a continuous operation or treatment especially in manufacture."[8] Processes have an input and output boundary; a beginning and endpoint (Figure 5.9). A "process" takes place or is set in motion because "something" a problem needs to be solved or something needs to be accomplished. The process provides some physical transformation to the product and/or emotional transformation to the patient going through the process. The goal within the Lean System is to expend resources only on activities that are "value-added to customer." Processes can also be broken down into sub-process steps. We categorize each sub-process/activity or step within a process into one of three categories of perceived customer value:

1. Value-added work
2. Non-value-added but "necessary" work
3. Unnecessary work or idle time

VALUE-ADDED

There are three criteria that must be met in order to determine if there is "value" within a process[9]:

1. The customer is willing to pay for the perceived value-added activity.
2. Physically changes the product or physically or emotionally changes the patient for the better, as perceived by the patient.
3. The activity is done right the first time.

When a step or activity meets all three criteria, we consider it value-added. We are often asked how to categorize when a patient asks a nurse a question or the nurse spends time with a patient because the patient is distraught or in need of emotional support. We consider any of these types of activities value-added because they are perceived by the patient as emotionally changing for the better.

Lesson Learned

A "nurse's touch" is considered value-added.

FIGURE 5.9   Process Description. Source: BIG Files.

---

[8] *Webster's Dictionary*, http://www.merriam-webster.com/dictionary/process.
[9] As defined in the AMA video *Time: The Next Dimension of Quality*, by the American Management Association; featuring John Guaspari and Edward Hay.

Non-Value-Added Activities/Work

If a process step/activity does not meet all of the above criteria, it will fall into the non-value-added category. Non-value-added activities generally rob us of time and/or resources, contribute to staff frustration and do not add value to the service or product from the customer's perspective. Non-value activities can be divided into three sub-categories:

1. Non-value-added but necessary work
2. Unnecessary work
3. Idle time

Needless to say, one can get into very heated arguments over what is value-added and what is not.

Non-Value-Added But Necessary Work

The largest cause of discussion and sometimes outright arguments during analysis sessions are process steps/sub-process activities which don't meet all three criteria, but meet one or two criteria. These steps we call not value-added but necessary. "Non-value-added but necessary" tasks provide an alternative if the evaluating person or group determines the majority of the criteria are met and/or the process cannot be eliminated and is needed to achieve the end result. Many times, these steps are regulatory requirements or hospital policy. In some cases, technology has not yet advanced to the point of eliminating the process step or task, but it may in the future. Sometimes the process controls are not in place to do it right the first time. Examples could be filling out a medication reconciliation form, performing x-rays, or laboratory tests.

Unnecessary Work

Unnecessary work does not fit any of the three value-added criteria. They are simply tasks that shouldn't be done. Unnecessary tasks normally emanate from the following:

- Unclear or unwritten procedures.
- "Non-standard work."
- "It's the way we've always done it."
- There was a good reason for it at one time, but the reason for it no longer exists.

Idle Time

Idle time is different than unnecessary work. Idle time is whenever we are not working on anything but just standing there watching. We constantly see idle time when we watch videos of staff. This can be due to employing a full time worker when in fact only "fractional labor" or a few hours of an employee was needed, and there is literally nothing for the person to do at that point (workloads are not balanced), the job was not designed well, or the person is lazy. It can also occur because of a misalignment between scheduled resources and customer demand. In any case, we don't normally view idle time as the person's fault; we view it as a fault of the system.

Warranted IDLE Time Exceptions

In healthcare, we run into situations one would seldom run into in a factory, such as having to notify a family member their loved one is dying or when caring for a patient who has become a friend, passes away. Healthcare staff have difficult jobs that should be especially valued in our society. It takes not only a highly trained and skilled person, but also an exceptional kind of person to be a nurse. In these situations, we build this time into our analysis. Nurses, especially on oncology units or in high-stress areas such as the intensive care (ICU) or trauma units, need time to recover and recharge. The standard work should build this time in.

Lesson Learned

Just because an activity "has to be done" does not necessarily make it value-added. We have to give the patient a nursing assessment, but the assessment, while it may be necessary, is still an inspection step. If you think about it with a very open mind, there is no physical change to the patient so it is considered non-value-added but necessary because it doesn't meet all three criteria.

THE PATIENT PHYSICAL EXAMINATION

One somewhat controversial example of value-added vs. non-value-added is the physical examination performed by a physician. Even between Lean book authors there is disagreement over what is considered value added. Obviously, one would have to agree that the physician examination is necessary in order to identify physical changes which may aid in determining the course of treatment and/or patient care plan; however, it does not meet the strict value-added criteria. This is because the examination in and of itself does not physically change the person. We would argue that the examination is actually an inspection step by the physician to try to ascertain or identify the patient's presenting problem. Shigeo Shingo refers to the doctor examination this way when he describes "judgment inspection... feeds information back to processing. It is like a medical examination... The sooner a symptom is identified, the more quickly and efficiently the problem can be treated... In summary: Judgment inspection discovers defects, while informative inspections reduce them."[10] Deming said, "You cannot inspect quality into the product,"[11] and Henry Ford said, "There can be no quality without a standard."[12]

A customer, however, may perceive value since the "physical inspection" or examination can reveal a problem or "no problem." Even though it may not meet the strict three criteria definition of value-added in which physical or emotional change occurs, it is perceived as necessary by the customer, so we would categorize the examination as non-value-added but necessary. While the doctor examination is technically inspection, the words spoken by the doctor to reassure the patient ("you are going to be OK") are perceived as emotionally adding value by the patient. Therefore, we do agree that any communication regarding the diagnosis or plan of treatment anywhere during the process would be considered value-added. This is because we believe the dissemination of information to the patient at any stage is value-added, assuming it is emotionally changing the patient for the better.

STEP 1: PROCESS FLOW ANALYSIS (PFA)—FOLLOWING THE PRODUCT/PATIENT

Following the product/operator flow was first utilized by Frank Gilbreth, but Gilbreth viewed the product and operator on the same axis. The approach we use today was developed by Shigeo Shingo, who first realized that "production constitutes a network of process and operations, phenomena that lie along intersecting axis. Improving production, process phenomena should be given top priority."[13]

---

[10] Shigeo Shingo, *A Study of the Toyota Production System from an Industrial Engineering Point of View* (New York: Productivity Press) 1989.

[11] Mary Walton, *Deming Management Method* (New York: Putnam Publishing) 1986.

[12] Henry Ford, *Today and Tomorrow*, Reprint edition (New York: Productivity Press) 1988.

[13] Shigeo Shingo, Japan Management Association *Non Stock Production:* The Shingo System for Continous Improvement, 1987 (New York: Productivity Press) 1988.

That is why the heart and premise of this Lean improvement system is to separate the two (product and operator), study them independently and then integrate them. We refer to this as the Shingo methodology. We will analyze the product process axis first, and then we will analyze the operations axis or what the operator does to the product.

The PFA follows the product through the value stream. This tool cannot be done in a classroom or conference room. One has to go to the area (*Gemba*) and "become the thing, information, or patient" as it travels through the process and experience its path first-hand, asking questions as you go.

This process exposes the next layer under the value stream map of what is actually happening to the "product" throughout the process.

MAPPING THE PROCESS—IDENTIFYING PROCESS BOXES

In order to understand the PFA tool, one needs to understand "what defines a product." Lean publications refer to the "product" in various ways depending on what business problem you are trying to solve. The product can take many shapes or forms in the healthcare environment and is defined by what the customer desires.

When starting the process flow analysis we need to consider the business problem. What processes need to be analyzed in order to find what caused the business problem and what opportunities exist for elimination of waste or improvements? Sometimes, following the product as product transformations occur is not as easy as it may seem. It is important to remember that you must "become the product" at each step of the process to make sure that you accurately capture events from the product's perspective. This sounds easier than it is as just about everyone mixes up the product and operator when they are first exposed to this tool.

For example, a patient who presents to an Emergency Department (ED) is the "product" of the process flow of "delivery of care" in the ED.

In the ED setting, the "end product" from the customer perspective is the ED course of treatment. To determine the treatment, we need the results from the laboratory tests ordered by the physician. The test result starts as "a physician order," turns into a blood draw by the nurse, is then transformed into "test tubes" that are sent to the laboratory where they are placed in a blood analyzer, and finally transformed into "the result." The result is then reviewed by the physician to determine the proper course of treatment, which is what the customer desires.

In the pharmacy setting, the end product is the medication taken by the patient. The medication starts as a complaint by the patient, once verified, turns into an order by the physician, moves to the pharmacy, is reviewed, then (filled) picked from the shelf, then sent to the floor, retrieved by the nurse, taken to the patient's room, and finally given to the patient by the nurse. The customer "value-added" is in taking the prescribed medication assuming it fixes the patient complaint.

The concept of understanding "the product" in this context is sometimes difficult but extremely important as you begin to apply Lean tools to identify waste. In the beginning, we all tend to mix up the product piece and the operator piece.

PRODUCT PROCESS FLOW ANALYSIS TOOL

PFA is performed by following the product through the defined process. The PFA tool facilitates the identification of wastes through analyzing each process step required to get the product to the end of the defined process. We denote what happens at each step, where, and how far the product travels in each step. It is important to assess "customer value" at each step, assigning the appropriate designation as to whether it is a value-added process or a non-value-added but necessary process. This will help to determine which steps should be eliminated, simplified or combined with another step, also note any improvements that could help the process. Additionally, time increments and travel distance are measured for each step as applicable to determine the total throughput time and

FIGURE 5.10   Lean Pieces - product.

distance traveled by the patient or product (in other words the time it takes the product to complete the process), as well as any time a rework occurs. The combination of information flow and product flow provides a comprehensive analysis of the current state of the process from the "product" or "patient" perspective (Figure 5.10).

A PFA can be performed by observation and documentation or by video. There are advantages to video.[14] Shingo stated in his book, *The Toyota Production System from An Industrial Engineering Standpoint*, "We recently purchased a video camera and began filming operations on the shop floor. After each recording session, we'd invite the worker we had filmed, the improvement team concerned, and the worker's immediate supervisor and play the tape for them... We usually came up with lots of suggestions for improvement... and we'd implement the good ones immediately."

We follow the same process. As the product is tracked through the process, each step is analyzed individually. The tool uses an acronym we call TIPS,[15] which stands for the industrial engineering terms transport, inspect, process, store. TIPS is utilized to analyze and categorize what is truly happening to the product at each step within the process.

Once we have baselined the existing process, we go through what we call the OMITs process. During the process we review each step to determine if it can be eliminated, rearranged, simplified, or combined. Once completed, we have a new baseline product flow and potential future time for total throughput.

The use of the PFA tools is described in Shigeo Shingo's *Toyota Production System From an Industrial Engineering Viewpoint*, and also in his book, *Non Stock Production*. Process flow analysis is also described in the book, *IE for the Shop Floor: Productivity Through Process Analysis*.[16]

THE FOUR COMPONENTS OF PFA - TIPS ANALYSIS

There are four things a product/process can do:[17]

1. Transport
2. Inspect
3. Process
4. Store

1. *Transport* is the act of moving the "patient, product, or information" from one place to another. We look at both distance and time as the product or patient travels through the process.

---

[14] Shigeo Shingo, *A Study of the Toyota Production System from an Industrial Engineering Point of View* (New York: Productivity Press) 1989.

[15] Shigeo Shingo, *A Study of the Toyota Production System from an Industrial Engineering Point of View* (New York: Productivity Press) 1989.

[16] Junichi Ishiwata, *IE for the Shop Floor: Productivity Through Process Analysis* (New York: Productivity Press) 1997.

[17] Shigeo Shingo, *A Study of the Toyota Production System from an Industrial Engineering Point of View* (New York: Productivity Press) 1989.

2. *Inspect* is the act of checking or examining the "patient, product, or information" during the process. Inspection steps are highlighted to make problems in the process visible. As an example, if laboratory tests are ordered and the physician reviews the results, the testing itself is a process and the review of the results is considered inspection. Some inspection is needed at critical failure points of a process; however, if the process is optimally constructed, then no inspection should be needed. As stated in the book, *The Elegant Solution*,[18] in most companies today "getting it right has been replaced by getting it out." We must return to "getting it right" the first time. Processes should facilitate activities being done right the first time and should include mistake-proofing methods within the process whenever possible to eliminate errors and the need to inspect. In theory, inspection is really a non-value-added process step. We think Shingo separated out inspection (as it could be considered a non-value-added process) in order to highlight it because things were not being done right the first time.

3. *Process* or processing is the act that physically changes the product in form, fit, shape, size, or function. Changes to fix or correct the product—what we call rework—can typically be measured with amount, time, cost, yield, weight, etc. Only process steps have operations that can be considered value-added. The other three criteria of TIPS (transport, inspect, and store) by definition are non-value-added. Our experience is that value-added processing is only a small fraction of the total time a product or patient spends in the process. It is not unusual for value-added to be less than 5%–10% of the total time the patient or product is going through the process.

4. *Store* stands for storage. In healthcare, we use the word "store" to designate wait-time or idle time for the product in a process. Our experience is that patients (and family members) spend most of their time in storage, normally alone, waiting for something to happen. We have found in all the analyses we have performed that it is not unusual to have storage (wait times) in the 50%–80% range or more (Figure 5.11). In their book, *Competing Against Time*, Stalk and Hout had a rule called the .05–5 rule.[19] This rule "…highlights the poor 'time productivity' of most organizations since most products and many services are actually receiving value for .05%–5% of the time they are in the value delivery systems of their companies." In other words, 95%–99.5% of the time nothing is actually happening to the product or, in our case, the patient.

They also go on to describe what they call the 3/3 rule. This rule states that during the 95%–99.5% of the time the products are waiting, they are waiting for one of three things:

1. Completion of the batch
2. Completion of physical or intellectual property
3. Management to make a decision as when to move the batch on to the next step in the process

In healthcare, we have found both of these rules to be true, even though they were originally constructed around manufacturing. With all this non-value-added activity, no wonder patients are frustrated as they go through the healthcare continuum of care.

We need to be careful as we identify and assign some activities or steps as storage. If a patient's body is recovering from an operation, we would argue this is not storage but value-added since the body is physically changing, or if a patient is receiving an IV medication, the waiting may be part of the treatment. The key is to be able to define at which point we move from when our body is

---

[18] Matthew May, *The Elegant Solution* (Free Press) 2007.
[19] Stalk, George/Hout, Thomas, *Competing Against Time*: *How Time-Based Competition is Reshaping Global Markets* (Macmillan) 1990.

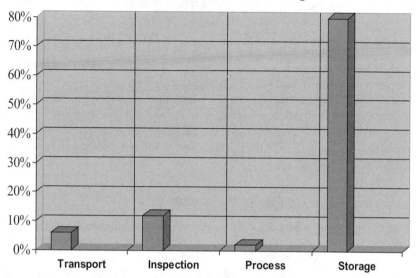

FIGURE 5.11   PFA Analysis Graph. Source: BIG Files.

recovering into storage or waiting. In some cases, we add an extra code to our spreadsheet to track recovery time. It is also worth noting that recovery time can be reduced, e.g., using non-invasive surgery techniques. This shows even value-added steps can be improved. Since storage in a process tends to be where the majority of waste occurs, storage can be defined with more granularity.

BASIC LEAN TOOLS UNDERSTANDING TYPES OF STORAGE

We said earlier that storage can be broken down into more minute detail. There are three types of storage:

1. RM—raw material
2. WIP—work in progress
3. FG—finished goods

RAW MATERIAL STORAGE

"Raw material" is a product or patient that has had no direct labor added to it. An example of raw material in healthcare would be the physician blood test order waiting to be assigned to a phlebotomist for collection. Another example is the patient's initial arrival into the waiting room prior to speaking to anyone.

WORK IN PROCESS STORAGE

The definition of work in progress or process (WIP) is a product or patient that has had direct labor added to it.

An example of this would be a patient in the ED who was registered or triaged, or had some blood tests drawn and is now waiting for results. Another example is our package of blood test tubes that was moved to a desk waiting to be opened and received into the computer system.

FINISHED GOODS STORAGE

Finished goods is a product or patient where all direct labor has been added to it and the product or patient has completed the entire process. In a product's case, the only thing left would be to ship it to the customer or, in the patient's case, it may be where they are waiting for their ride to leave the hospital. Another example of finished goods might be a completed radiology test "dictation" waiting to be seen by the ED doctor. Finished goods for the package of blood test tubes would be when testing on the package was completed and the package was waiting in storage to be properly discarded (or go to the hazardous waste landfill).

FURTHER DELINEATING STORAGE—TYPES OF WORK IN PROCESS

WIP is a critical component within a process—especially in healthcare—because many services are time sensitive. Understanding WIP within a healthcare process is important as it contributes directly to customer service and expectations.

WIP translates to waiting or idle time for patients and families and delays in treatments. In essence, WIP is stored labor capacity or stored cash flow tied up in the delivery system that cannot be valued until it is completed and billed.

To better understand this conceptually, we need to understand the three categories of WIP. The first two were explained by Shingo[20] and the third we have added:

1. Lot delay: one piece or patient is waiting for the rest of the lot or the "linear batch to complete" prior to going to the next step.
2. Between process delay: the piece, patients or entire lot is waiting together for next step in the process.
3. Within process delay: where patients or things going through the process were interrupted, but it did not fit the criteria of a lot or between process delay.

Let's consider some examples of each delay.

LOT DELAY

Let's use the illustration of physician rounding again to describe the concept of a "lot delay." A physician arrives on a unit to perform morning rounds. The complete process of rounding encompasses the patient examination, documentation, and writing orders. The physician could have 10 patients on the unit and, because of the centralized location of the charting station, the practice is to examine 4–6 patients sequentially in a batch, one after another without stopping to document or write orders. When reaching the charting station, the physician proceeds to write their notes and orders for all 4–6 patients at once or in a "batch." Let's assume we are following and analyzing the first patient. The first patient is now waiting while the next 3–5 patients are seen. We consider the all patients now in the process to be in a "lot delay" state, as their orders and notes are waiting until all the other patients are examined and orders written. We say the first patient or product is now waiting for the rest to be completed prior to moving on to the next step.

---

[20] Shigeo Shingo, *A Study of the Toyota Production System from an Industrial Engineering Point of View* (New York: Productivity Press) 1989.

POTENTIAL LEAN SOLUTION EXAMPLE #1

One improvement might be to implement computerized order entry (CPOE) by the physician to facilitate the elimination of "lot delays" through "real-time" computer documentation and time-order entry. The orders would be completed prior to leaving each patient room. This eliminates the batching of the patient's orders. When you multiply this times several hundred beds at each hospital, this can improve the process dramatically. Charts and nurses stationed outside the unit or at bedside (provided they are available there) help to eliminate the "batching" of documentation and orders.

POTENTIAL LEAN SOLUTION EXAMPLE #2

Another batching issue we discussed earlier in the book is the fact that most physicians make rounds at about the same time each day. This creates a bottleneck of orders and nursing duties which need to be completed and batching of discharges. There is typically a large disconnect in coordinating discharge times. The batching process results in a large bolus of discharges late in the morning after orders get processed. This affects staff significantly by forcing them to try to get all their patients ready to go home at approximately the same time. Then housekeeping gets requests for a group of rooms to clean (turnover) at the same time.

This is a difficult Lean problem to manage, but it can be dealt with by trying to get physicians to round at different times or by changing some of the staffing ratios to coordinate with patient needs and physician preferences. If you think about it, the discharge process should start with the initial patient visit to their physician. The physician generally knows how long the patient is going to require in the hospital or it can be suggested by their insurance company. The expected discharge date and time should become part of the patient's chart right from the beginning. Some hospitals provide patients with schedule discharge times in an attempt to level load the discharge work. It can also be addressed by changing the discharge process as organizations move to proactive planning in the days prior to discharges and how physicians and nursing floors track and time their discharges. This would also help with patient and family expectations and improve customer satisfaction.

BETWEEN PROCESS DELAY

Between process storage delay is defined as any delay, waiting, or idle time that occurs while the entire lot of products, patients, or information is waiting for the next process to begin. Once again, in the manufacturing world, the use of the word storage is common. You will find that, in healthcare, there will be some resistance to the use of the word "storage" when referring to processes where the product is a "patient."

As an example: A patient presents to the laboratory for a routine blood draw. The process for the blood draw from the patient's perspective is

1. Sign in
2. Complete registration
3. Receive blood draw
4 Pay for visit or co-pay

If the patient has to sit idle in a wait or "storage" state in between any of these steps, it is an example of a "between process delay."

An example of information flow for a pharmacy or drug store is:

1. The order from the doctor's office waits on the fax machine in email, or electronic queue
2. Then it waits to be entered into the system

3. Then it waits to be filled
4. Then it waits to be picked up

When the order waits (by itself, if one-piece flow, or in a group with all the other orders, i.e., batching) in between any of these steps, it is considered a between process delay.

WITHIN PROCESS DELAY

We created the "within process delay" because, particularly in healthcare, it was found that many processes begin but then get interrupted at critical times. Interruptions in the middle of processes create unique challenges. Many times, errors occur when a standard process "flow" is disrupted. This can create rework (or the need to redo some of what was just done) or workarounds to make sure the process was in fact completed and performed correctly. Sometimes it's not till later when the nurse or physician discovers the problem do we realize the process was never finished, or worse, we discover it when the patient brings it up or reminds us.

We find this with medication administration where a nurse may have been interrupted then got sidetracked and forgot to return to the original patient. Another example might be the patient/nurse discharge process. At the time of discharge, the nurse provides comprehensive discharge information, which includes going through each medication and having the patient read back the instructions to make sure the patient has full understanding of what was discussed. In the middle of the instruction about one of the medications, she receives a call about another patient, causing a delay in the discharge instruction process, creating idle or a within process storage/wait time for the patient in the discharge process. Because of the delay, the nurse found she had to start over when she went to go back through the medication read-back, which we refer to as process "rework." Because of the nature of healthcare interruptions, "within process" delays generally cause some rework or redoing of part of the process to ensure it is completed properly. Within process delays need to be minimized as interruptions create opportunities for errors to occur, thus compromising quality and outcomes.

WHY BREAK DOWN TYPES OF STORAGE?

Since storage or waiting is non-value-added, being able to clearly identify what type of storage is occurring throughout the process is beneficial to determine the process improvement opportunity (Table 5.3). If one were to categorize all the steps as storage, one would miss the opportunities to improve on the throughput opportunities that exist in the process. For example, batching is only found where lot delays are present. Between process delays can normally be eliminated up front because they are normally hand offs where no value is added.

But once we implement one-piece flow, any remaining delay will be a between process delay. As we stated before, within process delays generally signify some type of interruption in the process and generally create rework. When we eliminate the interruption, we eliminate the delay. All these delays impact customer satisfaction and make the overall process more costly.

After going through the OMITs process we construct the TO BE Process Flow. Eliminating steps eliminates opportunities for defects (errors) to occur, thus working toward improving quality.

TOTAL THROUGHPUT TIME

A primary goal of the product analysis is to determine the total throughput time of the process. This will become important later, as it will tell us what the total amount of inventory or patients should be in the process. The total throughput time is the sum of all the time the product, patient, or information spends in the process.

TABLE 5.3

PFA Quick Reference

Quick Reference Notes	Product Flow Analysis (PFA) Flow
When to use	Next Level of detail after VSM to determine opportunities to identify and eliminate "waste"
What it delivers	• Follows the product through the process "value stream" used to identify:
	• Waste in the process
	• Determine Value added, non-value added activity and non-value added but necessary
	Baseline Metrics – Throughput, Critical path process metrics, Value added activities
How is it performed	Manually transcribed and/or videotaped
	• Walk through the process
	• Document product flow
	• Perform Analysis
Analysis Steps	Product activities/process steps have four categories
Transport	• Transport
Inspect	• Inspect
Process	• Process Types
Store	• Value Added
	• Non Value Added
	• Non-Value Added but Necessary
	• Unnecessary or Waste
	• Storage types - Captures rework and Cycle times
	• delays
	• Between process delays
	• Within process delays

Source: J. Kerpchar.

PRODUCT FLOW ANALYSIS WORKSHEET

At first we build a manual worksheet to capture the PFA steps (Figure 5.12). We capture each step and note where it fits into our TIPS definition. We break down each step if it is a process as to whether it is value-added, non-value-added but necessary, or unnecessary, and we identify which type of storage the step fits. We also have spreadsheets designed to accumulate the times the product or patient spends in each step and the distance traveled. The process analysis should yield a 20%–40% productivity improvement to the overall process vs. a batch environment.

PRODUCT FLOW POINT-TO-POINT DIAGRAMS

Point-to-point diagrams are utilized to show the path of the product or patient through the layout of the area. This differs from the spaghetti diagram we use for operators. It is utilized to identify only product flow patterns. Because our layout will come from the PFA, this diagram is used to guarantee the product always moves forward in a point-to-point fashion. The product should never move backward. If any stations are out of order, they will immediately show up as you draw the point-to-point flow of the product. Stations that are out of order or force the product to move backward should be corrected in future revisions.

Lesson Learned

The product or patient should never move backward. It is OK for the person to move backward but never the product.

From the product's perspective, the point-to-point diagram assists in creating a logical grouping of operations or machines based on the flow of the product. Anytime a renovation or new

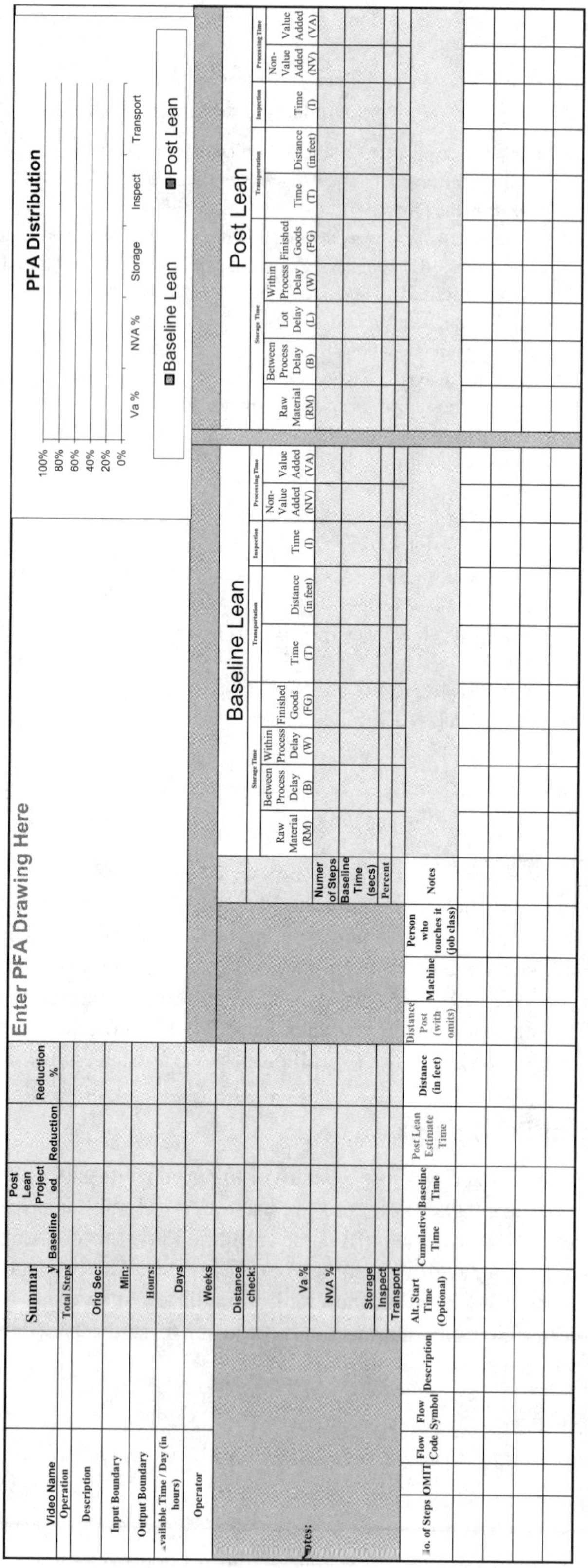

Enter PFA Drawing Here

PFA Distribution

100%
80%
60%
40%
20%
0%

Va %   NVA %   Storage   Inspect   Transport

■ Baseline Lean   ■ Post Lean

Summary

	Baseline	Post Lean Projected	Reduction	Reduction %
Total Steps				
Orig Sec:				
Min:				
Hours:				
Days				
Weeks				

Video Name
Operation
Description
Input Boundary
Output Boundary
Available Time / Day (in hours)
Operator

Distance check:

	Baseline	Post Lean Projected	Reduction	Reduction %
Va %				
NVA %				
Storage				
Inspect				
Transport				

Notes:

No. of Steps	OMIT	Flow Code	Flow Symbol	Description	Alt. Start Time (Optional)	Cumulative Time	Baseline Time	Post Lean Estimate Time	Distance (in feet)	Distance Post (with omits)	Machine	Person who touches it (job class)

Baseline Lean

		Storage Time			Transportation			Inspection	Processing Time	
	Raw Material (RM)	Between Process Delay (B)	Within Process Delay (W)	Finished Goods (FG)	Time (T)	Distance (in feet)	Time (I)		Non-Value Added (NV)	Value Added (VA)
Numer of Steps										
Baseline Time (secs)										
Percent										

Notes

Post Lean

		Storage Time			Transportation			Inspection	Processing Time	
	Raw Material (RM)	Between Process Delay (B)	Within Process Delay (W)	Finished Goods (FG)	Time (T)	Distance (in feet)	Time (I)		Non-Value Added (NV)	Value Added (VA)

FIGURE 5.12 Product Flow Analysis (PFA) Spreadsheet. Source: Authors – BIG Files.

construction is being considered, the layout should be tested utilizing point-to-point diagramming for all products/patients flowing through the process to ensure whatever is being conceptualized will result in a good flow through the area from the product and operator's perspective.

How to Do a Point-to-Point Diagram

The same teams who have participated in the PFA analysis should be involved in the point-to-point diagramming activity. The product point-to-point diagram is performed independently.

A team member is provided with a construction layout or sketches the layout on paper. As the product flows through the area, each movement is noted on the layout (Figures 5.13 and 5.14). Point-to-point diagrams should be created for both the base and revised "to be" layouts. We have also found that if the sequence is numbered in the point-to-point diagram, it helps in reviewing and utilizing the data to assist in sequencing equipment and supplies within a layout. We also recommend that the diagram is time- and date-stamped, as you may find varying product flows at different times, i.e., days vs. nights, weekdays vs. weekends.

Network of Process vs. Operations Defined

We have attempted to expand Shingo's separation between product, operator, and changeover and take it to the next level. We studied this for literally years before it dawned on us that each analysis tool (product vs. operator's axis plus changeover) provides different answers for Lean improvement. We would like to propose that analyzing the product axis will provide the following pieces of the Lean implementation:

- Total throughput time
- Flow, flow, flow

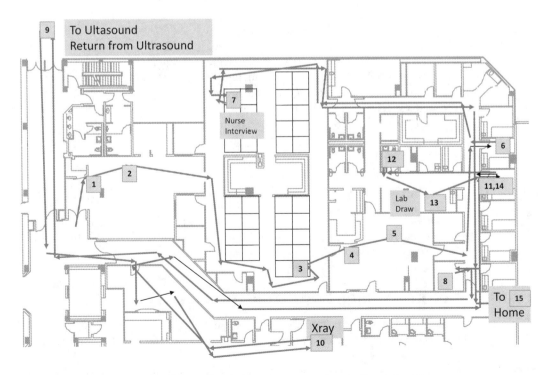

FIGURE 5.13   Point-to-point diagram surgical services pre-testing cardiac patient flow.

PTEC – Point to Point Non - Cardiac Patient

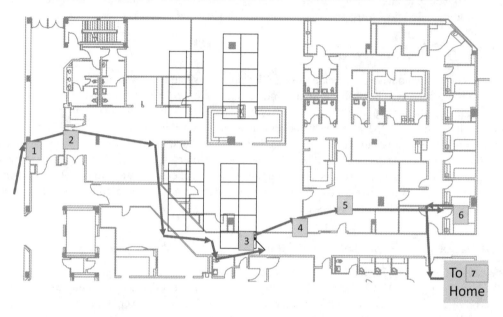

FIGURE 5.14   Product Flow Analysis (PFA) Point to Point – Non-Cardiac patient after Lean. Source: BIG Files.

- Layout and workstations
- Where rooms should be located in relation to the activity that is occurring
- Where the workstations should be located and the proper ordering of equipment and supplies
- The location of where standard WIP will be needed
- The standard WIP locations
- Machine times (running time of the process within a piece of equipment)
- Examples: How long does it take to run a centrifuge in the laboratory, run a laboratory processor for a given test, send a fax or make a copy, wait for an elevator to open, ride an elevator, or send a specimen through a hospital tube system?
- Routings: which are the paths or sequence of steps the product or patients follow as they progress through the process?
- Travel distance for the product

Lesson Learned

Using Lean tools enables you to understand and optimize what happens to the product or patient as they move through the process. Just analyzing and fixing the product axis piece of the network can yield as much as a 20%–40% productivity improvement.

GROUP TECHNOLOGY MATRIX—STRATIFICATION ANALYSIS

There are books dedicated to group technology[21] in manufacturing. Our goal here is to familiarize the reader with this concept and provide an insight into how this can apply within the healthcare

---

[21] John L. Burbidge, *Group Technology* (London. Mechanical Engineering Publication) 1975.

domain. The group technology or group tech matrix allows one to view processes or products that may be similar, to be "grouped" into "like-families." We analyze volumes, product/process steps and equipment, skill sets utilized, service lines, or other criteria that may apply in order to try to find families of products.

The first step is to develop a product/process matrix and group the parts or activities into like-families based on the machines or processes utilized and in the order in which they use each machine or process.

An example would be to consider laboratory processing. In most cases, when comparing all the process flows for a specimen tube in the laboratory, we find that they break into families like chemistry, hematology, urine, and others. When getting a little more detailed, we find that many hematology specimens get centrifuged where a number of chemistry specimens get aliquoted. As we drill down on "categories," we can place specimens that are "processed" similarly or/and need the same analyzers together in the same "cell." Once we break down all the equipment that is utilized with each family, we determine if we have enough to support making a "cell." The centrifuges are now placed in front of each piece of equipment (this may mean smaller centrifuges) instead of being in a batched area.

Look at nursing unit rooms and determine what they may have in common and how they might be "grouped" in "like-families" with similar features to optimize flow, layout, and sequence. The goal is to move like products or things into the same "work area," potentially eliminating (or at least reducing) changeover (setup) times. These groupings can also occur based on geography and are sometimes referred by the term "unit based."

In another laboratory example, a new hematology test is being offered to the market. The test requires a new piece of equipment. This new piece of equipment can do the new test as well as several other tests that are currently done on another existing machine.

Typically, the machine would be purchased and placed wherever it would fit in the existing layout without consideration of the optimal placement of the machine. Optimal placement would consider the following:

- Where is it used in the overall flow?
- What specimen preparation might be required prior to processing
- The new tests that will be performed and the volume of tests able to be utilized by the equipment
- The machines before or after it
- Features of the existing tests performed on other machines should now be considered for the new machine
- The old machine may no longer be needed

The group tech matrix provides a mechanism for you to determine what the "product feature" similarities are and how to maximize these similarities to improve layout design, flow, and setup.

EXAMPLE: GROUP TECHNOLOGY APPLIED TO A SURGICAL SERVICES UNIT

Most hospitals have ORs dedicated to certain types of surgeries; however, we have found the number and locations of OR allocations that are dedicated to particular service lines are generally mismatched (Figure 5.15). The OR rooms have normally not been analyzed based on similarities such as volumes, equipment supply use, turnover time, size of OR required to perform a given procedure, or the actual minutes of OR times used. These are all potential "features" that can be included in a group tech matrix to optimize the use of OR rooms. Once the appropriate number of rooms is determined to dedicate to a given service line, then the information in a group tech matrix can help you determine which surgical rooms to dedicate based on size and materials shared, again leveraging "features" or similarities and grouping to optimize layout and flow. A dynamic tool can be created

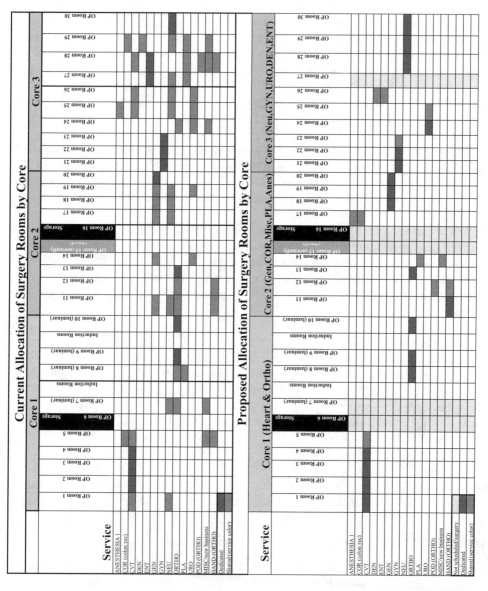

FIGURE 5.15 Group Technology Surgery Room Allocation before vs. after. Source: BIG Files.

so changes in case mix can be monitored and updated as surgical OR use changes, and room allocations can be adjusted accordingly.

Author's Note

Technically, group technology is somewhat of a compromise between batch and Lean. For example, in the Lean world we would want universal patient rooms on the floors or universal OR rooms. Since it is not practical to have every room outfitted for an ICU patient or every OR room outfitted with laminar flow hoods and robots, we leverage this by creating families of rooms using group technology criteria. The idea behind group technology is to still implement flow but in "family-like grouped" areas. A surgical example would be grouping vascular with cardio-vascular as they utilize similar equipment and supplies, both types of procedures deal with vascular structures, although some surgeons specialize in peripheral vascular procedures others generalize and perform cardio-vascular (which can include peripheral vascular) procedures.

An example: The laboratory is, in essence, a big group technology or centralized area supplying all the hospital. The goal with Lean is to first streamline the centralized laboratory by using group technology; then the next level of Lean would be to have mini-laboratories or point of use testing solutions wherever they were needed, where they fit in the department flow or, worst case, adjacent to the area and eliminate the centralized laboratory.

STEP II: ASSESS THE PROCESS—OPERATOR ANALYSIS OR FULL WORK ANALYSIS[22]

In this section, we refer to the operator as any person who is part of the process (Figure 5.16). The operator term is unfamiliar to most in healthcare, and we must caution you to clearly articulate the definition of operator. When speaking to frontline staff, you may need to interchangeably refer to the operator as a staff member to bridge the language barrier from manufacturing to healthcare.

Once again, we need to be reminded that we separate the product axis from the operator axis when doing analysis, and this is the secret for improving operations. Many times, focus is placed on what the person was doing, but not the product or patient going through the process. These must be looked at independently first, and then together after waste is eliminated from the process.

Lesson Learned

It should be noted that any step that was eliminated in the value stream mapping or PFA no longer requires operator analysis. This is why we do the analysis steps in the order of value stream map, product, operator, and changeover.

Lean

FIGURE 5.16   Lean Pieces – operator. Source: Authors.

---

[22] Kenichir Kato, *Productivity through Motion Study* (New York: Productivity Press) 1991.

TABLE 5.4
Full Work of the Operator Analysis

Step #	Omit	Description	Key Points	Reason for Key Points	Current TLT Each (sec)
1		grab marker, fill in board, put marker back	Visual control	Charge nurse knows who is in each room	9
2		walk to the outside of the counter			11
3	x	sift through papers			6
4		go get armband			5
5		put stickers on armband	Patient must be identified correctly	So we prevent I.D. mistakes later in the process	17
6		Update Checklist with date, orders, blood consent, ID labs, and verify requisitions are same from what DR. ordered			10
7		Sign Signature Sheet			10
8		Place Checklist, signature sheet, label sheet, and orders in order			35
9		Finds consent and reviews procedure and updates the checklist			27
10		Verify all lab work			24
11	x	Search for Blood Consent	Should not have to search needs improvement		30

Source: BIG File.

The operator analysis starts with filming the operator (i.e., nurse, doctor, technician, administrator, volunteer, etc.) and then reviewing the video with the operator, supervisor, industrial engineer (if one exists), and someone who knows nothing about the process. The outside observer's job is to ask "why" each step is performed since they don't have paradigms associated with the process. When reviewing the video it is important to communicate to the team that the video review is for process improvement only and that no disciplinary actions are ever to be taken from a video analysis session. The goal of watching the video is to analyze each step as to why it is done and then once again using the OMIT's process to question each step to see if can be eliminated, rearranged, simplified, or combined (Table 5.4).

We review each step on the video to the second, unless we know we can eliminate it. We then categorize each step as to whether it is value-added or non-value-added. If it is non-value-added, we break it down into:

1. Necessary but non-value-added work
2. Unnecessary work
3. Idle time

When the analysis is done, we basically have created a set of rather detailed job instructions. This becomes the basis for standard work later in the improvement process. The criteria for value-added is the same as for the product.

Why Make the Operator's (Staff Person's) Job Easier?

Think about it, who really impacts the customer and whose performance will drive outcomes and financial viability? The answer is the person on the frontline (floor) closest to the patient. Does it make sense to have the people who interact with the customers (patients) frustrated? In a time of nursing shortages, wouldn't it be easier to retain and recruit to an organization that strives to make the employee's job easier? Anyone in a management or support role doesn't directly make money for the organization; therefore, what is management's job? One of our favorite quotes is from Mike Walsh in the video *Speed is Life*, where he said, "Management's responsibility is to be worthy of its people."[23]

Why does management exist? The whole concept of middle management was started by the railroads back in the late nineteenth century. Frederick Taylor benchmarked the railroads and brought middle management and cost accounting practices from the railroads to manufacturing and, eventually, service industries like hotels and healthcare. He took the supervisor's job and split it up into eight different positions: planning, production, route, inventory stores, instruction card and time study, order of work, recording and cost accounting, and disciplinarian.[24] This was the beginning of the functional organization we have today. At the time these jobs were created, they were designed to help the operators (staff) get more product out the door, and they were co-located in the production area with those that did the work. Yet, where are most overhead indirect staff and managers located today? The answer would be "in their offices," normally far away from the frontline. All one can do in an office is manage history, answer e-mails, and write reports. Does any of this make the operator's job easier? When you think about it, in a truly Lean organization, staff positions need to be located on the floor wherever possible.

Lesson Learned

Management's goal should be to work on making the frontline person's job easier by removing waste and making improvements. They should know, own, and constantly be working to streamline their processes.

Total Labor Time

One of our major deliverables of operator analysis is total labor time. Total labor time is the amount of labor or work performed during the process by the operator to get to the end result. Machine time is not included in the labor time. The operator analysis should provide the baseline current "labor time," which is the total amount of both value-added and non-value-added labor time the operator performs throughout the task or process being analyzed. Calculating total labor time of a process will give you a picture of how much labor and, ultimately, how many staff members are needed to complete the one piece of whatever is being processed. The operator analysis should yield a 20%–40% productivity improvement to your overall process vs. a batch environment. In addition to capturing the labor time, the distance traveled is also captured as a baseline and future state.

Workload Balancing

Some staff members may be perceived as inefficient, are not able, or do not have the desire to do work at the same level as others. In general, in order to minimize the resistance we may encounter, we subscribe to Deming's belief that most people want to do the right thing and want to keep busy.[25] When we are idle for periods of time, the day can really drag on, especially if there is a clock right in front of you. We argue that, in most cases, it is the fault of management, not the staff that these perceptions occur. We normally find staff has not been provided with clear expectations nor have they

[23] Mike Walsh, at the time CEO of Northern Pacific railroad, "Speed is Life," Tom Peters, a co-production of Video Publishing House and KERA © 1991.

[24] Wrege, Charles D, *Frederick W. Taylor* (Irwin Publishing) © 1991; Copley, *Frederick W. Taylor* (Harper and Brothers) ©1923; Kanigel, *The One Best Way* (Penguin Books) © 1999.

[23] Mary Walton, *Deming Management Method* (New York: Putnam Publishing) 1986.

been held accountable to any performance metrics or targets. In general, if there are clear expectations and good training for the job or task, the person will feel better and do what is required. In addition, if a person has not been empowered or trained in every operation, or does not have the right equipment or supplies, it may not be possible for them to do the task at hand effectively or perform additional work. Occasionally, you may find the individual that just doesn't want to work or do their fair share, but as Deming said, 95% of the time the "system" is the problem not the employee.[26] We find people will generally do the best job they can with the tools management gives them.

With Lean, we implement workload balancing, which means we try to distribute the same amount of work to each person. We also use a concept called bumping whenever possible to eliminate any factional labor or idle time conditions.

This helps promote a sense of fairness among staff and generally improves department morale. We often find stars among the workforce who never shined before, simply because they were never given the proper training or were not given the opportunity to shine.

There are several components that we need to understand to achieve load balancing with a process or a given set of activities with a process:

- Available time
- Total labor time required
- Standard work
- Cycle time

To do this, we must understand how many operators are needed to do the work within a given cycle time. Number of Operators = total labor time required ÷ cycle time

How to Balance the Work

If we have a process in which there is 30 min of total work and six people working, how much work should be done by each person? The answer is 5 min (or 30 min ÷ 6 people).

This requires each person to be given the same amount (5 min of work) and each person, in turn must "do" his/her fair share of the 5 min worth of work. In order to accomplish this, we need to consider the skill set of the operators or staff performing the tasks or activitities. This works well if everyone in a work area can all do the same level of work from a competency, licensure, and training perspective. It is important to provide role clarity for each person and ensure each has appropriate cross-training to enable flexibility across processes and between tasks, processes, and equipment. The process re-design and benefits must be outlined to the staff so that clear expectations are set and they have a clear understanding of their new roles and responsibilities related to the process. In addition, targets and expected results are explained and definition in role clarity is outlined. At this point, this should not be new to the staff, as frontline staff and supervisors should have been an integral part in redesigning the new process, identifying waste, and helping to create the "new work". This participation is critical to a successful implementation, as frontline staff has a clear understanding of the day-to-day value-added and waste within the activities they perform. If we do not leverage their knowledge in the analysis and redesign, we will not obtain the expected results. Frontline staff and stakeholders must be a part of the redesign if the implementation is to succeed. Staff members need a full understanding of what is being done, why it is being done, "what is in it for them" if they go along with the changes. When we are line balancing, we must allow enough time for staff to perform each task. In Figure 5.17, the left hand graph shows the workloads for each person. Operator 1 has 40 sec, 2 has 45 sec and 3 has 30 sec and 4 has 65 sec. Based on this simple load diagram, we can determine that work is accumulating between operator 1 and 2. Operator 3 immediately performs any work received and proceeds to really back up operator 4 who is the

[26] Mary Walton, *Deming Management Method* (New York: Putnam Publishing) 1906.

Operator Line Balancing

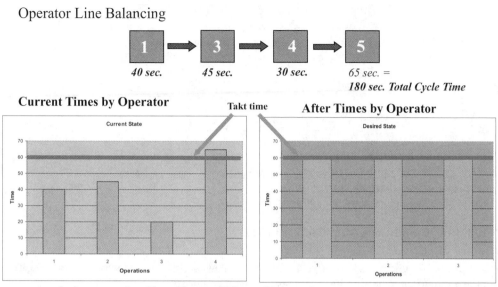

- *work is evenly distributed for all workers to meet Takt time.*

FIGURE 5.17   Operator Line Balancing to Takt time. Source: BIG Files.

bottleneck (technically people can't be true bottlenecks because we can always add more people). We can predict that the cycle time based on the theory of constraints[27] is going to be 65 sec. This means operator 1, if forced to wait for operator 4, would have 25 sec of idle time, operator 2 would have 20 sec of idle time, and operator 3 would have 35 sec of idle time each cycle. But instead of being idle, they continue to work (batch) so the inventory will pile up. Remember, idle time is one of the things that can force us to batch. As before, we can predict how much work will pile up and where. Since operator 2 is the next slowest operator and they are 20 sec slower, then every four pieces we will back up a full piece prior to operator 4.

The line in each graph in Figure 5.17 shows the 60 sec Takt time. If we divide 180 sec of total work (40 + 45 + 30 + 65) or labor time by the Takt time of 60 sec, it shows we need 3 operators. We can then rebalance the work across the 3 operators to meet the Takt time and free up a person. What do we do with the person we free up? This is normally not a problem in healthcare, where well-trained, highly skilled resources are difficult to come by; however, it is very important that we never lay anyone off due to continuous improvement activities, and there is a proactive plan in place to redeploy and retrain workers to other jobs or areas as this occurs.

Whenever we are training staff in the "new" or revised standard work, they often think we want them to rush. This is not the case. Staff should be coached not to rush, because if activities/tasks are rushed, mistakes and defects will occur. If we rush, quality will suffer, processes will need to be "reworked" and any time that you might have saved in elimination of waste will be lost in reworking defects. In addition, rework creates a financial burden that is not tracked and will lead to decreased customer satisfaction. The saying that we recommend posting in each new Lean system implementation is "Quality first; the speed will come." The other challenge we often face is while the work flow may be revised, the actual work is not and staff become so concerned with following the "new process" that they forget to do what is normally required as part of the job "that did not change." When this occurs, it can inadvertently lead to unjustified misgivings about Lean. As staff

---

[27] The theory of constraints basically states that one can only go as fast as the slowest machine or person in a process. This is from a book by Eli Goldratt called *The Goal* (Great Barrington, MA: North River Press) 2004.

Name	Sign In	Triage	Interventional	Discharge	Room RN	Charge Nurse
Joe Smith	1	2	1	2	1	
Jane Doe	2	3	2	4	1	1
Mary Jones	5	5	4	3	2	2
ED Educational Training Grid (One Patient Flow)						
Not trained in clinical area					1	
Exposed to clinical area					2	
Limited training in clinical area					3	
Proficient in clinical Area					4	
Trained in the Clinical Area as Trainer					5	

FIGURE 5.18   Cross Training Matrix. Source: BIG Files.

are cross-trained in new workflows, revised work, or new work, standard work and role clarity are extremely important to ensure that this does not occur (Figure 5.18).

Performing Lean implementation and applying Lean tools will enable us to become knowledgeable about how long tasks actually take to perform and enable reasonable targets to be established. An increase in productivity occurs when the process is redesigned with work in the proper sequence and balanced across the staff with the right tools, at the right time, in the right place, to eliminate waste in the process.

Lean uses the terms "Mura" for uneven pace of production, and "Muri" for unreasonable/excessive workload[28]. It is important to remember that people are not robots. There are some situations that cause cycle-to-cycle imbalances, such as defective materials, slower patients, and unanticipated distractions. All these will impact the balance of work and flow of the process. The staff in each clinical area must be flexible and empowered to overcome these imbalances.

To facilitate work balancing, we utilize a concept Ohno referred to as "Baton Zones,"[29] or flex zones, which are areas where hand offs occur (Figure 5.19). The above examples, where the same amount of work is allocated to each person is called "station balancing". In this case when the person is done his/her work they simply stop and start on the next patient or product. Baton zones utilize a concept we call "bumping" where employees continue to work on that patient or product until

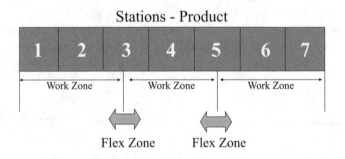

FIGURE 5.19   Baton Flex Zones. Source: BIG Files.

---

[28] Tachni Ohno, Setsuo Mito, *Just-In-Time For Today and Tomorrow* (New York: Productivity Press) 1988,

[29] Taiichi Ohno, *Toyota Production System* (New York: Productivity Press) 1988.

the next operator closest to the end of the process "bumps them" and takes over. Now the operators stay busy all the time and WIP is limited to one product or patient per operator.

The layout must be designed with short, easily shared steps around the zone for this process to work. Avoid staff using their hands as fixtures because operator flexing will be constrained. When there is a significant mismatch between the planned balance points where service is being transitioned, the team should investigate to find a root cause and generate a corrective action.

Work imbalance occurs typically because a staff person did not follow the standard work, may not be bumping/flexing to assist a co-worker, or a "stop the line" strategy was not initiated so that an unexpected problem could be addressed. This can be a challenge in healthcare as we deal with patients and deliver services rather than build products. Patients, due to their disease processes, may individually take longer to perform a task such as a difficult blood draw, obtain a history, complete an examination, or a patient who just needs extra time for support or encouragement. People should understand that they still need to work as a team and flex as required even though they have an order in which tasks should be performed. We are still requiring them to "think" and "do" the appropriate activities to get the job done.

Standing/moving operation also promotes operator/staff flexibility and health. A staff member who sits is more likely to either build inventory or to wait (adding seconds or minutes to a process), as it takes more effort to get from a chair rather than rotate around when standing. You will find that staff members who are "used to" sitting for tasks may resist the suggestion of standing and vice versa. From an ergonomic viewpoint, sitting is bad for you. It can lead to back problems and obesity, which can eventually lead to the possibility of early mortality.[30] You may need to transition from sitting to standing by adjusting counter heights that will allow the option to stand and perform activities. These will make the transition easier, as staff will find the task or activity they are performing easier to do if they stand. A general guideline for allowing "standup" chairs on the line is for operations or tasks where a person would have to stand in one place with no movement for 10–15 min at a time.

SEPARATE WORKER FROM MACHINE

It is important, during analysis, when operators interact with machines to separate the work performed by the machine from the person. Machines should do hazardous, dangerous, boring, or repetitive work. People need to be "used wisely." We have run into several situations where people actually perform the work better than robots and others where the robots performed better than people. People should have challenging work and be taught to constantly look for and identify improvements.

MACHINE TIME VS. LABOR TIME

When performing a WFA (Work Flow Analysis), we do not include machine time because the operator is not performing "the work" of the machine. An example of this would be centrifuging a specimen in the laboratory. The preparation of the specimen, placement of the specimen in the centrifuge, closing the lid, and turning on the machine are all part of the total labor time. The 8 min the machine is spinning, however, is not considered part of the labor time because the machine is doing the work and is captured in the PFA analysis. While the machine is working, the operator may be "waiting" for the spin cycle to complete or, hopefully, performing another task in parallel to the machine running. Examples where you might break down operator from machine time in healthcare would be hemodialysis, sterile processors, nebulizers, MRIs, and lab.

---

[30] "Sitting Time and Mortality from all causes, cardiovascular disease, and cancer," Katzmarzyk PT, Church TS, Craig CL, Bouchard C. Pennington Biomedical Research Center, Baton Rouge, LA. http://conditioningresearch.blogspot. com/2009/04/too-much-sitting-down-is-bad-for-you.html. It's Dangerous, Charles Osgood on the CBS Radio Network. The Osgood File. June 10th, 2010; "Don't Just Sit There—It's Dangerous," Charles Osgood on the CBS Radio Network. The Osgood File. June 10th, 2010.

Diagrams: Spaghetti Diagramming—Operator Walk Patterns

When we map the walk patterns of operators throughout their work process, we call this spaghetti diagramming. Spaghetti maps highlight and aid in the identification of system waste in the areas of transport, location of supplies and equipment, rework, and poor flow that may not be readily apparent when performing operator analysis. Creating spaghetti diagrams helps drive future state: improvements to process flow, placement of equipment (adjacencies) and supplies. The goal is to have the right equipment and supplies at the right place, in the right order to optimize flow. From the operator perspective, we can create work zones. Work zones are based on the cycle time each operator must meet. So, in the example pictured in Figure 5.19, operator one may cover stations one, two, and part of three. If our demand increased, reducing our cycle time and requiring us to add an operator, then operator one may end up working at station one and part of station two before handing off to the next person. Operator one would wait for operator two to "pull" the part from them vs. working up to a point and setting the part down or waiting for operator two. This again is called "Bumping". This shows work zones can change based on the number of operators and sequencing of units (equipment, adjacent processes, services, etc.). The goal is to create logical stations based on the PFA and then flex workers (flex zones) across the stations in order to balance the work.

How to Do a Spaghetti Diagram

The same teams who have participated in the operator analysis should be involved in the spaghetti diagramming activity. The spaghetti map for the operator is performed independently generally through observation or videotape. When performing the operator spaghetti diagram, it is helpful to number the steps as the operator goes through his/her tasks (Figure 5.20). We recommend that the date, time, operator, and operator skill level are documented. The team should determine the length of time to follow and map the operator's activity, which would be a true representative sample. For instance, you may follow a nurse for 1 or 2 hrs and when the nursing pattern begins to repeat, it means you have clearly reached a "representative sample of activity." For instance, you may note that the nurse may have already walked out of the area two or three times to get supplies, which clearly indicates that the location should be moved closer to where the actual work is occurring.

You may choose to spaghetti diagram at different specific times of the day, i.e., shift change or on a surgery floor at the time when most patients are being prepped to leave the floor, in order to get

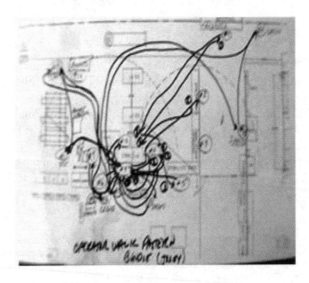

FIGURE 5.20 Operator Spaghetti Chart. Source. BIG Archives.

the most benefit from the time the team is able to devote to the tools. You may consider providing a pedometer to the operator so that a baseline distance traveled can be calculated. "Travel" time is waste, inefficient and, more importantly, can be tiring on staff. Proper planning of what you are trying to accomplish is key as you perform these tools.

The operator analysis helps focus on what to spaghetti diagram and highlight areas for future improvement. While the layout primarily comes from the product, bringing the point-to-point and spaghetti diagrams together will help solve the overall layout.

Next, we will take the information and determine a new layout based on all the information gained from each of the tools utilized thus far. Once a new layout is proposed, a simulated PFA and spaghetti diagram of the operator should be performed. Numbering should be used for each step on the new layout to see how the "new" Product Process Flows.

The next step after this would be to take the layout and understand how the operator will work within the new layout and where the supplies should be located.

Spaghetti diagramming can be very powerful in helping leaders, managers, and staff understand visual collision points, repetitive steps, travel time, and enable effective communicating of improvement opportunities at the "baseline level." Then post-diagramming reveals the results and additional improvements in the quest for elimination of waste.

NETWORK OF PROCESS VS. OPERATIONS DEFINED

We have attempted to take Shingo's separation of product, operator, and changeover to the next level. To our knowledge, no one has broken down these processes into the pieces of Lean thinking each one provides. It was years before it dawned on us that each analysis tool (product vs. operator's axis plus changeover) provides different answers for Lean improvement. We would like to propose the following "pieces" of Lean that will be determined by analyzing just the operator piece:

- Ergonomics/safety/fatigue
- Number of operators
- Line balancing
- Capacity planning
- Motion study
- Scheduling flexibility
- Standard WIP quantity
- Workstation design—tools and supplies sequenced in proper order of assembly
- Total labor time
- Operator walk patterns
- Ten cycle analysis
- Operator buy-in
- Baton zones/bumping
- Standard work
- Operator travel distance

Lesson Learned

Using Lean tools enables one to understand and optimize what the staff (operators) does to the product or patient as they move through the process. Just looking and fixing the operator axis piece of the network can yield as much as an additional 20%–40% productivity improvement.

MOTION STUDY—JUST WHEN YOU THOUGHT YOU WERE "THERE"

If you think you have improved all you can, let us provide you with another thought.

Shingo has an example in one of his books where he takes a towel and soaks it in water. One by one, he asks his students to come up and wring out the towel. The first person squeezes out a lot of water, the next squeezes some water but not as much. But even the last student was able to squeeze out some additional drops.[31] This exercise applies to waste as well.

Once you are trained to see the waste for what it is, there is much to see. But sometimes waste is hidden by batching, excess material, and just because that is the way we have always done it ("boiled frog" syndrome). Once you "Lean out" the area, it becomes easy to see where there is variation and waste. But as you continuously improve the area, the waste becomes harder to find, yet it is definitely there. In some cases, it would be easy to say we have improved enough and we don't need to improve anymore; however, just like the towel example above, the waste is always there. You just have to keep squeezing the towel.

The tool for this is Frank Gilbreth's motion study.[32] Motion study involves analyzing what we do to the fraction of a second. Gilbreth did his work with bricklayers. Gilbreth filmed and studied the motions of his bricklayers and developed what he called "Therbligs," or the 18 fundamental motions of the worker. He analyzed their work down to the right and wrong way to pick up a brick (Figures 5.21 and 5.22). He totally standardized how the wall should be built, brick by brick. He hired people to make sure that the cement was always the right consistency (Figures 5.23 and 5.24). This was all part of the scientific management movement of the Industrial Revolution in the early twentieth century. Gilbreths's Therbligs are listed below (Figure 5.25 for Therbligs):

Gilbreth's original work was done with bricklayers and is documented in a book called *Motion Study*, circa 1911. Gilbreth also used the techniques we are describing in a hospital setting. He created a hospital OR in his home, which was depicted in the original film "Cheaper by the Dozen."[33] Gilbreth videotaped the tonsillectomy operations on his children and himself so that he could study the motions that the doctors were utilizing and work to streamline them. He also recorded operations in hospitals such as removing tumors.

Our approach is to typically analyze operations to the second and, when we have exhausted improvement opportunities at that level, move to motion study. We have come across operations in healthcare where each person only has a few seconds worth of work in their process. We have successfully used motion study techniques to reduce these times by more than 50% per operator,

FIGURE 5.21 Gilbreth Bricklayers - Wrong Way to Pick Up a Brick. Source: Motion Study, Gilbreth, Hive Publishing © 1911.

---

[31] Shigeo Shingo, Japan Management Association, *Non Stock Production: The Shingo System for Continous Improvement*, 1987 (New York: Productivity Press) 1988.
[32] Frank Gilbreth, *Motion Study* Boston (USA; Stanbope Press) 1911.
[33] "Cheaper By The Dozen," 20th Century Fox, 1950.

FIGURE 5.22 Gilbreth Bricklayers - Right Way to Pick Up a Brick. Source: Motion Study, Gilbreth, Hive Publishing © 1911.

FIGURE 5.23 Gilbreth Bricklayers - Material Presentation Before. Source: Motion Study, Gilbreth, Hive Publishing © 1911.

effectively doubling their capacity. The concept of eliminating waste in motions and transforming them into work is known as labor density. The formula for this is work divided by motion with a goal of 100%.[34] One thing to keep in mind is that not all motion is work. Only work that is value-added or necessary should be considered true work.

---

[34] Japanese Management Association, *Kanban Just-in-Time* (New York: Productivity Press) 1986.

FIGURE 5.24 Gilbreth Bricklayers - Material Presentation After Material Handlers (or referred to as water spiders) made sure cement was always mixed properly so brick layers did not have to stop and could concentrate on just laying brick. He could construct buildings much faster than his competition so he won most of the bids. Source: Motion Study, Gilbreth, Hive Publishing © 1911.

Therbligs

Class	No.	Name	Symbol	Description
1	1	Assemble	‡	Shape of combined rods
	2	Disassemble	++	One rod removed from a combined shape
	3	Deform (use)	U	U for "use," or a cup placed upright
2	4	Transport empty (extending or retracting your hand)	∪	Shape of palm opened up
	5	Grab	∩	Shape of hand grabbing
	6	Transport	◡	Shape of object being transported with hand
	7	Release	⌒	Shape of object with hand facing down
3	8	Search	◯	Symbol of searching eye
	9	Find	◉	Symbol of eye having located object after search
	10	Select	→	Symbol of finger pointing at selected object
	11	Inspect	0	Shape of a lens
	12	Regrasp (reposition)	9	Symbol of regrasping object held by finger tips
	13	Hold	Ω	Shape of rod held with hand
	14*	Prepare	ß	Shape of a cuestick standing erect
4	15*	Think	⸮	Shape of a thinking person with hand by head
	16*	Rest	⸝	Shape of a person sitting on chair
	17	Unavoidable delay	⌢o	Shape of tripped person on ground
	18*	Avoidable delay	⌐o	Shape of person lying down

Note: An asterisk indicates a therblig that does not usually arise during normal tasks.

FIGURE 5.25 Gilbreth Motion Study Therbligs. Source: Shingo The Shingo Production Management System, CRC Press ©1990.

TIME IS A SHADOW OF MOTION[35]

With Lean, excess material and idle time always hide problems; however, not all problems result in extra inventory or idle time. When we watch videos, we look for safety and ergonomics first, but we

[35] Shigeo Shingo, Japan Management Association, *Non Stock Production: The Shingo System for Continuous Improvement*, 1987 (New York: Productivity Press) 1988.

also look at motions the operators take. The more motions a person uses to do their job, the longer it takes. Remember, Gilbreth said, "Time is a shadow of motion." If you can reduce the motions, the person is happier because the job is easier and management is happy because they are getting more done with the same person. It is a win-win solution.

Video allows us to see waste we might not normally see and gives us a chance to see some of the hidden waste (waste behind the waste), which is the most difficult to see. It is important to never turn off the video camera once filming starts or you will lose chances to see and remove waste in the process (even if the person tells you to turn it off because of a problem).

One of the advantages to video is there is no disputing the information. What you see is what was done. Many times we hear, "Oh, I didn't realize I did that" or what we filmed was "unusual" and doesn't normally happen that way. Based on our experience, don't believe it. If it happened when you filmed it, you can bet it happens more than people think. We also spot other wastes in the video, such as over-processing, excess motion, searching, and transportation, to name a few.

Lesson Learned

Management needs to support the video technique. You will get pushback on video from some employees, as this is new to many in healthcare and can be intimidating. You can document a process through observation and written documentation; however, the video yields the best results as there is no dispute and other wastes can be identified (Table 5.5). If video is allowed with staff

---

TABLE 5.5
Operator Quick Reference Guide

Quick Reference Notes	Operator Analysis
When to use	Next Level of detail which looks at each PFA remaining activity from the operator or staff member's perspective to determine the "value" of each step.
What it delivers	Identifies what operator activities are value added throughout the process and provides the labor time needed for each step and total labor time for the overall process.
Used to Identify	Waste in process leading to improvement opportunities • Determines Value added, • Non-Value Added but Necessary • Unnecessary or Idle Time
Baseline Metrics	Value added activities related to the operator Total labor time needed to optimize product flow Productivity opportunities for ROI
How is it performed	Manually transcribed from video by follow the operator through the process as the activities are being performed
Analysis Steps	Walk the process Document Operator activities Perform analysis (with frontline staff/operators) determining • Value Added • Non Value Added • Unnecessary or Idle time • May also analyze paperwork, searching, retrieving supplies and equipment or other categories as applicable Capture rework and labor (current and future) Distance traveled (current and future)
Combine PFA and Operator Analysis	Determine and note on the analysis what steps can be eliminated, simplified and combined within a process. Update the PFA as applicable with the operator process times.

Source: J Kerpchar.

review, in most cases the staff will gain an understanding of the value, when they participate in the review process. Then it is much easier to obtain "buy-in" to recommended changes and from others to be filmed.

It is important to analyze each task to the second so it can be recorded correctly and split into the appropriate category. How we split the work varies depending on the area we are reviewing. In some areas, we may break down times for computer input or retrieving supplies into separate categories. It is important to break the steps up into what makes sense for the area in which you are studying. We always do the task by hand first and then on the computer.

100% EFFICIENCY WITH HUMANS

Looking from a very analytical Lean or motion study purest point of view, an operator who uses both hands and feet at the same time is 100% efficient (a drummer is a good example). How close can we get to this in healthcare? Normally, we look at use of both hands simultaneously as 100% efficient, but technically it is only 50% efficient since we are not using our feet. People who use one hand as a fixture to hold something while the other hand is working on it are only 25% efficient and are also a common reason that operations cannot be split between two persons. Watch the work being performed. Can a fixture be made to hold the part for the person and free up the other hand? In healthcare, think of the daVinci robot®, where the surgeon sits at a console and simultaneously uses both hands and feet to manipulate the robot. It has robotic arms that, in fact, free up assistant surgeons' hands; they no longer have to be exposed to ergonomic challenges associated with laparoscopic instrumentation. So always look for ways to use both hands (or feet) at once or introduce foot petals to assist in reducing operator motions.

OPERATOR RESISTANCE

In healthcare, clinical personnel are trained to "get the job done" despite any obstacles and are encouraged and rewarded to perform workarounds. Since they have become accustomed to workarounds in their day-to-day life, we encounter resistance in redesigning processes and re-allocating work activities. Proactively sequencing "work" in the order it needs to occur, providing the right tools at the right place at the right time, and standard work may be very challenging concepts, and personnel may find it difficult to believe that it will actually occur. We often find that because they are trained to deal with emergencies and "rewarded for saving the day," it is often challenging for them to change from a reactive work model to a proactive model in which "workarounds and saving the day" are essentially eliminated.

STEP III: ASSESS THE PROCESS—CHANGEOVER ANALYSIS

Changeover analysis is the third assessment tool and it is performed in that order (Figure 5.26). The analogy we use for turnover is that of a pit stop. How long does a NASCAR pit stop take? The fastest

FIGURE 5.26 Lean Pieces Changeover. Source: Authors.

NASCAR pit stop on record is around 12 sec.[36] On the Winner's Circle[37] tape it takes about 14.7 sec. It is important to note that 14.7 sec is the clock time. In Lean changeovers, we make a distinction between clock time and labor time. While the clock time is 14.7 sec, we look to see how many operators there are to determine the labor time. If there are seven persons doing the changeover, we calculate the labor time by multiplying seven times 14.7 sec, which equals 109.3 sec. Could the pit stop have been done with one person? The answer is yes, but how long would it take? At least the 109.3 sec, but probably longer owing to travel distance and extra movements which would be required. Since races are typically won by fractions of a second, we would probably lose the race. What characteristics make the pit stop concept successful? Doing things in parallel, standard work for each person, and lots of practice all contribute to the Lean formula.

INTERNAL VS. EXTERNAL TIME

Another concept we use is to break the work down into internal time vs. external time. In the pit stop example, anything done while in the pit is considered "internal time." Examples would be changing the tires or refueling. Anything we can do while the car is going around the track is considered "external" time. For example, we could get the tires ready and located in the pit area ahead of time. So, if you think about it, the 14.7 sec is only a measure of the internal time, not the external time. Why do we focus on internal time? Because this is the amount of time the asset is not available for use, i.e., the car is not racing around the track.

FOUR PARTS OF A SETUP/CHANGEOVER PROCESS

The next step we use in setup analysis is to break down each step into its component parts or categories. Shingo describes these in his book, *A Revolution in Manufacturing: The SMED System*.[38] The four components of setup reduction are: 1) preparation (P) and organization, 2) mounting (M) and removing, 3) calibration (C) measurement and testing (positioning), and 4) trial (T) runs and adjustments. These terms are challenging for healthcare workers, so being able to convert the language and thought process to healthcare is essential to adoption.

The process we use for changeover reduction then is to video the changeover. This means we need a video camera to follow every person involved in the changeover. Examples in healthcare are the ED (changeover of rooms), housekeeping, or surgical rooms. Once we have the video, we break down each step from the video, preferably with the person we filmed, a supervisor, and someone who knows nothing about the process present. We initially break it into what we call the "As Is" condition. Each step is divided into either internal or external and one of the four categories we outlined earlier (PMCT). We also note distances traveled where appropriate.

Healthcare Setup Translation

We normally refer to setups in healthcare as turnover or changeover.

When analyzing room turnover, each person that has a role within changeover will need to be analyzed and have his/her work deconstructed. We divide up tasks in the video into the following categories:

---

[36] http://en.allexperts.com/q/NASCAR-Racing-2068/Pit-Stop.htm. Copyright ©2008 About, Inc. AllExperts, AllExperts. com, and About.com are registered trademarks of About, Inc. All rights reserved. There is no official record. It is estimated to be around 12 sec.

[37] "Winners Circle" was produced originally for Cosma International, an automotive components manufacturer, to help its workforce understand the power and simplicity of quick changeover techniques. However, it was so well done that it was subsequently released for the general marketplace. The film brilliantly blends clips of racecar pit crews with a Cosma work team attempting to reduce the changeover time of its 800-ton press from 2 hrs to 10 min.

[38] Shigeo Shingo, Andrew Dillon (translator), *A Revolution in Manufacturing: The Smed System* (New York: Productivity Press) 1985.

1. Preparation (P) and organization, which is gathering and preparing tools, information, or anything needed ahead of time for the "changeover." For example:
   - Is the bed available with an IV pole and a "roller" to move the patient (technicians, assistants)?
   - Does the patient need blood for potential transfusions on standby (nursing personnel)?
   - Is the next patient prepared to enter the room (by the surgeon, OR staff, and anesthesiologist)?
   - Is the anesthesia equipment prepared?
   - Are the clean supplies ready (support staff/assistants)?
   - Checking to see if the correct case cart is pulled, any additional instrumentation is needed, especially if there are implants involved.
2. Mounting (M) and removing includes removing or taking down the previous setup and preparation for the next activity, which could include removing the patient, changing beds, and cleaning up, which can only be done while the patient is out of the room. For example:
   - Removing the patient from the room
   - Cleaning the room
   - Making the bed (unless the patient is prepared in an induction room)
   - Moving the next patient into the room
3. Calibration (C) measurement and testing (positioning) includes making sure things are accurate and ready for setup and that machines are ready for use. Normally these occur after the patient is in the room. For example:
   - Calibrating equipment or pre-testing required for anesthesia monitoring or surgical equipment to make sure it is functional and functioning properly.
   - Positioning the patient for surgery (ortho cases).
   - Getting the bed to the correct height.
4. Trial (T) runs and adjustments. Normally these occur after the patient is in the room. For example:
   - Actions needed to be taken as a result of "pause for the cause." This is where the surgeon stops to make sure everything is correct and in order prior to beginning the operation.
   - An instrument set is not ready so another one has to be retrieved to use in its place.

Multiple screws and fittings required for knee replacement.

The next step is to invoke the SMED process, which Shingo developed from 1950 to 1969.[39] This can be thought of in healthcare as SMER (single minute exchange of rooms). There are three steps to the SMED process.

1. The first is to identify internal vs. external work. We do this in our video analysis.
2. The next step is to convert internal to external work wherever possible. So we question every step as to whether it can be converted from internal to external work. This enables us to shorten the clock time on the changeover.
3. The third step is the OMIT's process to look at each step to see if we can eliminate, rearrange, simplify, or combine all the remaining work.

To complete our analysis, we go back over each step to determine what the "to be" state will look like if we can make improvements to the changeover. Initially, it is not unusual to find that most of the internal time is spent on preparation and organization; however, preparation and organization

[39] Shigeo Shingo, Andrew Dillon (translator), *A Revolution in Manufacturing: The Smed System* (New York: Productivity Press) 1985.

should be almost totally external time and completed before the patient enters the room. Our goal with the other two steps, calibration and trial runs, is to eliminate the need for them. This means the 14.7 sec in our pit stop should only be for internal steps that are related to mounting and moving the patient or product.

In healthcare, SMED can get confusing. The concepts, however, are very applicable to many settings, such as laboratory changeover of equipment/reagent changes, turning over patients such as bed or room cleaning, or radiology, catheterization laboratory and surgery room "turnovers." In addition, the non-clinical areas of laundry, nutritional service areas and even engineering services may have equipment setups.

WHY REDUCE SETUPS? BENEFITS OF SMED/SMER (SINGLE MINUTE EXCHANGE OF ROOMS)

Reducing setup time immediately increases capacity. The goal is to reduce the time it takes to do a changeover so that the fixed asset can be freed up and utilized as quickly as possible. In surgery it may be an OR that we need to turnover quickly so we can maximize the surgeon's time and get patients in and out faster. In ORs, we have been able to get surgeons one or two more operations a day in the same amount or less time with less waiting between cases. On the floors and in the ED and radiology, it is turning over the room between patients. In the office, it can simply be reloading paper or toner in the copying machine.

We propose that analyzing just the changeover will provide the following pieces of Lean:

- Enabler for one-piece or one-patient flow or smaller batch sizes
- Immediately increases capacity
- Enabler for mixed model and ability to supply in sets
- Provides quick response to demand changes
- Enabler for more reliable delivery of care
- Capital asset utilization rates increases (if demand is there)
- Reduces material handling
- Results in standardization
- Improved operator safety
- Improved patient/product quality and integrates five S and mistake proofing

SUMMARY

We began with an overview of Lean Concepts, then we moved into surveying our customers and finding out what was important to them and what challenges they experienced with the current process. We also interviewed the staff and constructed fishbone diagrams to help categorize and determine the root cause of the problems they faced. Problem is not a bad word; in fact, identifying and bringing attention to problems needs to be encouraged. We need to surface problems by lowering the inventory, eliminating storage or waits, and rework to uncover hidden wastes, remembering that waste hides more waste.

We then determined our customer demand and peak demand (in some cases to the hour) and calculated our Takt time. The demand is the number of patients, products, or services that need to be "processed." Demand could be the number of customers who present to the Emergency Room for treatment in a particular hour, day, month, or year. From the pharmacy's perspective, they would be more interested in the number of medications they need to "fill" in 15 min, 60 min, or daily, so the demand from the pharmacy's perspective might be medication fills per hour or average number of medication filled per patient. Takt time is equal to the available time divided by customer demand or the beat to which we need to construct our new system.

Next came the value stream map, which provided a high-level systemic view of the overall process, identifying process vs. non-process based activities and a baseline view of throughput for the overall process. Part of our calculations included determining value-added vs. non-value-added time, cycle time, and throughput (LOS) time. The findings and opportunities identified through the value stream map helped us to gain insight into what areas needed improvement and where to focus the next level of tools. Our assessment tools included the PFA, operator analysis, and changeover analysis. It is optional at this point to go back and update the value stream map with the analysis-based data. Utilizing the PFA tool, we looked at how the product or services "flowed" within and throughout the process.

Information was gathered on the time and distance it takes to go through the process or service. We used the eight wastes to identify the value-added percentage along with the process steps that could be eliminated, rearranged, simplified, or combined. We now look at the remaining steps to see which ones can be done in parallel. The product also gives us total throughput time, which we can use to calculate how much inventory (product or patients) needs to be in the system to meet the Takt time. In healthcare, the ability to measure and track throughput as a metric is key to improving processes. There are many processes for which throughput is uniquely defined; one example could be "a stat medication order," where the throughput metric could be defined from the time the medication was ordered by the physician to the time the patient actually received the medication from the nurse. In radiology, an example of throughput would be the arrival of a patient in radiology at the registration desk to the completion of the examination or, better yet, the patient receiving the examination result. Throughput is a key metric in Lean and should be a key metric for every department in every organization. We also pointed out that just because we have to perform a step does not make it value-added. Determining the new flow and new layout begins with the knowledge gained from the PFA analysis.

Next was performing the operator analysis, which looked at the process from the operator's or staff's point of view and provided a baseline for "labor time." We were then able to eliminate, rearrange, simplify, or combine the steps as they relate to the staff member doing the work. This helped streamline the work of staff persons to make sure that the activities being performed were value-added based on what is "really" needed to achieve the results. Observations during this process provided opportunities to make sure that the staff person had been provided with the "right tools or parts" at the "right place" to get the job done with the least amount of effort, thus the least amount of wasted motions and activity, again using "the eight wastes" as a guide. This provides the basis for standard work and balancing our operation steps. The operator analysis gave us total labor time, which we can now use to calculate how many staff we will need in our newly designed process and area layout.

Then we performed the changeover analysis, which looked at the turnover of the room between patients and the opportunities that existed to convert internal steps to external. Reducing turnover time frees up capacity (beds) throughout the system. It also makes our surgeons much happier as they can get more cases done in the same amount of time, which can be financially rewarding as well.

The overall goal is to achieve a new process flow, free of waste and non-value-added activities. In healthcare this often equates to improving both patient and information flow. Improving flow is fundamental to achieving customer value and delivery of expected results.

Remember, it is essential to ensure that we have clear definitions of each metric. These include precise starting and ending points for the process, how, when, where, and who is collecting it, and over what time frame. It is important that consistency in the metric collection process is obtained. The definitions need to be discussed and clearly understood by all stakeholders to avoid downstream confusion of what exactly is being reported.

To summarize, we have the following key process metrics coming out of the analysis phase: available time, Takt time, throughput time, total labor time, and changeover time.

Lesson Learned

The real key with Lean is figuring out the product axis vs. the operator axis and changeover axis separately and developing the solution for all of them together.

6 Putting It All Together

Focusing on the first S in our BASICS model (which stands for suggest solutions), the goal of this chapter is to introduce the balance of the tools and how to proceed once the analysis is completed. There are many pieces to a Lean implementation and they are all interconnected. The material in this chapter will walk through the relationships and how the data collected up to this point can be leveraged to prepare you for your implementation. It will discuss suggesting solutions for improvements and making recommendations to management to secure their buy-in and approval (Figure 6.1).

The information obtained from the staff during the value stream map, product process flow, operator analysis, and changeover analysis helps us develop the key data elements: cycle time, Takt time, demand, available time, and TLT. We then use the analysis to develop standard work, calculate SWIP, design the new layout, and create the new work station/area design. Materials/inventory management supports the new flow of delivering the service or product to the customer. It is important to note that this is a ready... aim... fire... approach, but it is not analysis paralysis. With enough practice, the tools can be applied quickly (in the span of hours, depending on scope).

USING THE FUTURE STATE "TO BE" AND FUTURE STATE ANALYSIS TO DESIGN THE NEW PROCESS AND IMPLEMENTATION

The key elements that need to be considered in your optimal flow design are all derived from the analysis tools we described earlier.

- *The future state value stream map helps provide a road map for areas and projects to focus process improvement identify wastes and throughput opportunities and our current state metrics.*
- *Knowing the current and forecasted customer demand and "peak" demand is critical.* We should design our new processes and layouts to 50% of the current demand or to the demand forecasted in the hospital strategic plan in order to encompass future growth.
- *Determine the available time, which is the amount of time available to do work or perform an activity.* An example might be the pre admission testing area which operates from 6:00 a.m. to 5:00 p.m. for an available time of 11 hrs or 660 min of operation, while an area such as an emergency room, which is open 24 hrs, has an available time of 1440 min.
- *Understand the Takt time (customer demand divided by available time).* This helps determine the "beat" or "pace" of the activity that needs to performed as well as assists in balancing the workload.
- *The future state or what we call the "To Be" process flow analysis and point-to-point diagram showed us how the flow should look.* This is where we begin to design the new layout for the area. This can be done with a computer-aided drawing (CAD) system, but it is usually best to get a "to-scale" diagram of the area and use "paper dolls" or "cutouts" to see how everything fits. It is not unusual to go through many versions of the layout before getting it right. Each time we develop or change the layout, we need to draw a new point-to-point diagram of how things are going to flow using the layout guidelines. We need to optimize the layout and work station design to create a "Lean" layout that places the sequence of steps/activities in the correct and/or parallel order.

Phases

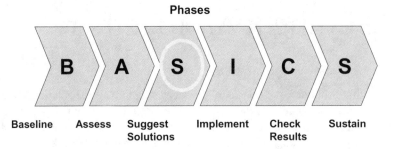

FIGURE 6.1 BASICS Model – Baseline. Source: BIG.

- *The "To Be" work flow of the operator analysis and spaghetti diagram showed us how to optimize operator walk patterns, locations for point-of-use storage, and work station design.* The work station must have the "right tools at the right place" to perform the activities in the proper sequence within the process.
- *The "To Be" changeover analysis showed us what our additional capacity can be.* The key now is to determine if we have the resources necessary and determine the time frame to implement the changeover ideas. We need to calculate the capacity for the areas before and then after to determine if they can support the input to and from the area implementing the turnover project. For example, if we can do one or two more surgeries per day per surgeon, can Pre-Op and post-anesthesia care unit (PACU) support the new demand numbers?
- *Calculate the total labor time (TLT) from the work flow analysis.* The TLT is equal to the sum of the total value-added and non-value-added labor time. It is the amount of time staff members spend on activities within a process. The demand, available time, and TLT will drive the number of staff or operators needed to run your process and impact your work area design.
- *Understand the desired cycle time and new staffing model.* The cycle time comes from the operator analysis, the demand, and the Takt time. We need to figure out how many operators are needed to support the current peak demand and forecasted demand. We then need to make sure we can balance the workload for the staff. After balancing the workload, we will have the cycle time (the amount of time each person must meet to complete their part of the operation or activity within the process). It is calculated by dividing the available time by the volume demand of the new process. It also equals the TLT divided by the number of operators/staff members (if work is balanced evenly). The new layout needs to be reviewed to ensure we have room for the number of persons required to support current, peak, and future demand.
- *Determine if standard work can be applied.* Have the employees in the area help develop the standard work and train to the defined standard work. Make sure to plan for demand fluctuations related to staff and resource (supply) requirements. This often requires a new staffing model for the area. The plan should include how to run the area with one or two less in case the demand drops or one or two more persons in the event the demand increases.
- *Determine the standard work in process (SWIP).* This calculation determines the minimum amount of inventory that is necessary to perform the task safely and meet the required cycle time. Be aware that batch operations normally require at least double the inventory. The quantity of SWIP may change with revisions to the throughput time, cycle time, and number of operators or staff in the cell or changes in customer demand. In healthcare, often the SWIP is actually patients going through or waiting during the process. We can design the waiting areas based on the projected waiting times divided by the cycle time we plan to run. Keep in mind that we want to design these areas to incorporate present as well as future demand. Consider any innovations or changes from current state such

as deploying "pagers for family members," which may decrease space needed in waiting areas (as long as you are actually going to implement).

- *Adjust inventory and understand materials and supply chain management.* Make sure the layout has enough room for the "right amount" of supplies available at the "right time" at point of use, in other words available when needed and room to grow if necessary.
- *Create a plan for every part with a focus on how and where each item will be replenished.* Some options for replenishment include fixed time or fixed quantity *Kanbans.*
- *The layout needs to be flexible.* Put work stations on wheels, don't hard pipe machines, and install flexible utilities wherever possible so that if we have to move equipment or work stations in the future it is not a barrier.

One can now see why we spend time analyzing the process. The analysis of the data will lead you to the optimal solution.

UNDERSTANDING DEMAND AND RESOURCE NEEDS

When converting a process from batch to one-piece flow, there may be some substantial time savings just from running one piece or one patient at a time. Customer demand, cycle time, TLT, and standard work are directly related to one another. In earlier chapters, we discussed calculations relating to staffing to demand. Now it is time to put the calculations into practical use.

EXAMPLE 6.1

If on average, 120 patients per day come to the Emergency Department (ED) and need to be signed-in, triaged, and seen by the physician, then the average daily demand (ADD) would be 120 patients per day. The hourly demand would be 120 ÷ 8 hrs (for an 8-hrs shift) or 15 patients per hour. This can be extremely important to understand, as this will impact how and when one might want to schedule staff in a clinical area. Since it is difficult to adjust staff to smaller than hourly increments, we normally use hourly demand when looking at staffing resources and balancing labor. Resources can be optimized by scheduling staff to the actual customer demand or arrivals by hour. In healthcare, we have found that managers fall into the routine of scheduling staff in routine shifts—7:00 a.m. to 3:00 p.m., 3:00 p.m. to 11:00 p.m., 7:00 a.m. to 7:00 p.m.—without really understanding when patients arrive or when peak patient services are required.

In the emergency department example, the waiting room is normally filled with patients waiting for care because demand by hour and cycle times of activities have not been analyzed. Often, the physician and staff scheduled hours do not align with the patient arrivals by hour. Therefore, the correct number of staff, scheduled at the right time, performing the right activities is not available, and bottlenecks occur. Working in the healthcare environment, we have found that demand in most areas, even the emergency room, is very predictable. There will always be times when emergencies occur, such as the "bus accident"; however, if the manager or supervisor reviews hourly, daily, and seasonal demand, the right resource scheduling is possible.

Using the same demand in the emergency example above, let's examine the initial two process steps in the emergency room arrival: patient sign-in and triage.

Patient sign-in and triage cycle times are determined by performing an operator analysis on each process and understanding the specific tasks involved and the cycle time necessary to perform these activities. An example of sample data is outlined in Table 6.1.

The next step is to review the information in the chart to determine the number of staff needed per shift and the ability to schedule them to fit the hourly demand. We calculated the available time for performing activities for the 7:00 a.m. to 3:00 p.m. shift at 480 min. Understanding the available time, we can now calculate the number of staff needed.

To meet current average shift demand:

Method 1: Total shift labor time ÷ available time = # of staff or operators to meet current demand

TABLE 6.1

Sample Data Sign-In and Triage

Patient sign-in	Available Time (min)	Total Labor Time For 1 Patient (min)	ADD (Average Daily Demand: 7:00 a.m. to 3:00 p.m.)	Hourly Patient Demand: 7:00 a.m. to 3:00 p.m.	Takt Time (min)	Required Labor for all patients (min)	# of Staff Required Method 1 · Required Shift Labor/ Available Time	# of Staff Required Method 2 · TLT/TT
Patient sign-in	480	5	120	15	4.00	600	1.25	1.25
Triage	480	6	120	15	4.00	720	1.5	1.5

Sign-in 600 min ÷ 480 min = 1.25 staff
Triage 720 min ÷ 480 min = 1.50 staff.

In the example above, the TLT to perform the task contains both value-added and non-value-added activities. When determining final staffing for a given process, be careful that you take into account all the activities or tasks the individual is performing. Another way to calculate number of staff is to take the TLT divided by the cycle time or Takt times (see method 2).

Method 2: Takt time = 60 min/hr ÷ 15 patients/hr = 4 min/patient
TLT for 1 patient ÷ Takt time = # of staff

Sign-in 5 min ÷ 4 min = 1.25 staff
Triage 6 min ÷ 4 min = 1.50 staff.

Takt time will give you the theoretical, whereas cycle time will give you the actual, unless Takt time = cycle time.

Since we have a person and a fraction of a person (we call this fractional labor), we can't necessarily utilize a fraction of a person, which means that for sign-in the person will be idle 75% of the time. If we only had one staff member assigned to each of the tasks, we would fall behind the pace and the beat of the process would be disrupted, creating bottlenecks or "wait states." So, the solution would be to cross-train the staff to flex from work area/activity to work area/activity, if possible, and capitalize on minimizing fractional labor.

In hospital environments, this is difficult, as only certain people can do certain jobs. When we divide out the numbers, anything above 0.9 people can be rounded up to a full person. The challenge is to eliminate enough work from the area to get the fractional person somewhere between plus and minus 0.1. The key is to divide the work as evenly as possible and have the people in the areas flex to cover minor variations in cycle times. Sometimes, some of the steps can be offloaded to other areas when appropriate to facilitate the balance. Imbalances that are less than about 10% of cycle time will usually not be a problem and are handled by flexing staff or operators. Flexing Staff or operators can take two different forms. Ohno uses the analogy between swimming relay handoffs and baton relay handoffs[1] to describe the differences in flexing. Swimming relay handoffs require the next worker to wait until the person prior to them completes their work, whereas a baton relay handoff allows work to be handed off before it is completed but requires the operator to be able to perform that work.

In order to do this, we need layouts that support flexing, and each person has to have the necessary skills to carry out each of the tasks involved. At many hospitals, this creates an initial barrier; for example, registration may be centralized, located in partitioned cubes (isolated), or doesn't want to cross-train non-registration personnel. Sometimes, to flex labor we may decide to staff a level up or

---

[1] Taiichi Ohno, *Toyota Production System* (New York: Productivity Press) 1988.

even create a new higher-grade position. For example, staffing with a nurse vs. a technician as the nurse could carry out additional duties where the technician could not. This involves a cost-benefit decision. Is it worth paying a higher skilled salary vs. having a technician idle 50%–75% of the time? Often we find this analysis doesn't take place, and many times finance discourages this line of thinking.

In the example listed above, an option would be to add a second triage nurse as a backup for times when there are more patients waiting than one nurse can handle or if triage takes longer than the average 5 min, as there are variations in the time it takes. Another option would be to add up the TLT of 600 min for sign-in plus 720 min for triage and then divide by 480 min of available time to determine the combined labor needs, which would equate to 2.75 operators or staff. This again assumes that staff are interchangeable and again assumes that the layout is flexible and the work can be balanced.

Every time there is a change in demand, a change in products or services offered, a change in process, or new machinery introduced (i.e., robots or new diagnostic equipment), it necessitates recalculating all the numbers in order to re-balance the work flow. World-class companies see these changes as opportunities to improve and eliminate even more waste in the process. Be careful with elements of a job that may have been categorized as a group of operations with a large chunk of time. Sometimes these can be split up to get the work to balance. As a normal rule of thumb, we analyze operations down to the second to avoid this problem. Bottlenecks may also be caused by machines that require extended machine cycle times or that have larger capacity to run multiple tests or processes. Ask yourself, what can be done to separate the machine work from the human work or to divide up the machine tasks across different machines?

Now consider the following ED example, which will pull together the concepts of a target metric, cycle time, Takt time, demand, and available time.

APPROPRIATE RESOURCING CAN DRIVE METRICS

EXAMPLE 6.2

Patients present to the emergency room for critical care, urgent care, and for non-urgent treatment care. Urgent and non-urgent patients (patients who leave the same day) expect to see the physician within 20 min of arrival, which is defined as the time the patient sign in to the time the physician examination is started. So, we need to ensure delivery of value to our customer by making improvements to achieve a door-to-physician time less than or equal to 20 min. A value stream map was created and the data revealed the demand through the ED was 15 patients per hour (average) for 7:00 a.m. to 3:00 p.m. shift. Ten of the 15 patients per hour were non-urgent. The average baseline cycle time from door to physician was 79 min (5 + 10 + 5 + 6 + 0 + 45) (Figure 6.2).

- Sign-in: 5 min (with a range of 1–15 min)
- Triage: 6 min (with a range of 0–25 min)
- Registration collection of demographic information: 8 min (with a range of 2–20 min)

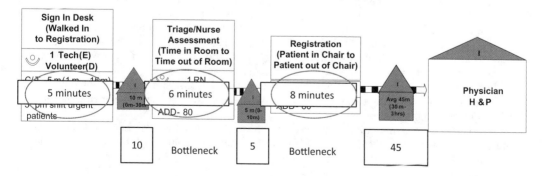

FIGURE 6.2   Value Stream Map ED Process boxes before with opportunities. Source: Authors.

To calculate demand for non-critical patients:

- Available time = time per shift 7:00 a.m. to 3:00 p.m. = 8 hrs × 60 min = 480 min (note: lunches are covered by staff or charge nurse)
- Hourly non-critical demand = 10 patients per hour (note: demand by hour does not always = the average)
- Daily shift non-critical demand (8 hrs shift 7:00 a.m. to 3:00 p.m) = 80 patients per day
- Total process time from the process boxes = 19 min (5 + 6 + 8)
- Total storage times (or wait times in the triangle boxes) = 60 min (10 + 5 + 45)
- Total process time from the process boxes = 19 min (5 + 6 + 8)
- Total through put time door to MD = 19 min process time + 60 min storage (patient wait time) = 79 min on average (range 33 to 234 min)

Since the Take time is:

60 min ÷ 10 patients = 6 min

We need to design a process where every 6 min a patient sees the physician to be able to achieve the Takt time or "pace" of how the patients are arriving to the emergency room.

If each process step is not completed at or below the 6 min Takt time, then a "bottleneck" or wait state will occur creating excess WIP, i.e., patients waiting.

Remember, any excess WIP or idle time is the sign of a problem within a Lean system. A bottleneck is the constraint, (where the capacity of the machine cannot meet the demand) in any series of operations in a process. Per the theory of constraints, which is explained in detail in a book entitled *The Goal*,[2] the cycle time will always be equal to the slowest machine or slowest person in the process. We refer to these constraints as "Herbies." In theory, a person (Herbie) should never be a constraint as we can always add people but we cannot always add or speed up machines. In essence, only machines should be bottlenecks in a process. This is a good and bad news story. The bad news is we have a backup or bottleneck. The good news is we not only know we have a backup, but we also can now predict when the backup will start, how long it will last, and how many patients will queue up.

Bottlenecks occur in the process if each of these tasks is sequential and we have only one work area for each process staffed with one person. The sign-in process is 5 min and the subsequent processes are 6 and 8 min, respectively. So the slowest process is 8 min, which means we can't go faster than 8 min cycle times unless we add people to or speed up the registration process, thus becomes the rate limiting step.

We cannot meet the 6 min Takt time as the process is currently configured. So the backup starts at registration (8 min CT). Sign-in has an average of 1 min of idle time compared to the Takt time but is 3 min slower than registration. So every cycle, we get 2 min behind per person (6 min per arrival vs. 8 min for registration). For every 4 patients, one will back-up after triage and before registration. Assuming no variation, we would never have a back up at sign-in. Hence, we can predict the queue (Figure 6.3).

Let's say our demand changes to 12 patients per hour. Now patients arrive every 5 min (new Takt time), which would create a backup starting at the triage nurse (6 min CT). Now there is no idle time at sign in. Now for each patient, we lose 1 min at triage and 3 min at registration. We can predict that every 6 patients we will back-up a patient before triage because the triage nurse is losing 1 min for every patient that arrives. Registration is losing 3 min per patient arrival (8 min–5 min). So for every 8 patients, Registration gets 3 patients behind.

In the above example, the cycle time for a history and physical examination by the physician is 5 min, so we are not going to meet customer expectations or the 20 min target metric owing to the bottlenecks in the process.

In real life, because we experience these bottlenecks and the added complexity of acuities in the ED, the triage nurse will start to shuffle the order of patients sent through the process in order to treat "sicker" patients first (i.e., the essence of the word triage). This then changes the first-in,

2 Goldratt, Eliyahu & Cox, Jeff. *The Goal* (North River Press) 2004.

Queuing Example			Queuing Example		
# of Patients	6 min Takt time Arrivals	Registration Cycle Time Queue	# of Patients	6 min Takt time Arrivals	Registration Cycle Time Queue
1	6	8	1	5	8
2	12	16	2	10	16
3	18	24	3	15	24
4	24	32	4	20	32
5	30	40	5	25	40
6	36	48	6	30	48
7	42	56	7	35	56
8	48	64	8	40	64
9	54	72	9	45	72
10	60	80	10	50	80
11	66	88	11	55	88

FIGURE 6.3   ED Queuing Example. Source: Authors.

first-out sequence of the patients to "see the physician," which further impacts the ability to meet the customer-defined 20 min target and contributes to even more bottlenecks within the process. Once the sorting of patients begins, the wide variation in "waits" in the ED occurs as the patients that are perceived as less urgent get "sorted out to wait for care" often are placed behind several less urgent patients leading to patients "left without seeing Doctor "LWSD". Understanding Takt time and process cycle and wait times will help assess the resources and staffing required to balance the workload.

Sometimes, we may be in a situation where we cannot "run to customer demand." An example of this might be if we had an employee out sick. If we could not find a replacement, we would run to a slower cycle time than Takt time and we would fall behind, and patients would wait. If later in the day additional staff came in, then we might be able to run at a faster cycle time than our Takt time and whittle down the queue.

The next step would be to perform either an analysis of cycle time through observation with a stopwatch or perform a formal product process flow and operator work flow analysis with a video camera to determine if any of the activities that occur in each of the sub-processes of door-to-physician could be eliminated, simplified or combined, or rearranged to be done in parallel.

In the example (Figure 6.4), it was determined the "wait states" between processes could be nearly eliminated once we analyzed the Takt time, cycle times, and resource needs. In addition, the staff felt, since the value proposition was in seeing the physician, "full" registration could be done in parallel later in the process. Operator work flow analysis (WFA) was used to determine

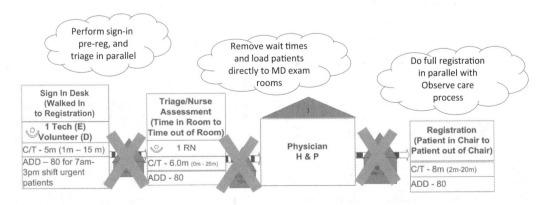

FIGURE 6.4   VSM Process Boxes Future State. Source: Authors.

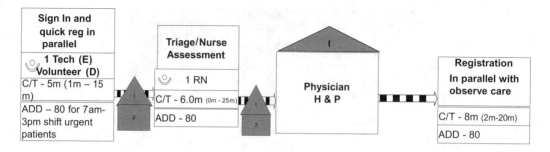

FIGURE 6.5 ED Value Stream Map Process Boxes After Lean. With improvements in parallel processing we now have 11 min process time and 4 min of storage (wait) = 15 min cycle time (to see the MD). Source: Authors.

standard work and provide cycle time information that will be used to calculate the amount of staff needed to meet the customer expectations (Figure 6.5).

TRUE BOTTLENECKS

A true bottleneck is defined as a machine that runs 24 hrs a day and cannot meet Takt time. In healthcare, the ED room can be a true bottleneck, as witnessed when the ED goes into inpatient "hold" status, where patients are unable to be moved to units and therefore remain in a "wait-state" in the ED resulting in lengthy delays or diversions. How we handle a true bottleneck is different from other constraints. Other constraints can be made up with overtime or speeding up the machine, etc. But true bottlenecks must be managed intensely to mitigate any lost time. It is important during the analysis phase to look at the processes as an overall system and determine whether there are any true bottlenecks lurking.

CROSS-TRAINING

Having staff cross trained can help alleviate bottlenecks as staff can "flex in" when needed. Staff need appropriate cross-training to perform the tasks and have a clear understanding of the benefits to the customer and the organization and to address "what is in it for me" as it relates to each person. Cross-training is normally the first thing needed in order to achieve the desired workload balancing. Staff members must be multi-process capable to fine tune the work distribution. This necessitates that they learn more tasks or operations within a cell or work area. One way to facilitate this training is to use a cross-training matrix and post it on the team communication board to keep track of which staff members are trained up to what level in each task.

HOW TO CONSTRUCT A CROSS-TRAINING MATRIX

Each staff member that works in the area is rated based on a set of objective measures (0–4). These ratings should be continually monitored and revised. If a staff member has not worked in a particular area or performed the task for a given period of time (i.e., 6 months), they should either be re-certified or lose their status for that operation (Table 6.2).

In an environment where continuous improvement is practiced, the tasks or operations will be continually improving and changing. This requires the staff to be trained on the latest developments and standard work in the area. The goal for the area should be to have all staff at a status "3" or above on all operations/tasks. This is just one example of cross-training matrices that can range from simple to complex.

TABLE 6.2
Cross-Training Matrix Sample

Name	Task 1	Task 2	Task 3
Jane	3	3	4
Karl	4	1	0
Loretta	0	4	2

Legend: 0 = untrained, 1 = in training, 2 = produces quality tasks, 3 = meets cycle time, 4 = can train others

---

HEIJUNKA—SEQUENCING ACTIVITIES, LOAD BALANCING

Production leveling, also known as *production smoothing* or—by its Japanese original term—*heijunka* 平準化[3], 平 means "a plain, flat, level," 準 means "standard, level," and 化 means "change."

Level loading is a technique for reducing the *mura* waste and is vital to the development of production efficiency in the Toyota Production System and Lean manufacturing. The general idea is to produce intermediate goods at a constant rate, to allow further processing to be carried out at a constant and predictable rate.[4]

In manufacturing, this concept is utilized to level out production of various or "mixed" models. This concept allows Toyota to run multiple car types down the same line one model after another. This can only be accomplished with flexibility built into the layout, equipment, utilities, and people. The idea behind this concept is to schedule your patients evenly so as not to create batches of patients coming in at one time. In some areas of hospitals this is easy to do, and in some areas it may be near impossible to do.

In a hospital setting, this mixed model concept could be interpreted as running multiple types of surgery at the same time or running various levels of acuity down a Lean care track in an ED. In order to properly sequence activities within an operation, one must understand the order of the activities and in most cases, the information flow. Often, the information flow will actually pace the progress of the patient through the process. The product process flow analysis gives us this data and then we combine it with the "amount of demand" and type of demand in products or services to determine the sequence.

Once the proper sequence is determined, the flow of the patients must be balanced and evenly distributed to the extent possible. In Lean, we call this demand smoothing, level loading, or *Heijunka*. We then need to match the product process flow (understanding the "critical value-added and non-value-added but necessary activities") to what is "required" by the operator or staff person within the amount of time (cycle time) it takes to perform those activities that come from the work flow analysis. We need to be able to optimize the delivery of products or services within the time frame the customer desires or that which is demanded by the process Takt time.

When all the patients arrive at the same time, it creates a domino effect across the system, pulling on all system resources at the same time, disrupting first-in, first-out and the ability to concentrate and effectively prioritize the work. A simple example might be pre-admission testing. 40 patients were scheduled by the physicians' offices to come to the clinic as outlined in Table 6.3.

The majority of the patients arrived for pre-admission testing between 6:00 a.m. and 9:00 a.m. If the total cycle time (and labor time) for the visit was 60 min, to meet the early morning demand we needed 10 staff members; this resulted in more staff and more labor costs than needed throughout

---

[3] Translation provided by Professor William Tsutsui, Associate Dean for International Studies, Professor of History, College of Liberal Arts & Sciences, The University of Kansas.
[4] Taiichi Ohno, *Toyota Production System* (New York: Productivity Press) 1988.

TABLE 6.3
Before Pre-Testing Schedule

Hours	Available Time per hour (min)	Patients Scheduled	Cumulative patients	Percent of Total Daily Patients	Takt Time	TLT Per Patient (min)	Appointment Total Labor Time (min)	# of Staff Needed Method 1	# of Staff Needed Method 2
6:00 a.m. to 7 a.m.	60	10	10	25.0%	6.0	60.0	600	10.0	10.0
7:00 a.m. to 8 a.m.	60	8	18	45.0%	7.5	60.0	480	8.0	8.0
8:00 a.m. to 9 a.m.	60	6	24	60.0%	10.0	60.0	360	6.0	6.0
9:00 a.m. to 10 a.m.	60	3	27	67.5%	20.0	60.0	180	3.0	3.0
10:00 a.m. to 11 a.m.	60	3	30	75.0%	20.0	60.0	180	3.0	3.0
11:00 to noon	60	4	34	85.0%	15.0	60.0	240	4.0	4.0
Noon to 1:00 p.m.	60	2	36	90.0%	30.0	60.0	120	2.0	2.0
1:00 to 2:00 p.m.	60	2	38	95.0%	30.0	60.0	120	2.0	2.0
2:00 to 3:00 p.m.	60	2	40	100.0%	30.0	60.0	120	2.0	2.0
Daily	540	40			13.5		2400	40	40

the day, as the majority of work was performed in the initial 3 hrs. If the area was staffed to handle only the average workload, then a bottleneck would occur and some patients would wait for over 5 hrs, ultimately resulting in dissatisfied customers. The process owner of the area surveyed the customers and found that patients didn't mind coming in throughout the day. By still providing the desired morning appointments and revising the open slots, they were able to level out the rest of the day (Table 6.4). Staffing was improved, morale was better, and they were able to make their targeted times and output to meet demand.

Another example of level loading would be to set up the clinic schedules at an even rate each hour and then staff to that rate. Figure 6.6 shows the patient is in and the chart is ready.

Another example is the *Heijunka* box we used in the pre-testing department (Figure 6.7). Each slot represents half-hour increments. The night before, it is loaded with each patient by schedule time. In the back is a no-show and cancelled slot. We immediately know by hour who is late and how many are scheduled for that hour. Each slip contains spots to fill in process times so we can track the cycle time of each step and the overall throughput time. The times were manually entered into an Excel spreadsheet and goals were set for the overall time the patient spent going through the process. The goals were based on obtaining a complete and thorough assessment of the patient along with collecting all required labs and x-rays.

The fact that hospitals, in general, do not level load their schedules creates a tremendous amount of waste in their systems in extra labor and overtime costs. In many cases, all their resources are needed at the exact same time. Examples of this are getting patients ready in Pre-Op for 7:30 a.m. surgery starts and the morning collection run for the phlebotomists. In most hospitals, the a.m. phlebotomist collection or "morning run" requires that blood draws are performed over a short interval of time for a large number of hospital inpatients as the results need to be available for physicians morning rounds. This causes an extreme burden for laboratory services and resources from 2:00 a.m. to 7:00 a.m. every morning. It is very difficult for a hospital to hire phlebotomists to work 4 to 5 hrs per day from 2:00 a.m. to 7:00 a.m. to meet this peak demand. This is one of the cases where demand and staffing is difficult to modify. One might consider cross-training to flex phlebotomist staff during off-peak times to other laboratory tasks such as receiving, or review by floor the time that the laboratory results are truly needed for the "internal customers" (physicians) by reviewing the physician rounding schedules to see if there is any potential to level the workload.

Level loading surgical cases throughout the week and throughout the day has been shown to be very beneficial in some hospitals, improving the ability to free up bed capacity and improve ED flow. Level loading the cases directly impacted the number of beds needed on the same days of the week, spreading the need throughout the week. Remember, hospital services and resources are inter-mingled and adjustments in one clinical area can directly impact other clinical areas. This concept, while simple, is very important to making our Lean processes run smoothly. The goal in Lean is to staff the process based on data, thus managing by fact. Then work to improve the process and layouts to take out costs. If you focus on the process, instead of cutting costs, you will get the results.

STANDARD WORK

The "Holy Grail of Lean" is standard work. Without standard work there can be no improvement in the process, no flexibility, and no guarantee of quality from the process. If we are going to create a continuous improvement environment, standard work must be the foundation of every process. Each operator must be trained and must execute the steps in order for each operation the same way, every time. Taiichi Ohno said, "The first step toward improvement is standardization; where there is no standard, there can be no improvement."[5]

---

[5] Japan Management Association, *Kanban Just-in-Time at Toyota*. (New York: Productivity Press) 1989.

TABLE 6.4
Heijunka (Level Loading) After Pre-testing Schedule

Hours	Available Time per hour (min)	Patients Scheduled	Cumulative patients	Percent of Total Daily Patients	Percent of Total Daily Patients Per Hour	Takt Time	TLT Per Patient (min)	Appointment Total Labor Time (min)	# of Staff Needed Method 1	# of Staff Needed Method 2
6:00 a.m. to 7 a.m.	60	5	5	12.5%	12.5%	12.0	60.0	300	5.0	5.0
7:00 a.m. to 8 a.m.	60	5	10	25.0%	12.5%	12.0	60.0	300	5.0	5.0
8:00 a.m. to 9 a.m.	60	5	15	37.5%	12.5%	12.0	60.0	300	5.0	5.0
9:00 a.m. to 10 a.m.	60	5	20	50.0%	12.5%	12.0	60.0	300	5.0	5.0
10:00 a.m. to 11 a.m.	60	4	24	60.0%	10.0%	15.0	60.0	240	4.0	4.0
11:00 to noon	60	5	29	72.5%	12.5%	12.0	60.0	300	5.0	5.0
Noon to 1:00 p.m.	60	4	33	82.5%	10.0%	15.0	60.0	240	4.0	4.0
1:00 to 2:00 p.m.	60	4	37	92.5%	10.0%	15.0	60.0	240	4.0	4.0
2:00 to 3:00 p.m.	60	3	40	100.0%	7.5%	20.0	60.0	180	3.0	3.0
Daily	540	40				13.5		2400	40	40

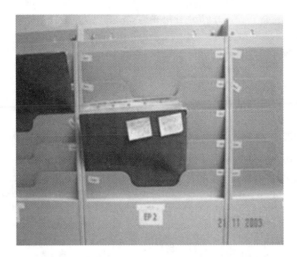

FIGURE 6.6 Heijunka appointment scheduling box in EP laboratory. Source: BIG Archives.

FIGURE 6.7 Heijunka scheduling box unused in surgical services pre-testing department. Source: BIG Archives.

Story

Excerpt from *The Five Patients*, by Michael Crichton[6]

Surgeon: "Give me the smallest Fogarty you have."

Circulating Nurse: "Here is a number four"

Surgeon: Let's have a look at it, opens it up, "it looks too large, are you sure you don't have something smaller?"

Scrub Nurse to Circulating Nurse: "I know we have a six at least"

---

[6] Michael Crichton, *The 5 Patients* (Books) 1970.

Circulating Nurse: But a six is larger than a number four" (she said it hesitantly because numbers do not always run the same way. For instance, urinary catheters nasogastric tubes run in proportion to size—a number 14 is larger than a 12. But needles and sutures run in the opposite direction, an eighteen is much larger than a 21.

Circulating Nurse: "Well see if there is something smaller." There wasn't. The Surgeon made a small cut in the artery wall, and found he could slip in the number four Fogarty without difficulty.

This story illustrates problems have existed with standardization for years within healthcare. When increasing numbers could mean larger or smaller products there is more chance for error and confusion among staff. This does not mean that staff are robots. In fact, batching makes staff robots. As the staff get into a rhythm doing standard work, we want them to constantly think about how to improve the processes. It is the supervisor's job to spend at least 50% of their time encouraging and implementing process improvement ideas. All improvements should be documented by updating the standard work and then training all the staff. Then every staff member must use the new method until it is improved again.

Policy and procedures are not the same as standard work. A policy and procedure dictates what we do and, sometimes, what is expected and who is responsible. How does this compare to standard work? Standard work is defined by Ohno[7] as three items:

1. Cycle time
2. Work sequence
3. Standard inventory

JOB BREAKDOWN/WORK FLOW ANALYSIS

Behind or underneath standard work are job breakdown instructions with detailed steps and times so anyone can perform the work.

DEVELOPING STANDARD WORK

When planning standard work, it is important not to overburden or overwork employees. Once the waste is eliminated, the goal is for employees to work at a normal pace and create an environment where employees are able to take on additional tasks and become multi-skilled and multi-process-capable. Productivity increases and employees become more valuable and more marketable without working harder.

A good analogy for standard work is a pass play in football. Each time, the operator (receiver) must run the pattern (sequence of operations) in the same amount of time (cycle time) in order to complete the pass. If an operator does not follow the play or is too slow or too fast, they will not catch the ball. As a result, football teams video plays, review the tape to look for improvements, and practice, practice, practice. Another good analogy is an orchestra. Have you ever heard a fifth grade orchestra play? How do they sound compared to a symphony orchestra? Let's look at our three components of standard work. What is the sequence of operations or steps? If you answered the music or each note, that is correct. Think about it. Every note must be played in the exact order and the right note needs to be played. What if everyone in the symphony orchestra did what a lot of our employees do and decided to play the notes in the order they want to play them? After all, forcing them to play the music as it is written would make them robots, wouldn't it? The next component of standard work is cycle time. What represents cycle time in our example? Cycle time is represented by the length of each note and the need to play the note for exactly the correct amount of time. It is important to differentiate

---

[7] Taiichi Ohno, *Toyota Production System* (New York: Productivity Press) 1988.

cycle time from Takt time. Standard work must be based on cycle time because to run to Takt time may not always be feasible. For example, Takt time may dictate that the line or area is run with 1.5 people, but we can't run with half of a person. Therefore, we must run with two people. This means we have to recalculate the time using two people, which is going to give us a cycle time that will run faster than Takt time. This means we will over produce unless we stop the line when we meet the required output or we find something else for the half a person to do each cycle.

In the hospital environment, this is further driven by the difference in skill sets and the need to have additional people (not just fractional) to run the area. In addition, since there is so much variation in some cases with how certain patient care must be delivered, we may have to have a range of cycle times in the standard work.

The SWIP (Standard Work In Process) inventory can be viewed as the instrument the musician is playing. In some cases, a musician may have more than one instrument in the inventory due to the demands of the musical score.

The difference with the fifth grade orchestra is that they don't always hit the right notes, they don't always get the timing right, and they may not have exactly the right instruments. Like a symphony, standard work first has to be created (i.e., the musical score or the football play). Then it takes training and education and lots of practice to make sure we hit the notes correctly and follow the beat. The beat in our musical example is like the Takt time, which is comparable to the time signature of the score (i.e., 4/4 or 3/4 time). Standard work is actively being deployed in healthcare to improve quality; examples include: the process in administering pause for the cause, post-surgical notes, blood products, SBAR, and handoff communication.

Most good operators will intuitively see the need for standard operations once you start to try to balance the line. The line cannot be balanced without standard work. Standard work cannot be implemented until all the parts and tools are available in the correct order (product process flow) for the operators to do their job.

Standard work is the foundation for continuous line improvement, line flexibility, and quality improvements. Each staff member must be trained and must execute the steps in each operation the same way every time. Does that mean we can never improve the process? No! We can improve the processes and, in fact, encourage process improvements by suggesting that line staff come up with improvements, try the improvements (to ensure results), document the improvements, train the staff on the improvements, and make sure each person uses the new method until it is improved again.

Lesson Learned

The only way this system can work is if we give the supervisors time to carry out the improvements.

STANDARD WORK FORM

Standard work is derived from the work flow analysis we did earlier. After documenting the operator steps, key points and reasons for key points, we go back and look for items to omit or items where we can save time through the improvements brainstormed during the analysis process, i.e., eliminate, rearrange, simplify, or combine. The steps that are not omitted are then rearranged into the proper sequence and become the basis for how to do the job. This becomes the standard work.

Table 6.5 shows a standard work form. The standard work form is primarily designed for the supervisor. It is constructed at a higher level than the work flow analysis (job breakdown). We have added columns for key points and reasons for key points, which were derived from the TWI.[8] We have also merged what is called a standard job sheet, which depicts a layout of the area. The standard job sheet is used to show the operator walk patterns, denote safety items, WIP storage, number of operators, quality checks, and pipe locations. This form can be adapted to any area. We normally

---

[8] Donald Dinero, *Training Within Industry and Training Within Industry Manual* (New York: Productivity Press) 2005.

TABLE 6.5
Standard Work Form

Nurse Job Standard Work

Area	Total Labor Time	Available Time Minutes	Daily Demand	Takt Time Minutes

HEAD COUNT: 1   3   4   5   6

CYCLE TIME:
HOURLY OUTPUT:
DAILY OUTPUT:
Layout Area and Walk Patterns

Standard Work Area:

Job Step #	Nurse Description (what they do)	Key Points and Quality Notes (how they do it)	Reasons for Key Points	Min Time (secs)	Max Time (secs)	Avg Time (secs)	Cumulative Avg Time Minutes
1							
2							
3							

create standard job sheets for plus or minus one or two operators so the supervisor can run the process short or with additional staff.

WORK STANDARDS

Work standards are different than standard work and are designed around jobs that do not repeat or only repeat every so often. In some cases, the work standard may not have times for each step or a range of times for each step. Remember, we can only implement true standardized work where we have constant repeatable operations with little or no variation. This means all tools, materials, supplies, and equipment are ready in their proper locations and in the right amounts necessary and on hand exactly where they will be needed.

In healthcare settings, this is not always possible. No two patients are exactly the same, and since we are generally in the repair business, we can encounter substantial variation between patients and what is required to treat each patient may be different. For example, in the emergency room, some patients may simply need a prescription for an antibiotic while others need a full workup of diagnostic tests and x-rays. In the clinic setting, elderly or immobile patients take longer to process. So, in many cases we have to implement work standards in addition to or as part of standard work. Sequence of operations, SWIP, and/or cycle time may vary. We have often struggled to even get to a work standard because every patient is unique.

Lesson Learned

The Lean tools are a guide and cannot be "cookie-cuttered" into every healthcare application, even from site to site. You have to do what makes sense for the area in which you are working and use the tools appropriate to that area.

EVENTUALLY STANDARD WORK CAN LEAD TO SEMI- OR COMPLETE AUTOMATION[9]

As we standardize work and activities, we can now see opportunities to semi-automate or completely automate tasks. This concept, especially in the United States, is met with resistance. Yet, this is the nature of technological change. People should not have to do mundane, repetitive, boring jobs all day long. If a machine can do it, we should let a machine do it. We cannot let the fact that a person's job may be eliminated get in our way of improving a task. We need to make sure we don't lay anyone off due to continuous improvement and that we invest in re-training those displaced for new or revised jobs. Our experience is jobs can be semi-automated (i.e., using a power screwdriver vs. a manual screwdriver) and realize 80% of the improvement for about 20% of the cost. It normally takes the other 80% of the cost to get 20% more improvement by fully automating tasks. The Shingo chart shows this path from manual to semi-automation to full automation (Figure 6.8).[10]

Lesson Learned

It is not until machines are doing tasks that we can start truly mistake-proofing operations.

LEADER STANDARD WORK

The concept of leader standard work supports the overall system. This means every employee up to and including the CEO has standard work as a basis for their jobs. The work is less standardized the higher one is in the organization. David Mann, in his book *Creating a Lean Culture*,[11] describes "leader standard work" in detail.

---

[9] Shigeo Shingo, *A Study of the TPS From an Industrial Engineering Viewpoint* (Productivity Press) 1989.

[10] Shigeo Shingo, *The Shingo Non Stock Production: The Shingo System for Continuous Improvement* (New York: Productivity Press) 1988.

[11] Mann, *Creating a Lean Culture.*

	Type	Hand Functions				Mental Functions			
		Principal Operations				Marginal Allowances			
		Main Operations		Incidental Operations		(Usual Method)		(Toyota Method)	
Stage		Cutting	Feeding	Installation / Removal	Switch Operation	Detecting Abnormalities	Disposition of Abnormalities	Detecting Abnormalities	Disposition of Abnormalities
1	Manual operation	worker	worker	worker	worker	worker	worker	worker	worker
2	Manual feed, automatic cutting	machine	worker	worker	worker	worker	worker	worker	worker
3	Automatic feed, automatic cutting	machine		worker	worker	worker	worker	Machine that stops automatically (worker oversees more than one machine)	worker
4	Semiautomation	machine	machine	machine		worker	worker	Machine (worker oversees more than one machine)	worker
5	Preautomation (automation with a human touch)	machine	machine	machine		machine	worker	Machine (automation with a human touch)	worker
6	True automation	machine		machine		machine	machine	machine	machine

FIGURE 6.8 Shingo Model of Transition from manual to automated operations. Source: Reprinted from Table 3 on page 71 of *A Study of the Toyota Production System*, by Shigeo Shingo, © 1989 Productivity Inc, PO Box 13390 Portland, OR 97213, 800-394-6868, www.productivyinc.com, with permission.

Whether you are a supervisor or CEO, you may wonder why you need Leader Standard Work. One reason is it truly helps manage your day, and the other is to set an example and role model the behaviors desired from the rest of your organization. It doesn't mean everything is done to the second, but starts to allow the groundwork for *Gemba* walks or "rounding," which used to be called "managing by walking around," and blocks out your calendar so it is done each day. When a leader rounds several times each day they are:

- Checking visual controls
- Attending huddles
- Encouraging improvement suggestions
- Sitting in on a quality circle
- Performing a Five S, standard work, or *Heijunka* audit
- Answers a question from a supervisor with "what do they think they should do"
- Suggests an A3 root cause analysis

It shows the staff that these things are important and reinforces the desired behaviors and helps develop their ability to think.

CAPACITY ANALYSIS—PART PRODUCTION CAPACITY SHEET

Ohno said capacity is equal to work + waste[12]. Throughput time is how long it takes for a patient or product to get through the entire process. It is composed of process time, transport time, and wait times.

Lean has a tool called the part production capacity sheet (Figure 6.9). Once we have analyzed the area, this sheet is the vehicle to pull all the data together. This sheet is described in many books but is well-documented in the book, *Toyota Production System*.[13]

---

[12] Taiichi Ohno, *Toyota Production System, Beyond Large Scale Production* (New York: Productivity Press) 1978.
[13] Yahsiro Monden, *Toyota Production System* (Institute of Industrial Engineering) 2002.

Part Production Capacity Sheet (PPCS)	Available Time (hrs/day)	Available Time (min/day)	Available Time (sec/day)	Customer Demand (units/day)	Takt time (sec)	Factory Demand (units/day + scrap)	Required Cycle Time	Total Labor Time	Number of People Required
Description Histology	24.0	1,440.0	86400	990.0	87.3	990.0	87.3	245.0	2.8

Basic Time   ***Capacity***

Specimen / Work sequence	Manual operation time (sec)	Machine processing time (sec)	Completion time (sec)	Loads per day based on completion time	Max container batch size	Machine container capacity per hour	Max machine capacity per day	SWIP	Number of machines required
Description of process									
Cumulative times	245	33302	33547						
Percentage manual op. and VA time	0.7%	99.3%							
1 Tissue prep	60.0	30,501.0	30,561.0	2.0	150.0	2.0	600.0	350.2	1.7
2 Embed	10.0	21.0	31.0	2,787.0	1.0	1.0	2,787.0	0.4	0.4
3 Cutting	60.00	80.0	140.0	617.0	1.0	1.0	617.0	1.6	1.6
4 Staining	10.0	2,700.0	2,710.0	31.0	30.0	6.0	5,580.0	31.1	0.2
5 Signout	105.0		105.0	822.0	1.0	1.0	822.0	1.2	1.2

FIGURE 6.9 PPCS (part production capacity sheet) histology.

LAYOUT DESIGN

The PFA and WFA help to determine the proposed changes to the product flow and how the operator activities will be improved within the new flow. The point-to-point and spaghetti diagrams help to show how the product flows through the current layout and the challenges the operator experience in the current state. The next analysis peels down one more level to workstation design. It is critical to look at the layout and work station design as part of the process improvement. Most base layouts are generally full of the waste of transportation, which leads to the waste of over production (batching), waste of inventory, and waste of idle time. If the layout is not fixed or the work station design corrected, it may be virtually impossible to achieve the targeted results.

MASTER LAYOUTS

Typically, we recommend companies begin our implementation approach with a pilot area. Once the BASICS tools are implemented, the companies now have an idea of the time and dedication required to pursue this implementation strategy. When the first project is completed, we suggest they put an overall implementation plan together. Part of that plan should be to develop a master layout early on in the process. The advantage of creating this master layout is, as we implement ongoing improvement we can work to begin to move or place the new lines, machines or work stations where they fit in the overall new Lean master layout. We have seen companies save a tremendous amount of time and expense getting their layout right the first time as opposed to moving entire areas multiple times per year. In manufacturing, we utilized this strategy when we purchased companies and moved their manufacturing to our plants. We use the BASICS tools to figure out how to move and transition their batch processes to Lean processes. This forced us to run the new area Lean. Many hospitals will move the batch processes "as is" and then try to Lean them out; however, this requires more space initially and loss of productivity until or if the area is converted over to Lean.

In hospitals, moving areas is very expensive and difficult because of the need for containment and patient safety. The biggest opportunity for Lean master layout development is during a re-design of an area or a totally new hospital or clinic construction.

Lesson Learned

There is an inherent danger in initially value stream mapping only a "sub" process. This danger presents itself in the fundamental concept of the value stream itself. If we only look at one sub level value stream, we are not necessarily seeing the "big picture." This is why it is important to do a high-level value stream map for the overall organization, which depicts how all the individual value streams work together. There should be an executive position in the organization that is always looking at how all the value streams (processes) function and work together and assess improvement opportunities to streamline the overall organization. The master layout should be considered at this level. If individual value streams are working on improvements but are isolated, then, essentially, we are still supporting silos even though they have been "Leaned." Too often we see layouts implemented by well-meaning managers or teams, but because there is no "knowledgeable Lean review," they are not really Lean but still implemented.

CREATIVITY BEFORE CAPITAL

When we begin a process improvement project, we always recommend the concept of "creativity before capital." Money doesn't solve every problem. We can generally make many improvements for no investment or minor expense dollars; however, it has been our experience that most hospital layouts are in need of some type of major construction as part of a Lean project

The best time to design a new layout is when a new building is designed, but most hospitals miss this opportunity because either the hospital or the architect are not aware of Lean layout and work station design principles. This oversight can cost hospitals millions a year in hidden costs.

It is recommended a budget or dedicated "funds" for potential layout or equipment improvements be established and set aside, in the event they are required. If this is not done prior to the start of a project, the approval process may delay the project timeline and, if the funds for the improvement are not approved, it may impact the ability to achieve the outlined results.

The optimization of the layout and work station should be performed in conjunction with the front-line staff for the new process. Leveraging the knowledge of the frontline staff will provide an overall better design and, in addition, help facilitate the adoption of the new process and layout. Remember the change equation, which includes both the "change" and the "acceptance." One can develop a great process change or re-design, but if we do not continually work on the change side of the equation, the result may be zero. The following can impact flow related to layout and work station design.

Lean Layout Design—Configurations—Determining the New Flow for the Area

Most healthcare managers have not been exposed to the concepts widely deployed in manufacturing related to layout design. Understanding these basic design concepts and their benefits and then applying them to healthcare design will provide significant opportunities in process improvement. When reading material related to Lean, particularly in the manufacturing domain, there are references to "cell" or "work cell." This is a foreign term to most healthcare managers. The definition[14] of work cell is the physical or logical arrangement of all resources (people, machines, and materials) associated with the performance of an activity or task. As we discuss layout, we may refer to this cell-related definition. An example of a cell could be the work area that performs all chemistry tests in a large laboratory or the area where all hematology tests are performed, i.e., the "hematology cell." The patient unit on the floor could be referred to on a large scale as a work cell as well.

The main goal in layout design is to design areas that flow and do not contain isolated islands. Figure 6.10 shows three people who cannot flex or help each other out. We see these designs all the time in hospitals. Each of these workstations is an isolated island which prohibits flexing and leads to fractional labor.

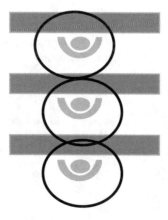

FIGURE 6.10   Layout Isolated Islands. Source: BIG Files.

[14] Businessdictionary.com.

From a workflow perspective, particular "cell" shapes have been identified that facilitate work or process flows. Generally, the shape of a cell is mostly determined by the requirements of the process. Functional layouts may require that the product is moved within the department many times to get processed. For example, the blood sample or test tube is delivered to one spot, dictated by the tube system location in the department, and then "received' adjacent to the tube system, and then transported to another room where it is centrifuged and then another room where the test on the blood sample is performed and resulted. In this example, the operations are isolated by functions, and functions occur in silos. If there are errors in the processing, it is normally difficult to locate where the error occurred. In addition, if there are questions about the sample, communication is hindered by the functions occurring in different areas in isolation.

The staff at the beginning of the laboratory process (receiving end) does not really understand how long it takes from the time the specimen is received until the result is sent because the total process is divided functionally in different rooms or areas of the laboratory. When the processes are located in cells or workspaces that are in sequence and adjacent to each other, the team members understand their part in the total process. We normally find that the most utilized areas are, for some reason, located farthest from the beginning of the process.

The "U-Shaped" Layout

Layouts can be in an L shape, S shape, C shape, etc. Shapes such as A, T, F, E, or R layouts, for example, would contain isolated islands. The U-shaped layout has some advantages over other shapes (Figure 6.11). The main benefit is the ability to share resources. The staff is better able to help each other should the need arise. Communication among the staff is easier, especially between the beginning and end of the process or part of the process that you are trying to improve. Walking distances are shorter and the person can work while they are standing and moving. Staff will be more productive yet potentially feel less fatigued. This layout maximizes the ability to flex the staff across operations. It can be run with one person or multiple persons. If, for example, it is run with three persons, one person could do stations 1, 9 and 10, or 1, 2 and 3. If one person runs 1, 9 and 10 then that person controls the input and output of the area, so we can never start more than we finish.

Materials and supplies are replenished from the outside so there is no interruption to those working inside the area. When building new layouts or work areas, effort should be made to have most of the operations take place in the same area with one team. This facilitates communication, as errors are found and communicated among team members. This motivates team members to problem solve to avoid mistakes. U-shaped layouts do not have to run counter-clockwise. The advantage to counter-clockwise is to those of us who are right-handed. It is important to note that accommodations need to be made for left-handed people, as applicable, especially in work station design.

Materials Replenished from outside the line.
No interruptions to operators.

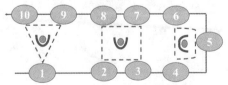

Operators on the inside of layouts ensure
maximum flexibility and teamwork.

FIGURE 6.11   U Shape Layout. Source: RICi Files.

STRAIGHT LINE LAYOUTS

Straight lines or linear layouts allow resources to move down the line sequentially for the process (Figure 6.12). Staff can still flex in a straight line, but the flexing is limited to the operator immediately before or after. The drawback to this layout is that, with one staff member, the travel distance is longer from operation one to operation six; however, the process generally dictates the layout.

PARALLEL LAYOUTS

Parallel layouts are designed with the staff on the inside to facilitate resource sharing as staff can move across to the other parallel line or down the same line (Figure 6.13). Materials and supplies are replenished from outside the work area or cell to minimize interruptions. This layout works well in a high-mix, low-volume environment.

OTHER LAYOUT CONSIDERATIONS

Layout and work station considerations should include baton zones or flex spaces in between work process zones. These areas are located before or after standard work zones in which operators/staff can flex to absorb minor variations in time. From a healthcare perspective, consider the pre-admission testing visit that we will discuss in further detail later. Some patients may require an electrocardiogram (EKG) while others may not, so there can be variation in how one might move a patient through activities that occur during a pre-admission testing visit.

Since all patients are not created equal, one must consider areas where the layout can handle a "back-up." Back-ups are normally patients, and since they represent excess inventory, then the goal should be able to eliminate the backups in the process. Again, consider the pre-admission testing department. If the blood draw/EKG area is short a person, patients may back-up and require chairs in which they have to wait. If the nurses draw blood in the same room where they interview the patients then patients will normally back-up in the pre-admission waiting area.

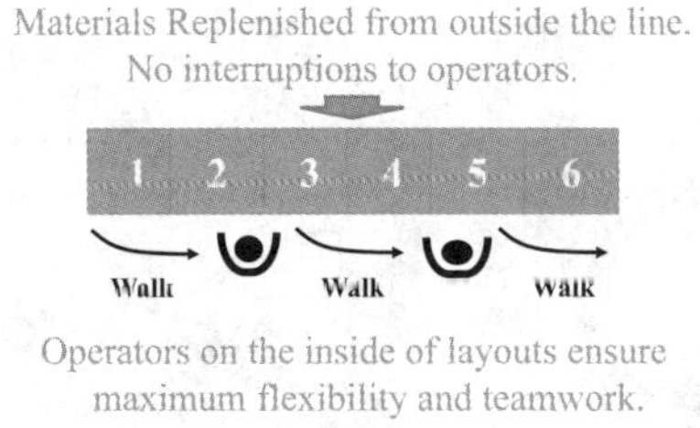

Materials Replenished from outside the line.
No interruptions to operators.

Operators on the inside of layouts ensure
maximum flexibility and teamwork.

FIGURE 6.12   Straight Line Layout. Source: BIG Files.

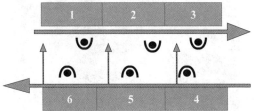

Materials Replenished from outside the line.
No interruptions to operators.

FIGURE 6.13   Parallel Line Layout. Source: BIG Files.

Lean layouts should promote flexible workspace and design. Layout re-designs should result in a decrease in overall space and travel distance needed to perform a task and minimize fractional labor. If the re-design does not save space, then we need to understand the variables that caused the space to increase. In most cases, space increase would be due to changing technologies for new equipment or dramatic increases in projections volume.

GUIDELINES TO LAYOUT RE-DESIGN—NON-NEGOTIABLE

Guideline #1: No isolated islands

Rationale: The golden rule is not to build isolated islands into your layout. Isolated islands are areas where we isolate workers and prohibit flexing. We see this in hospital settings all the time. Isolated islands create the need for fractional labor, which means that a person may only have 50% of their time assigned to a task. They may not be able to be assigned any more duties because they either aren't capable, may not want to do another job, or cannot flex to help someone else out because they are too far away (distance). They may have a barrier that precludes them from flexing; an example of this is the nutritional tray line (Figure 6.14). Notice that the operators (staff) are boxed in by equipment and carts of dishes or food, and the layout prevents them from performing other tasks.

Guideline #2: No or limited use of doors, drawers, and walls

Rationale: Walls are bad! Drawers hide clutter and provide a space for "just in case" supplies, which increase inventory and impact the organization financially by having hidden excess cash in "un-needed" inventory. If cabinets need to be installed, remove the doors. If doors or drawers have to be installed, make them "see through," so when looking for items, they are clearly visible. This will also assist with Five S to de-clutter and keep the area clean.

There will be much resistance to this guideline. Staff and especially supervisors and managers will come up with many reasons for why we need walls, doors, and drawers. They have become accustomed to what they have today and are challenged to make the paradigm shift to an open "shared" environment. The hospital will have to define what a "customer" area is and what it needs.

FIGURE 6.14 Nutritional Tray Line Isolated Islands. Source: BIG Archives.

We have designed many "customer" areas without doors and drawers and we tape out items and areas, where allowed.

We have found that there is seldom a true need for walls, doors, and drawers.

Lesson Learned

Have the courage to challenge conventional guidelines and regulations, as many are antiquated and can be overturned. Some are misinterpretations of regulatory requirements or The American Institute of Architects (AIA) guidelines. There are times when we have had to go to accreditation agencies to get clarifications, additions, or changes to existing guidelines to facilitate Lean designs.

Guideline #3: Flexibility

Rationale: What you are building today may change tomorrow. Build "flexible grids" for water, electric facilitates flexibility and extended use (Figure 6.15). Providing utilities in a grid enables flexibility in future space use. Grid-type layouts allow for "plug and play" air, water, and gas connections. In addition, should you need to move a piece of equipment to another location to improve the flow, or take on a new line of business, it makes sense to change the sequence. Flexible utilities can make the change cost effective. Maintenance should move each piece of equipment with the paradigm "that it can be moved twice as fast the next time." There will be resistance in general to grid utility construction, which can cost more up front but will provide huge savings in future re-designs. Many organizations start projects with limited budgets and have difficulty justifying future cost avoidance measures when they have limited funds available for a basic project.

Guideline #4: OBA Gauge

Rationale: The rule is that racks and partitions should be no higher than four foot, where possible. This is called the "Oba Gauge." A four-foot-tall Japanese Lean sensei named Mr. Oba was notorious for insisting that nothing in the factory be taller than his eye-level. This resulted in the "Oba Gauge" for a visual workplace. The idea is to avoid creating view-blockers in your workplace whenever possible. It is also called the "four-foot rule" or "1.3 meter rule." Five and six foot high cubicle walls and doors create "isolated" islands or silos in work environments. Cubical walls should be no

FIGURE 6.15   Flexible Utilites - Clean Room. Source: BIG Archives.

FIGURE 6.16 Lean Layout-No 5 foot walls, open conference room and offices. Source: BIG Archives.

more than three or four foot high offices to encourage line of sight management (Figure 6.16). Use modular furniture to facilitate ease of movement, cell or work area re-design and configuration. We are seeing more organizations adapt to the use of modular furniture. Use clear glass for offices to encourage open door policies.

Guideline #5: Review layout and work station design for travel distance and "ergonomics," limit reaching, and have staff stand, if possible

Rationale: Travel and motion are non-value-added activities identified as "wastes." They also cause fatigue and impact your workforce, so whenever possible, they need to be eliminated or minimized. Sitting may cause staff to reach unnecessarily and the up and down activity may be more detrimental ergonomically than standing. There will be resistance to "stand and move rather than sit." When staff is provided with the appropriate mechanism, such as padded mats and high counters along with health safety and environmental reviews, we can overcome most, if not all, objections. We have even found when areas are set up for one-piece or one-patient flow and staff members are allowed to sit, they find themselves preferring to stand and walk. This depends solely on what activity they are required to perform and how long they may be standing in one place. If the activity requires a constant up and down movement or someone has to stand in one place for a long period of time (10 or 15 min), then they should sit because standing and not moving is bad for you. Each situation needs to be assessed on an individual basis. Overall, our analysis shows standing and moving in properly designed layouts to be up to 30% more efficient than sitting at one station.

Guideline #6: Staff should be located on the inside of the "work cell" and replenishment should be from the outside

Rationale: Locating staff on the inside facilitates movement of staff as they are able to flex across process steps, promotes resource sharing, and provides shorter travel distances. Replenishing supplies from outside the work cell or area limits interruptions of "cell activity" when supplies are needed.

Guideline #7: The layout should be designed with flow and visual controls in mind

Rationale: Point-to-point diagrams must be constructed for all proposed layouts. These diagrams should include both the flow all products and inbound and outbound materials. Cell layouts should remain constant regardless of the amount of operators (within reason).

Guideline #8: Co-locate executives and office staff on or near the floor or areas with their products/patients

Rationale: How can an executive manage a hospital from a separate building or floor? We need to be co-located on or near the *Gemba*. This aids in assisting any interruption of flow on the line and ensures a quick response to any staff problems.

Guideline #9: Don't plan rework inside a cell

Rationale: If you absolutely must have a rework area, make sure it is painfully visible and that someone is accountable. Statistics on WIP and cash flow, and cost of poor quality (COPQ) for the area should be posted and visible.

Guideline #10: Develop a master layout early on in the project

Rationale: The master layout can be constructed in less than a day but sometimes can take a week or more to get it right. It does not have to be perfect, but will serve as a guide to the core team and a vision to the rest of the organization of how things may look in the future. We typically get it 80%–90% correct the first time.

Guideline #11: Layout approval

Rationale: Establish a Lean layout review board. There should be a Lean layout expert developed at your site with the power to say "no." This person should be thoroughly trained in the Lean principles and be able to offer an explanation and suggestions for layouts that are not acceptable. The layouts should be explained in a meeting to the staff, facilities or engineering department, supervisors, and process owners prior to submittal for approval. Reasonable suggestions, which do not violate the principles, should be incorporated. Be careful with new installations not to add additional workspace if data does not support it. Every time we have added additional workspace that people just had to have, it has resulted in the additional workspace collecting junk. An analogy for this would be the exercise bike which becomes a clothes hanger.

Guideline #12: Housekeeping

Rationale: A place for everything and everything in its place! Each place should be labeled with the equipment name, supply or part name, and location. Consider appointing someone or a team to implement Five S Kaizens frequently and sponsor shredder days or housekeeping days several times a year. Take before and after pictures of each project area. Video a baseline of your entire plant prior to starting Lean improvements.

How Do We Know When the Layout Is Right?

This is a difficult question to answer, but we find it to be somewhat intuitive. You just know when you get it right and when all point-to-point diagrams work and the metrics support it. Some metrics we use are total space, travel distance, minimal distance between consecutive machines, number of operators, inventory, percentage of fractional labor, etc. When the product flows in one direction and never goes backwards, the operator travel is minimized, changeover can be performed quickly, and there is room for expansion, we know the layout is close to being correct. Keep in mind that, as we continue to implement improvements or expand capacity, the layout may need to change. This is why walls are never in the right place and it is important to have work stations and equipment on wheels with quick disconnects, etc., to facilitate easy and ongoing layout changes. As improvements are implemented, most layouts continue to shrink over time. In developing the layout, it is important to separate human work from machine work. Once the layout is in place, we need to immediately implement and audit standard work methods where possible, balance work across all operators, and train and cross-train operators as soon as possible to minimize the number of staff required to support the operation. The layout should provide for standing/walking, moving operations, and have room for SWIP.

WORK STATION DESIGN

We always get frontline staff involved in the work station design. When we watch the videos, we find the staff actually shows us how to set up their work. The goal is to set up standing moving operations where possible. Any good ergonomics and safety person will confirm that moving and walking is better for you than sitting all day. Standing in one place is bad for you. When we set up work stations, we design them for standing up and, if sitting is necessary, we put in "standing height sit down chairs." We want work stations to be as flexible as possible. This means wheels with no hard piping, conduit, or tubing. Work stations need to be safe and ergonomically designed with standing mats. Lean, ergonomics, and safety all work very well together.

We have already discussed the importance of engaging frontline staff, frontline supervisors, and managers in the process of layout and work station design. Often, we find work stations are changed on the fly at every shift change based on how the next employee performs their work. It is critical that the frontline staff is fully engaged in the re-designing of their work stations, as it reinforces acceptance. Once the base layout is determined by re-designing the process flow, each work station or area within the new layout needs to be designed. To do this we will construct a block diagram with each major process having a block. Underneath of it we include the following:

- What supplies are needed?
- What utilities are required, i.e., electric (voltage), gas, air, water, etc.
- What is the placement, order, or sequence of the supplies for each work area or station? and that each is labeled by location.
- What equipment is required? Larger pieces of equipment may tend to drive the overall layout. We call these monuments. One has to take into consideration mechanical and electrical "fit up" requirements like high voltage electrical connections, water lines, air lines, gas lines or venting/ducting requirements. Some equipment when initially considered doesn't take into account other pieces of equipment which may be necessary to support it like manifolds, cooling addons or hydraulic modules.
- What should be near each work station (fax, phones, copiers, etc.)? (Again, the larger layout will drive adjacencies, but remember what may be needed related to support these in the adjacent work areas.)
- What size and amount of supplies are needed?
- How many work stations are needed?
- The cycle time for each block in the diagram.

We recommend team members consisting of frontline staff and supervisor plan out the work station and locate all supplies and needs on the drawing. Work stations should be designed to the product flow (not the operator time). The team needs to decide on quantity and location for inventory and "buffer" or back-up supplies, and discuss the replenishment or restocking of supplies to determine the impact to work station design. If during the process a "collection area" needs to be considered, such as in a laboratory re-design where there may be multiple collection points for specimens within a larger "work cell," discussions should take place to make sure that appropriate locations are built into the work station design. It is recommended that, if multi shifts and staff are sharing work areas, each person on each shift has the opportunity to review the work station re-design and process and that there are standards and audits put in place to ensure compliance.

The list of tools and supplies was documented when we did the work flow operator analysis. When setting up work station designs, we will normally run a pilot with the staff person. We literally go step-by-step, where applicable, lining up their materials and supplies in the proper sequence in order to minimize reaching and excess motions. We then draw an outline around it or tape it out and label it. This is a very time-consuming process that requires much patience by the staff person and the Lean team. Once we get everything in place, we have the operator run the work station and then make adjustments, since operators will normally forget something or something will not be in the right place. When we are comfortable that everything is set up correctly and they have practiced, we will video them and then sit down and review the video. After reviewing the video, we will make other improvements or adjustments as necessary. Once we are satisfied that things are running well, we will look at formally re-designing all the work stations.

There may be cases where we duplicate equipment or supplies on the work stations so that the product keeps moving forward and allows the opportunity for other operators to flex. If we were to set everything up on one work station with the supplies not in the exact order, i.e., we put a fixture in the middle of the work station, this would force the operator to stay in one place, probably sitting, and would not allow anyone else to flex in and help.

STAND UP VS. SIT DOWN STATIONS WITH CHART FLOW

In a pre-testing clinic at Hospital X, we designed a new flow and work station for assembling patients' surgical charts. This involved essentially setting up a line where all the forms were placed on a counter in the order they were assembled. The clerks simply grabbed a hard chart and then picked up and placed each form from the form bins into its proper position in the hard chart. In the current layout, due to the configuration of the nurse work station counter, we could not set up the forms properly so the clerks had to slide their chairs back and forth, and they hated it. Of the three clerks, one had some physical issues that made it difficult to stand up, so she resisted the stand-up operation. We brought in a health, safety, and ergonomics expert who agreed the operation should be "stand up." We ended up suggesting a compromise solution, which was to install a new stand-up height counter, but provided a "stand-up–sit down" chair for the other operator. We have designed lines in the past to accommodate staff with wheelchairs.

Lesson Learned

Standing and walking is normally up to 30% more efficient than sit down operations. We also need to be able to develop solutions that work just as well for our physically challenged individuals.

WORK STATION DESIGN SUMMARY

Work stations do not have to be designed to meet the Takt time as long as operators can flex across the stations. The problem with designing stations to Takt time is that the Takt time may change and then we are faced with changing the work stations every time the Takt time changes. Do we have the right amount of inventory? We need a minimum amount of WIP to meet the Takt time and do it safely. The SWIP at the line or in the area is based on Takt time and the throughput time. Stations are initially designed based on what logically makes sense to build the product or process the patient. Work zones need to be designed for plus or minus two operators based on the number of operators required to meet the current cycle time or Takt time. Stations should be designed to support peak demand with maximum options. The layout should not change based on changing the number of staff. The layout may change based on ongoing improvements. Supplies and tools should be in the exact order of use and should be within reach, even if duplicate supplies are required. Determine appropriate inventory amount required.

As you design your workspace, ask yourself the following questions:

- Do you have doors and drawers as hiding places?
- Is the furniture bolted or is it readily movable?
- What is the state of the infrastructure? If a new piece of equipment had to change location, how difficult or costly would it be to partially re-design the work area?
- Have you calculated the distances that the product and staff need to travel between processes and to get the supplies they need to do their jobs? Where are the staff members located in relation to the flow of the work that needs to be performed? Are there collisions which may occur between staff members or opportunities for products to get mixed up?
- Are there walls or doors impeding flow?
- Can you visually identify bottlenecks with the process?
- Are tasks or processes that occur sequentially located near each other to enable flexing of resources?

MASTER LAYOUTS AND LEAN DESIGN

Lean and Architects

There is a real need for architects to learn Lean because just about every hospital design today is not Lean. Many hospitals ask us to review a new design that is so far along in design stage 4 or 6, (see Table 6.6), that any changes would be impossible owing to the high cost of the changes.

Lessons Learned

Now we ask at what stage the design is in and, if it is in the final stages, we politely refuse to comment. Why? Because at this stage all we will do is frustrate and upset anyone involved in the process unless they are really willing to spend the money on the changes. Lean should enter at stage 1 and latest at stage 2.

When designing buildings with multiple clinics, don't design a central registration area. Registration should be located within each clinic. Central registration areas create bottlenecks and delay patients and ultimately the physicians.

In new buildings or construction, there may have been thought given to layout adjacencies and equipment placement. We have found that, in many instances working with architectural firms in healthcare over the years, the architects believe they have given consideration to equipment placement and process when designing workspace. More often than not, the architects increase space based on volume projections and then apply square foot multipliers to determine the amount of space needed to support the project. Recently, there has been an increase in the number of architectural firms now utilizing Lean principles to help guide their design process, still they may be reluctant to push back when managers and staff ask for "non-Lean" designs. When analyzing the architect's layout, do point-to-point diagrams for every product/patient in the process. Again, the

---

TABLE 6.6

Stages of Design

1. Conceptual development
2. Block Diagram
3. Rough Layout
4. Area Design
5. Initial Schematics
6. Detailed Schematics

---

overarching goal is to provide a flexible work area and work station designs to be able to adapt to future needs and provide an environment conducive to continuous improvement.

DO WE REALLY NEED TO ADD MORE ROOMS OR SPACE?

Most hospitals underestimate the need for Lean design. The first question asked should be if we really need to add rooms or space. In the pre-Lean environment, the need for additional rooms, which appear to be required, may, in fact, not be needed once the Lean project is completed.

At Hospital X, we were working on Leaning a laboratory, both core and non-core (Figure 6.17). The architects were told the laboratory expected to double its output over the next 3 years. So what did the architects do? They doubled the floor space for both laboratories. Once they doubled the floor space, there was no longer room for both laboratories on the same floor. As a result, the decision was made to move the non-core laboratory offsite to a two-story building. By the end of our Lean laboratory project, we were able to reduce the architect's footprint for the core laboratory by close to 30% and the non-core laboratory by the same margin. In addition, both laboratories could have remained on the same floor. But since the new building was so far along, they continued down that path. By moving the non-core laboratory to another building, a whole set of additional waste was created.

Lessons Learned

When we do need more space or rooms? It is important to Lean out the processes first and then, and only then, make changes to the layout. It is important to remember that each layout needs to be as flexible as possible. Hard piping, hard walls, and immovable equipment, are bad, as are centralized nursing stations, materials, and supplies. To the extent possible, we need grid work in

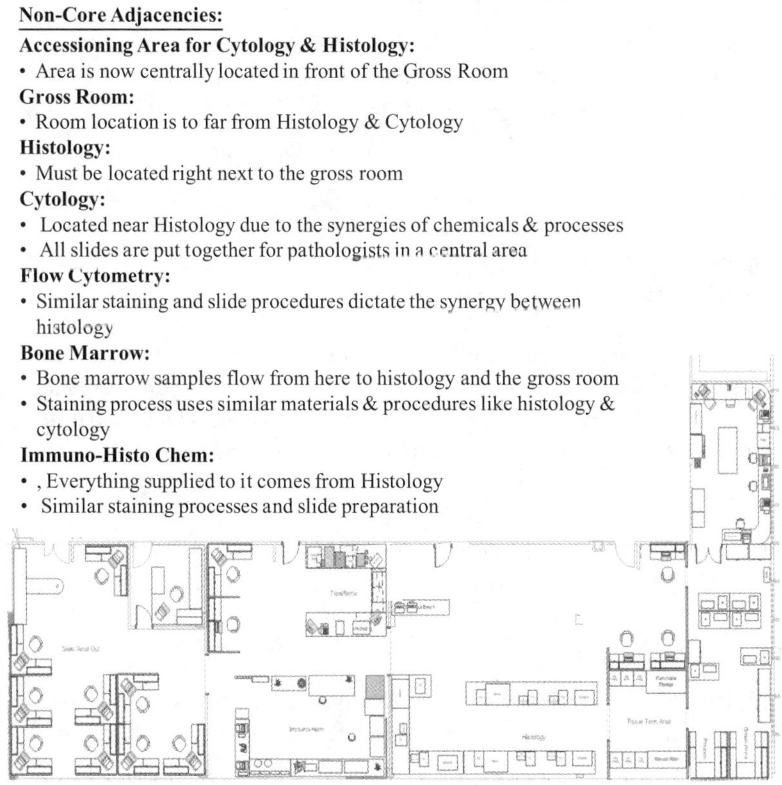

Non-Core Adjacencies:

Accessioning Area for Cytology & Histology:
• Area is now centrally located in front of the Gross Room

Gross Room:
• Room location is to far from Histology & Cytology

Histology:
• Must be located right next to the gross room

Cytology:
• Located near Histology due to the synergies of chemicals & processes
• All slides are put together for pathologists in a central area

Flow Cytometry:
• Similar staining and slide procedures dictate the synergy between histology

Bone Marrow:
• Bone marrow samples flow from here to histology and the gross room
• Staining process uses similar materials & procedures like histology & cytology

Immuno-Histo Chem:
• , Everything supplied to it comes from Histology
• Similar staining processes and slide preparation

FIGURE 6.17 Lean Master Layout – Non-Core. Source: BIG Files.

the ceiling so utilities can plug and play. This may be more expensive up front but saves significant dollars in the future.

LAYOUTS DRIVE WASTE IN THE FORM OF INCREASED LABOR COSTS—CONSIDER ADJACENCIES

Next to the batching mindset, and sometimes because of it, layouts are the biggest driver of the 8 wastes. It is amazing to see how much waste can be built into a layout. How does this happen? While some architects may consider the flow, most don't. They tend to put things where the customer wants them and then work to make everything else fit, which doesn't always mean it flows.

When isolated islands are designed, we end up paying for the fractional labor of that person who then ends up being idle. There is not a cost for this in the architect's proposal. A significant amount of thought is provided from the implementing department; however, many times there is not much thought given to how the new design may impact other departments.

Layouts should be designed to support the overall flow of the support area, clinic, or hospital. Overall flow is just as important—if not more important—than the flow within a department. Hospitals need to be thought of as a system with many departments and information flows interacting all the time.

Hospital X asked us to design a new hospital ED with Lean tracks but then decided not to Lean out the ED in the existing hospital. We advised them that if they did not implement Lean in the existing ED, there is no way they would be able to run it when they moved to the new Lean ED design. The new Lean area would run much worse with the old processes, if at all.

Lesson Learned

The hospital must be prepared to run Lean if they are going to design Lean. One cannot design a Lean hospital and run it with the old batch-driven systems!

For example, when designing an ED, we need to consider the location of radiology and laboratory in the master layout. Ideally, we would build these areas into our ED layout. If this is not possible, they should be considered when viewing adjacencies.

Layouts should:

- Minimize travel distance and excess walking
- Avoid isolated islands and support flexing
- Include point of use storage
- Incorporate IT systems at point of use

EDs are one of the two main front doors of your hospital. The other front door is the routine entrance for surgery patients and visitors. It may also be the door to your outpatient facilities and services (i.e., pharmacy). The ED should have a front door for patients and a separate door for ambulances. One may want to consider separate entrances for outpatient radiology or laboratory testing.

Lesson Learned

If you are going to compete with stand-alone outpatient facilities, you have to offer similar parking and easy access as the outpatient facility.

SOME PRACTICAL EXAMPLES OF LEAN DESIGNS

Surgery should have admitting (registration) as part of the waiting area or be able to provide the functions of registration at the surgery area to eliminate the step of going to registration.

- The waiting area should be on the same floor as surgery or preferably adjacent to the surgical area.

- Sterile processing and materials should be located on the same floor as surgery, Pre-Op, and PACU.
- Surgery should form a U-shaped. Unless designing encapsulated surgery flows, i.e., individual surgery tracks, then Pre-Op and PACU should be adjacent so resources can be shared.
- The ideal surgical layout would have all rooms the same (universal). For cost and practicality reasons this is not always possible. Otherwise, assign rooms geographically by family-based demand.
- Surgical suites should have cores in between where materials and equipment can be stored based on the families of rooms located within the core.
- There should be pass-through access to enable restocking of materials without having to enter the rooms.
- There should be a clean and a dirty side, with an entrance for patients and an entrance for staff.
- Each room should have point-of-use materials and equipment (based on the group tech matrix).
- Consider adding induction rooms so anesthesia can prepare the patient prior to surgery. One room can be shared between two ORs.

NURSING FLOORS

When designing nursing floors, one should consider adding point-of-use material storage in the room or, worst case, immediately outside the room. Many hospitals are already doing this. Remember centralized storage areas; whether they are for materials, nursing station, medications, etc., bring the "centralized" waste along with them.

Large centralized nursing stations, in general, are "waste attractors." We have to travel to them and we socialize at them. Many hospitals are moving to smaller point-of-use nursing stations or getting rid of them altogether in favor of in-room or room-side charting. These are often called "pods." Open units so staff and readily move throughout and across the unit where ever possible.

ICU floors should be close to surgery. Patient floors can be grouped by service line, where possible.

OTHER DESIGN CONSIDERATIONS

Surgery should be near the ED in case an emergent surgery is required, especially in level 1 or 2 trauma hospitals. Laboratories should be near both the ED and pre-testing areas, or have point of service testing available. Radiology may be divided between inpatient and outpatient. If there is a high outpatient volume, it should have an outside entrance. It should also be located near the surgery pre-testing unit. Demand should drive location of the radiology areas. All layouts should allow for the process owner and staff to be located in or near the area.

LEAN AND REGULATORY ENVIRONMENT

In Lean designs, you must be willing to challenge the convention. We have had instances where we had to go back to regulatory bodies, like the Joint Commission on the Accreditation of Healthcare Organizations (JCAHO)[15] or the State Agency for Health Care Administration (AHCA),[16] and have

---

[15] What is JCAHO? The Joint Commission on the Accreditation of Healthcare Organizations sets standards for healthcare organizations and issues accreditation to organizations that meet those standards. JCAHO conducts periodic on-site surveys to verify that "an accredited organization substantially complies with Joint Commission standards and continuously makes efforts to improve the care and services it provides."

[16] About the Agency for Health Care Administration (AHCA): "This Agency was statutorily created by Chapter 20, Florida Statutes as the chief health policy and planning entity for the state. We are primarily responsible for the state's $16 billion Medicaid program that serves over 2.2 million Floridians, the licensure of the state's 36,000 health care facilities and the sharing of health care data through the Florida Center for Health Information and Policy Analysis. Our mission is Better Health Care for All Floridians."

them approve our designs. We occasionally come up with rooms that don't necessarily fit existing criteria. For example, EDs had provisions for examination rooms and waiting rooms (non-patient care area), but did not have a classification for the "observe care" area we created. This was where patients who were waiting for test results or, in essence, didn't need a formal bed or room, could wait and have limited care as needed until all the tests and results were complete. Patients were monitored but they were not in an actual room. If care was given, it was provided in a room attached to the area. There was no criteria for this in the AIA, AHCA or JCAHO guidelines.

EXAMPLE: CLINIC VISIT

Scenario #1

Let's examine the process of the clinic visit, which would include the following components: having blood work drawn (laboratory testing), EKG, x-ray, consent signed, and medical history taken. The goal would be to have all this completed with preliminary results from the laboratory tests back within 85 min, before the patient leaves, in case additional laboratory tests are needed. This ensures that the patient does not have to make a return visit.

In this example, an appropriate layout or design can significantly impact the clinic's ability to achieve this result (Table 6.7). These are the average times for the steps at a high level. If the current process was done in this order, without reference to how long each of the activities needed to be performed, they would never be able to achieve their goal of 85 min. This excludes looking at the eight wastes and the activity and time between each process step, like the travel between clinical areas or laboratory specimens, which have to get transported to another location for processing.

Scenario #2

If we just reorder the "line" of work, we can get closer to our overall goal. The example in Table 6.8 illustrates that, conceptually, a healthcare process can be the same as an assembly line's activities linked together to achieve a customer result. This example did not go into the detail of the transport or co-location of services and adjacencies of departments in order to achieve maximum throughput and minimum cycle time. It did provide a very simple view of how looking at one process can be performed linearly while the steps in two different sequences can provide different end results. By moving the laboratory draw up to step #3 in the process, it enabled "parallel" processing of the remaining activities that had to occur to meet the goal of 85 min.

This would be very easy to do if this were the only component that impacted a customer going through a process; however, there are many variables that influence a process, such as hourly demand and the number of patients or services being provided.

Using the example above, what if the specimens were not taken immediately to the process area or the laboratory test ran in "batches" and the specimen had to "wait" for the next batch cycle to run? These may be items the clinic process may have not considered when setting the original goal. In using average cycle times, you may end up with significant variability from average

TABLE 6.7
Clinic Steps Before

Steps	Time (min)	Cumulative Time
Enters the clinic, signs in	1	1
Patient Registration (demographic and financial)	8	9
Medical History Taken	25	34
Consent Signed	5	39
EKG Taken	10	49
X-Ray Taken	30	79
Laboratory Draw (results take 70 min)	6	85
Lab Results Received	70	155
Total Goal = 85 min		155

TABLE 6.8
Clinic Steps After

Steps	Time (min)	Cumulative Time		
Enters the clinic, signs in	1	1		
Patient Registration (demographic and financial)	8	9		
Laboratory Draw (results take 70 min)	6	15	Lab Results Time Starts Here	
Medical History Taken	25	40		25
Consent Signed	5	45		30
EKG Taken	10	55		40
X-Ray Taken	30	85		70
Lab Results Received		85		
Goal = 85 min				

process time (yielding a large standard deviation) in results when you do not fully understand what is going on in "interdepartmental or between process work cells." There may be downstream opportunities to improve as you go beyond the area over which you have control. In order to optimize the process flow, the following are criteria required as you look at your process re-design.

RATE COMPANIES ON THE ABILITY TO SUSTAIN CONTINUOUS IMPROVEMENT.[17] PLAN FOR EVERY PART—AMOUNT OF SUPPLIES/INVENTORY NEEDED

The plan for every part (PFEP) provides a mechanism to track and determine the supplies needed, current demand, and the current state inventory information. We need to know where they are located, how many will be replenished, and a buffer plan to ensure that supplies will be available to meet peak demand. While many of us have created Lean materials spreadsheets in the past, they didn't seem to have an official name until the book, *Making Materials Flow*, was published.[18] The PFEP can be created manually, but is easier to manipulate in an Excel spreadsheet. The PFEP involves literally listing every single part used in the process or area. Then we look at each part to determine the lead time, daily quantity required, days of supply on hand, safety stock, and appropriate Kanban sizes. This rather large spreadsheet is dynamic and needs to be maintained at some frequency in most areas because volume or mix of cases can change, thereby impacting the minimum, maximum, and reorder quantity levels. The charge nurses or service team leader should have the final say on the minimum, maximum, and reorder quantities.

How many "quantity" at the work station "at the right place" is generally based on the demand for the supply, how long it takes to replenish it, supplier minimum ordering size, supplier quality issues, and demand variation, which create a beta or risk factor associated with re-supplying the part. We generally add a small buffer of supplies called safety stock to cover this risk.

Each clinical area should understand what it is that they have in the way of inventory of supplies, and how much they use based on their demand (daily). In addition, for each supply, they should understand the replenishment process from the supplier, including how it is supplied to them (i.e., by box and the number in the box or the unit) and the lead time to obtain additional supplies, which will impact the minimum, maximum, and reorder point of each type of supply required.

The amount of supplies and bins or containers and the size of the equipment or supply bins will determine the size and number of shelves which impact the layout. We need to "right size" the bins

[17] Richard Schonberger, *World Class Manufacturing: The Next Decade* (New York: The Free Press) 1996.
[18] Rick Harris, *Making Materials Flow* (Cambridge, MA: Lean Enterprise Institute) 2006.

or containers which supplies are utilized to the actual demand. If the containers or bins are too large, the tendency will be to overstock the bins. This can lead to organizational cash flow issues, due to money being tied up in excess inventory. In addition, over-ordering and over-stocking raises the potential to purchase supplies that will only become expired.

All shifts should have input into the work station layout and design. This sounds simple; however, there can be a significant amount of "change management" with the people component involved. In addition, there are techniques utilized in Lean to help sustain work station design, such as labeling and outlining, where supplies and equipment should be located to provide visual cues when equipment is misplaced. Supplies that are needed all the time should be at point of use. Supplies needed once a day can be further away and supplies used once a week or month further away still.

LABELING

Labeling of supplies and where they are placed, such as shelves and bins, is important (Figure 6.18). The front of the bins should have the bin location and the quantity and description of the supplies in the bin. Labeling is an important part of visual controls and is a critical component when implementing Lean initiatives, to help eliminate the waste for searching.

KANBAN

Kanban (watch over a board), where kan, (literal—watch over a board for a period until one) is a concept related to Lean and Just-In-Time (JIT) production. Kanbans facilitate inventory supply replenishment. The Japanese word Kanban is a common term meaning "signboard" or "billboard." According to Taiichi Ohno, the man credited with developing JIT, Kanban is a means through which JIT is achieved.[19]

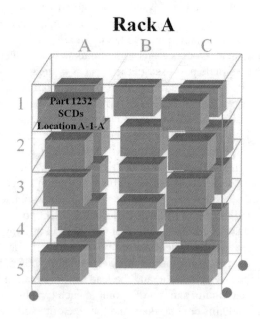

FIGURE 6.18 Rack Labeling Example of how to label a specific location on a shelf on a rack. Source: BIG Files.

---

[19] http://dict.regex.info Japanese to English dictionary, http://www.saiga jp.com Kanji to English.

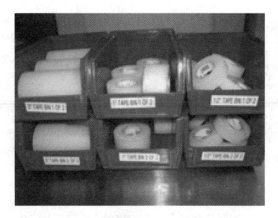

FIGURE 6.19 Two-bin Kanban system example: Operators take from top bin first. An empty bin signals replenishment needed. Drawback to this setup is operators can draw from both bins and could have FIFO issues when second bin is returned. Source: BIG Archives.

The purpose of a Kanban system is to control the flow of material by providing inventory as a buffer in order to synchronize two disconnected processes. Because Kanbans are inventory, we need to constantly work to minimize the amount of materials. A Kanban trigger or signal can be an empty space, an empty bin, a piece of paper, an electronic signal (lights, electronic data interchange), or an icon (e.g., rolling golf balls down a tube).

A Kanban is a signal designed to trigger an event. The term Kanban is used not only to describe the system, but also the individual bins or cards in the system. A Kanban card or empty bin can signal the need for the material to be replenished or it can serve as an order for production to begin in order to replenish the parts. The simplest type of Kanban is called a two-bin system (Figures 6.19 and 6.20). A two-bin system is composed of two separate bins containing the same parts, with one bin placed behind the other. When the first bin empties, the bin is removed and the second bin, full of parts, slides down into its place. The empty bin is now the Kanban, or signal to replenish it. Kanban is similar to the re-supply of milk when the milkman would take your empties and replace them with full bottles. We utilize a material hander (sometimes called a water spider) to replenish the bins.

The Kanban system can be a one-bin system as well, if the parts are replenished every day (Figure 6.21). Normally in a one-bin system, the bins are refilled to the top, as one might refill bread

FIGURE 6.20 Two-bin system operator draws from first bin then 2nd bin slides down. The first bin is the signal to replenish. Operators could still draw from second bin but this bin setup is more clear. Source: BIG Archives.

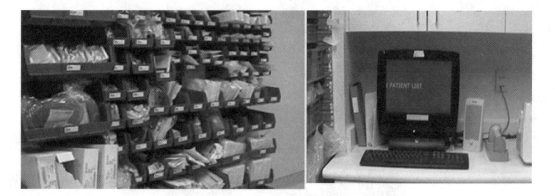

FIGURE 6.21 One bin system with terminal. Supplies are replaced nightly based upon POS system. Source: BIG Archives.

in a store. This is called a "breadman" system. In some areas, the nurses scan into a terminal the quantity of supplies taken. This information is immediately passed to the stockroom or supplier as data for replenishment. This is called a point of sale system. Another way to trigger replenishment would be a water level line drawn or painted in the bin. When the parts go below the line, then it needs to be replenished.

WHAT PARTS DO WE KANBAN?

Kanban systems are sometimes referred to as supermarkets since they were the premise for the idea. The simplest way is to consider any part for Kanban that has a consistent demand over a user-defined period. This may be daily, weekly, monthly, or sometimes even quarterly. Parts that are specially ordered or ordered once a year are normally not good candidates.

CONSTANT TIME OR CONSTANT QUANTITY

Kanbans can be replenished in two ways. Constant time means they are replenished the same time each day or several times a day. This is referred to as a "breadman" type replenishment, which is similar to grocery store shelves being restocked each night (Figure 6.22). Constant quantity may empty out at any time, but we refill it with the same quantity every time.

FIGURE 6.22 Supermarket Replenishment System. Source: BIG Archives.

There are many components to consider in creating lean workflow. It is important to understand how to leverage and integrate the different analysis tools. The application of lean concepts and tools can help you optimize your flow and help you move from your current to future state.

In summary, we have described how you can leverage the data collected and information obtained through deploying key Lean tools to enable you to manage by fact, and move from your current to future state to design and implement and improve your process.

7 Implementing Lean in a Healthcare Environment

HOW TO IMPLEMENT LEAN METHODOLOGY

You can do it to them or with them. We would rather do it WITH them than to them.

We are now into the implementing phase of the BASICS model (Figure 7.1). To recap, we have baselined the project, assessed the project, and developed and suggested solutions. We typically report out to the senior leadership team. The report outs can be held after each phase (letter in the BASICS model) or based on agreed up-front milestones in the team charter. Some hospitals call these report outs "tollgate or phase gate reviews."

This chapter deals with the implementation of the new layout, workstations, and materials piece explained in earlier chapters. We are also going to discuss Five S, visual controls, and mistake proofing, along with the checking and sustaining phases of the BASICS model. Part of sustaining is ongoing Kaizen and we will discuss the differences between Kaizen and Point Kaizen events in detail later in the chapter.

THE LEAN SYSTEM IMPLEMENTATION—ARE YOU READY FOR IT?

Do you have a compelling need to change your organization? Do you have a burning platform? Do you have a fundamental dissatisfaction with how things are done today and the waste that is prevalent in all your processes? Are you willing to get the entire organization involved, including your board of directors? If so, then you are ready. If not, in the long run, you will not be successful. Remember: 40% to 80% of companies do not sustain the Lean journey.

WHAT TYPE OF COMMITMENT IS REQUIRED?

We tell companies that Lean is a minimum 5 year commitment that never ends! It is a journey, not a "quick fix" solution. It requires resources, a plan, and an unwavering commitment. We recommend budgeting up-front for Lean and paying for it with savings.

The term "project" is somewhat of a misnomer with Lean, in that the word "project" has an ending connotation to it. Technically, once we end a Lean project, we are really just beginning the improvement that is necessary for the area, process, or changes to the overall system being implemented.

Implementing Lean changes is not always easy. While it is important to coach and motivate to help these people buy in, it is not worth spending all your time on the 10% or so who will refuse to change. Taiichi Ohno ran into the same problem when he first started implementing his new system. In his book, *The Toyota Production System*, Ohno states that one has to "Use your authority to encourage them."[1] "When he (Ohno) introduced Kanbans to the Toyota production process, he was forced to resort to holding his position against many complaints from his foremen to his boss. He had to rather forcefully urge his foreman to go along with the system resulting in a number of

---

[1] Taiichi Ohno, *Toyota Production System* (New York: Productivity Press) 1988.

Phases

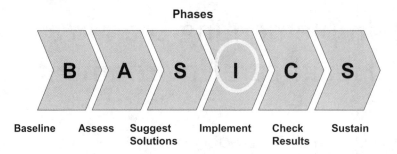

| Baseline | Assess | Suggest Solutions | Implement | Check Results | Sustain |

FIGURE 7.1   BASICS Model–Implementation Phase. Source: BIG.

complaints that he was doing something ridiculous and should be stopped. Fortunately the top manager trusted him and told him not to stop."[2]

By sticking with his new system, he eventually introduced it company-wide, even though it was not a smooth transition. Had top management not backed Ohno, the system we know as Kanban today probably would not exist. This passage from Ohno's book, *The Toyota Production System, Beyond Large Scale Production*, now considered the "Father of the Toyota Production System," supports the notion that top management must change its way of thinking, make a commitment, and show strong support for Lean if it is to be successful.

Lesson Learned

Whenever implementing Lean, people are going to resist changes. As leaders you have to hang in there and support the changes, and maybe even for a period of time, "brute force" the changes, until the new culture "sticks."

What Is *Kaikaku*?

Kaikaku, 改革, reform or reorganization.[3] It is a term noted in Jim Womack's book, *Lean Thinking*,[4] and is the subject of a book of the same name. In the book, *Kaikaku*,[5] it is described as "A great transformation in awareness and in actual business. It is a large fundamental change of policy, practice or awareness."[6]

Kakushin[7]

Kakushin 革新 is a serious blossoming improvement plan, defined as revolutionary change driven by the leadership including at board level. An example would be in 2006, Toyota was even questioning its basic Kaizen approach. The result was the initiative by then CEO Mr. Watanabe to cut the number of components in their car by half. This was on top of the 2004 initiative to improve 173 system components and to cut procurement costs by 30%.[8]

The BASICS approach we use to transform cultures from batch to Lean described in this book is a different implementation approach than the Point Kaizen approach. It is more along the lines of the *Kakushin* and *Kaikaku* approach, utilizing Lean system implementations or what some call System Kaizen. When converting processes from batch to flow, we use the BASICS tools described

---

[2] Taiichi Ohno, *Toyota Production System* (New York: Productivity Press) 1988.
[3] http://dict.regex.info Japanese to English dictionary, http://www.saiga-jp.com Kanji to En.
[4] James Womack and Dan Jones, *Lean Thinking* (Simon and Schuster), 1996. www.lean.org.
[5] Norman Bodek, *Kaikaku* (PCS Press) 2004.
[6] Norman Bodek, *Kaikaku* (PCS Press) 2004.
[7] http://dict.regex.info Japanese to English dictionary, http://www.saiga-jp.com Kanji to En.
[8] "Evolving Excellence," December 2006, http://www.evolvingexcellence.com/blog/2006/12/toyota question.html.

in the earlier chapters in order to assess and improve the entire system. Then we use Kaizen (ideas from the floor) and Point Kaizen events to sustain and drive continuous improvement. The goal is to create a culture within the hospital where most of the improvement suggestions emanate from the staff on the floor and giving supervisors and managers time to implement the improvements.

When we do Point Kaizen events, we do them a little differently than traditional Kaizen blitzes, in that we continue to use the "ready-aim-fire" approach vs. the typical point Kaizen approach of "ready-fire-aim." We pick an area to improve, assemble a team, video and analyze it, and then make improvements. We get more proficient in the tools the more we utilize them. In some cases, on smaller projects, we can get through all the necessary BASICS tools in a day or less.

IMPORTANCE OF LEAN PILOTS

We recommend using Lean pilots. We start off with small pieces within the project, apply the Lean tools and work out the "kinks" and test the change prior to converting the entire area. A phased approach gives everyone time to voice their opinions and secure the necessary staff buy-in from the area. We also suggest involving the engineering/maintenance and health safety and environmental departments on the team full time or part time.

KEEP THE OWNERSHIP WITH THE LINE ORGANIZATION

The real key to implementing and sustaining Lean is to create a "PULL" for Lean from the top. The CEO needs to set goals and expectations for the line organization, which can only be met by implementing Lean. It is important to keep the ownership with the process owner and not let it fall to the Lean team. The Lean team can unknowingly take the ownership by simply doing the charter or doing the scheduled report outs. These tasks must stay with the line owners in order to be successful.

LEAN IMPLEMENTATION OBJECTIONS AND RETAIL SALES TECHNIQUES

OBJECTIONS ARE GOOD!

Many feel that if they object or want to discuss proposed Lean ideas, they will be perceived as negative. This couldn't be more off target, because we need people to ask the difficult questions. Just because people ask difficult questions does not mean they are negative. But once the questions are answered, are they on board with the changes?

To start the discussion, one needs to understand the true nature of an "objection." There are three answers that one encounters when trying to sell an idea: yes, no, or the objections, i.e., what about this or that?

Remember, if someone objects to an idea, they have not said "no." Objections come from our paradigms that we discussed earlier. Objections are actually a way for the person to try to buy in to the change. If one can satisfactorily answer all the objections, they get the sale. Therefore, we look forward to objections. When someone does say "no," one normally responds with "why?" The question "why" is designed to solicit the objection. Once we have the objection, we must work to overcome it. Sometimes it can be overcome quickly, while other times it may take training, a series of long discussions, or showing the person an example of where their objection was overcome, i.e., benchmarking. Some of us just need to see it to believe it. Once we see it, there is no stopping us from going after it. Once we overcome all the objections, we need to go for the "close."

Lesson Learned

It is key that each objection is individually addressed or you will not be able to gain complete buy-in or closure.

Types of Closing Questions

There are several closing processes taught in retail sales. Some of them are:

The direct close
The indirect close
The positive negative close
The assumed close

These techniques work with change management as well because we are trying to "sell the change," or in this case, "Lean," to the organization. Let's explore the different types of closes. It is important to remember that in selling once a closing question is asked; "He who speaks first loses". You must wait for the person to answer.

The *direct close* is simply asking the person if they are willing to go along with the change. Then be silent until they answer.

The *indirect close* is accomplished by answering an objection. It goes something like this… The customer found a tile they liked. I asked if they liked the tile. They said they did but wanted it to be "no wax." The response was, "So if I were to tell you it was 'no wax' you would take it with you tonight?" They said yes, I said yes, and we closed the sale.

The *positive negative* close is taking into consideration what a customer initially states is a key characteristic they are seeking. For example, I had a customer that stated as soon as I met them that they wanted a tile that had to be glued to the floor. We looked at several tiles and they found one they liked. My closing question was, "Well, it's a great tile and will work perfectly for you based on all the criteria you need. The only problem is you have to glue it!" Well, the customer looked at me like I was an idiot and said. "But that's what I want. I want one that needs gluing." I said, "Oh, alright then" and wrote up the sale.

I used this in healthcare. I was told by a manager that they wanted to implement Lean in the emergency department (ED) so they could increase their volume. When we were done touring the area and talking with the staff in the area, I said my assessment is that Lean would work very well in their area but he needed to understand that if they implemented Lean, he needed to be careful because word of their improvements would get out and spread. I showed him data to prove we had seen an initial 10% bump in initial volume each time we improved the ED processes. He said, "That's not a problem for us; that's what we want!" I said OK and we implemented Lean in their ED; they saw a 10% bump in volume with an empty waiting room for the first time, even after their waiting time which used to be at 2 a.m.

The *assumed close* is accomplished by just starting to write up the sale. While writing up the order, it is not uncommon to hear the husband and wife saying, "Are you happy with it? Are you sure you want it?" They agree they want it and sign on the bottom line.

These same closing techniques can be utilized in selling the change you desire and help overcome the resistance to change. The most important thing to remember is that most of us are only good at selling something we really believe in. When someone does object to implementing Lean in their area, the first thing we try to ascertain is the objection. If the objection is that it is "going to make my job more difficult," our response might be, "so what you are saying is, if we could show you how it would make your job easier, you would buy in to the change? OK, let's show you how it will make it easier to do your job in the long run." Once the discussion is complete, we are ready for the closing question: "so now that we have shown how much easier your job will be to manage in the new Lean environment, are you willing to work with us on the change?" Then be silent because he who speaks first loses.

Lesson Learned

Don't badger. Sell your case based on data and facts, not what other people think. Be confident, believe and be passionate in your responses, back them up with data and past results, answer the objections, and close the sale!

GENERAL OVERARCHING LEAN IMPLEMENTATION TIPS

- Get all the employees involved in the process. Make it fun. Five S contests, Spaghetti mapping by each other, keeping track of the person with the most travel distance etc.
- Treat people like people—we can't emphasize this rule enough!
- Encourage, Communicate and Engage staff throughout the process.
- Gain empathy to understand the challenges (this is a critical step to get the the "right solutions!").
- Listen, Listen, Listen to employees and patients who are captive in your processes.
- Do Gemba walks - go to the actual place and see for yourself.
- Design out the frustrations and barriers.
- Link changes to empathy received from patients and staff.
- Work really hard to keep it simple.
- Manage by exception wherever possible.
- If you can't do it all at once… phase it in.
- Pareto rule (80%…. 20%….). The Pareto[9] principle normally applies to Lean implementations. Focus on the 80% you can impact and save the 20% to work on later.
- Skeptics are good, cynics are bad. We encourage skeptics. After all, they keep us honest. Cynics are convinced it will never work, thus anything you do will be wrong. If you can turn a cynic, they become zealots, but it takes a tremendous investment in time but they can become your best sales people.
- Leverage your informal leaders as they can significantly influence your ability to achieve buy-in and acceptance.
- Naysayers are not always against you. Many times, they just honestly believe it won't work. It is OK to be negative as long as they are not cynical. We can normally bring them along once the new process is up and running and they physically see it working.
- Dedicate as many resources as possible. We find that each person you can dedicate to improvement pays for themselves ten times over. In the long run, we need to free up 50% of our supervisor and managers' time to implement improvements.
- Always start closest to the customer. This rule has never failed us, but it is somewhat counterintuitive. People say that if the sub-process isn't working, then the final process closest to the customer won't work. While this might be true, by acting on the later process we create the true pull requirements for the earlier process. If you attack the earlier process first, then all you do is bottleneck the process prior to the later process.
- Demand, Takt, flow, balance (flex), standardize, improve.
- It's not unusual to find that what you think is the bottleneck, is not the bottleneck. People only think they know where the problem is until they study and analyze the root cause of it.
- No one should lose their job directly due to continuous improvement.
- Don't try to do everything at once. Prioritize and stay focused. This does not mean you can't multitask, but too many projects at once can be a recipe for disaster.
- Don't waste too much time on concrete heads (batchards). Give them some time and coach them to buy in, but in the end, you may have to find a new home for them—in or out of the company.

---

[9] http://en.wikipedia.org/wiki/Pareto_principle. The Pareto principle (also known as the 80–20 rule, the law of the vital few, and the Principle of Factor Sparsity) states that, for many events, roughly 80% of the effects come from 20% of the causes. Business management thinker, Joseph M. Juran, suggested the principle and named it after Italian economist Vilfredo Pareto, who observed in 1906 that 80% of the land in Italy was owned by 20% of the population. It is a common rule of thumb in business, e.g., "80% of your sales come from 20% of your clients." Mathematically, where something is shared among a sufficiently large set of participants, there must be a number k between 50 and 100 such that $k\%$ is taken by $(100 - k)\%$ of the participants. k may vary from 50 (in the case of equal distribution) to nearly 100 (when a tiny number of participants account for almost all of the resource). There is nothing special about the number 80% mathematically, but many real systems have k somewhere around this region of intermediate imbalance in distribution.

TEAM CHARTERS

Team charters are a necessary tool prior to starting any project. Team charters include entry and exit strategies, budgets, and detailed scopes. They are contracts with the teams, implementing department, and the leadership or steering committee.

At Hospital X, Bill, the Lean specialist, was working with his second clinic. The first had been very successful and was even toured by other hospitals. As the second clinic kicked off, Bill met with the leadership to review the charter his team had prepared. The leadership took the position that they had already done one clinic and there was no need for a formal charter for the second team. How wrong they were! About 3 to 4 weeks into the project, the team champion/sponsor was on vacation for several weeks. During this time, certain members of the team took over, alienated Bill and ostracized him from the management meetings. Meanwhile, the clinic leadership team decided they wanted no part in the changes and the effort stalled. Because there was no charter (the result of an uncommitted leadership team), there was no escalation plan. As problems surfaced, the team started "in-fighting." It was further complicated by a new hire whose job was to project manage (micro-manage) the team. The project manager was not familiar with Lean or Six Sigma. Instead of meeting with Bill and learning the Lean implementation process, the project manager met with the team and laid down his rules and how his project was going to run. The 2nd project became a total failure.

Lessons Learned

The significance of the team charter is not just to provide a road map for the team, but also to create a "pull" for the team, provide a structured approach for leadership interventions, and create a vehicle for leadership to follow-up and sustain during and after the initial implementation.

The charter is a symbol of management commitment and provides an escalation process and ultimate ownership for the team and its results in the event that they run into any resistance to change.

Guidelines for the Supervisor

- Be a leader and lead the work area.
- Create an atmosphere that encourages adherence to standard work.
- Run the daily team meeting/huddle.
- Make timely and effective decisions.
- Be able to prioritize and delegate.
- Be the role model for the work area (i.e., attitude, breaks, etc.).
- Make the numbers and meet the schedule.
- Understand how the area should run and run it properly. Make sure people have tools and materials to do their jobs. Know each job thoroughly and be able to train others in standard work and hitting the times. Manage the standard work in progress (WIP) in the area. Manage breaks, lunch, and start times.
- Ensure the day-by-the-hour chart and the month-by-the-day chart is filled out.
- Deploy people properly, make sure people stay in their areas, and flex as required. If you have extra people in the work area, make sure to move them to another area.
- Discipline people as required.
- Clearly display the standardized work sheet in the area.
- Keep the area clean. Make sure tools are put back after each shift.
- Cross-train everyone in the area and rotate jobs at some frequency—daily, weekly, or monthly.
- Create a top ten problem action item list for both the team and upper management.
- Take swift and effective action on ideas generated by the team.

- Update the standard work as suggestions are implemented.
- Attend production meetings and update management, escalate as appropriate.
- Float into the line as needed or ensure someone is available to float.
- Be responsible to immediately respond to problems in the area with appropriate action and then document on the day-by-the-hour chart.

Train the Staff in the New Process

The next step is to train the staff in the new process. This is done by taking the standard work developed by the team based during the video analysis and communicating it to the rest of the staff. We typically do this in small groups and ask for their input as we go. Sometimes, it is necessary to pull the whole staff together in order to get everyone to agree on what the steps for the standard work are going to be. Most of the time, the person's job doesn't change, just the order or when they do the steps in the job.

Types of Training

It is important to train your organization with an overview of batch systems vs. Lean systems, Lean principles, Six Sigma, Total Quality (TQ) tools, and change management. Training should focus on tools 50% and people 50%. For those of you who have implemented changes, you already know that the tools are easy to learn compared to getting people to change. Training should always be followed by some type of Implementation so the learning can be retained.

Overview Training

Lean overview training can run anywhere from 1 hr to 5 day sessions. We recommend basic overview training for the entire organization. It should be part of the training and communication plans. While it is true that Lean cannot be totally learned in a classroom, if the classroom training is done properly, many tools can be implemented on leaving the class. There are also advanced Lean training classes and a variety of Lean certification options available. The participants are exposed to Lean principles in several ways.

In the 5 day overview training, participants learn through lectures, interactive exercises, and a small Kaizen event. They experience teamwork and team building and typically meet new people inside or outside the organization. Participants include those who are going to be working on their first Lean project, key stakeholders, suppliers, and customers of the pilot project. We have run the classes with everyone from the president to floor personnel. Prior to the class, we normally video a process from the pilot project and analyze them in the class.

Participants not working on the project team are always tasked to implement at least one improvement when they leave the class. This results in an opportunity to get the class back together to follow up on the improvements. When we get them back together, we encourage them to make another improvement and to get someone else to make an improvement as well. When everyone in the class is exposed to Lean, it makes it much easier to implement each project. This training becomes part of a larger, more comprehensive training and Lean Implementation plan. Interestingly enough, we have many people who have repeated our 5 day training a year or two later. The advantage is that once a person has implemented and learned Lean principles and tools, they continue to get something new out of it. We have had all levels of healthcare personnel attend our manufacturing 5 day classes (normally a year or so after they started their Lean journey).

Lesson Learned

Where an overview training session is not utilized, it is much more difficult to implement and sustain the project.

ON THE JOB LEAN TRAINING

On the job training is provided during an event or implementation. It is important to review the Lean principles and whatever specific tools are going to be involved prior to implementation. Essentially, Lean system Kaizen implementations are ongoing training in each of the Lean tools that are necessary for the project. This training is invaluable, as it is totally based on real-life implementation as opposed to the classroom. The overview classroom training should be a pre-requisite for an implementation. It saves a lot of time covering the principles and reasons for implementing Lean.

EXECUTIVE TRAINING

Executive training should be the same as for implementers; however, this is difficult to accomplish. The best way to learn Lean is by doing it. Most executives don't feel they have time to learn, so we prepare overview training for them. This training is generally 1 to 2 1/2 days. We have had many executives get much more involved and attend 5 day overview training, drop in during implementation training, and lead training and Point Kaizen events. Again the best adult training is tied to some type of implementation.

THE LEAN IMPLEMENTATION MODEL

The implementation methods model describes the different approaches to Lean and compares them to Toyota (Figure 7.2). This whole discussion is confusing as the word Kaizen appears in all four methods. In order to clarify, let's examine each method.

- Method 1 - is the implementation model we have been promoting in this book based on the BASICS model and followed up with PDSA (plan, do, study, act). Most companies today use Method 2 for conversion from batch to flow. Once the processes are stable we start working toward the Toyota Culture model with the percentages mentioned for Methods 2, 3 and 4.
- Method 2 - is made up of Point Kaizen events.

	This is the Goal!!	95% Consultants	5% Consultants
Method 4	Method 3	Method 2	Method 1
Good Idea (GI)Club Board/Executive Level Chartered Strategic Kaizen Teams	True Kaizen	Point Kaizen Events	System Kaizen Implementation
Continuous Learning	Ideas Flow From Floor & Implemented by Team Leader		
CI System Responsibility	Sustain	Initial Sell Sustain	Should be used for Batch to Flow Conversions
Toyota uses 10%	Toyota uses 80%	U.S. uses 80% to 100% Toyota uses 10%	
CEO & Board should own	CEO & HR should own		

FIGURE 7.2   Lean implementation methodology.

- Method 3 - is the goal of a Lean culture. This is where 80% or more of the ideas are generated from the floor every day and implemented by the team leader or supervisor.
- Method 4 - is composed of high-level chartered teams that are looking at benchmarking the rest of the world and constantly assessing the overall continuous improvement system of the company.

GENERAL DISCUSSION OF THE FOUR METHODS

Once the area has been converted to flow with the BASICS model, we utilize method 2, Point Kaizens, as one method of sustaining. We also use Point Kaizens occasionally as a way to introduce a new company to the power of what a dedicated team can accomplish in 1 week. Most companies and 95% of consultants have been using method 2 to try to convert from batch to Lean. Most of their training material and certifications are developed around this Point Kaizen approach. We will discuss the pros and cons of this as an approach to convert batch to flow. What took seven Kaizen events and 2 years at one company to implement flow on one line was surpassed at the same company using the BASICS approach during one 8 week system Kaizen implementation in another area that looked at the entire product line from beginning to end. It is a very powerful system. Just using the Point Kaizen approach seldom leads to method 3, which is the overall goal of a Lean culture. Method 4 uses the Good Ideas club to sustain and continuously improve the other three methods.

KAIZEN (METHOD 3) VS. THE TRADITIONAL POINT KAIZEN (METHOD 2) EVENT APPROACH

What is Kaizen?

Kaizen is a Japanese word, Kai meaning change and zen meaning gradual. Kaizen is loosely interpreted in English to mean continuous small or incremental improvements. The terms Kaizen and Point Kaizen often get confused or used interchangeably. Point Kaizen events and Kaizen are *different* concepts. Toyota's Kaizen approach is based on the Toyota House with the two pillars of JIT and Jidoka supporting the roof (respect for humanity) with the foundation being standard work, Heijunka, visual controls, TCWQC and TPM (Figure 7.3).

Kaizen

Kaizen is the idea that every employee is contributing ideas and small improvements every day. Supervisors and managers are given time, at least 50% of their day, to implement these changes. These small ideas each day turn into thousands of suggestions and significant bottom-line profitability on an annual basis.

FIGURE: 7.3   Toyota House. Source: BIG Slide.

Point Kaizen Events

A traditional Point Kaizen event requires a team of 6–8 people who are dedicated for a week to an improvement effort. Point Kaizen event training is typically a 5 day event, with the first day being training, the next 3 days on the floor or in the office making changes with a report out, and "celebration" on the fifth day. In reality, we have found Kaizen events can range from a 1 hour event to 2 to 3 week events, although this is rare. The events require a full-time dedicated team during this time.

Point Kaizen events require very specific, focused, realistic goals that can be accomplished within the event's time frame. These are typically sold by consultants as "ready-fire-aim" events and contain the same day of training for each Point Kaizen event forever. Each event ends with the team going back to their regular jobs and a 30 day list of actions to complete. Ready-fire-aim means you just go do it without any planning.

POTENTIAL PITFALLS OF THE TRADITIONAL POINT KAIZEN APPROACH

Many consultants today use Point Kaizen events to implement Lean. There can be problems with this approach when doing large conversions from batch to flow. It is important to understand that Point Kaizen events are an easy sell to company management because they only tie up 6–8 people for a week, and they get management on board with Lean. Management doesn't have to do anything but give up a person here or there for a week and attend the report out. They are initially amazed at what a dedicated cross-functional team can accomplish in a week. The team appears, based on the PowerPoint presentation, to get great initial results.

The next pitfall is that most Point Kaizen event report outs contain a 30 day list. Unfortunately, the dedicated teams are only put together for a week so there is no one left to follow up the 30 day list. Then the company assigns the list to the area supervisor, but this doesn't work either because the supervisor is too busy fighting day-to-day problems or can't get the list done. As a result, many Point Kaizen events don't sustain the improvement. The other problem using Point Kaizen events as an implementation strategy is there is only so much one can accomplish in a 1 week event. Point Kaizen events are designed to make small and large improvements within the week and rarely lead to organizational cultural transformations.

On large healthcare service lines, like inpatient, laboratory, ED, or operating room (OR), only a small part of a line can be attacked in a Point Kaizen event. For instance, changeover of one surgery room might be targeted for an event. If you don't hit a process that is on the critical path, roll it out area or system-wide and sustain it, then the results don't get to the bottom line. In addition, the old processes still exist. In many cases, you are still batching into and out of the improved area. This also makes it difficult to sustain.

Our results are not getting to the bottom line… We are having trouble sustaining the improvements… We are not able to complete our Kaizen newspapers and 30 day lists… I can't put that many people in the Kaizen Promotion Office or run all the events required based on 1 event per 100 persons in the company. These comments were common at all of Company X's sites. While weekly events were very successful in the short term, they were typically difficult to sustain in the long term or even the week after the event. The consultants told us that this was normal. We were also told that we may end up changing the layout up to 10 times a year and that was normal because each event is looking at a different piece of the process. The important thing was to just go out and change something; don't study it, just try it.

If you are a hospital administrator in the middle of a typical week in the OR, imagine I come to you and say we are going to do a Point Kaizen event in your area this week. We are going to change your whole process design around, and it may work or it may not but that's normal. We want to just ready-fire-aim and "go do." Or imagine you are in construction and I say, "Let's just change that steel to plastic; it's cheaper and we can get it quicker." Or "Let's just change this layout. After all, if we don't get it right the first time, we will just re-do it ten or twelve times this year until we get it right." Or I am a doctor and I say let's not do the operation the standard way;

let's improve it by just trying something new. We don't need to study or plan for it; after all, it might work. Point Kaizen trained JIT Consultants told us it's not unusual to take 3 steps forward and 2 steps back. After all, you can't expect to get it right the first time every time. Doesn't this type of logic sound absurd? Yet, we are letting ourselves be reeled into this type of approach with traditional Kaizen events.

Sound management techniques and training typically would reject and, at most, discourage this type of thought and approach. In fact, when we explain this approach during our Point Kaizen event training sessions, it is often met, at first, with disbelief and amazement; however, owing to the reputation of Kaizen consultants and films showing great results, we are often misled to believe that this panacea exists and that our sound judgment should be replaced with a "just do it" philosophy. The films do not show where these efforts fail and the potential costs of failure.

We believe, as a stand-alone improvement philosophy, the Point Kaizen approach to Leaning out entire companies is dangerous not only to American but also global manufacturing, healthcare, and service industries. If the Point Kaizen event approach is not completely understood, it can result in the opposite of the desired effect. It then becomes a failed effort or a very expensive (the consultants time is not cheap) yet failed proposition. We believe many companies have failed, leading to scrapped Lean initiatives owing to their experiences with the traditional Point Kaizen event approach. We have often heard, "Oh, yeah, we tried that Lean stuff before and it won't work here!"

DISADVANTAGES OF POINT KAIZEN EVENTS USED FOR FIRST TIME IMPLEMENTATION

1. The term "event" in and of itself does not signify continuous improvement and the typical Point Kaizen event approach is "ready-fire-aim, not ready-aim-fire." The Point Kaizen event has to be scoped to something that can be accomplished in a week (really three or three and one-half working days), but, typically, companies try to tackle too much at once. They tend to sub-optimize processes because only so much can be accomplished in a week. Sometimes this is not enough time to make it work or for staff to understand or learn the new way. Staff are typically not trained well in new procedures and many times the new procedures are poorly documented, if at all. So, if they do get it up and running but someone is out sick, the supervisor doesn't know what to do. The process introduces variation and some areas have been shut down for days, weeks, or even months after a poorly planned event. Area staff are left with the results of a Kaizen event (and in some cases all the mess), but no support to clean it up. Many times, in people's haste "to do" or make changes, safety, ergonomic, and local and state regulations are violated.

2. They are difficult to rollout as an overall system strategy. They are a slow approach and don't work well for initial batch to one-piece flow conversions. Changes to a system are not normally planned well and opportunities exist for many unintended consequences after the team leaves. During an event, there is only time to work on a piece of the process; we don't have time to take a step back to look at the whole process, i.e., to look at the big picture. We found with Point Kaizen events, TQ teams, or Grass Roots Teams, sometimes spent a week trying to improve a process that, when we looked at it from a system view, could have been eliminated. Instead, we wasted valuable time trying to improve it.

3. Most Point Kaizen events are based on what management thinks are the problems, but have not collected data to know for sure. It is difficult to sustain improvements if an event is done in the middle of a process and supporting systems are not improved. We still have push systems before and after the new Lean part of the process; therefore, it is very tough to maintain. 30 day lists are typically not followed up or require extensive resources to complete. On average, 50% or less of Point Kaizen events sustain over time. There are normally no audit systems to follow up.

4. Teams get in line for "events," delaying improvements. *At one company, a supervisor came to me and said, "I bought all the quick-change tooling we need for this one machine but*

I can't get on the Kaizen event calendar to get it installed!" There is normally not enough time to get standard work in place and sustain it and the supervisor doesn't know how to run it.

Many companies form Kaizen promotion offices. These contain the trainers for Kaizens and people freed up as part of the Kaizen events. While, in concept, Kaizen promotion offices make sense, they are seldom successful and become easy targets for layoffs. In addition, since the Kaizen trainers are dedicated, they end up spending a lot of time in the office instead of on the floor making improvements or training line management how to lead events.

5. Kaizen events feed the CEO's desire for quick returns for little investment. They tend to turn into Friday "shows" for management, free lunch for the team, and a checkmark off the list that the kaizen event has been completed for corporate. Some companies are measured on the number of Kaizen events instead of the continuous improvement measures they should be monitoring.

6. Some companies have "Initiativitis." They try to implement different pieces of the Toyota process system (TPS) separately. Over several years, a Fortune 100 company had launched separate initiatives with Five S, Focused Factories, Kanbans, Process Flows (TQ Speed), Process & Wall Mapping, not to mention 4 days of TQ tools training, facilitator training, and Point Kaizen events, etc. But they never put all the tools together and integrate them with the Lean culture. As a result, the improvements became difficult to sustain and most people figured they could just "wait it out."

7. Reward systems are not changed to support continuous improvement.

8. In many cases, the Kaizen event approach typically makes one more dependent on consultants. Once management sees the first report out and the enthusiasm of the team, they are hooked. They immediately want to roll out more events. This is reinforced by the notion that we only need to dedicate a team for a week to get great results. The consultants provide 1 day of the same training for every event, which is not enough to learn Lean or understand the philosophy behind it. Therefore, the teams become dependent on the consultants' knowledge. Since the consultants encourage creation of a Kaizen promotion office to coordinate the events and the company does not have enough trained personnel, the consultant can typically expect 1 to 2 years worth of engagement. Many companies use the number of events as a measure vs. process-based continuous improvement measures.

Lesson Learned

Ready-fire-aim is a good way to get management to do something and to start changing, but the Point Kaizen approach has a poor chance for true success as a stand-alone strategy. A new approach is needed other than Point Kaizen events if the United States or any other country is going to be truly successful at sustaining Lean. Once the consultants leave, most companies revise their Point Kaizen event approach and Kaizen Promotion Office because of the sustaining issue and lack of getting to the bottom line. I still hear the same complaints today from manufacturing companies and hospitals. The BASICS system Lean approach is the answer, but it takes time and resolve to implement because it is a ready-aim-fire approach and requires a significant commitment up-front of project and training resources.

ADVANTAGES/RESULTS OF KAIZEN EVENTS

With all these negative comments, one might think we are against Kaizen events. But we are not! Kaizen events have their place and should be a part of your improvement strategy, but not your entire improvement strategy. We believe Point Kaizen events should be utilized and can be extremely valuable as a management introduction to continuous improvement to get people on board with Lean. As long as the expectation is set up front to encourage "try", fail fast, and learn from your failure to achieve the right result, it can be extremely beneficial as one of the tools for sustaining Lean to augment the continuous improvement program to foster the Lean cultural transformation.

- If properly scoped and chartered with the right expectations, Kaizen events can provide great results, and a lot of change can be accomplished in a very short time frame. We have completely changed entire layouts overnight.
- Significant productivity and space improvements can be made within the specific area being targeted.
- They promote organizational team building with visibility to the senior leadership team. They showcase the power of dedicated cross-functional teams to make quick changes, which help break down functional barriers.
- They can be a good training and sustaining tool to help develop a continuous learning organization.

We find that there are many projects that lend themselves to the Kaizen event approach. Some of these are:

- Setup/changeover reductions
- Five S
- Poka yoke, etc.
- TPM pilot
- Visual displays or controls
- Smaller area layout improvements
- Processes that can be improved within the week time frame, employees trained and the supervisor left with a complete standard work package

In order to utilize Point Kaizen events as an overall implementation approach, there has to be a cohesive strategy with multiple sequential events in one area and a ready-aim-fire approach. Toyota did not get Lean doing Point Kaizen events. Point Kaizen events came much later, after the company was converted to flow.

Lesson Learned

Based on all the reading we have done, it seems that at Toyota about 10% of improvement comes from Point Kaizen events, 10% from leadership-chartered improvement teams, and 80% from employees and supervisors (team leaders) on the line every day.

We have developed a new, revised Kaizen approach in order to convert the Point Kaizen event to more of a ready-aim-fire style event with training tailored to the event. We recommend against generating a 30 day list, as it has been our experience that these are seldom followed up unless the proper resources are dedicated and management has the discipline to bring the outstanding items to closure.

Our revised Kaizen approach is composed of the following:

- Senior leaders should lead the event and the training.
- Charter the team properly.
- State the target improvement and expectations up-front.
- Focus the team and provide the right team members and resources.
- The Kaizen team must be dedicated during the event.
- Give the team priority over resources, especially maintenance.
- Act on fact, use the BASICS tools, videotape, and utilize a ready-aim-fire approach.

- Utilize a ready-aim-fire approach.
- Provide overview training to all participants.
- Follow up each day with the team or team leader.
- Make sure all changes are documented prior to the end of the event.
- Make sure changes are communicated to the product team ahead of time and secure their buy-in.
- Implement changes.
- Report out to the senior leadership team at the end of the week's event.
- Make sure that any remaining action items are turned over as recommendations to the area or functions responsible.
- Have a follow-up meeting with management to ensure all actions are closed out.
- Have a follow-up audit or review in 1 week or at 1 month intervals (as needed) to ensure the improvements in the area are sustaining.

VISUAL MANAGEMENT SYSTEM COMPONENTS

There are four components of a visual management system. These are:

1. Five S
2. Visual displays
3. Visual controls
4. Visual management

FIVE S

Whether or not Five S (5S) is implemented as a separate initiative, it becomes a part of every implementation. As we make changes to the layout and workstations, we implement Five S as we go. Some organizations add an S for safety and call this 6S. Five S is the beginning step and part of a larger whole, called visual management systems. The goal of visual management is to make problems jump out and be visible.

When a work area is neat, clean, and orderly, it is a more efficient and safer work area. The Five S's are a method for creating and maintaining this type of work environment. Listed below are the Five S's with original Japanese words and different American definitions, depending on the source:[10]

Seiri—整理[11]—proper arrangement, sort, clean up, clearing up, organization: The first step is to separate and consolidate those items that are necessary for the proper functioning of the work area (tools, fixtures, work instructions, parts, etc.) from the unnecessary items. Get rid of those items that are unnecessary.

Seiton—整頓—arrange, put in order and store, set in order, order, orderliness, organize logical order, neatness: Arrange items so they can be retrieved immediately in the order required. Make a place for all the necessary items and put them in their place. Identify their appropriate place by outlining the area (shadow boarding) or labeling the space.

Seiso—清楚—neat, tidy, shine, cleanliness, cleaning, pick up: Operators clean the work area daily. Sweep the floors, wipe off the machines, and keep a sanitary work area. Make sure everything is neatly in its place.

---

[10] Nelson, Mayo and Moody, *Productivity Five S Series, Powered by Honda*; Shimbun, *The Five S's, Visual Control Systems*; Hirano, *Putting Five S to Work;* and Ohno, *Workplace Management.*

[11] Translation provided by Professor William Tsutsui, Associate Dean for International Studies, Professor of History, College of Liberal Arts & Sciences, The University of Kansas.

Seiketsu—清潔—Create standard work procedures which standardizes and helps maintain a spotless workplace. Find ways to keep the overall environment neat and clean. Are there ways to reduce dust, dirt, and debris that make the cleanup easier? How are old documents purged from the area? Can we eliminate safety hazards?

Shitsuke—躾—discipline, sustain, conduct, changing work habits, training: Discipline and training. The most important step of all is to maintain the area once it has been created. Everyone must follow the standardized procedures for cleaning and organizing. Continue to look at the whole area, not just your workspace.

Many areas audit regularly to track their improvement. The area team uses the audit results to focus their improvement efforts and increase their score on the next audit. The area team should review the audit results, brainstorm suggestions for improvement, and take the necessary actions.

The observation form can be tailored to the plant. A plant that does chemical processes will have some different items than a plant that only does assembly. Remember to include safety as part of your Five S audits.

Five S is about two major items—housekeeping and discipline. Housekeeping is about the old saying "a place for everything and everything in its place," but it is also about discipline. Putting things back in their place is the most difficult part of Five S. The leader of the area sets the standard for Five S and Lean overall. If someone does not put something away where they should and the leader says nothing, then effectively the leader has just rewarded that behavior. We all need to be part of setting the standard at the highest levels if we are to be considered world class.

VISUAL DISPLAYS

Visual displays are signs and bulletin boards that communicate information. They do not enforce any action, only communicate the name of an area, machine, or some other type of information.

VISUAL CONTROLS

The analogy for visual controls is the human body.[12] When the body has a problem, it lets you know. It may be in the form of a fever, pain, bleeding, blister, etc. Once your body signals a problem, it needs to be taken care of right away or it tends to get worse. This is true in the hospital or clinic as well. The goal is to make problems visible so they can be fixed right away and then fix them so they don't come back. The work area should "talk to you" and communicate its condition as you walk around it.

Visual controls are different than visual displays as they help remind us but usually don't force certain actions. For example, a stoplight tells a driver to stop, but it doesn't force the driver to stop. The driver stops because they know if they continue there may be some negative consequence, like an accident or a ticket. They are communication tools to help the systems within an area respond to customer demand and changes within the environment. These controls come in many forms, but the common denominator among them is that they cause an appropriate action when a visual signal occurs. The following is a list of examples.

- When a Kanban card is placed in the post office box, it triggers the right number of parts to be made or replenished.
- In a laboratory, when an LED light is turned on, it may signal to a technician that the processing line needs attention or to a supervisor that a machine is down.

---

[12] Taiichi Ohno, *Toyota Production System* (New York: Productivity Press) 1988.

- Electronic whiteboards or tracking boards in an ED may signal when a new order has been written that needs action or an abnormal lab has been resulted.
- In surgery, electronic tracking boards may signal where the patient is in the process, signaling what actions need to be taken.
- In pharmacies, empty bins or water level marks prompt a visual cue that supplies need to be replenished.

Measurements of the process in the area are visual controls that are updated by team members and are used to drive improvements. Day-by-the-hour charts are a simple form of area metric. When the area is performing to the Takt time, it is meeting its target metrics. When the area misses its Takt time, comments are noted on the chart to help the teams follow up with countermeasures and root cause corrective actions. The charts are used to facilitate team meetings and become the primary communication tool.

The goal is to create visuals so anyone can walk around the area and know what's going on and how we are doing without asking anyone.

Story

Ironically, when we create our Lean environment in factories, we use the emergency room as an example. We ask 5 day training class participants the following questions regarding creating a Lean environment:

1. *Does every second count?*
2. *Do I need all my tools and supplies at point of use (POU)?*
3. *Do I need standing and walking operations?*
4. *Does everyone need to know their jobs and have standard work?*

The answers are a resounding "yes" to each question. Then I go on to explain and ask what the difference is between a factory and an emergency trauma room:

1. *Does every second count? Yes.*
2. *Do I need all my supplies at POU (Point of Use)? Imagine the doctor says, "Scalpel," and the nurse says, "Wait a minute doc, it's in the cabinet over there!" After searching, she can't find it and says, "It must have been moved out of the room to the 'core' supply area!"*
3. *Do I need standing and walking operations? Imagine they wheel you in to the emergency department and all the doctors and nurses are sitting on chairs.*
4. *Do we need standard work? Imagine if all procedures were not standardized.*

We were able to observe a trauma case in action. There were actually two trauma bays in one big room. As we waited for the patient arrival, the number of staff in the room increased, filled with excitement and anticipation.
While watching, it was obvious that:

1. *Every second counted.*
2. *The trauma doctor asked for an instrument, and the nurse proceeded to search through all the case carts and couldn't find it (seconds lost). The nurse asked the doctor if there was something else she could use. The doctor indicated there was and told her what to get. The nurse found it and handed it to the nurse assisting the doctor.*
3. *Everyone was standing and walking and seemed to work well as a team.*
4. *Everyone seemed to know their jobs and tried to anticipate the doctor. But they were all over the place. Several times, the doctor asked for something and either it wasn't there or a nurse had to run out to the hall supply closet to get it (again seconds and minutes lost).*

After the trauma was over and the room was cleaned, we took a look at the layout and the nurse walk patterns that I had drawn during the case. Some questions immediately popped into my mind:

1. *Why couldn't the nurse find the instrument or supply requested?*
2. *Why did another nurse have to go outside the room several times for supplies? We talked with the nurse, who said they frequently run out of materials due to empty bins. We asked what happens if materials are not in the closet. She said she has to run downstairs to central supply. This is with a critical patient on the table!*
3. *What would happen if there were two traumas going on at the same time in that room?*

We reviewed the materials bins, and noticed several were empty. At that point, the materials person showed up to inventory the bins.

We asked him why the bins were empty. He said they only refilled the bins once a day. We asked what happens when there is a patient on the trauma table and the bin is empty. He said, "Oh, they just run down the hall to the supply closet and get what they need." We said, "But the patient could be dying!" He said, "Well, that's how we've always done it since there was a cut back on FTEs 5 years ago!"

We then asked who set the PAR levels on the bins. He didn't know but guessed it was someone in materials. So now, we hesitate to use the trauma room as an example with factories.

VISUAL MANAGEMENT SYSTEM

The goal of a visual management is to make *abnormal* conditions immediately visible using Five S, visual displays and visual controls, and taking the premise one step further by incorporating root cause, countermeasures, andon, risk mitigation, TPM, and mistake proofing. The goal of the system is to prevent or mitigate the defect. An example of each component can be found in automobiles.

Let's say you leave the headlights on in the car. What happens? The car has a light that shows your headlights are on (visual display). If you take the key out of the ignition it makes a noise (andon) to make you aware that your lights are still on. The next level is where it mistake proofs it by turning off your lights for you after a pre-programmed length of time. The lights going out is the final signal of the visual management system. The car now prevents the defect by mitigating the error and preventing the defect (dead battery). We discuss visual management from a supervisor's perspective later in the chapter.

LEAN GOAL IS ZERO DEFECTS—DIFFERENCE BETWEEN AN ERROR AND A DEFECT

Lean tools are designed to measure, highlight and eliminate defects; the only way to get to zero defects is to eliminate the error before it occurs. Therefore, it is important to understand the difference between an error and a defect. An error is a mistake that is made; a defect is a problem that occurs as a result of the error that was made. Shingo often referred to this in his books as the importance of separating cause from effect. An example would be as follows: the error was leaving the lights on in the car, while the defect is that the battery died. Mistake-proofing is a critical component of Lean and provides a mechanism to eliminate the errors so defects won't occur.

Many organizations use statistical process control (SPC). SPC is a good program but will not ensure zero defects since the defects are detected after they are made. The goal of Lean is 100% defect prevention at the source. Lean processes require defect-free patients and processes to support a JIT system. JIT is getting the right "good quality" part or the "properly prepared" patient. If this is not the case, then the system breaks down and delays occur.

Ultimately, the need for control plans in a truly Lean environment should disappear as any abnormalities should be clearly and immediately visible in the workplace in real time. However realistically, control strategies are needed as it is difficult to "mistake proof" 100% of the opportunities where errors can occur even though that is the goal. Shingo conveys these in his book, called *Poka yoke*.[13]

Poka Yoke

Poka yoke—ポカヨケ—distraction proof, is a Japanese term that means "fail safing" or "mistake proofing." A *Poka yoke* is any mechanism in a Lean process that helps staff avoid (*yokeru*) mistakes (*poka*). Its purpose is to eliminate product defects by preventing, correcting, or drawing attention to human errors as they occur. The concept was formalized, and the term adopted by Shigeo Shingo as part of the Toyota Production System. It was originally described as *Baka yoke*, but as this means "fool proofing" (or "idiot proofing"), the name was changed to the milder *Poka yoke*.[14]

Types of Control and Warning Devices[15]

- Contact device: contact is established between the device and the product.
- Fixed value method: part must be a certain weight or it won't work.
- Motion step method: product must pass inspection before proceeding to the next step.
- Design-out defect: the ultimate goal is to eliminate errors by designing your products or processes Lean.

Once you clean up the areas and standardize the work, then the variation sticks out. Six Sigma tools are designed to fix the variation. The Lean tools and Six Sigma tools integrate nicely.

Examples of Cause and Effect

- Process: car crosses over railroad track.
- Error: car crosses railroad track when train is coming.
- Defect: train collides with car at railroad crossing.
- Warning device: use a signal or sign and/or sound to warn the driver of the car.
- Control device: put up gates to prevent the car from crossing.
- Design-out defect: design a bridge over or under to the railroad track, which prevents the error and the defect.

Lesson Learned

Goal is defect prevention at the source.

---

[13] Nikkan Kogyo Shimbun, *Poka yoke* (New York: Productivity Press) 1988; Singo, *Zero Quality Control* (New York: Productivity Press) 1986; Hinckley, *Make No Mistakes* (New York: Productivity Press) 2002.

[14] www.Wikipedia.com. Harry Robinson (1997) "Using Poka yoke Techniques for Early Defect Detection," http://faculty-web.berry.edu/jgrout/pokasoft.html. Retrieved May 4, 2009. Shigeo Shingo and Andrew P. Dillon, *A Study of the Toyota Production System from an Industrial Engineering Viewpoint* (Portland, OR: Productivity Press) 1989, p. 21–22. John R. Grout and Brian T. Downs. "A Brief Tutorial on Mistake-proofing, Poka yoke, and ZQC," MistakeProofing.com. http://www.mistakeproofing.com/tutorial.html. Retrieved May 4, 2009. "Poka yoke or Mistake Proofing: Overview. The Quality Portal," http://thequalityportal.com/pokayoke.htm. Retrieved May 5, 2009. Nikkan Kogyo Shimbun, *Poka yoke: Improving Product Quality by Preventing Defects* (Portland, OR: Productivity Press) 1988, p. 111, 209. "'Pokayoke.' The Manufacturing Advisory Service in the South West (MAS-SW)," http://www.swmas.co.uk/info/index.php/Pokayoke. Retrieved May 2, 2009. 8. http://dict.regex.info Japanese to English dictionary, http://www.saiga-jp.com, http://thequalityportal.com/pokayoke.htm.

[15] Shingo, *Zero Quality Control* (Productivity Press) 1986.

TOTAL PRODUCTIVITY MAINTENANCE

Total productivity maintenance (TPM) involves everyone in the organization, from top management to the staff person on the floor. With TPM, the staff members now share in the maintenance and upkeep of the equipment. They take care of day-to-day checklists (adding oil to a machine, changing over reagents) and maintenance takes care of difficult problems. The analogy for this is like taking care of your car. You wash it, check the fluids, put gas in it, but when there is a big problem, you take it to a mechanic.

TPM has all sorts of application in hospitals. There are machines everywhere, but we don't always think about them. Sterile processing has washers and sterilizers, radiology has x-ray equipment, surgery has "C" arms and anesthesia equipment, and the floor nurses use medication storage machines and have machines at the bedside that monitor vitals. All of this equipment has to be maintained. With Lean, the nurses become the front line for maintenance when reporting problems or making minor fixes to machines.

Total Productivity Maintenance Goals

- Eliminate unplanned machine downtime
- Increase machine capacity
- Have fewer defects
- Reduce overall operating costs
- Allow for minimum inventory
- Increase operator safety
- Create a better working environment

Overall Equipment Effectiveness

The goal of overall equipment effectiveness (OEE) is to take metrics that individually might look good and look at them together. The metrics are:

1. Scheduled available time (any unplanned downtime or changeover time counts against this)
2. Operating rate—rate or speed at which the machine is scheduled to run
3. Defect rate—percentage of good parts

Let's say we were running a piece of laboratory equipment. Ninety percent of the time, we had planned for the machine to be down for normal maintenances. We had to slow the machine down due to a service issue so it was operating at 90% of what it was rated and we had 95% good results, i.e., 5% had to be retested.

These numbers by themselves look pretty good, but they hide the true utilization of the machine. OEE multiplies these percentages together (0.9 x 0.9 x 0.95) to determine the true capacity (77%) of the machine.

New Maintenance Paradigm

In the Productivity Series entitled TPM,[16] there is an interesting quote: "Maintenance should be looked at as Capacity Generators." Really think about this quote. When it is time to cut heads, where do we normally start? We normally start with "indirect labor." The first indirect labor target is normally maintenance. After all, what do they really do? We can outsource them if we have to, right?

---

[16] TPM, Productivity Video Series©.

Sometimes this perception is unwarranted, but other times it is due to poor management of maintenance resources or lack of discipline and accountability. Laying off maintenance first is easy to do because it is quick money on paper, but what does it cost us in the long run? When we let maintenance go, all the little day-to-day problems don't get fixed or, sometimes, even worse, well-intentioned people try to fix them. Over time, our equipment shuts down or stops running all together.

Lesson Learned

Look at maintenance not as a cost center but as a profit center. After all, they are capacity generators.

LEAN AND MAINTENANCE IN HOSPITALS

Lean creates job security for the engineering and maintenance of hospital facilities. We are constantly asking maintenance to remove doors on cabinets, install flexible workstations, remove walls, reposition and resize nursing stations, make us POU locations, and do mock-ups for pilots. So maintenance really wears two Lean hats. One is helping us with Lean changes. The other is working to Lean the maintenance processes themselves!

CONSTRUCTION CHALLENGES

When implementing Lean there will be construction challenges; regulatory agencies, permitting bodies, joint commission requirements[17], and AIA guidelines[18] all impacting construction projects. It helps to get maintenance involved early on the team and to train them in Lean principles and make sure they are always in the communication loop and planning. TPM should not be just a maintenance initiative; it should be a company-wide initiative. The best way to start TPM is by creating simple checklists for each piece of equipment.

HOSPITAL AND IT SYSTEMS

Whenever we value stream map hospitals, it becomes apparent how many different and unconnected information systems typically exist. Contrast this with most factories, which have typically one material requirements planning (MRP) system or enterprise planning (ERP) system. Hospitals tend to have laboratory information systems, registration systems, insurance verification, surgery system, ED system, bed management, pharmacy and stat system, scheduling, overall hospital information system, electronic record software, instrument tracking systems, billing systems, materials management systems, marketing or forecasting systems, desktop software and bar coding and other scanner support. This is not a complete list and does not include all the manual information that is charted.

IT also provides services: data backup and retention, risk management, help desk, software loading, computer maintenance and upgrades, software control, network installation and support, and shared drives.

IT has potentially three hats with Lean:

1. Streamlining the internal IT processes
2. Connecting and streamlining the overall information flow
3. Supporting Lean system implementation and Kaizen teams

Streamlining internal IT processes utilize the same BASICS tools we have discussed throughout this book. The first step is to value stream map the processes and then apply the product and operator

[17] Joint Commission on Accreditation of Healthcare Organizations
[18] http://info.aia.org/nwsltr_aah.cfm?pagename=aah_gd_hospcons.

tools. Streamlining overall communication involves building interfaces so all the different IT systems can talk to each other. This is not an easy task. There are ERP systems available now for hospitals.

Lean teams require varying levels of IT support throughout their improvement journey. Other support needs involve POU printers and supplying software needs to the team.

The real key when improving processes is not to purchase software to fix problems or streamline a process until after the process has been "Leaned" out. In addition, the software needs to be flexible. It needs to support Kanban applications and frequent changes or modifications to support ongoing improvements to standard work. It is important to remember that software does not solve everything. In many cases, we have suggested holding off on purchasing additional systems or scrapping them altogether. A major Lean tenet is don't tie operators to machines; use check blocks or boxes or touch screens, etc. There are several books on Lean and IT now, including *Easier, Simpler, Faster*[19] and *Lean Software Strategies.*[20]

BASICS—Checking the New Process

The Lean team and the supervisor must prove that the new process implemented in the area performs as expected and document the new process (Figure 7.4). It is the leadership's job to continually check the process in order to make sure it is running properly. In order to check the process, we need metrics, standard work, and visual controls in place. After the area has been run for a short time, some ongoing "fine tuning" will be necessary, followed by continuous improvement. Make sure the area has appropriate metrics in place (e.g., a day-by-the-hour chart) visible for all to see, accompanied by daily huddles to monitor progress and solicit employee suggestions. When we experience a problem, we need to address it in real time by working through the problem-solving process.

BASICS—Sustaining the Process

It is up to the team assigned to the work area (including the supervisor, planner, engineer, etc.) to sustain the gains and continuously improve the operation of the targeted area. The team should debrief the staff and other stakeholders on the improvements that have been made. Any follow-up items should be small and easy actions.

SUSTAINING TOOLS

Sustain Plans/Control Plans

While we have created sustain plans, control plans, and combinations of the two, one needs to realize that the term sustain plan is somewhat of a misnomer and not sufficient for a Lean implementation

Phases

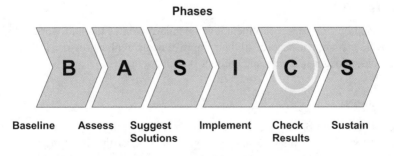

| Baseline | Assess | Suggest Solutions | Implement | Check Results | Sustain |

FIGURE 7.4   BASICS Model – Check Phase. Source: BIG.

[19] Jean Cunningham, *Easier, Simpler, Faster* (New York: Productivity Press) 2007.
[20] Peter Middleton, *Lean Software Strategies* (New York: Productivity Press) 2005.

Phases

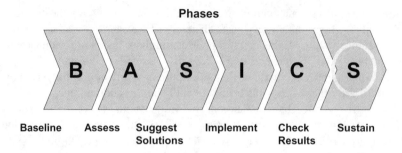

FIGURE 7.5   BASICS Model – Sustain Phase. Source: BIG.

(Figure 7.5). When a Lean system implementation is completed, there is generally an exit strategy for the dedicated Lean resources. This is the point where the consultant, internal or external, leaves the project. The exit strategy should contain the conditions and deliverables that must be in place prior to that exit.

A control plan generally has a list of metrics that the area must continue to meet. When one of the metrics falls out of control, then some predetermined action that is noted in the control plan is followed until the metric is back "under or in control."

The sustain plan is a little different in that it contains the control plan and includes actions necessary to sustain the implementation. But the idea behind Lean is that we do not just sustain, but continuously improve. Therefore, the sustain plan should be renamed "the continuous improvement plan."

In his book *Creating a Lean Culture*,[21] David Mann describes four necessary criteria to sustain Lean:

1. Leader standard work
2. Visual controls
3. Accountability
4. Discipline

These criteria are combined with the notion that the role of the team leader or supervisor must change from 100% running the business to a combination of running the business and improving the business. Toyota actually builds in 50% time for the supervisor[22] to continually improve the business. In the United States, if two supervisors had 50% of their time available, we would probably work to lay one of them off.

LEADER STANDARD WORK

We have expanded on this concept to include all standard work. Standard work is the vehicle that has helped Toyota capture and sustain all their improvements. It also provides the vehicle to transfer areas from an old manager to a new one without skipping a beat.

VISUAL MANAGEMENT

We discussed this concept briefly earlier. In the context of creating and sustaining a Lean environment, we expand visual controls to visual management. At first this is a tough concept for hospital administrations and doctors to comprehend. Most hospital administrations utilize reports to

---

[21] David Mann, *Creating a Lean Culture* (Productivity Press) 2005.
[22] Jeffrey Liker, *Toyota Culture* (McGraw Hill) 2008.

manage their areas. What's wrong with reports?[23] Reports are history, and usually so much time has transpired that one cannot get to the root causes of any problems. In addition, based on our experience, the data in many reports is so suspect that it is scary to think that anyone uses it to manage or make financial decisions.

The goal with Lean is to manage in a REAL TIME ENVIRONMENT. This has many implications for hospital administrators. We need to go to the floor, get our information first hand, manage by fact, and encourage and challenge our people to think through and solve problems.

Imagine you are a director who is told by your boss to go to the floor and do a Gemba Walk. On your first trip, you will find your people are busy all the time. In fact, when you first go out to the floor, you will probably be in their way. Most of your managers are probably spending 80%–90% fighting fires and 10%–20% running the area. You look around to see what is going on, but all you see are whiteboards or maybe an electronic screen.

You go over to the charge nurse and ask what is going on. The charge nurse says, "Why are you here? Is something wrong?" In any case, she tells you to wait until she is free to talk to you. During that time, a surgeon tells you his case was delayed because his instruments weren't ready. An anesthesiologist grabs you and complains that the Pre-Op nurse did not have his/her patient ready. A nurse tells you that she was yelled at by the surgeon because the preference card was not right, and she had to run to three different supply areas/closets to find what was needed. That was after she called Materials, who said they had no one who could run it up to her.

I knew of one charge nurse who was suddenly reporting to a new director. The new director held daily status meetings in her office, which the charge nurse was told to attend. Because she was attending so many meetings, her area started slipping and the status meetings got longer and longer. As a result, her area continued to slip more and more and she was eventually terminated for mismanagement of her area.

Lesson Learned

In Lean we have a saying. Convert Staff jobs to Line jobs whenever possible. *When "overhead" office staff people aren't busy, they create work to justify their jobs. This creates more work for the people on the floor who are already busy. We need to evaluate the value-added from the office environment and review every report to see if it is value-added.*

Does any of this sound familiar?

This example represents typical surgical areas in most hospitals. Everyone works in a reactive atmosphere and crisis management dominates. Our managers are congratulated and rewarded for working around the system to fix problems.

So how do we set up a visual management system? First we have to "Lean out" our processes so they flow. We need to get all supplies and materials at POU where they are needed. We need to Five S the area and organize our equipment. We need to reduce any unnecessary equipment and supplies. Once we establish flow and clean up and organize the area, we need to start putting process focus metrics in place and make them visible.

ACCOUNTABILITY

We have already discussed the importance of accountability. This is, in some cases, a foreign concept to healthcare supervisors and managers. Many will require coaching and training to beef up their analytical skills and business acumen. Accountability is a big problem in most hospitals. People are typically not held accountable and don't have metrics for which they are responsible.

At Hospital X, I interviewed every leader in the surgical services area. One of the questions I asked each person was, "how are you measured?" Most said they are told during their annual

---

[23] Brian Maskell, *Making the Numbers Count* (New York: Productivity Press) 1996.

reviews if they are doing a good job. I couldn't believe that virtually no one had any metrics. They were not held responsible for anything. If they did have a metric, they could not tell me how they were currently performing against the metric. No one knew any of their cycle times or quality metrics. One person told me that they had a budget to meet and was grilled on it each month, but there were never any positive or negative consequences if they did not meet their target. Many Lean companies no longer utilize the traditional annual review.

If we are going to follow a clinical management model, we need to train our clinical staff in business processes, analytical skills, supervisory and leadership training, and financial management. We also need a probationary period where clinicians can see if they like management or would prefer to stay in a caregiver role.

Many hospitals have lost their chain of command and respect from the staff for their leaders. After all, the leadership doesn't really know what goes on every day. As a result, they react and dictate edicts in order to change things. The HR movements of the 1960s and 1970s[24] have left us with little or no discipline in our work areas. People think discipline is a "bad" word and processes are not documented. In many cases, supervisors and managers are not properly trained or developed to manage others. As a result, we continue to promote leaders who have no clinical knowledge or clinicians who have no business savvy. This results in an organization where the leadership is unable or literally does not know how to hold people accountable.

We need to return to the days of promoting from within. We need supervisors who have done the job, know the job, and can train in the job. This tribal knowledge is the basis for standard work. Most hospital procedures are poorly documented.

When hospitals, or any company for that matter, have leadership running the company who don't know the business or service line, then the organization is in jeopardy. When a consultant has to be called in to help with restructuring the organization or provide (vs. facilitate) strategic planning, then there is, potentially, a weakness at the top.

DISCIPLINE

Discipline is key in Lean environments. Without discipline, there is chaos. We need people to have the discipline to follow standard work, put things back where they belong, follow through on audits, conduct root cause analysis, and create the continuous improvement environment.

STAFF INVOLVEMENT

The importance of including staff in the Lean analysis and journey cannot be overemphasized, as most organizations don't fail in analysis, waste identification, and process re-design; they fail in sustaining the "change." The ability to sustain the process is related to communication, staff participation, training, role clarity, reward programs, and clear expectations of expected results and the importance placed on sustaining and improving from every level of leadership.

YOU GET WHAT YOU EXPECT; YOU DESERVE WHAT YOU TOLERATE[25]

ADDITIONAL SUSTAINING TOOLS

Once the Lean system Kaizen implementation is completed, there are several sustaining tools:

- Training within industry
- QC circles

---

[24] Henry Ford and Samuel Crowther, *My Life and Work* (Garden City, NY: Garden City) 1922.
[25] Unknown, *Reader's Digest.*

- Point Kaizen events
- Ongoing Kaizen (ideas generated from employees on the floor)
- Company-chartered continuous improvement groups

The ultimate vehicle for sustaining, regardless of the approach, is the constant updating of the standard work to capture all improvements.

Lesson Learned

Implement Lean first, then Six Sigma. As you Lean out the process and establish flow, clean it up and begin to get work standards in place or standard work; the variation now stands out and is immediately obvious. That is when we bring in Six Sigma tools.

REPEAT THE CYCLE!

Remember that "continuous improvement" must become a way of life. After a line has been converted from batch to one-piece flow, use Kaizen events as a way to sustain the cycle. Kaizen events can be hours or days, but have a cross-functional dedicated team working on improvement.

LEAN PRACTITIONERS

Many companies, hospitals, and manufacturers have positions called Lean Specialists or Lean Masters. We believe these terms are really misnomers. We have seen many Lean Masters that have not read any Shingo books and can't implement a pilot Lean activity on the floor or even know the three components of standard work. We have seen Lean Masters certified based on doing 6 or 7 kaizen events. How is this even possible? Most Lean Practitioners don't even like the title Lean Master or Lean Expert. We don't believe anyone can be a true expert in Lean. We also like the term Lean sensei or Lean teacher, but we now favor using the term Lean Practitioner. In order to be a Lean Practitioner, it means you have to practice and actually implement Lean on a continuous basis. A Lean Practitioner Level 3, for instance, would be defined as someone competent in the Lean tools with an understanding of the culture who has implemented in several environments such as assembly, machining, transactional processes, etc. In Healthcare, they may have implemented in the Lab (which has assembly and machining), Radiology (setup reduction and flow) and a transactional flow. This takes an average of 6 to 9 months working with a sensei (Lean Practitioner Level 5) who is well-grounded in the tools of scientific management, Lean principles, well read on Lean literature (Shingo Books) and change management.

The Level 5 Practitioner would replace the other categorization called a Lean Master, and someone who is well read in Lean and has implemented system and Point Kaizens and established a track record of sustained improvement for 3 to 5 years.

LEAN HOSPITAL IMPLEMENTATION (SYSTEM KAIZEN AND POINT KAIZEN) LESSONS LEARNED

CREATE THE LEADERSHIP ROAD MAP

It is important to have a leadership Lean/Six Sigma implementation road map. Lean should be part of the strategic goals and, as such, should be tracked and measured the same. Failure to have a map is like driving with no compass or shooting arrows without a target. It leads to pockets of success and fractured results.

MAKE SURE YOUR ORGANIZATION IS READY

Some organizations are just not ready and shouldn't implement Lean. If there is no compelling need to change or fundamental dissatisfaction in how things are done today, it will not be successful.

Creating and having everyone involved formally sign a contract for change which includes the Lean vision is a good tool for this. Part of the leadership road map should include a communication, training, and resource plan. The contract for change is designed to put everyone on notice of the go forward plan and expectations, and secure the buy-in up-front. Failure to do this can lead to failed implementations.

CREATE A LEAN STEERING COMMITTEE—BUT MAKE IT THE SENIOR LEADERSHIP TEAM

Part of the leadership road map should be the creation of a Lean steering committee. I can hear you say that the last thing we need is another committee. Yet this committee can and should be made up of the senior leadership team or some subset of the team. Since Lean should be a goal in the strategic plan, it should be no different than reviewing any other strategic plan goal to see if the company is on target.

The Lean steering committee should review the team charters to make sure the projects align with the overall vision and that the teams are on schedule. Each senior leader should be a champion and participate in the implementation with the team. The goal of the steering committee is to break down the most difficult organizational barriers, the sacred cows, and assist in any way possible to make the teams successful and work to develop the Lean culture.

LEAN CONSULTANTS SHOULD REPORT TO THE CEO

In many companies, we have reported to someone other than the CEO. We normally end up reporting to the process excellence leader or the director of operations. We find this is a short-sighted approach. If Lean is a strategic goal, and the goal is truly cultural transformation then the consultants should report to the CEO. Only the CEO is empowered to break down all the barriers in the organization. Consultants can only be effective and successful to the level of leadership to which they report. If they report to the director of operations, then much can be accomplished in operations, but none of the other functional silos will participate directly.

CREATE A LEAN ORGANIZATIONAL INFRASTRUCTURE

There needs to be a basic infrastructure in place for implementing Lean and it should be part of the leadership road map. The process excellence team should eventually fold back into the organization in staff jobs. A key failure mode is when finance identifies the process excellence group as "easy pickins" to be laid off to increase profits in the short term.

COMMUNICATION PLAN (FIGURE 7.6)

There is a saying that "you cannot communicate enough" during any type of organizational change. Our experience is that this could not be a truer statement. A communication plan should be established up-front detailing the tools, frequency, method of delivery, and responsibility for the item. For example, we are going to publish a Lean newsletter, twice a month, via email and hand out at the cafeteria and the process owner is responsible. The importance of ongoing communication cannot be emphasized enough! Communication can determine whether a project will be successful and sustain. It can impact how Lean cultural transformation will be viewed.

TRAINING PLAN

To be successful, development of a training plan is crucial. The training plan should include short- and long-term plans as well as some type of auditing or assessment process. It should also include development of an infrastructure to support the ongoing training required with a continuous improvement, learning organization.

				Surgery PI Project Proposed Communication Plan					
Meeting	Purpose	Owner	Key Tasks	Frequency	Duration	Delivery Via	Date	Location	Attendees/Distribution
Kick-Off Meetings									
Data Support	To discuss the data needs of four OR projects and how to support: 1. Material/supply. 2. OR Metrics green bell project. 3. OR Scheduling VSM/baseline performance 4. PASS Phase 2		Meet to allocate data support resources		1 hr	meeting	Week of 9/18	OR admin	
VSM participation	To seek black bell and green bells who may be available to support data collection for the creation of VSM in OR scheduling		Communication requesting available resources to assist with documentation of VSM of OR scheduling		Once	email	9/18	Main - OR	13B
OR Scheduling VSM and Baseline Performance	To inform of plan for VSM and baseline performance assessment in Or Scheduling. Secure team members and time commitments		Inform of role as process owner and secure team members, inform of timeline		1 hr	meeting	Week of 9/18	OR admin offices	
PASS Phase 2	To discuss with the PASS project, his role as process owner and time commitment. Also, identify team members and time commitments		Meet to discuss PASS Phase 2 project		1 hr	meeting	Week of 9/18	OR admin offices	
PASS Phase 2	To discuss scope, charter document, and overview of process. Specifically discuss team members and time allocation to project		Set Date and Create Agenda For Meeting		1 hr	meeting	Week of 9/22	PASS breakroom	
VSM validation/PASS Phase 2	To interview for OR information (VSM) and inform of failure Or project plans		Interview for VSM information (VOC) and inform of failure PASS projects, order sets		30 min	meeting	09/22/08		
All Employee PEP (Lean) Kick off Meetings	Formal Kickoff of Project with all employees in Surgery, SPD, Materials, Other areas impacted		Need Script to answer change questions		Utilize 1/2 hour of weekly staff meeting (scripted)	meeting	Week of 9/22		Surgery Staff including SPD and Materials
Physician Kick Off Meetings- TBD	Formal Kickoff with Surgeons and Anesthesiologists		Need Script to answer change questions. Select Physicians and Choose Venue		Utilize existing Board or Staff meetings	meeting	TBD		All Physicians

FIGURE 7.6 Communication plan example. Source: BIG Files.

LEADERSHIP CANNOT STAY IN THEIR IVORY TOWER

The CEO cannot manage a Lean transformation from their office in an "ivory tower." The CEO must get involved and go to the *Gemba*. CEOs who truly "get" Lean participate in the training and are involved as teams implement throughout their organizations. They talk with the staff and join them in the lunchroom. In some cases, they move their offices to become more accessible. They don't listen to hearsay or accept excuses; they hear issues first hand, and they eliminate leadership "perks." They talk to their patients in addition to their physicians. They see laying people off as a failure on management's part. They are the first to take a pay cut, if necessary. Leaders must role model the culture they are trying to create.

LEADERSHIP MUST LEAD AND DRIVE LEAN CHANGES, NOT JUST SUPPORT THEM

If the CEO is not trained properly or does not support Lean, it will ultimately fail. An untrained CEO, even in a support mode, can be dangerous because the culture change starts at the top and the decisions made at the top are still based on the old batch environment. So, even if the CEO believes they are supporting it, they may be doing irreparable harm and not realize it. This is because a Lean management system requires different reactions and behaviors than the old batch-driven systems.

LEADERS MUST PARTICIPATE IN LEAN. YOU CANNOT "GET IT" IN A TWO HOUR OR FOUR HOUR POWERPOINT PITCH

It takes time to understand all the implications of Lean thinking to develop and sustain a Lean culture. It takes benchmarking, reading, and understanding what a Lean culture is in order to be successful in creating one. It takes leading a Point Kaizen event or participating in an implementation and attending training to even begin to understand the Lean tools and concepts.

DON'T LET LEAN TURN INTO FINANCE-DRIVEN FTE WITCH HUNTS

Lean can easily turn into finance-driven FTE witch hunts. Finance is normally the first major barrier we run into in Lean implementations. This is again because the old ways of measuring and cost accounting normally make the Lean initiatives initially look poorly. If all the organization desires is a way for the financial department to eliminate FTEs, the word will get around and people will resist participation in Lean initiatives, any videotaping or making improvements for fear their jobs will be eliminated.

WORK TO ESTABLISH THE LEAN CULTURE, NOT JUST THE TOOLS

Some organizations just focus on the Lean tools. The tools are easy compared to the people piece. If we just focus on the tools, you may realize "pockets of excellence," but it will ultimately not sustain because the Lean culture was not created.

INSIST ON UPDATING STANDARD WORK

Without standard work, Lean will fail. Standard work is the glue that holds the entire system together. Without standard work, there can be no ongoing improvement nor can one capture the improvements made. Improvements become person dependent and disappear with that person when they leave.

DO NOT REWARD WORK AROUNDS

If the old "hero of the day" and "work around" culture prevails, Lean will fail. When we work around a problem, we don't solve it, so it ultimately comes back! Lean only sustains in cultures that learn to address root cause and fix problems so they never come back.

The Paranoid syndrome

At Hospital X there was a medical director who had outlasted several administrations. He chaired the surgeons committee and was the "go-to" guy for all the surgeons and anesthesiologists in the hospital. He basked in the glory of being the person all the surgeons confided in and loved to complain to management about all the problems.

He had participated in numerous process improvement projects in the past, none of which were successful, to the point that only one or two action items might have been accomplished on each. This shielded him from any changes and kept him as the "go-to" person for his peers.

As we implemented Lean we started making changes fairly quickly. He could not believe things were actually changing this time and the changes were sustaining. On the surface, at our weekly steering committee meetings, he told us what a great job we were doing; however, he became very concerned and paranoid that his role would change and he would no longer be the go-to guy. He viewed the changes as a threat vs. an opportunity. This became very unsettling to him and he started to resist the changes. Eventually, he stalled our project, made life very difficult for the Lean team with management, and refused to approve many of our changes. Because the team was successful, despite his efforts, management finally saw him for what he was, a "concrete head." Senior management tried to coach him through it, but he felt he didn't need to change with 1 year left before retirement. We ended up having to work with him until he retired.

Don't Encourage the Victim Syndrome

This person, the victim, like Eeyore,[26] tends to have that "cloud over their head" all the time. They cannot accept the changes nor take responsibility for them in their area. Although they were involved in the changes, they felt threatened and turned everything we did together into something that was "done to them" even though they agreed with all the changes.

Physician Resistance to Lean

In manufacturing, we have found machinists tend to fight Lean the most. They are very independent and typically start out not wanting any part of standard work. In the hospital world, the machinist seems, in some cases, to be replaced by the physician.

At hospital X, we were piloting our new ED system approach. The physicians involved with our team were part of and embraced the changes. The medical director, however, would not get involved and totally disagreed with our changes. He refused to speak directly with the team and purposely distorted our very positive results from their ED medical group during a budget presentation to the hospital CEO. This set the team and the ED rollouts back several months. After much coaching from his own physicians and finally witnessing first hand the changes, he reversed his position with the CEO, but by then the damage was done.

While some physicians truly embrace Lean and some actually drive the changes, most tend to initially resist or downright fight the changes. When they see the positive impact of Lean, they eventually come around. This brings up a point. Most Lean consulting is sold through the administrative side of hospitals. There is a real need to sell Lean through the physician/clinician side.

Dr. Nelson, a physician trained in Lean and author of the book Sustaining Lean in Healthcare: Developing and Engaging Physician Leadership, states, "The likelihood of a successful implementation in a hospital or clinic setting is directly proportional to the time spent engaging the physicians prior to initiating change. It is critical to understand their needs, to demystify Lean and to get their commitment for involvement in making tests of change. Sustaining a successful implementation may be as dependent on physician recognition of the improvement in their professional work lives

---

[26] A. A. Milne, *Winnie the Pooh* (London: Methuen) 1926.

as continued senior leader commitment. Value for physicians from more efficient and safer patient care processes can be a powerful force for sustainment."[27]

Get Everyone Involved in the Analysis Phase

Get as many people as possible in the targeted area involved in any Lean implementation from the beginning. The analysis tools are designed for that purpose. Many times we are told that people cannot be pulled to watch the videos. Without the people who actually do the work in the room during analysis, we can only guess at what they are doing. Even if we have someone else there that does that job, they still don't necessarily know what the person we filmed is doing. This is especially true in environments where everyone does it differently.

The other point here is that people will try to cut the analysis time by having the team do the analysis first and then bringing the person in to discuss the video. While it can be done this way, it is a poor process. The person who was filmed does not get to participate in the enlightenment process that occurs watching what they do on the video nor do they participate in any of the discussions leading up to the idea. You lose any opportunity to get their buy-in to the new process because they are not involved in creating it. So now you are doing it "to them". They will also fight the results when they are told that they should be able to do that job in one-third to one-half the time they do it now. When they participate in the analysis process, they are part of omitting steps and the subsequent suggestions and are then part of the reduction in time and can go back and trial the new process and work to improve and sustain it.

Give Lean System Implementation Time to Work before Trying to Change the Underpinnings

With any new process, it takes time to work. Everyone tends to resist the new process because it is different. We also fall victim to the systems thinking law of "unintended consequences." This law states that whenever we implement changes, no matter how much planning, there will always be something we forgot. Don't worry though, because the people in the area will be more than happy to point the mistakes out to you. As a result, we need time to work out the "bugs" and get the new processes working before scrapping it to go back and do it the way we have always done it before. It is very important not to over-react to comments or feelings people initially have prior to giving the new system a chance to work.

Dedicate Resources up Front

When starting the first Lean projects, we recommend a 100% dedicated cross-functional team of people to go through the BASICS process. We have tried the "part time" approach, and it NEVER works. The reason is that the day-to-day problems always win out over the needs of the improvement team. While we know it is very difficult, it is critical to backfill these people so that they can participate 100% of the time learning the tools and implementing the new Lean process.

Include a Strategy for Accountability and Sustaining as Part of the Continuous Improvement Road Map

In the overall implementation plan there has to be consideration given to how the project will be followed up and sustained. Keep in mind, sustained means ongoing improvement. We typically implement control plans and sustain plans with every project. Since the Lean management system

---

[27] Dr. Michael Nelson, Blue Corn Professional Services, Personal Communication, From Introduction to *Sustaining Lean In Healthcare: Developing And Engaging Physician Leadership, (Productivity Press),* 2011.

is new to the organization, we have learned that the process owners do not have the discipline, Lean knowledge, resources, or accountability to hold the gains and continually improve.

At Hospital X, this became a big problem. Once the project was done and the Lean team moved on, the organization believed it was the process owner's job to sustain and continue to drive improvements. We agreed! However, if the process owner, from a Lean maturity standpoint, doesn't know what needs to be done and there is no one to coach them on their standard work, it will ultimately fail. Finance said it was not their job to sustain it or make sure they met the ROI, which finance drove up-front. The process excellence staff organization said it was not their job to make sure it sustained because they were moving on to the next project. In addition, there was a major reorganization in the works within the hospital. This created quite a quandary, which by the time we departed, was never resolved.

Listen to Your Lean Consultants/Experts

Many companies get to a point after 3 to 6 months where they think they know enough to do it all themselves. Every company seems to go through this phase. People get to a point where they know enough to be dangerous and dangerous they become. Why do companies hire Lean consultants? Many times we have asked ourselves the same question. They refuse to put the Lean steering committee together; they stop listening to the Lean consultants and do what they want to do. Then, they come back to the Lean consultants and ask why Lean isn't working and blame it on the consultants.

Adopt and Integrate Standard Work and Create a Suggestion and Reward Systems

Toyota first learned about suggestions systems from Henry Ford. Toyota's suggestion system is described in the book, *40 Years, 20 Million Ideas*.[28] It is a fascinating read. Their model is not based around a suggestion box, but by having suggestions encouraged every day by the team leaders (supervisors) and implemented in real time. If it doesn't work, then they continue to try until it works or they go back to the way it was before and then try another improvement idea the next day. Once suggestions are implemented, the team leader updates the standard work in order to permanently capture the idea.

Don't Leave Managers in Place Who Aren't Going to Get It

One of the biggest obstacles we face is the manager or supervisor who is just never going to "get it." They don't buy in to Lean. They are normally from the "my way or the highway" philosophy of managing or they just plain look at this whole Lean thing as a threat to their job and the way they have always done it before. Our policy is to coach and mentor, coach and mentor, but eventually it becomes pretty obvious the person is not going to "buy in." Many times they go into a "stall" mode where they are always talking how great Lean is and outwardly agreeing with the team, but behind the scenes, they are stalling and doing everything they can to thwart the team.

Our experience is that 40%–70% of frontline supervisors and managers can't make the switch from cop to coach. If you keep them, they will kill the project and blame it on Lean or Six Sigma. It is important to move them to another area where they can be an individual contributor or moved out of the organization. It is difficult to do and most organizations wait way too long to address the problem and then wonder why they don't get the results.

This ties in with the ongoing review to see if we have the right people on the bus and if they are in the right seats to take us to the next level. With Lean, the need for the hero has gone away. It is also difficult when this person, who has so often been the "hero of the month," has to let go and focus on the process.

---

[28] Yuzo Yasuda, *40 Years, 20 Million Ideas* (Cambridge, MA: Productivity Press) 1991.

DON'T LAY PEOPLE OFF AFTER LEAN IMPLEMENTATION

As stated before, our goal is to never lay off anyone as a result of continuous improvement. This does not mean there cannot be layoffs due to a recession. Toyota and other companies have found a way to deal with recessions by hiring temporary part-time people. When you work for Toyota, it is a lifetime commitment. When you leave Toyota, they don't invite you back.

DON'T SHORTCUT THE TOOLS

If we shortcut the tools, then we shortcut the results. It is really that simple.

ENCOURAGE LEAN ARCHITECTURAL DESIGNS

Traditional architect designs are not Lean. If a Lean consultant is brought in, it is best to bring them in during the conceptual phase of the project prior to drawings.

INCLUDE A "GO FORWARD" PERSON ON THE TEAM

When implementing multiple sites or campuses, it works best if the prior campus team contains a person from the next campus to be implemented. We call this a "go forward" person. This is a great way to load the next campus team for success.

TRAIN, TRAIN, TRAIN

One cannot train enough with Lean. There is so much to learn. There are more than 500 books on Lean as we speak, many of the best now out of print. Creating a training plan up-front and following it is critical to success. The training is no substitute for the experience of implementing on the floor, but good interactive classroom training does have a role with Lean. Initial training can be as short as an hour or up to as long as 3 months or more at different intervals.

Ultimately, the training and ongoing continuous improvement culture becomes the role of the team or group leader with the assistance of HR and management. *You don't really learn the material until you have to train the materials!*

CREATE AN ESCALATION PROCESS

It is critical to have an escalation process in place to help the improvement teams or supervisors remove barriers to improvement. Many times, people are afraid to complain to their bosses or their bosses may be the problem. Failure to have this process in place will force these issues to be hidden and not surface. The escalation process should go to the CEO. Several times, we have had to go to the CEO during Lean implementations to make the final call.

IDENTIFY THE PROCESS OWNER AND THE TEAM LEADER UP FRONT

Document and communicate roles and responsibilities for everyone in the organization.

At Hospital X, we were speaking with a manager and asked to whom he reported. He said he reported to two different directors in the department. I asked each director who the manager ultimately reported to, and neither was sure. I asked the administrator over the area who the manger reported to. He said he reported to Director 1 and why was I asking. I told him that no one I asked was sure. Then he said, "Well, he also sort of reports to Director 2 as well." One director was administrative and one was clinical. This caused a lot of confusion and resulted in little accountability.

Lesson Learned

When all else fails, ask, "Who owns it?" If there is even a moment of hesitation in the response there is a problem.

CHANGE REWARD SYSTEM

If we implement the new Lean system but leave the old reward system in place, what will be the outcome? The new system will never sustain. We must change the reward system to align with the new desired Lean behaviors. This should be part of the Lean road map.

IT'S JUST A BUMP IN THE ROAD

Many times, especially during suggesting solutions, or implementation, the team will run into problems and setbacks. A legal or compliance person will tell you something can't be done, or somehow the team has inadvertently upset someone. We have come to refer to these as "bumps in the road." At the time, they may seem like major issues or problems, but once we work through them, they become minor. This is a time to consider the communication model. Sometimes face-to-face communication is best during these "bumps."

MULTIPLE SITE ROLLOUT STRATEGIES

SITE/AREA SELECTION

We generally suggest putting a cross-functional team of individuals together to form the team. We pick a pilot site and pilot line based on the following criteria[29]:

- Most important, it must be successful.
- We must have open-minded leadership willing to participate on the team, take ownership, drive and sustain the change.
- We need the process owner to spend 80%–90% of the time on the team.
- The pilot should prove that the BASICS tools work.
- Where it makes sense, we should be able to transfer results to other campuses and standardize the processes.

TRYING TO IMPLEMENT SEVERAL PROJECTS AT ONCE WITHOUT SUFFICIENT RESOURCES

Resources become a critical ingredient when implementing Point Kaizen events or Lean implementations. If you can't resource it, don't launch it! We have seen and been part of many efforts that failed because the implementing area, while really wanting to make the changes, couldn't free up the necessary or the right staff to make the changes successful.

---

[29] Influenced by Mark Jamrog, principal, The SMC Group.

8 Executives and Lean

INTRODUCTION

Lean and other quality initiatives often do not find their way into a company through senior leadership. These projects normally start at the middle-management level and trickle up and down. Senior managers usually believe they have a good understanding of quality initiatives while often their understanding is not as deep as they believe.

You do not need to go to Japan to see Lean at work. There are many companies to tour in the United States, including Toyota. Most associations offer tours of companies working on Lean, including the Association of Manufacturing Excellence, the Society of Manufacturing Engineers, the Institute of Industrial Engineers, the Society for Health Systems, and the Institute for Healthcare Improvement. There are many good books to available to read.

BEEN THERE, DONE THAT

It is important to understand that senior leaders have been through many quality initiatives over the years. Many can still remember the days when total quality management (TQM), continuous quality improvement (CQI), and the other alphabet soup initiatives were the quality programs *du jour*. While many senior executives may have only fleeting memories of most of these initiatives, they seemed to come and go on the whim of consultants. It is understandable why many senior executives are skeptical and perhaps even cynical of new quality initiatives that come in the vernacular of a new group of initials or new "sound bite." In addition, many of the results derived from other quality initiatives are not culturally transformational nor do they mirror results seen through Lean initiatives.

Along with this superficial understanding of quality initiatives, it is not surprising to find that many senior leaders and executives believe they have a better understanding of these programs than they do, and most think they have a good understanding of how to deliver high-quality patient care. It is not until they get personally involved with Lean and other Process Improvement methodologies that they begin to understand what they do and do not know. In these difficult financial times, the cost of implementation is also a significant barrier. Healthcare entities are facing challenges not encountered before with the inception of the Affordable Care Act, Bundled Payment Programs, the growth of Accountable Care Organizations, and overall consolidation in the marketplace. Everyone recognizes the need to change. There is building pressure to create customer value, to do more with less, while maintaining high quality, exceptional patient experience at a lower cost.

Learning Lean can be difficult for most executives since many are busy addressing these current operational challenges and leadership functions. Even the thought of taking the time to sit down and understand Lean and other quality initiatives is quite daunting with everything else piled up on their plates. Often, one of the most difficult tasks of getting Lean into an organization is the "coaching up" that executive high-level staff must do to their most senior leadership to get them to understand the level of value, level of commitment, and the investment in time and energy to realize a Lean organization. If executives somehow find the time to truly understand Lean and its impact, they will discover it is not just another quality improvement initiative. Lean provides concepts and tools that will fundamentally change the way organizations do business and ultimately make their jobs as leaders much easier in the long run.

MORE THAN JUST A COMPETITIVE ADVANTAGE

Our current healthcare spending model in this country is unsustainable. Additionally, safety of healthcare is being called to question as the IOM Institute of Medicine[1] estimated that up to 98,000 American patients die each year from medical errors. Further evidenced in the recently published article, in the *Journal of Patient Safety*, "A New, Evidence-based Estimate of Patient Harms Associated with Hospital Care" by John T. James, PhD, which utilized the global trigger tool to flag specific evidence in charts that point to adverse events that may have harmed a patient, "the findings revealed a lower limit of 210,000 deaths per year was associated with preventable harm in hospitals. Given limitations in the search capability of the Global Trigger Tool and the incompleteness of medical records on which the Tool depends, the true number of premature deaths associated with preventable harm to patients was estimated at more than 400,000 per year. Serious harm seems to be 10- to 20-fold more common than lethal harm."[2]

The ability to provide increasing quality of care at decreasing cost through organizational efficiencies is paramount. As healthcare focuses on the Institute for Healthcare Improvement's (IHI) Triple Aim which is framework to optimize healthcare system performance of improving the patient experience (quality and safety), improving health of populations and reducing the per capita cost of healthcare[3], the need to provide "value based care" will become more critical as the market gets more competitive and unit cost reimbursements decrease. It will become more imperative for organizations to become more efficient. Not only will executives need to understand the potential financial impact from a bottom line perspective, but they will also need to be able to lead the organization in understanding that eliminating waste will reduce the number of steps, thereby reducing the opportunities for defects or errors to occur. This will ultimately lead toward improving the overall quality of the service and care delivered to the customer (both internal and external) and the end result, over time, will positively impact the organization.

With the creation of the Hospital Consumer Assessment of Healthcare Providers and Systems[4] (HCAHPS) survey, hospitals are becoming increasingly aware that their reputation for quality and patient satisfaction can drive consumer choice. They are now recognizing that it is necessary to view patients as customers because they are held accountable for their customer service track record in a very public forum. Executives need to place emphasis on the importance of obtaining the voice of the customer (VOC) to fully understand what is value-added from the patients' point of view, which may be different from how they have viewed their organizations in the past. Medicare is also reimbursing hospitals based on these "value based metrics". Gaining an understanding of Lean concepts and principles and deploying Lean tools to optimize operations will become a competitive model that enables corporate sustainability in the long run. Over time, Lean will move from being utilized to achieve a competitive advantage to a way that companies operate in order to survive.

Lesson Learned

Lean is the competitive advantage today and a way of survival tomorrow.

BOARD OF DIRECTORS TRAINING

Every Lean system implementation or journey should be supported by the guiding principles and values of the organization.

---

[1] TO ERR IS HUMAN: BUILDING A SAFER HEALTH SYSTEM, November 1999; http://www.nap.edu/books/0309068371/html/; Copyright ©2000 by the National Academy of Sciences.

[2] A New, Evidence-based Estimate of Patient Harms Associated with Hospital Care, John T. James, PhD, www.journalpatientsafety.com; 2013 Lippincott Williams & Wilkins.

[3] http://www.ihi.org/offerings/Initiatives/TripleAim/Pages/MeasuresResults.aspx

[4] http://www.hcahpsonline.org/home.aspx

The board of directors is playing a more active role in organizations, both strategically and operationally. As boards become more accountable, not just for the financial health of an organization but also for the quality and outcomes of that particular institution, it becomes imperative that the board understand the quality and improvement initiatives taking place in the company. The board of directors is responsible for setting the strategic direction of the organization; therefore, they must receive training in Lean in order to understand the value of Lean and drive the Lean transformation from the top. Top-down leadership is critical to rolling out and sustaining Lean and a commitment of significant resources to achieve organizational improvement. One needs to recognize the executives on the board have many of the same challenges as other executives in terms of time commitment, prior quality improvement experience, etc.; however, it is imperative they understand the potential impact Lean can bring to an organization in order to fully support the initiatives. It is interesting to note many hospital boards have members from industries other than healthcare which are practicing Lean such as manufacturing or service based companies who are now enlightening fellow hospital board members as to the benefits of introducing Lean programs. In addition, for Lean to permeate the organization, the process excellence organization should report directly to the CEO and the board. This will place attention to the importance of the transformation, while providing the most senior executives direct access to what is occurring in the deployment.

DIFFERENCES BETWEEN LEAN AND SIX SIGMA

Executives often find themselves in a position where they have to explain why they are advocating Lean and/or Six Sigma and the differences between Lean and Six Sigma. While both tool sets start with the Voice of the Customer (VOC), Lean is focused on improvements to flow and throughput velocity through standardization of tasks and improving efficiency by reducing non-value-added activities and removing waste. In a Lean culture, small incremental improvements are made every day by everyone in the organization.

Six Sigma is a more methodical model aimed at improving processes by reducing variation. Healthcare organizations often find it difficult to begin with Six Sigma tools, as the processes are ridden with waste and a significant amount of variability. In order to achieve the greatest impact toward improving the process, we recommend applying Lean concepts first, in order to eliminate waste and streamline processes, and then apply Six Sigma tools to reduce variation.

Most projects or initiatives use a combination of both Lean and Six Sigma tools, since they both work well together.

DEFINE REALITY FOR THE LEAN INITIATIVE

Executives can become familiar with Lean concepts, tools, and benefits by attending healthcare forums, reading literature, or formal training. They begin by identifying areas within the organization in which there is a compelling need to change. In most circumstances, these are areas in which there is poor performance based on either patient complaints, poor satisfaction scores from patients, physicians or staff, falling volumes, or an area's inability to move its metrics.

Occasionally, Lean projects are initiated prior to potential capital investments to validate, consolidate, or redesign an expansion. Senior executives must select Lean projects that carefully align with corporate goals and strategy to allow buy-in from the entire healthcare team. It is the executive's responsibility to engage in the process of "project or initiative selection" to make sure the area and the potential initiative being considered has a proper scope with clarity in the project definition, with expectations that are realistic and aligned to the strategic plan of the organization.

We have had many executive-level conversations on where in the organization to begin Lean initiatives, as in many cases the areas with the most opportunity for improvement has experienced ongoing organizational challenges. There may have been weak management or they may not have had the appropriate support to make the necessary changes to be successful. It is critical for the executives to assess and understand potential challenges a Lean initiative may encounter and be willing to remove barriers and provide the support needed to enable success.

A key component of any initiative or project selection is setting in place accountability along with roles and responsibilities for the initiative. The executive must make sure that all the stake-holders understand the initiative, timeline, expectations, and deliverables. They need to be realistic and clearly communicated with area leadership and staff prior to the implementation rollout. It is important that the executive demonstrates an ongoing strong and active level of support to show that the Lean effort has the highest priority.

Communication is critical! Everyone, including front-line staff, supervisors, managers, and team members, should understand the goals and objectives to be achieved, how the Lean initiative will help the clinical area achieve the goals, how they (staff and managers) will be impacted by them, and what is in it for them if they meet the deliverables. These are basic change management questions that need to be addressed and re-addressed throughout the initiative. The staff needs to clearly understand what the organization is trying to accomplish and what role they play in helping the organization reach that goal. This can be done by attending departmental meetings with the area management personally kicking off the project, holding weekly update meetings, making department rounds, and continually interacting with the staff in the area in which the initiative is occurring.

It is critical to review the objectives, goals, and timeline during status update meetings, allowing time for key designated team members to discuss challenges, successes, and lessons learned.

RESOURCES AND ACCOUNTABILITY

It is up to the leadership to work with the area managers, supervisors, and even the finance depart-ment to make the necessary resources available. Often, staff feels overwhelmed with the amount of work they have to do and it is a very difficult transition to take time out of one's daily work to be 100% dedicated to a Lean team. The senior leadership is responsible to select the teams and encour-age multi-disciplinary cooperation to bring the right people to the table. They must dedicate the resources and time needed to change processes, to carefully set the stage, and identify appropriate roles and responsibilities for these teams.

Lesson Learned

Leadership must be prepared to "backfill" those on the team, as these projects don't work well with "part-time" resources. The day-to-day tasks always win out.

It is the responsibility of the executive and critical to the success of the Lean initiative to allow the time needed to change culture. Executives need to be aware that the teams engaged in these initiatives spend 20%–30% of their time in training concepts and tools and 70%–80% of the time in change management responding to the cultural component. Some organizations create a separate "budget" so that the time for employees who are engaged in the initiative are not "charged" to the department budget.

At multi-national company X, the CEO boldly challenged all of their plants to be 80% Lean within five years. Then over the course of the next year the goal changed from five years to two years. Anyone that knows anything about Lean would tell you five years is extremely aggressive for a multi-national company, but to cut it to two years is ridiculous. As a result, it started driving irrational behaviors at the company.

Lesson Learned

Culture changes normally take 5 years with a passionate and dedicated CEO and senior leadership team communicating the vision, consistent message and adhering to a strong value system centered on adding customer value along with respect and appreciation for their employees. Eventually, everyone is on the Lean team, as Lean becomes the way we do business.

In healthcare settings, managers are often promoted from within and may have little experience in these areas. Frontline nurses and ancillary support personnel who are excellent clinicians are often placed in management positions with limited management experience or training. This is somewhat unique to the healthcare profession. Thus, the selection of projects and the setting of appropriate expectations and goals become even more critical. The culture in many organizations has not fostered an allowance for staff, managers, and team members to take chances and learn from their mistakes.

LEAN SHOULD BE WHERE THE ACTION IS

It is important that the Lean team, process excellence organization, and the area leadership are co-located where the action is. Many companies have put their process excellence or quality departments off-site in other buildings and sometimes even at other hospitals or clinic locations. It is critical the Lean group is on-site and any Lean activity be visual to the frontline staff. This is a very important piece of the cultural change. The Lean change program must be in front of everyone, every day, and successes published throughout the organization.

REMOVING BARRIERS

It is the responsibility of the executive to listen attentively, ask questions, and be prepared to help to remove barriers to keep the Lean initiatives on track. Barriers often encountered are cultural, territorial, accountability challenges, team resource availability, and financially driven such as budgetary constraints or capital needs. There may be times when new equipment or funding for layout reconstruction are identified, and executives can play a pivotal role in championing resource needs.

Lean is a different way of thinking and managing. Some areas may have performance issues with managers or staff who may be competent, but may not have the necessary skills needed or may not be receptive to adopting Lean as a new way to do business.

Executives are constantly faced with determining if they have the "right people on the right seat on the bus." Our experience has been that every Lean initiative has staff "changing seats" or "leaving the bus." In most cases, managers or staff members recognize that they do not want to engage in the cultural transformation and opt to move to other areas or leave the organization. As these challenges present themselves, the executive leader will play a key role to make sure the right leaders are in the right place to drive the initiative to the next level. The area leadership must be held accountable to sustain any improvement and drive continuous improvement activities forward.

Executives must be willing to work through personnel changes and engage human resource managers to help resolve staffing barriers. If the area executive believes that the outcome of the Lean initiative may be staff reductions, there must be a plan to move staff to other areas. Normally, attrition will provide open spots for those freed up. We do not recommend layoffs during or surrounding a Lean initiative. This will prove counterproductive and rumors will travel like the plague relating Lean to layoffs. It will then be extremely difficult to engage other areas within the organization in Lean initiatives.

If Human Resources is engaged early on, they can provide advice on opportunities for employees as reductions occur and provide counsel on options for staff or managers who may resist the cultural transformation necessary for the Lean initiative's success. We put people we "free" up on future process improvement teams until we can find a home for them.

MEASUREMENTS TO DRIVE OUTCOMES

The next major issue for leadership is to set up processes for measurements. This is particularly critical in healthcare, where, often, quality measurements can be difficult to evaluate. Measures should be directly driven from your organizational vision, strategic plan and the objectives that are set forth outlining what you in to accomplish to attain that vision. Many organizations leverage Hoshin planning (policy deployment) as their strategic planning methodology. As your strategic plan is developed, each objective identified should include measures defining success related to quality, cost and delivery. Lean initiatives should be aligned to the objectives within your strategic plan. If this alignment process is absent, projects tend to emerge based on immediate issues, rather than being strategically prioritized. Establishing organizational measures and alignment to Lean project measures creates a process and disciplined set of checks for monitoring performance, and accountability, both in the workplace and at the project level to assess progress. In healthcare, accountabilities and measures are critical to a Lean initiative; without this, Lean will not be sustainable. "Floor" management and daily huddles are necessary to facilitate communication with frontline staff to "debrief" daily operations and receive feedback for continuous opportunities of improvement.

Outcomes measurement is the gold standard in healthcare; however, in healthcare we must often measure processes or level of care. However, a flawed process with too many steps or steps not aligning with evidenced based care paths can negatively impact outcomes. Therefore, developing process measures should go hand in hand with clinical measures. There can be many process steps in the care of a patient. By improving these process steps we assume or in many cases, the literature supports improved outcomes. An example might be a patient with a heart attack (a code STEMI) that is seen in the emergency room and because the clinical literature supports better outcomes, aspirin is prescribed. The morbidity and survival of the patient become the outcome measure. The literature supports many of these processes. They lead to positive outcomes and it is under this assumption that we look at these "process" of care metrics.

It is critical that leadership set up a dashboard where these measurements are tracked on a regular basis to actually prove that our pre- and post-results are what we expect. In many cases the numbers are not large enough at a single institution or the time frames long enough to look at outcomes; this is where benchmarking can be helpful.

It is also very important to set up a measurement system that looks at measurements in real time so that effective changes can be made immediately. Patient care and quality outcomes are time-sensitive factors. There is little value in looking at measurements at the end of the month only to find out "after the fact" that we have a problem. Additionally, we have to look at individual measures, not just averages or extremes. It is not helpful to look at only extremes of measurement, since variation can be an issue. One of our sayings is "variation is the enemy of Lean,"[5] and we have to focus on keeping the standard deviation to a minimum.

The challenge, initially, is that very few processes within healthcare follow a normal distribution. There is extreme variability as standard work has not been deployed and staff may perform tasks differently on different shifts. We must stabilize the process through a Lean initiative and gain an understanding of what is important to the customer. This is accomplished through eliminating non-value-added steps, which will result in decreasing variability and "clean up" the process, which then highlights the remaining variation.

Who Is to Blame?

The measurement piece must be focused on improving the process. It is sometimes very tempting and easy to find someone or something to blame when there is a problem. We have to recognize that at least 90% of the time, the process or "system" is at fault, and focusing on people only misleads and slows down the ability to determine the real root cause.

An example often used in healthcare is when something goes wrong; we default to "more education" and focus on individual learning. This is often not the correct approach. Often, when we look back at the process, we find out that it has been broken for some time and that simply re-training will

---

[5] Influenced by Six Sigma saying.

not solve the problem. We have to go back and analyze the process to determine the true systemic root cause.

We need to discover what in our system allowed the "error" by the staff person to be made. How do we "people proof" or mistake proof critical processes to prevent the error and resulting defect from ever occurring again? We have to get beyond depending on the individual's personal knowledge, training, experience, skill, and memory. No one intentionally decides that they are going to come in to work today and purposefully make mistakes. Many industries have deployed mistake proofing to eradicate unwanted behaviors, fully understanding that people don't want to make errors and feel terrible when they make them, especially when people's lives are at risk.

YOU ARE WHAT YOU MEASURE

Executives need to set the standards! They need to choose the metrics that they want to achieve, that are aligned to the organizations goals, and provide clarity to management about what is being measured, who is responsible, how (baseline, targets, and stretch goals) results are going to be evaluated, and how often the results should be reported (timeline, daily, monthly, quarterly). It is important that these results are posted real time in the department, not just on a cluttered bulletin board or mixed in with other paperwork. You must set the bar high and visible.

In healthcare, we often suffer from information overload. We are so busy trying to get so much information out to the line level staff that we are naïve to the fact that very little is grasped. We need to whittle the data down to information and train our staff in the vital few metrics that are important. Hourly patient and leader rounding are becoming more prevalent in many organizations. Critical information should be shared at standing "huddles", during rounds and/or at the department meetings every morning in a very visible graph-like fashion so it can be looked at and evaluated quickly. The ability to select representative data points to measure core processes, with clear definitions, with real-time reporting on an executive dashboard to monitor performance is critical to continuous process improvement and to achieve organizational excellence.

CONTROL OR SUSTAIN PROCESS

Executives must supervise the creation of a "control or sustain" process for all improvements. If the executive does not follow up on Lean changes, managers and supervisors will assume that it is not a priority. If you think it is important, they will think it is important!

This means that once a change is put in place, a real-time measurement process must be put in place to keep track of the process. The most difficult part of Lean/Sigma is to make sure the process stays in "control" and continues to improve. The process should be measured before and after on a continued basis, or one cannot determine if the improvements to the process are sustained. It is the responsibility of the executive to review the measures and make the area managers and staff understands the expectations and set accountabilities in place. This may mean the initiation of both positive and negative consequences for the staff in order to create accountability and discipline for the measures.

The target measures must be established at the beginning of a Lean initiative ("baselined"), and once the improvement is established, constantly improved, otherwise things have a tendency to backslide to the old less efficient "way we have always done it" (Figure 8.1).

If the expectations are not met, then the executive must work with the process owner (i.e., department leader) to identify the root cause and put a corrective action plan in place.

Any process deployed should have key metrics and/or measures that are reported through the chain of command starting at the frontline, to supervisor/manager to director to senior executive, so the senior executive can gauge how well the process is performing and be able to identify challenges. These metrics and/or measures should be incorporated into the leader standard work. The senior executive should work with their leaders to help them grow and develop by holding them accountable to sustain and improve the process measures.

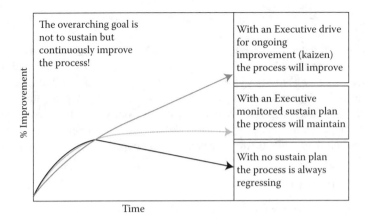

FIGURE 8.1   Improvement Curve. Source: Authors.

Lesson Learned

When the executive's bonus rides on the measure, the measure normally improves. The question is: "Is it the right improvement?" The answer is: The right improvement is driven by giving the process owner the right tools to determine how to improve the process. The wrong improvement is driven by the senior leaders providing all the answers and focusing only on results.

LEAN AND AUDITS

Looking at the Toyota model, there are a number of key areas emphasized in the development of their Lean process. The first one was auditing. Auditing can be utilized in a variety of ways and it can play a key role in identifying opportunities for improvement on a day-to-day basis. It can be leveraged to monitor a recently implemented improvement in order to understand the level of control or adoption.

Auditing can take the form of a written audit assessment or can be a form of "rounding." An example of this being implemented in many organizations, such as at Sharp Healthcare, is "leader rounding" utilizing a leader rounding form[6]", where the executive's focus is on mentoring the area leadership on key initiatives that it desires to "hardwire" in the organization (Figure 8.2). This is a form of ongoing and visual process improvement. The premise is that key process metrics are reviewed on a day-to-day basis by management and leadership in "real time." This allows for immediate corrective action and achieves the best results.

Executives can set a clear line-of-sight accountability from the frontline staff to the executive, by incorporating audits, measurement reporting, action plan updates to resolve challenges, monitoring the results of audits, feedback mechanisms from staff, suggestion implementation, and incorporating continuous improvement into leader standard work, where the executive "leads by example" to drive ongoing performance and improvement.

"PROJECT-ITIS"

One of the challenges in many corporations is to get out of what is called a "project mentality." Companies launch project after project, hoping something will "stick." Even if these are Lean oriented, sooner or later, they run out of staff to continue these projects or the same staff members may

---

[6] http://www.sharp.com/choose-sharp/sharp-experience/leader rounding.cfm

Unit Leader Weekly Linkage Grid

Expectation: completed and turned into supervisor by late in day on Friday each week.

Leader:		Unit:		Week ending:		
Top Priorities Employee Opinion Survey	▸ ▸ ▸		Must Haves	▸ Smile, greet, hello ▸ Take people where they need to go ▸ Leader rounding ▸ Thank you cards ▸ Key words key times		
Top Priority Pt. Satisfaction	▸		AIDET	▸ Acknowledge, Introduce, Duration, Explanation, Thank You		
Top Priority MD Satisfaction	▸		Monthly Behavior Standard	▸		
Rounding for Staff Satisfaction	▸ Ask staff: do you have tools to do your job today? ▸ Ask staff: any special patients/visitors I need to know about? ▸ Remind staff which priority or priorities they are working on today ▸ Tell staff what your expectations are. ▸ Spend time to ask/observe staff for desired behaviors		Keywords at Key Times	▸ ▸ ▸ ▸ ▸		

DATE & LOCATION					
# OF PTS /STAFF/MDs VISITED	/ /	/ /	/ /	/ /	/ /
EMPLOYEE ISSUES	Followed-up	Followed-up	Followed-up	Followed-up	Followed-up
ENVIRONMENTAL / EQUIPMENT/ SAFETY ISSUES	Followed-up	Followed-up	Followed-up	Followed-up	Followed-up
SUGGESTIONS FOR IMPROVEMENT	Followed-up	Followed-up	Followed-up	Followed-up	Followed-up
DATE & LOCATION					
STAFF TO RECOGNIZE (Be specific, build confidence and don't overwhelm)	Completed	Completed	Completed	Completed	Completed
WINS					
SECRET SHOPPING Staff publicly recognized					
Registry staff signed AIDET & Behavior Standards					

People/actions to manage up (to director) for thank you notes:		Scouting report (dept accomplishments, new equip, staff to recognize, issues, MD activity, current patient sat results):			

Employees Contacted At Home (LOAs & Worker Comp.)	NAME				
	DATE				
30/90 Day Interviews Completed	NAME				
	DATE				
High/Medium/Low Reviews completed	NAME				
	DATE				

Connect the Dots After Rounding (Mirror Image)	What's going well?
	What is improving?
	What could be improved next?
	How did you recognize the staff for the behaviors that support the priority initiatives?

FIGURE 8.2   Leader Rounding Tool Example, Sharp Healthcare, Grossmont Hospital, http://www.sharp.com/choose-sharp/sharp-experience/leader-rounding.cfm.

be assigned to every project. We have been at several companies where they have many projects going at the same time. The oldest project seems to fall out of control once the staff readjusts their sights on the newer projects. This is why a change in culture is so critical. We must move out of the "project-itis" mentality and move toward creating an environment of change based on process-focused improvements.

HUMAN ERROR FACTOR

Current hospital culture and training combined with years of tradition, paradigms, and poor hospital information systems have all contributed to the broken hospital systems we see today. Physicians have had to react and deal with these systems, getting reimbursed less and less for their services, while malpractice insurance skyrockets. A number of states have capped their insurance judgments.[7,8,9] Since 1986, 38 states have reformed joint-and-severe liability rules; 23 states have enacted statutes limiting non-economic damages, and currently 18 states have such statutes in place; and 34 states have restricted punitive damages. Yet doctors are human, hospital staff are human, and all doctors and staff, even the best, make mistakes. Why? Because humans are, based on a poll of several Master Black Belts, at best from less than 1–3 Sigma. This means doctors average 66,800 mistakes per million or more. While most are probably minor, every once in a while a major one is going to occur, even to the best.

The temptation not to report a medical error should never be underestimated. One published study disclosed that only 50% of house staff physicians who admitted making serious clinical errors disclosed their errors to medical colleagues, and only 25% disclosed them to the patients or their families. In another published survey of laypersons, only 1–3 of respondents who had experienced medical errors said that the physicians involved in the error had informed them about it. Still another survey, asking European physicians whether they would disclose a medical error to patients, found that although 70% responded that physicians should provide details of such an event, only 32% would actually disclose the details of what happened. A similar percentage of American physicians (77%) echoed the same opinion.

A British researcher explains this reluctance to disclose by pointing out that physicians who commit medical errors frequently question their own competence and fear being discovered; they know they should confess but "dread the prospect of potential punishment." These reactions are "reinforced during medical training; the culture of medical school and residency implies that mistakes are unacceptable and point to a failure of character."[10]

Nurses, hospitals, and anyone who works within a hospital are subjected to malpractice risk. Hospitals are struggling with how to create a "just" culture of honesty with patients, while trying not to increase malpractice claims. How do you push a "just" culture when society is always looking for blame (especially within the U.S. legal system)? Doctors have years of habits—both good and bad—influenced by society and our legal system, as well as ethical dilemmas created constantly by new technology. When we implement Lean, we start to bump up against these old habits. It is interesting to note how much medicine and medical technology has changed over the years, yet, in most cases, our processes have not!

Lessons Learned

The ability to deploy Lean is directly related to the culture within your organization. Culture change is the biggest obstacle to implementing Lean and lack of systems thinking is the biggest obstacle to implementing the right tools and improvements.

---

[7] Liker, Toyota Culture.

[8] http://www.webmm.ahrq.gov/perspective.aspx?perspectiveID=50.

[9] Source: http://uspolitics.about.com/od/healthcare/a/01_tort_reform.htm.

[10] http://uspolitics.about.com/od/healthcare/a/01_tort_reform.htm

Fair and Just Culture[11]

The Lean cultural change needs to include what used to be called a "blame-free" culture. This is probably not practical since a blame-free culture is not practical. The new terminology is more accurately called a "just" culture. This is a culture where, when things do not go right, they are looked at critically from an operational standpoint. If it is a hospital systemic process issue, it is dealt with at that level. If it is truly an individual person's accountability, such as the person refuses to follow the standard work or abide by the new system, then appropriate action should be taken. Thus, it is not really a blame-free culture, but a fair, just, and accountable culture that focuses on dealing with problems at an accurate level and in an efficient manner, keeping the patient at the forefront of everyone's concerns. If a process has been broken and not followed for years, it does not seem right to punish an individual for not following it when something goes wrong.

In the Lean model, the culture is based on "Respect for Humanity." Whether we call it "just" or "blameless," this new culture is critical in order for Lean to work.[12] A Lean environment should encourage employees to feel free to uncover and share problems. The goal is to have every problem exposed, identify the root cause, then act on and fix the problem so it never comes back. If the employee is too afraid to admit to a mistake, we will never know a problem existed or, worst case scenario, the problem manifests itself and eventually results in something serious, such as a hospital-acquired infection or the death of a patient. If employees do not feel comfortable identifying wastes within their processes and exposing problems, Lean will not permeate the organization.

A good model for making sure that all aspects of a project are clearly evaluated is to focus on evaluating the critical areas of safety, quality, delivery, cost, inventory and morale.

A new worker on the Toyota line had accidentally scratched the underside of a front fender of the car as he carried out his operation.[13] He debated whether to tell the team leader because, after all, no one would probably see it. He pulled the andon cord and the supervisor came over. The worker told the supervisor the problem. The supervisor asked him how it was caused. The worker told him. Together they came up with both a short-term (counter-measure) and longer-term solution to fix the problem so it would never come back. At lunchtime, the team leader pulled everyone together and congratulated the worker for pulling the cord and telling him about the problem. Everyone clapped.

Lesson Learned

Does everyone on your healthcare staff feel free to admit to problems immediately as they occur? If we don't surface the problem, we can't fix it. If your culture is based on fear and retribution, employees will not surface problems and everyone loses.

As we can see from the story above, there are two ways to approach problems—one is positive and the other is negative. Some hospitals have been very successful at creating this "just" culture.[14] Other hospitals may just be beginning the journey; however, this may truly be one of the most difficult programs to implement, as it will require an organizational culture change.

---

[11] Joint Commission on Accreditation of Health Care Organization 10/07 vol 33 #10.

[12] Mann, *Creating a Lean Culture*. (Productivity Press) 2005.

[13] Liker, *Toyota Culture* (McGraw Hill) 2005.

[14] http://www.webmm.ahrq.gov/perspective.aspx?perspectiveID=50.

COMMUNICATION, COMMUNICATION, AND MORE COMMUNICATION

An important piece of a Lean environment is that leadership should set up a two-way communication process where line level staff can use their experience to safely identify existing problems and comfortably contribute ideas that they feel are valued and should be acted on. These ideas should be acknowledged by management. One way to do this is by putting up a bulletin board that tracks, open and honestly, any employee suggestions and creates a dialogue to get more information about particular suggestions (Figure 8.3). This dialogue must then be acted on, putting a process in place to take the suggestion and operationalizing it. All this should be in a public forum, so that people feel that their ideas are taken seriously and have value. Providing staff with a mechanism to make recommendations and publicly displaying the impact of their suggestions will drive cycles of continuous improvement, foster employee engagement, and help sustain Lean.

Communication is a critical enabler and can be facilitated by holding regular meetings every morning. This should be a brisk meeting, 5–10 min, also called "standup meetings or huddles." These meetings should deal with issues of the day, talk about difficult problems, and talk about changes in patient's status. They also need to address efficiencies of care, which is not necessarily a standard topic in today's environment. These meetings can also be where new information is shared from a process change and where results can be shared with the group.

In addition, in order to achieve a transformational change, executives must create ongoing lines of communication with managers and staff to share the organization's strategic goals and to reinforce the organization's priorities. They must ensure that each employee understands how each can contribute to help the organization to achieve its goals. If reinforcement is not continued, attention and priorities will fade, and the progress to achieving the strategic goals will diminish.

GEMBA[15] – WHERE THE TRUTH CAN BE FOUND

"*Gemba* 現場 translated to "on the spot," the actual place," or "the real place" where value is created." One of the most important aspects of Lean is the "walk around" or going to the *Gemba*. The *Gemba* should be a visual workplace and it "should talk to you" by making problems immediately visible (Figure 8.4). Going to the *Gemba* provides the opportunity for executives, managers, and supervisors to develop their employees by reinforcing organizational priorities and encouraging them to think through the problem-solving process. This is done by the executive going to the area and seeing what is actually occurring on the frontline. The executives can engage employees in

FIGURE 8.3   Idea Board. Source: BIG Archives.

---

[15] www.saiga-jp.com, kanji to English dictionary, http://diet.regev info Japanese to English dictionary.

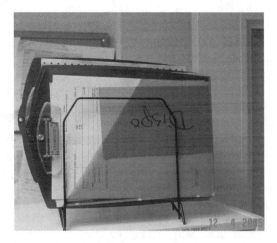

FIGURE 8.4   Visual Control ED Disposition Rack first-in-first-out order (FIFO). Source: BIG Archives.

active communication related to topics important to the organization and obtain direct feedback from the staff.

The executive or manager may choose topics for each *Gemba* to drill down on potential issues that have been identified and then encourage the area leaders to take the opportunity to ask why five times to get to the root cause of the problem. An environment of transparency and trust must be created. Clear, concise, open, and honest dialog must be continued. Suggestions and feedback must be accepted and evaluated without an initial reaction. No ideas are "stupid."

In a healthcare situation, walking around the hospital or a medical office, talking to patients, vendors, and line level staff helps to create critical communication both upward and downward. *Gemba* walks allow staff to see the commitment of the executive team and vice versa. The staff can communicate issues that are affecting them on a very real day-to-day basis.

When was the last time you had lunch with the frontline staff in the cafeteria? This is routinely done by Japan Airways President and CEO Haruka Nishimatsu. In both a CNN and CBS Sunday Morning[16] *interview, he stated he likes to eat lunch with the employees "in order to share and to raise morale and motivation." His philosophy is "there is no one at the top or bottom. A boss is in the same boat as their people. You either share the work and sacrifice together or the company will sink." He goes on to say, "If you have a problem, don't blame the person you are dealing with, blame the person in charge." In the same segment, Southwest CEO Gary Kelly says, "It won't work if leaders treat themselves one way and employees another."*

It is also important that the executive be among the patients, as they are the ultimate customers of the system. They can give feedback on the things that are working and not working in a very direct and meaningful way.

WHAT QUESTIONS SHOULD YOU ASK WHEN DOING A GEMBA WALK?

- What are your challenges, problems, issues?
- What have you improved today?
- Audits - Are they up to date? What problems are they having?
- How can I help you?

---

[16] CBS Sunday Morning, aired February 2009, entitled "Economy Class," produced by Marsha Cooke and edited by Randy Schmidt, CNN interview on You Tube, http://www.youtube.com/watch?v=858t44psmww&feature=rec-LGOUT-exp_fresh+div-1r-2-HM.

Lesson Learned

An executive must be open and accessible. Get out of the ivory tower and find out what is going on in your hospital first-hand at the Gemba.

MEETINGS

Meetings are often the bane of existence in a corporation. Meetings take up a tremendous amount of time and often take up most of many executives' day. Meetings in and of themselves are not necessarily bad; however, in many companies, both the number of meetings and the meeting inefficiency create a tremendous waste of time. In looking at this from a Lean perspective, if the time is not actually spent adding value to the customer, then one must question the value of the meeting(s). Meetings should be carefully orchestrated in terms of what their purpose is and what their outcomes will be, making sure that this will all add to a better product (patient care). Many organizations undergoing a Lean transformation actually "Lean" the meeting process by eliminating redundant or ineffective meetings that are not value-added to the internal or external customers, deploying structure and rigor in meeting design. Companies are moving to designated "no meeting days" to allow managers to dedicate more time to managing frontline operations and staff.

PAYING FOR SUGGESTIONS

One complicated issue is when to compensate for suggestions. There is no easy answer. Some people feel that paying for suggestions is paying people for work that they should already be doing. Other companies feel that the value of suggestions and savings should be transferred back to the individual employee. Many companies introduce some type of gain-sharing or bonus system in which all employees receive an equal amount vs. a percentage of their pay. This is an individual company decision, and there are pros and cons to all approaches. The goal of many Lean organizations is to eliminate all wasted activities, redundancies, and create error- or defect-free processes; doing this will eliminate steps and improve cycle times and rework, thereby increasing the productivity of each worker. By increasing productivity, we need less staff to do the same work so companies will become more profitable. These profits should be shared with employees. The goal should be to pay 20%–30% more than your competitors, thereby attracting and retaining the best employees and facilitating recruitment and retention of highly talented staff. Toyota's suggestion system is described in the book, *40 Years, 20 Million Ideas.*[17] Employees are generally paid small amounts for their ideas, but when they receive a payment, they share it with their co-workers. After all, without their co-workers they could not have implemented the idea.

PHYSICIAN ENGAGEMENT

One of the most difficult challenges for executives in the hospital and healthcare setting is engaging physicians. Increasingly, physicians feel pressures from the outside world, both financial and administrative. Rising administrative issues around healthcare coverage, patient financial engagements, and ongoing malpractice issues have clearly increased the stress and anxiety that weigh on physicians on a day-to-day basis. With the advent of Bundled Payment initiatives, and the increase in formation of Accountable Care Organizations (ACOs), physicians and Healthcare executives are having to understanding at greater depths the impact of hospital processes and physicians practices on "value stream of the patient". Bundled payments reach beyond the four walls of the hospital into the pre, post hospital stay and to re-admissions. Additionally leaders are having to look at the current hospitalist model to make sure there is the communication and coordination in place between physicians/consultants

---

[17] Yuzo Yasuda, *40 Years, 20 Million Ideas* (Cambridge, MA. Productivity Press) 1991

that optimizes evidence based "standard practice" to produce the desired outcomes and throughput. As these new arrangements arise, these are a few of the challenges encountered as physician's need to engage in challenges which historically were viewed as the hospital's focus. Most hospital processes were seen as hospital issues and not physician issues. It is becoming critical that physicians and staff focus on understanding the impact their activities have within the larger system and understand that fixing these processes will make their lives easier. In addition, physicians are now becoming employees of hospital systems forcing this necessary alignment.

When engaging in Lean initiatives, some organizations get the physicians involved up front with a "contract for change" where the expectations of the initiative and the physician involvement are clearly stated. The Lean tools apply to physicians' processes the same as any other process in the hospital. Some physicians have improved their independent office operations and are seeing the benefits. Videoing is a great way to surface improvements that Emergency Department (ED) physicians, surgeons, and hospitalists can make to improve their bottom line or be able to make the same revenue in less time. It is critical to bring physicians on the Lean journey and have them participate in Lean projects that directly impact their daily activities. Their feedback provides the physicians perspective of the process. It also serves to facilitate the acceptance of the new process and can be beneficial as the physicians can see that the hospital administration is working toward improving activities that directly impact their workflow. We have had staff who are resistant to the change go to their physician "allies" in an attempt to de-rail the proposed changes. However, if the area physicians are knowledgeable about what is occurring, they can assist in the change management and help to defuse these potential situations.

THE COG IN THE CHAIN OF COMMAND

We have learned over the years that every once in a while a middle management person can become a "cog" in the wheels of the organization. This person could be anywhere in between the CEO and the person on the floor, but normally they are director level or above. They are typically out to make a name for themselves. We call these people "career managers". They typically find ways to prevent problems from sticking to themselves but take credit for everything positive. It is all about them and managing their ongoing career advancement. They are not team players (but they talk like they are) and they are not interested in developing their people. Information from the top is filtered through this person to their reports based on what they desire to pass on and filtered up to their manager so that no information that makes this cog look bad goes any further.

At one company, an employee had information that there was no way they were going to meet a particular customer schedule. Even though they told their boss, their boss refused to let them tell his boss, the general manager.

At another company, a room full of "old boy network" directors outright lied to a new general manager about the production schedules. They confidently conveyed everything was on schedule when it was not. Why? In the past, the old general manager never left his office, so the directors could tell him whatever they wanted. If the new general manager had not gone to the floor himself, he would never have known the true production status. You would not want to have been in the next production meeting!

What does this say about our organizations? One can see why Toyota develops a leadership culture focused on going to the floor to witness problems first-hand.

VALUE STREAM MANAGERS IN THE LEAN ORGANIZATION

The goal in Lean is to create value stream managers who own and are accountable for the overall process. Functional managers are still required but should matrix to the value stream managers. In some hospitals, these are called service lines; however, the concept of service lines is different at different hospitals. In manufacturing, a value stream is equivalent to what used to be called a small business unit, where the value stream manager would have an entirely cross-functional organization reporting to him/her, but were responsible "soup to nuts" for the entire operations—from sales and marketing to delivering the product. In hospitals, the value stream is more difficult to determine. Some would argue that the operating room and ED are value streams, but they don't encompass the entire flow of the patient. So should they really be value streams? In our view, a value stream would be a service line or combination of similar service lines that own the patient from their arrival until the bill is paid.

As we transition to Lean, old traditional jobs change. We no longer need five or six supervisors in nutrition. Why? Because now the Lean line is contained in a much smaller area, visual controls exist, and visual signals like Kanban drive replenishment. Our demand becomes more predictable and waste decreases, which makes it easier to trigger orders from suppliers. We may now see the need to start combining roles, i.e., technician and secretary, etc., driving the need for more flexibility and cross-training.

ROLE OF THE EXTERNAL CONSULTANT

When first starting out, it can save a lot of time and money to hire an external resource to help lead you down the path. The consultant should base their business on transfer of knowledge and helping you develop your own internal resources. The consultant should be a change agent and a catalyst for change. However, the consultant cannot be responsible to sustain your Lean roll out!

At some point, the consultant should transition from a sensei to a Lean resource. Consultants come in varying price ranges. It is best to seek and check out the consultant's references prior to signing a contract. You should build in a clause that, if you are ever not satisfied with the consultant for any reason, you can immediately terminate them and only be liable for expenses incurred to that point.

Most consultants will pay for themselves within a year; however, this is difficult to measure when you are using traditional accounting measures. You should agree with your consultant up front what will be considered Lean savings, if this is a requirement of launching the effort. Over time (2–3 years), most hospitals realize that determining return on investment (ROI) for every project is not a value-added process and that it results in much wasted time to assemble and justify, with most never being followed up. CEOs and executives learn to implement Lean because it is the right thing to do. You may not see real bottom line results until several years into the process, as it takes time to implement the changes across the system.

SUMMARY

Lean transformations are cultural movements that need to be led by senior level executives. In order for this to occur, executives at all levels must be knowledgeable and achieve a full understanding of the impact Lean will have on the organization. Beginning with the customer, Lean can provide a strategic competitive advantage through improvements in quality and safety by reducing the opportunities for errors and defects and by eliminating wasted activities. The elimination in defects and waste will yield financial returns in patient safety and adverse events, and improvement in productivity, reduction in throughput, and enhanced capacity. Executives must communicate organizational priorities by "walking the walk," by going to the *Gemba* and setting first-hand, clear, line-of-sight accountabilities both vertically and horizontally throughout the organization. This will require patience, coaching, mentoring of supervisors and managers, and fortitude and perseverance when challenged by skeptics.

PUNCH LIST OF CONSIDERATIONS/IDEAS FOR THE EXECUTIVE LEADER

- *Lead by example.*
- Visit your project teams.

- Five S *your* office.
- Move your office or add an office on the floor.
- Drive problem-solving mentality by example.
- Participate in or lead a Point Kaizen event.
- Conduct a, Five S Heijunka, or standard work audit on the floor.
- Eliminate PowerPoint© presentations and switch to A3s.
- Don't waste time reviewing good things done by your reports—focus on problems, highlighting and telling managers to think and solve for themselves.
- Go to the *Gemba*—talk to your surgeons, talk to your surgeon's offices, talk to your surgeon's staff on the floor.
- Help overcome the "not invented here," "not our way," and "can't be done—regulations, legal, policies" syndromes. Understand that 40%–60% of frontline supervisors have difficulty making the change from "the old way to coach".
- Train your board members, staff, and your employees in Lean. Consider creating a training center. Create leadership development programs.
- *Create a Lean culture* that is action oriented and focused on execution. Make continuous improvement part of the strategic plan. Implement Hoshin planning. Create a Lean system implementation plan with an oversight Lean steering committee. Don't put expectations on the Lean team… put them on the line owners. Create a "pull for Lean" throughout the organization.
- *Encourage problem sharing.* Create feedback loops so you can hear what you need to know vs. what you want to hear. Conduct skip-level meetings with your employees or, better yet, have lunch with them. Have Town Hall meetings on Lean and Six Sigma. Create (with pay) a surgeon/anesthesia feedback committee.
- *Organize realignment.* Move staff jobs to line jobs. Conduct succession planning to lowest levels. Consider a move to value stream leaders. Eliminate layers in your organization. Don't put leadership in separate off-site buildings. Eliminate "employee of the month" and executive perks. Consider salary caps and bonus systems. Consider lifetime employment. Train and establish Lean accounting and convert cost accountants to Lean project leaders.
- Develop process-oriented metrics vs. results.
- Use Hoshin Planning to align strategic goal deployment with the staff in the workplace.

9 Roles and Responsibilities of Managers and Supervisors

If you're any good at all, you just know you can be better...

—Lindsay Buckingham
Fleetwood Mac

SETTING THE STAGE: ROLE OF MANAGERS AND SUPERVISORS

Supervisors and managers (hereinafter referred to as management team) need to be actively engaged in helping to develop the team charter, define and clarify the scope of the Lean project, establish metrics, and provide support and guidance throughout the Lean initiative.

The questions that need to be understood by mid-level management from the executive leaders as they engage in the Lean initiative are:

- Why was this department chosen?
- How visible is the initiative within the organization?
- Is this the first Lean initiative? Note: The perception of being "targeted" for a Lean project may be perceived negatively by a clinical area management team if not framed properly. If other attempts have been made with Lean, what will be different to make this one succeed?
- What is the problem, what needs to be improved, what are the deliverables, and what would success look like?
- What is the scope of the project?
- What is the timeline of the project?
- What is the role of the executive in the Lean initiative?
- What is the executive's perception/expectation of managers' and supervisors' roles and responsibilities for the success of the initiative, especially if they have not been exposed to previous Lean initiatives?
- Are they receiving Lean consultant support (internal or external) and training? What is the exit strategy for the dedicated resources?
- What resources will need to be provided to the clinical area managers and supervisors?
- Will the manager and supervisor be able to backfill staff or other resources to be engaged in the Lean initiatives?
- How will the cost of backfilling for the resources be accounted for? Many healthcare organizations are labor constrained and they do not, culturally, proactively accommodate for Lean initiative resources. (Will it be budgeted negatively at the department level?)
- Will the Lean initiative impact any bonuses?
- What is the communication expectation between the managers, supervisors, and executive related to the Lean initiative?
- What is in it for them? The fear of the unknown may cause reluctance to participate.
- How will the progress and results of the initiative be communicated throughout the organization?
- How will it be sustained? What metrics are in place to continuously monitor the results and ongoing improvement?

The level of support displayed by the management team throughout the Lean initiative makes a significant impact on the overall project success. It has been our experience that 40%–60% of mid-level managers initially resist Lean initiatives. Some managers and supervisors may fear they do not have the ability to do what they are being asked, and the Lean initiative may take them way out of their comfort zone. If you add the fact that the goal of Lean initiatives is to expose all the wastes in their area of responsibility, this can be paralyzing to many individuals and, as with any change, they can view this as potentially threatening to their job or how they are perceived as a manager. In many cases, they may opt to alter their roles either during or after the implementation and, in some cases, will sabotage the implementation in subtle ways.

Instead, managers and supervisors should view the Lean initiative as an opportunity to showcase their talents. They should embrace any feedback which helps to identify waste in their process and be recognized/rewarded for eliminating it.

To be successful, they need to become knowledgeable and proficient in Lean concepts and tools with the expectation that they will drive Lean continuous improvement initiatives within their clinical areas. Every supervisor and manager we know who has embraced Lean has actually improved their careers and moved up in the organization. A significant number have become internal Lean consultants and/or green belts. It can be a great career pathway, merging one's expertise in clinical care with process improvement.

DO YOU REALLY WANT TO KNOW WHAT I SEE? DO YOU REALLY WANT TO KNOW WHAT I THINK?

Charlie Chan used to say, "Your eyes see but they do not observe." We think this statement characterizes waste that is inherent in all our processes. One has to train to observe the waste that exists before one can start eliminating it.

When you hire or assign a Lean consultant and they tour your healthcare department, clinic, or administrative area, they see waste everywhere; in places you don't see or may not be able or may not be willing to recognize as waste (based on your current paradigms). There are different philosophies or strategies on how to communicate what the consultant sees to those whose area is being toured or, in the external consultant's role, to those who are their prospective employers. They can range from telling you what they really see, to "sugar coating it" and telling you what you want to hear.

We have found, however, the brutally honest approach doesn't always work. At some companies the executives were so put off with the response we were never invited back!

So now we always start out by asking, "Do you really want to know what we see?" If so, we will be happy to point out some of the waste we see and honestly tell them. If they say yes and become very defensive (normal behavior), we stop because we know they thought they could handle it, but really can't. The management team must learn to be able to put their Lean glasses on and take an objective look at the waste which is occurring in their work areas.

Authors Note: You can tell companies which are further down the Lean path because they don't want to hear about the good things they are doing; instead they insist any outsiders looking at their processes communicate any waste or problems they see!

KEY RESPONSIBILITIES AND TOOLS FOR MANAGERS AND SUPERVISORS

COMMUNICATION

It is equally important that the cultural change starts at the top and is communicated throughout the organization down to the line level staff. The management team can never communicate enough when going through any type of Lean change. This is where the action must begin.

Line level staff must start looking at their processes differently and must be attuned to the fact that just because they have always done it this way does not mean it is the right or the best way. They must start looking for waste and inefficiencies. The executive team must create an environment where their management team has the confidence to communicate freely and openly.

This is a major cultural change in most hospital environments which are extremely task oriented. The nurses must change their thinking from simply looking at the task of giving a patient a drug or moving a patient from A to B, to looking at the process from either a patient's and/or the hospitals' perspective. This is sometimes an extremely difficult change for any line level staff who may feel totally overwhelmed with the day-to-day functionality of their current role. Newer computer systems make this even harder by creating "task" lists as part of patient routines.

The management team plays a critical role in communicating to staff all the information related to the Lean initiative. The importance of communication cannot be over-emphasized. We have a saying: "When they are tired of hearing the message about the Lean initiative, they are probably just beginning to get it." Multiple means of communication should be used, such as daily huddles, communication boards, newsletters, intranet, e-mails, etc.

It is important to communicate with your staff so they understand the organization's Lean Vision, what it is you are trying to improve and why it is important to the organization and patient. The line level staff should not see this as a new project or initiative, but as part of an ongoing effort to improve and nurture the new Lean environment and culture.

In a healthcare environment, most line level staff members are very caring and patient-centric individuals and it is important they continue to view their role as improving patient care. They need to understand better care is not just about doing that particular task that day, but requires looking at the whole process outside their usual scope. They need to look at things from a multi-disciplinary perspective, which is a major cultural shift.

If Lean is viewed simply as a new project, it will not be very effective. It is important that leaders are seen on the floors helping to create this cultural change. However, leaders must ensure a "bottom-up" approach by encouraging the staff to look for improvement opportunities vs. always providing the answers. This begins to create the Leader as teacher concept and the Learning Organization.

Most staff will initially view Lean as an additional task to their job. In the beginning, this is true. Time is spent learning and implementing Lean tools, but day-to-day work still has to be completed. But over time, as the transformation occurs, Lean becomes "how we do our jobs." This sounds easy, but it's not. If you are a manager or supervisor going through the initial Lean system implementation and culture change, this can be a very difficult transition period.

The challenges a nursing manager will have to face include following their leader standard work, auditing their staffs standard work, holding staff accountable to the standard work, maintaining discipline all while driving continuous improvement. Some staff will embrace the changes while others will fight them. Nursing managers will encounter ongoing negativity and resistance to change from that portion of the staff fighting the change. Be prepared, as some staff may try to sabotage the change; some may even call to complain to the Joint Commission on Accreditation of Healthcare Organizations (JCAHO) and other state agencies, while others will go covert and fight you behind your back. It is not unusual to have to remove those who even after coaching are never going to buy or for others to request to be moved.

In the book, *Baptist Healthcare Journey to Excellence*, CEO Al Stubblefield gives the following example:

> *In October 1995, I walked into our board meeting and promised that we would raise our patient satisfaction scores from the eighteenth percentile in patient satisfaction to the seventy-fifth percentile in 9 months. This was a radical but (I hoped!) achievable goal, and I believed that creating some quick wins was crucial to our success. When I walked out of the room after making that announcement, one of my senior officers took me aside and said, 'Do you realize what you just did in there? You set us up for failure!'*

Part of my reason for sharing this is that 9 months later, when we had not only reached the seventy-fifth percentile but surpassed it, that officer was no longer with the organization. He and a handful of others who were unwilling to embrace our new culture had to be replaced.[1]

So why all the negativity? Implementing Lean is very unsettling to those who are comfortable in their jobs. Complacency is the mother of mediocrity. The more successful the organization the more difficult implementing Lean becomes. Anyone who has gone through change will admit that change can be very difficult. Despite all the talk about current problems, people tend to be generally happy with their jobs, and with the *status quo*. They love to complain about certain things or conditions, but deep down they either really like things the way they are or they are good at managing the informal workarounds developed over the years. This brings us back to the change equation,[2]

$$C \times V \times N \times S > R_{change},$$

Do you and your people really have the *C*… a compelling need to change? If not, they simply will not change. The senior leadership and management team must create the "burning platform to create the compelling need to change for their employees."

As a leader, you can't always be everyone's friend and also be a great supervisor. Someone has to hold people accountable, do the scheduling, discipline, documentation, etc.

You must remember that each person may be impacted differently and the answer to what is in it for them will change based on their perspective. For example let's say the Lean initiative reduces throughput in the Operating Room and we now get done in 9 hrs what used to take 10 hrs. The surgeon will be happy as their day will end earlier. But the staff will see it in different ways. Some will see this as a positive, a chance to leave on time, while others will see this as negative because they lose an hour of overtime which impacts their income. It is important to understand the changes from their point of view and work with them to overcome their objections and to see these changes in a positive light.

IDENTIFY AND PROVIDE RESOURCES

The manager or supervisor of the area may be asked to identify individuals to participate directly with the Lean consultant on the process excellence "core team." This is the group who become the subject matter experts (SMEs) for the team and will be driving the activities of the Lean initiative. The team members selected should be the informal leaders of their staff to help facilitate input from co-workers and help to communicate the changes which need to be implemented. Many times, we find managers or supervisors that select staff to engage in Lean initiatives just because they are available, expendable, or maybe on light duty. A manager who has not been exposed to Lean may not realize that selecting key employees who are viable as future leaders is the most advantageous approach.

Lesson Learned

Ultimately, the team is only as good as its members. If the best people are selected for the team, the best results will be achieved.

Many times, managers and supervisors view having to "give up" staff to be on teams as an imposition, as they may not be given additional budgetary dollars to backfill staff. Others may feel burdened if they take on the workload of their co-workers who are given what may be perceived as a work hiatus to be on the Lean team. These issues are all challenging but the quicker we fix our

---

[1] Al Stubblefield, *The Baptist Health Care Journey to Excellence: Creating a Culture that Wows* (Hoboken, NJ: John Wiley) 2005.

[2] This equation was modified from the $D \times F \times N > Rc$ from Gleicher, Beckhard, and Harris.

processes, the easier our jobs will become. Being selected for a Lean Team position should be seen as a job development opportunity and be part of your employees career planning. It is not uncommon for Lean team members to be promoted or given more responsibility once they return to their department roles. Remember, eventually we are all on the Lean team once we are fully transitioned to a Lean culture.

It is important managers and supervisors communicate to co-workers why they selected and who they selected along with the timeline to the rest of the staff. Being a Lean team member can be challenging. It is not uncommon for staff on the initial team to be ostracized by their peers. It is the role of the managers and supervisors to provide support to the team members throughout the initiative and work to communicate effectively and provide a positive work environment. The management team needs to provide continuous process improvement activities, driving quick wins, and ongoing Kaizen (changes for the better) once the initial Lean initiative has been implemented.

TIME MANAGEMENT AND THE "FIRES"

As part of the management team, you may personally experience or have to deal with an employee who pushes back before, during, or after the Lean initiative in response to the changes being made. The normal response from the nurse to our requests for changing the process is "we don't have time to do this!" But ask yourself; why don't they have the time? Normally, it is because they are too busy doing their normal job or just fighting the everyday normal "fires." Why do they have to fight fires every day? Where do the fires come from? The fires (or inefficiencies) seem to be everywhere.

Most people have a love/hate relationship with these "fires." Staff say they hate to fight them and will complain about firefighting, but yet, deep inside, they get great satisfaction from conquering and extinguishing (at least for the time being) these fires. In addition, most staff are rewarded or recognized for saving the day for coming through with the impossible. We call this the "hero syndrome". Firefighting is an inherent skill set in healthcare workers.

There is a saying: "Today's problems come from yesterday's solutions."[3] For example, the boss decides he or she knows how to fix a particular problem and tells the employee to implement the fix. Meanwhile, a patient complains, an auditor shows up and finds the nurses aren't following a procedure; someone calls in sick or has to leave early. Then, the directors want a report or analysis on a patient service issue, and on top of this, reports are due tomorrow, and you're late for a meeting. So where do all these fires come from? They come from behavior and variation inherent in the organization's or clinical area's current culture and processes… in essence, the overall system! Firefighting is a sign of a reactive, results driven culture. If you are not improving everyday you are getting further and further behind. Firefighting only leads to more firefighting! We need to change the system to a pro-active, process focused culture driving ongoing improvement and where firefighting is now seen as a management weakness.

Lesson Learned

Firefighting doesn't solve problems; only root cause analysis (PDCA) solves problems. As long as we firefight, we may extinguish the fire, but it is guaranteed to come back. With Lean, we replace firefighting skills with Lean management system skills.

So think of these "fires" as problems with our processes, problems with our staff's time management, or problems with behaviors or attitudes of our people. These are all ultimately problems with our "systems." These problems cannot all be solved by writing people up or blaming individuals. In fact, this only makes it worse because it hides the root cause of the problems. Remember, these are systemic problems and systemic problems require systemic solutions.

---

[3] Peter M Senge, *The Fifth Discipline*, Doubleday, 2006, p. 57.

Lesson Learned

To implement Lean, we need to change the systems. Fires eventually go away and managing becomes easier. Blaming people interferes with exposing the inherent problems in the system. Also remember, excess materials, wait times, and idle times are all signs of a problem in the system. Managers and supervisors need to gain a solid understanding of Lean concepts, principles, and tools so that when changes are made in Lean initiatives and staff pose questions and concerns, they can address them with confidence.

STANDARD WORK AND HEALTHCARE

One of the critical components of a Lean initiative is developing standard work for processes that are routinely performed, to eliminate errors, provide role and task clarity, and decrease variation within an activity, task, or process. It is not uncommon when rolling out standard work to hear, "Oh, you want us to be robots." We confront the perceptions of standard work directly. All employees from the executive level to the frontline staff must understand that the goal of standard work is not to make employees robots, but to improve the quality of our work and allow for the implementation of continuous improvement.

A good example of standard work is the checklist utilized by pilots. The pilots have probably done that checklist hundreds if not thousands of times. They go through simulators over and over again rehearsing standard work. Ask yourself, why do they have standard work? Does it make them robots? How would you feel if the pilot on your flight decided he didn't need to do the checklist, or she didn't need to follow the standard procedure because her way is better than all the rest of the pilots? How would you feel if the evening pilots did their work differently than the day pilots? Most non healthcare workers are amazed to find out that most hospital systems lack even basic standard work processes. How can you have or measure quality without a standard?

Another good example is a dollar bill. Is a dollar bill a standard? Of course. It represents 100 cents. What if the standard for a dollar bill changed every day? One day it is worth 95 cents and another it is worth only 85 cents. We have standards all around us. If not, we couldn't administer a litre of solution or buy a gallon of milk. Our systems around us each and every day are all dependent on standards.

Nursing schools train us to be critical thinkers and the U.S. culture is very individualistic.[4] Therefore, standard work meets much resistance in the United States, no matter what the setting. Yet, when we do not standardize, everyone does the job differently and quality suffers. We also lose our chance to improve the process. Let's say we have a process with steps one, two, three and four; we all do the steps in a different order and we find a way to eliminate step two. What will happen when we tell everyone to eliminate their second step? Everyone will eliminate a different step. Let's say we have a laboratory specimen in the process and we leave to go to lunch. How can someone pick up where we have left off if everyone does it differently? The person taking over will have to spend time assessing what's been done in order to move forward. What is the chance that a step could be missed?

A new laboratory technician started in a clinic. The standard work was to draw blood and immediately label the specimen with the patient's name. Instead of following the standard work, the technician put the blood tubes in his pocket (batching) and called in the next patient. Over the course of just 1 week, he mixed up patients' blood samples three times. We all know how dangerous this is! The technician refused to follow standard work and was replaced.

FOLLOWING STANDARD WORK DOES NOT MEAN WE STOP THINKING

We must spend time convincing healthcare workers they can still "critically think" while doing standard work. Clinical judgment and critical thinking will always be part of healthcare. This issue

---

[4] Liker, *Toyota Culture* (McGraw Hill) 2008; Mann, *Creating a Lean Culture* (Productivity Press) 2005.

is synonymous with convincing physicians that standard orders are not cookbook medicine. We may want our physicians to use checklists, but we need their expertise for the unplanned or unusual. We need to continue to innovate. The movement toward evidence-based medical care is aiding in the adoption of standard order sets. We still need physicians to deal with the undefined, the exceptions, and the large part of medicine that is still "art."

Lesson Learned

When hiring people, it is important, once Lean is in place, to communicate our new Lean expectations during the interview process. This should include Lean orientation training along with the expectation for all employees to follow standard work and to contribute improvement ideas daily.

Remember, standard work has been readily practiced in healthcare; physicians are taught and have always applied standard work in how they perform and document history and physical examinations. In addition, subjective, objective, assessment, and plan (SOAP) notes, situation, background, assessment, recommendation (SBAR), universal protocols, documenting times of patient orders and blood transfusion processes are also examples of standard work practices that have been readily adopted. Proper standard work methods help ensure quality and protect us legally. When encountering resistance to standard work, it is helpful to provide examples of how standard work has been applied in healthcare to improve quality, safety, and communication. The computerized physician order entry (CPOE) is helping to create standard work and mistake-proofing medication ordering and drug interactions.

Once developed and implemented, it is important to audit standard work. This is the supervisor's and manager's job. The frequency is negotiable, but auditing standard work is important for several reasons:

1. It is important to maintain quality and control over the process. Note: one can only sustain quality if it is built into the system, i.e., standard work.
2. Standard work is key to sustaining and maintaining a disciplined Lean environment. This is where the continuous learning organization captures its improvents.
3. The auditor should not only be reviewing to make sure the person is following the standard work, but also constantly looking for improvements or asking employees for ideas to change the process in order to make the person's job easier.
4. We need to make sure we are adhering to any new changes to the standard work.

At Hospital X, we implemented standard work in their pre-testing area. The charge nurse over the area stated she stopped auditing the standard work. When asked why, she said it didn't matter to her in what order people did things as long as they did them, and she saw no point to the audit. She also said she was told that since everyone was hitting their cycle times (and performance metrics), she no longer needed to do the audits. Consider what your response would be to her as her manager?

Our response: She was asked if she considered patient safety important. She was then reminded of all the problems that we had encountered with quality prior to implementing standard work. It was explained that auditing should not be looked on as another task added to her workload, or where she was to pass judgment on her fellow workers; but as an opportunity to ensure the quality and safety of our patients as well as a vehicle to discover additional improvements. When the audit is completed, the results should be immediately fed back to the individual being audited. If problems are found, we should view that as a positive! If we don't find the problems, we can never fix them. We then need to get the staff together and identify root cause and brainstorm and implement countermeasures. Auditing can be performed by any individual, assuming they are trained in the process of how to do the audit and document the results. By fixing the problems so they don't come back, it makes our jobs easier as charge nurses or managers. If we can find a way to mistake proof the problems, then the need to audit diminishes.

Lesson Learned:

When supervising and auditing, we need to make sure that the standard work steps are being followed in the proper order in the right amount of time.

Auditing standard work is like balancing your checkbook. You never know if the bank is going to make a mistake.[5]

Just because people are meeting or exceeding the cycle times or metrics doesn't mean they are necessarily following the standard work. The only way one can know for sure is to conduct the audit. There will always be some variation in cycle times, especially when the tasks involve interviewing patients, as each may require a different level of interaction. When we find huge variations in time, it normally means people are not following the standard work. It should be noted that we are using the term standard work in some healthcare areas somewhat loosely when compared to manufacturing. Some areas in healthcare are really using work standards vs. standard work owing to the lack of repeatability and variation inherent in patients; however, this should not be used as an excuse not to continue the pursuit of true standard work by using Lean and Six Sigma tools to reduce variation.

Lesson Learned

We can eliminate audits only when we eliminate the need for the audit. Auditing is not necessarily Lean but a counter measure. The goal should be to create visual controls with real time feedback so we can fix the problems as they occur. When the process is under control and feedback mechanisms installed, we should no longer need the audit.

IMPLEMENTATION

Once the Lean pilots are complete and first phase of the new Lean process is initiated in an area, we must give the implementation enough time to work. When the new process is fully implemented by the process owner and the team, it is normally 80%–90% "complete." During the early phases, due to the scope of some areas, we sometimes end up maintaining two separate systems: the old way of doing it in parallel with the new way of doing it. This is a very confusing and difficult time for the staff during the implementation. It basically ends up being what we call organized chaos; however, once the area is converted to Lean, the rewards will come. Managing the Lean way is easier and more fun than the old way; however, the way we manage in Lean must change from the old way.

Lesson Learned:

If we keep the old way of doing things in the new Lean environment, it will quickly revert back to the way it was before. Lean is a different system and requires a different management style.

Changes or adjustments to the new Lean process need to be based on fact, not on what people think. For some reason, when implementing changes to a process or creating a new process, some of the staff will immediately want to change the new process without giving it a chance to work or getting sufficient data to show a problem exists. If we allow this to happen, we end up making changes with no data, based on gut feel or opinion. In many cases, the changes they want to make, oddly enough, will tend to resemble the old process which they always complain about. What should we do in this case? Most of us are tempted to give into the changes; but, if we give in to the changes, we will go back to the way it was before. Is that an option? Keep in mind how the old process was before? Inevitably, we will have all the same problems we had before!

Lesson Learned

As the manager or charge nurse, it is important that the staff is guided and coached to make the changes based on data, facts, and sound Lean principles and to resist resorting to shortcutting the

---

[5] Willie Grace, Manager, Presbyterian Hospital, Albuquerque, NM.

process and making process changes "on the fly." Remember, the definition of insanity is expecting things to change when we never change anything.

The new Lean process which has just been implemented is very fragile and needs constant support, nurturing, and time to stabilize as it moves into the "control" or check results and sustain phases. Now is the time to get more ideas from the staff and continue with ongoing Kaizen to continue to drive improvement.

PROBLEMS WITH BEHAVIORS

There is a common phrase that one often hears when discussing behaviors: "You get what you expect; you deserve what you tolerate." This saying reigns true throughout many of life's situations, including the workplace. Ultimately, as a manager or supervisor, one gets the behaviors the organization or culture expects and rewards. However, these behaviors can be "desired" or "undesired".

Homework

Identify the most desired and least desired behaviors in the organization, area, or process. If desired, identify how those behaviors are being rewarded and keep those systems in place. It is important to realize we are rewarding the undesired behaviors as well. The next step is to identify any rewards behind the undesired behaviors and develop plans to eliminate them and replace them with our preferred behaviors and change the reward system to encourage the new desired behaviors.

A book called *Bringing Out the Best in People,* by Aubrey Daniels,[6] can help with this homework assignment. In this book, Mr. Daniels discusses "fact-based" performance measures and the necessary role of consequences, both positive and negative, when rewarding behaviors. This is a gross simplification of the book, but we have found this book to be extremely useful in dealing with organizations.

UNDERSTANDING EMPLOYEE SATISFACTION

Homework

List on a piece of paper ten things that would make you as an employee more satisfied, then as a manager, then as the CEO. Do you see any common items in these lists?

No matter what our role is in the organization, most of us want to understand what is expected of us and be empowered to achieve it. In order to be successful, we must be provided with clear direction, organizational priorities, and the ability to create processes to do our jobs safely and efficiently. We need the right tools and supplies to do our jobs and leave feeling like we accomplished something and we are part of a winning team. This is impossible to achieve if processes, areas, or people are out of control and not standardized.

Lesson Learned:

People will do the best job they can with the processes, tools and materials you provide, i.e., the four M's (Man (person), Method, Machine, Materials).

The combination of Lean and change management tools will help make us successful. Lean initiatives take place on the frontline, requiring managers, supervisors, and frontline staff to work together to develop a problem-solving culture. In order to make the appropriate improvements, all staff must learn to identify waste and be able to make suggestions and/or take action to eliminate waste and defects.

---

[6] Aubrey Daniels, *Bringing Out the Best in People* (New York: McGraw-Hill) 1994.

An additional benefit of a Lean culture and Lean environment is the employee satisfaction and commitment that comes with it. Employees like being involved in improving the organization, and ultimately, the better patient care and outcomes. This employee satisfaction can translate to less nursing turnover, as well as a healthier and more productive work environment. Increasing cultural change in this direction can increase efficiency, which increases satisfaction, thereby creating a positive directional change which saves or even creates jobs in the future.

Lesson Learned

The overall costs for our employees is significant and to replace them costs even more. Add up all the training, tribal knowledge and contributions made by employees. Why would we ever want to have to replace them? By implementing Lean and sharing the rewards employees can make more money in less time while helping to grow the business. There can be significant savings in adding a goal of increasing our employee retention.

MANAGEMENT AND SUPERVISOR PERFORMANCE

One of our Lean principles is to work to never be idle. We call idle time "pure waste." A good manager or supervisor can keep several balls afloat at once. For many, this is a learned behavior. One of our Lean goals as managers is to spend at least 50% of our time on continuous improvement and the other 50% running the business.[7]

Continuing with our firefighting analogy from above, firefighters don't have any time left at the end of the day for continuous improvement and eventually "burn out." The only way we can survive and improve is to get our fires under control and start putting them out permanently so the embers can't restart. Only then will there be time left to start improving our processes. The more we improve, the more we contain and eventually extinguish the fires. Managers may resist this and initially find it hard to believe, but putting out these fires permanently will ultimately make their job easier.

Imagine if everyone had what they needed when they needed it, if everyone did things the same way and staff was empowered to identify waste and come up with ways to eliminate it. How much easier would it be to manage the area? You would never have to even worry about failing an audit!

The problem we encounter here is outright fear. Some managers are concerned that they won't be needed anymore. In the past, they have held key information about the process "close to the vest" to make it difficult for anyone to replace them. Now they are being asked to share this highly prized information.

When their processes are videotaped, we expose their "dirty laundry" for everyone to see! Is it any wonder some resistance builds up! This is why it is so important to manage the "people" piece and change management piece of Lean, and teach managers to embrace the change as see it for the opportunity it really is.

But in the end, who would you rather hold on to? Would you rather promote the employee who is the micro-manager, constant firefighter, and hero of the day? Or would you rather promote the employee who admits he/she is no longer needed in that role and worked themselves out of a job by following the Lean principles? If you are the employee, do you want to do the same boring job forever or would you rather continue to grow, develop, rotate positions, increase your skill sets, and become more marketable?

DELEGATION

Lean initiatives require a level of comfort with delegation. Engaging frontline staff in problem solving and supporting them in the initiatives requires that managers must be able to empower and delegate activities they may not have in the past. Managers or supervisors may choose not to delegate

---

[7] Liker, *Toyota Culture* (McGraw Hill) 2008.

because they do not think anyone else is as qualified to do the task, or the right person wasn't hired and didn't have the right job description or appropriate role clarity. Some managers just like to do everything themselves. There is a comfort level knowing every detail and making every decision, i.e., "micro-managing," as it were. This manager is normally not very proficient in coaching or mentoring.

Part of the job of a leader is to develop those who work for us. How do we overcome delegation challenges? We encourage you to do it through empowerment. Managers need to have confidence in their employees to have the ability and skills to perform tasks independently. Confidence is achieved through the training and development of the staff. To do this, we use a tool called the empowerment or freedom scale.[8] The scale is composed of the following five levels:

1. Told what to do
2. Ask what to do
3. Recommend, then take action
4. Take action, notify at once
5. Take action, notify periodically

These represent the chronological order of our comfort levels between the manager/supervisor and their direct reports or team they are championing. This scale can be applied to individual tasks, job descriptions, and team projects, etc. Consider it the next time you discuss a task with your team member or charter a team.

THE JOURNEY OF A LEAN SENSEI WITH A STAR WARS∞ ANALOGY

At some point, Lean Thinking clicks, the light bulb goes on, and the young Lean Padawan starts to "Truly See." They begin to see the levels of waste and see how the Lean tools and principles really work to reduce the waste. They may not totally believe it will work yet, but they are on their way down the right path and the Force is with them.

Anyone who has experienced this Lean journey can probably think back to some experience, training, exercise, video, seminar, or conversation that opened their eyes. Once their eyes are opened, they continue down the path utilizing the tools, until they get enough training and experience to really believe it works.

The analogy of "The Force" in Star Wars[9] *is not too farfetched. It can take from several months to several years for people to get "it" and believe the Lean principles and philosophies really work. The Star Wars sayings fit well with Lean:*

- *"Try or do not, There is no try, only do*
- *Jedi Knight you think you are?*
- *You must unlearn what you have learned*
- *Mind what you have learned, save you it can*
- *Feel the force; beware of the dark (batching) side."*

We have found all these phrases apply to those going down the Lean Practitioner path. *There is no try.* When we implement Lean, we need to mistake proof the implementation so that there is no turning back. To go back to the way it was before *…leads to the dark side it will*!

Many times, especially if we have higher levels of education, *we must unlearn some of what we have learned.* I had to unlearn my entire cost accounting for operations class. Traditional cost

---

[8] Coopers and Lybrand. Allied Signal TQ Training Course - 1994
[9] *Star Wars.*

accounting gets in the way of Lean. Almost all of us are born with the "batch is better" paradigm. This is the "dark side" to Lean and our minds are always fighting us.

Lesson Learned

It is a powerful tool when the leadership team can conduct the Lean training course themselves with an expectation for their staff then to be able to conduct the future training sessions as well. Lean training was accomplished for each employee within the area, which allowed the implementations to proceed much more quickly and more smoothly with great buy-in and suggestions from the staff. Everyone thinks they understand Lean until you are put into the position of teaching it yourself. Do not underestimate the power of the Leader as Teacher concept.

Toyota didn't leave its protégés with NUMMI, the California joint venture between GM and Toyota, alone for over three years.[10] Yet, at most companies, they get one Lean project under their belt and management thinks they are done and can go it alone. After the first Lean pilot they want to cut back on the training and cut the implementation times in half and then blame the consultant when they have trouble sustaining it.

Lesson Learned

Shortcutting the Lean processes never works. The path to the dark side this is. We must allow each person to go on their own personal Lean journey otherwise they will not gain the learnings. There are two ways to implement Lean. Do it with them or Do it to them!

ON-LINE LEAN TRAINING

There is never a good time for training. You must make the time for training; however, don't think you can do all the training on-line.

At Hospital X, we were told to put all Lean training on the back burner. There was no time or money for training. We highly recommended against this approach but were told to implement it anyway. So we trained the persons on our team as we went, which worked fine. When rolling out to the rest of the area we, of course, met a lot of resistance as the untrained staff had no idea what we were trying to accomplish and didn't understand the concepts or the tools. The Lean training-on-line program they were developing was still not completed after a year. We told them on-line training will allow people to learn the terminology, but one cannot learn Lean without putting the terminology and concepts into practice. Eventually they agreed with us and we taught their management and balance of the staff our Lean training course.

Lesson Learned

The Lean journey is a constant journey of learning. Only by doing do we learn and, by sometimes failing, truly learn. Implementing Lean can save you, your job, and the organization by improving profitability through reducing waste and variation in healthcare processes. "Mind what you have learned" may the force be with you on your Lean journey!

---

[10] Jeffrey Liker, *Toyota Culture* (New York: McGraw Hill) 2005.

10 What It Means to Have a Lean Culture

The leadership has to get involved; you can't do this from the front office. You have to be there in jeans and work boots, moving the machines yourself.

—**Joe McNamara**
President at McNamara Manufacturing Holdings Dba Ttarp Co.

ORGANIZATIONAL DISSEMINATION OF LEAN

By now you have probably gained a better understanding of what it means to be Lean, the concepts, philosophies, and benefits an organization can achieve if Lean is adopted and deployed throughout the organization. In order to disseminate Lean across an organization, a cultural transformation must occur. In order to create a Lean culture, one must understand what makes up a Lean culture.

The customer should be the main focus of every Lean culture. This means the organization must have a way to tap the voice of the customer for each process and communicate it to the employees. Despite what we would like to believe, healthcare organizations have not historically focused around the patient; however, now with the adoption of publicly reported measures or HCAHPS and value based purchasing, a greater emphasis is now being placed around understanding the patient experience. Organizations are now being forced to understand and adopt process-focused metrics geared to improving the patient experience.

This topic is covered extensively in several recent publications. *Toyota Culture*, written by Jeffrey Liker, explores Toyota's Lean culture in much detail. David Mann's *Creating a Lean Culture* outlines the important components in a Lean culture. Dwane Baumgardner and Russ Scaffede's *Leadership Road Map*[1] lays out a guide for the CEO and board members of a company to implement a value based Lean culture. In the book, *The Baptist Health Care Journey to Excellence: Creating a Culture That Wows*,[2] Al Stubblefield describes his journey to change the traditional hospital-based culture. These are excellent references and, when taken together, provide a comprehensive road map on what and how to change the culture. The premise of each book explains that culture is a direct reflection of the beliefs and value systems embodied by the CEO and senior leadership team. Ultimately, others can influence the culture, but changes to the culture start with executive team.

We will briefly cover the following topics associated with implementing a Lean culture:

1. Understand what a Lean culture looks like—"the people piece"
2. Lean culture assessment
3. High-level steps to implementing a Lean culture
4. Barriers to continuous improvement
5. Work to sustain and improve it

---

[1] Russ Scaffede, owner, Lean Manufacturing Systems Group, LLC and management consulting consultant, vice president of manufacturing at Toyota Boshoku America. Past general manager/vice president of Toyota Motor Manufacturing Power Train, past senior vice president, senior vice president of global manufacturing at Donnelly Corporation, co-author of *The Leadership Roadmap: People, Lean & Innovation*, with Dwane Baumgardner and Russ Scaffede (Great Barrington, MA: North River Press) 2008.

[2] Al Stubblefield, *The Baptist Health Care Journey To Excellence: Creating A Culture That Wows* (Hoboken, New Jersey: John Wiley & Sons) 2005.

UNDERSTANDING WHAT A LEAN CULTURE LOOKS LIKE—"THE PEOPLE PIECE"

While you can read up on all these topics, there is no "one-size-fits-all" solution. Every organization is unique; however, there are several common principles, approaches, and barriers encountered, as well as lots of *lessons learned* that can be garnered from organizations going through a Lean cultural transformation.

As we have stated many times, the Lean culture is only attained when you are tapping into and implementing the ideas of everyone in the organization, every day. Everyone in the organization is continuously and relentlessly working to eliminate waste where we offer what the customer desires with the highest quality, just in time, with the lowest cost and great patient experience. It is a culture where people enjoy coming to work, they are not afraid of layoffs or census managing, and get paid more than the competition. The culture is role-modeled by the leadership, which is open and accessible to all their employees.

Standard work and work standards are developed by employees who are disciplined, accountable and take pride in everything they do. Standard work is prevalent in all layers of the organization and employees have what they need, when and where they need it; if they don't, they are empowered to work toward achieving it. Staff and physicians are encouraged to surface root cause problems with visual controls which provide a direct line of sight to their patients/customers and their expectations and quality.

The business incorporates real-time visual management systems with accountability and discipline where the front-line workers understand the chain of command and how they contribute to the specific goals in the strategic plan. Supervisors are promoted from within and are knowledgeable, accountable, and train their employees in standard work. Employees work as a team, with an understanding that each and every patient is "their" patient. Staff members are cross-trained with the idea that no job is beneath them (i.e., anyone can mop the floor or pick up trash). PowerPoint presentations are replaced by A3 reports (one-page standard form) to provide a common way to communicate and problem solve across the organization. The leadership is truly guided by a set of values and social responsibility to their communities. They respect and develop their employees, foster company loyalty, and encourage employees to think. The Lean organization is aligned by value streams (which breaks down the silos) with a focus on improving the overall process every day.

IMPORTANCE OF THE 50% PEOPLE PIECE

While some shrug off the need to bring everyone along on the journey, "the people piece," as we call it, cannot be underestimated and must be appreciated and constantly worked in order to be successful. Implementing the Lean tools, while not always easy, are child's play when compared to implementing "the people piece" of these culture changes.

Understanding that people will make or break an organization's ability to fully deploy Lean is even more critical if you are a service organization. This is because, in most cases, the elimination of waste in service organizations occurs through process changes and deploying standard work and cannot be achieved or assisted by just sequencing equipment and/or making "layout" changes.

This requires that people "buy-in" to the process changes and standard work being implemented. If there is partial or no buy-in, then sustaining will be difficult. While it is easy to talk about the people piece and values by which the company will live or principles which will guide it, it is a very difficult environment to create, takes an incredible amount of work and perseverance, and must be driven from the top to be ultimately successful. The amount of time that this will take should not be underestimated. Culture changes typically take 3 to 5 years or more.

PEOPLE VS. TASK—WE NEED A BALANCE

If the goal is to truly have a cultural transformation, each employee should perform activities as defined by the customer with the least amount of waste. The desired behaviors need to be embedded within the organization by communicating, training, and reinforcing from the highest level of the organization. Most companies are still unable or unwilling or uneducated in how to create this "people piece" of the Lean culture. Too often, we treat people as replaceable or expendable, and we don't work to develop their talents. We call this the eighth waste: the "waste of talent."

If one gets too focused on "the people side," however, we lose discipline at the frontline and people will tend to do as they please. We can lose productivity and will hear comments like "How can you expect that person to work all day?"

Once during a Lean system implementation, we had an employee express that he was emotionally distraught because he never had to work all day before. Sixty to eighty percent of his prior days were doing nothing as he watched and also complained about the person across from him working non-stop, shouldering the burden of the operation. This employee complained to us that we couldn't expect him to work all day; and in order to do so, he would need significant time, i.e., months, to work up to getting used to working all day. He then went to HR to complain.

You also see this phenomenon when managers have to just about "bribe" their employees to do a task that management cannot perform. At Toyota, almost everyone starts on the frontline. Even engineers start on the line so that they understand the systems, how the car is made and what their employees go through to make the car. What is interesting is that many of these principles were developed in the United States and were taught to the Japanese post-World War II as part of the CCS trainings. Unfortunately, the U.S. did not continue to leverage them.

In healthcare, we find managers often do not understand what employees have to do to perform their tasks. This is, in part, because licensure or specialized training is required to perform many activities. It is not always common practice for managers or other support staff to start on the frontline. When they join the company, they are placed at the level their licensure or degree dictates. In addition, it is not always common practice to have employees shadow each other to understand what they do or why they do it. While they may shadow the person doing their job, they do not take time to understand the entire process from the patient's perspective. For example, we have found staff in the operating room who do not understand what happens in the Pre-Testing, Pre-Op, or Recovery area. On the opposite end, many clinical staff members are promoted because they are "good clinicians" and are not adequately trained or prepared to manage employees. This may cause an imbalance between the people component and the "data" or scientific management component of a Lean Culture.

VISION

In order to have a cultural transformation, the organizational leader must be able to define and articulate where the company is headed and what the "next level" of improvement will look like. Joel Barker says, *"A leader is someone you choose to follow to a place you wouldn't go by yourself."*[3] Successful Lean companies articulate and spread their Lean vision across the organization. Toyota combines this vision with its ongoing worries to create what some call "healthy or cultural paranoia" or a never-ending "compelling need to change". They create this healthy paranoia throughout the company regardless of their position in the industry. They do not celebrate when they hit a major milestone[4] because it is expected. Yet, they always worry about the competition and are concerned that they are not changing fast enough or are growing too fast and use this "worry" to constantly drive improvement.[5]

---

[3] Joel Barker video, "Leadershift™ Five Lessons for Leaders in the 21st Century," American Media Inc, Distributed by Star Thrower.

[4] "CBS Sunday Morning, Under the Hood," Steve Glauber Producer, David Bhagat, editor, June, 2007 based on comments by Norm Buffano, senior vice president of Toyota.

[5] "Toyota's All Out Drive To Stay Toyota," Business Week Vol., December 3, 2007.

Organizational Value Systems

Does your organization have a set of values it truly lives by? Typical values are integrity, trust, etc. Successful Lean companies have a set of guiding principles and values that the companies truly live by. For example, as of this writing, other than the closing of the Numi plant and one small layoff (of 350 people)[6], Toyota has had no other layoffs since the 1950's, including during the 2008 and 2009 recession.[7] Most companies have values, but they seem to be in name only. They say they believe in the values; however, many of the decisions made are not necessarily based on their values, nor do they live by them. Organizational leaders must role model their values by example. If they don't, then employees start to lose trust and not live by them either. Companies that live by their value systems include their values in their employee evaluations as subjective criteria.

In the book, *The Leadership Road Map*,[8] the authors dedicate the first half of the book to principles and values creation systems. When we hand this book out to executive leaders, they tend to skim through the first half of the book. When we ask them what they thought of the first half, they almost always respond, "Well, I already knew all that and it was somewhat a waste of my time."

We feel the key to these chapters is that in the end, do organizations really put their value systems into practice?

We then ask the leaders the following questions:

- Can your employees state their company values?
- What would your employees say if we asked them the following: "Does your leadership live by those values?
- Do your leaders make decisions based on those values?
- Does the leadership put the values into action?"

How would you answer the questions? Be honest; in most cases the answer is "no!" This is such an important point. We all know values are important, but most companies don't "walk the talk." One company that does "walk the talk" is Barry-Wehmiller. *Target Magazine* profiled CEO, Bob Chapman, and the "unique management system that truly embodies the people-centric, sustainability-focused principles of the Toyota Production System."[9] In the article, Mr. Chapman proposes the equation: **"People + Process = Performance"**.

We feel this embodies how important the people piece is to Lean (Table 10.1).

Mr. Chapman expounds on this equation by saying,

We realized about 8 years ago that we didn't have any 'stated values'. We 'thought' we had a 'good culture', but if you asked someone what that was, it differed by individual. But, about 8 years ago, we gathered a few people together to understand some of the leadership initiatives we were trying and we decided to 'study' articles on leadership in preparation for this meeting. In the course of the meeting, we started talking about what 'good' leadership should look like and we articulated the guiding

---

[6] HANS GREIMEL - Toyota's 'lifetime employment' takes hit with Australian layoffs. Japan's biggest automaker announced the elimination of 350 of 4,600 employees at its Altona plant in Melbourne, or 8 percent of its workforce. The company blamed the cuts on tumbling demand that forced a 36 percent slide in production at the plant over the last four years. "The reality is that our volumes are down. What we assumed was a temporary circumstance has turned into a permanent situation," Toyota Australia CEO Max Yasuda said in a statement. Toyota's Australian plant makes the Camry, Camry Hybrid and Aurion sedans for Australia and export. The other reality is that lifetime employment has never been an iron clad proposition in Japan or elsewhere. But Toyota has been better than most automakers in trying to protect it.

[7] Employees were also let go as a result of the joint venture NUMMI plant closure. Temporary employees have seen layoffs; however, that is why they are temporary. Toyota has considered voluntary job cuts with early retirement options and has offered buyouts peaked at 149,000 units in 2007; the company expects 95,000 in 2012.

[8] Dwane Baumgardner and Russ Scaffede, *The Leadership Roadmap: People, Lean & Innovation* (Great Barrington, MA: North River Press) 2008

[9] "Capturing the Competitive Advantage of Employee Fulfillment," *Target Magazine*, Vol. 25, No. 3, 2009.

TABLE 10.1
What We Believe

We believe that business enterprise has the opportunity to become the most positive influence on our society by providing a cultural environment in which people can realize their gifts, apply and develop their talents, and feel a genuine sense of fulfillment for their contributions in pursuit of a common inspirational vision.

Barry-Wehmiller: "What We Believe"

At Barry-Wehmiller, our **Guiding Principles of Leadership** define our vision of a dynamic corporate culture based on trust, respect and a genuine commitment to the personal and professional development of our team members. By striving to live these principles each and every day, we put our organizational values into action and advance our goal of measuring success by the way we touch the lives of people.

We believe that creating a truly successful environment—one that brings out the best in people and translates into strong business results over time—is our leadership challenge.

We believe that in every interaction, our customers are entitled to proactive and insightful communication with competent individuals who care about our customers' needs and the quality of their experience with our products, with our services, and with us.

We believe it is our responsibility to help our team members learn not only the fundamentals of our business, our products and our services but also realize the leadership skills needed to create an empowering and fulfilling environment.

We believe that embracing the leadership tools of **Lean (L3)** will allow our team members to fully engage their heads, hearts and hands to create products and services that are competitive and responsive to our customers' needs.

We believe that the convergence of **Lean** and our **Guiding Principles of Leadership** is critical to securing a rewarding and sustainable future for our associates by allowing us to compete effectively.

We believe that the decisions we make when filling leadership positions are critical as these people are stewards of our unique culture.

We believe that the fusion of our unique culture with the clarity of our vision is a powerful combination critical for long-term growth.

We build *GREAT* people who do *EXTRAORDINARY* things.

PACKAGING • ENGINEERING & IT CONSULTING • CORRUGATING • PAPER CONVERTING

Source: Courtesy of Robert Chapman, CEO, Barry Wehmiller, January 10, 2009.

principles of leadership. We had a general vision of growth, value and liquidity, all financial before this time, and due to this articulation of our guiding principles of leadership, we refined our 'vision' to people, purpose and performance. It is fundamentally about how we touch lives of people, but to do so we need an inspiring purpose and then we need to execute/live this purpose by performing! It has totally transformed our sense of purpose. We have recently taken it to another level and now state what we believe! It is our sense that all of these statements are in harmony and have evolved over time. We call it L3, Living Legacy of Leadership, as we are striving to develop and live leadership principles that are so profound that they will become deeply imbedded in our organization and serve as a sustaining leadership practice for generations to come. We believe that business enterprise has the opportunity to become the most positive influence on our society by providing a cultural environment in which people can realize their gifts, apply and develop their talents, and feel a genuine sense of fulfillment for their contributions in pursuit of a common inspirational vision. We found the Toyota system, and most all Lean leadership practices, to be all about numbers, waste reduction, inventory turns, quality, improved financial performance and we 'realized' that the employee engagement aspect of Lean was a powerful leadership practice that could allow us to engage the heads and hearts of our teams, not just their hands, and create a more fulfilling environment for them daily. That is the problem with Lean. We do it for the wrong reasons. It is clearly a way to cure the decades old practice of paying people for their hands, when they would have given us their heads and hearts for free 'if' we just knew how to ask. Lean is a wonderful way to ask![10]"

---

[10] Correspondence from Robert Chapman, CEO, Barry Wehmiller, January 10, 2009.

Homework - answer the following questions:

> 1. *Does your organization live its values in its day-to-day operations?*
> 2. *Is it obvious to your ultimate customer, your patient?*
> 3. *Does the organization use its principles to truly measure and guide the decision making?*

Pearls of Advice

- Be patient with the process but insist on results.
- Don't confuse effort with results.[11]
- Create a "no excuses" environment (toward improvement).
- Pause briefly to reflect on your successes, and then move on to the next one.
- The consultant can't do it for you!

Managing Resistance to a Lean Culture Change

Every organization has resistance to change. This resistance to change is embodied in the trials, tribulations, and outcomes of past change efforts. If the organization has demonstrated historically that other initiatives deployed were unsuccessful, then there will be more resistance to change. If the change is not supported or driven by top management, it will not last because employees will not view Lean as a priority. Successful Lean companies overcome the resistance by creating a compelling need to change and providing a positive vision of where and what they aspire to as the future state or next level, and then display activities and resources to support the vision.

Lean Culture Assessment

Homework

Figure 10.1 is a self-assessment that can determine where your organization is on its Lean journey. We have selected attributes that align with each type of culture. This can be used to help assess your organization. Place an X where you think it best fits your organization.[12]

This assessment includes just a few of the attributes of a Lean culture. On which side does your organization seem to land?

Assessment Issues and Discussion

Are your people motivated to do a good job? Do they take pride in their work or just do enough to get by? Would they want to put in the extra effort because the organization makes them feel valuable? Is company loyalty encouraged? Company loyalty used to be coveted; today it is discouraged. It is no wonder we have the Enrons of the world. We seem to have lost our way!

Motivation and Continuous Improvement

That's the one nice thing about winning is you never second-guess yourself afterwards.[13] The way to truly motivate people is to give them a vision to which to aspire and lead them there. Make them feel part of a winning team, part of your successful organization. If you expect your people to put in extra time, do you put in extra time as well? Does the executive team role model the behaviors

---

[11] Vic Chance, vice president of worldwide operations, Cordis Corporation, a Johnson and Johnson Company.
[12] Includes input from Jim Dauw, president, ITT Control Technologies.
[13] Quote from Erik Seidel ESPN World Series of Poker 9-14-10.

Traditional Healthcare Culture	Mark "x"	Lean Six Sigma Healthcare Culture	Mark "x"	Traditional Healthcare Culture	Mark "x"	Lean Six Sigma Healthcare Culture	Mark "x"
Short Term Focused		Long Term Focused		Lots of searching for everything		FIVE S'd organized areas	
Results oriented metrics		Process focused metric		Lots of PowerPoint Presentations		One Page A3 presentations	
Metrics located on computers		Metrics visible for everyone to see		Employees good at one job		Cross trained and cross functional "flexible" teams	
Management owns the numbers		Everyone owns the numbers		No time for training... too expensive		Mandatory training minimum 40 hours per year	
Finance drives improvements		Quality and Voice of Customer - drive improvements		1st day – on the job training		1st two weeks learning culture prior to training	
Finance Driven Decisions		Analysis and value added data driven decisions		Hire anyone that breathes		Strict selective criteria - teamwork and discipline	
Many management levels		Few Management levels		HR backs employees that don't perform		HR backs managers and employees coached to "get them on the right seat in the bus"	
Autocratic		Participative and "Bottom up"		Subjective evaluations		Objective and subjective evaluations with development and succession planning incorporated	
Management Heavy		Empowered at the lowest levels		Special executive perks		No executive perks	
Management tells what to do		Management asks challenges staff and offers help		Executives considered "Suits"		Executives considered coaches and mentors	
Manage by "gut" and experience		Manage by Fact		Ivory Executive Tower		Executives and managers co-located with employees	
Shoot from the hip fixes (not "data driven")		Analysis data driven fixes		Executive Dining Lounge		Executives eat with employees in cafeteria	
Band-Aid type fixes		Permanent "root cause" fixes		Layoffs		Executives take pay cuts first, no one laid off	
Mistakes Punished		Mistakes Rewarded		People considered expendable		We invest in our people and cherish them	
People not paid to think		People expected to contribute new ideas daily		Organization Silos		Value Stream Organization	
People don't have goals		Hoshin Planning - line of sight to strategic plan		Normal Maintenance		Total Productivity Maintenance	

FIGURE 10.1 Traditional vs. Lean.

Traditional Healthcare Culture	Mark "x"	Lean Six Sigma Healthcare Culture	Mark "x"	Traditional Healthcare Culture	Mark "x"	Lean Six Sigma Healthcare Culture	Mark "x"
"it is the ED's patient, not mine" Batching Predominant		Every patient is "OUR" patient Flow driven		Receiving Inventory stores		point of use (delegate quality) Point of Use Materials Storage (POU)	
Overproduction		Produce what's needed when it's needed		Cost of quality as a percent of sales		Poka Yoke	
Erratic demand and staffing		Level loading and staffing to demand		Fake Lean		Lean seriously	
Reactive environment		Proactive environment		Finance		Lean Accounting	
Fire fighting rewarded Lots of inventory (nurse stash)		Fire fighting eliminated Minimal inventory, no stash		Manager Expedite Order Placers		Managers Spend 50% on Improvements Buyer/planner/scheduler	
Muda or waste everywhere Employees frustrated end of day		Improvements visible everywhere Employees feel sense of accomplishment each day		Physician Preference Cards Kaizen events		Generic Preference Cards True Continuous Improvement	
People talk behind others backs		Daily huddles surface employee concerns and ideas		HR		Lean Culture	
Little or No Standard Work		Standard work documented (and people follow it)		Self-directed teams		Hierarchical chain of command	
Few or No audits		Many audits		Managers 100% run business (fire fight)		50% manager time budgeted for improvements	
People have repetitive dull work		People have meaningful and rewarding jobs		Meeting goals		Never Satisfied with goals	

Source: Includes Input from Jim Dauw, President ITT Control Technologies, with permissions.

FIGURE 10.1 (continued) Traditional vs. Lean.

you desire from your staff? Would your people say they work for a world-class organization with world-class processes?

By all current standards, you may think your organization is successful, but remember—success breeds complacency. Do you *really* demand continuous process improvement every day, or do you drive strictly financial-based improvements that middle management accomplishes through census managing or ongoing service and staff cuts? When was the last time you improved your processes? When was your last innovation? In the words of Sir John Harvey Jones, "*If you are not progressing, then you are regressing.*"[14] The more complacent your organization gets, the more vulnerable you are to the competition.

There was a time when layoffs or census managing were considered a failure on management's part. Today they are commonplace tools used by the same management. After all, in the traditional model, people are considered expendable. It doesn't matter how much we have invested in training them.

How do we treat our customers? Some companies actually refer to their customers as "units" as opposed to patients. Which side currently best fits your organization?

A goal of the Lean culture is to have 20%–30% less labor than your competition but have a 15%–30% increase in market wages over your competition.[15] People should be rewarded for being more productive. What would be the advantages of this outcome? Employee retention would be at an all-time high. We all know how expensive it is to train people in their jobs and the culture. What is your employee turnover rate today? Job-hopping used to mean you weren't employable; now, if you don't change jobs, people perceive something is wrong with you!

Another key element of companies in the past was the notion of "promote from within." Toyota still follows this today. Yet, in the United States, it seems it is more often "promote from without," and employees' opinions are not as valued as those of external consultants.

In some companies, we have people constantly bidding and competing for their jobs. What type of environment does this create? Deming preached management must migrate away from managing by fear, yet at many companies this fear is embraced. In hospitals, we don't generally see management by fear but typically the opposite; there is little or no management accountability at all. Back to assessment. Did you rate yourself honestly? Would your employees agree with your ratings? Why not have some of them fill it out and see? An example is embedded in Hospital Consumer Assessment of Healthcare Providers and Systems (HCAHPS) a "willingness to recommend". Not only does management need to be concerned about whether a patient would be willing to recommend, but a gauge could be would your employees willingly recommend your hospital to customers in the community? Would your employees want to have services performed at their place of employment?

The first step to improvement is recognizing the need for improvement. But is it enough? Is there a compelling need to change? Remember the change equation:

$$C \times V \times N \times S = \text{Rchange}$$

---

[14] Video: "Trouble Shooter Series," BBC Television.

[15] *From Detroit Free Press*

The UAW is losing its edge in pay compared with non-unionized U.S. assembly plant workers for foreign companies, even as Detroit automakers aim for deeper benefit cuts to trim their losses.

In at least one case last year, workers for a foreign automaker for the first time averaged more in base pay and bonuses than UAW members working for domestic automakers, according to an economist for the Center for Automotive Research and figures supplied to the *Free Press* by auto companies.

In that instance, Toyota Motor Corp. gave workers at its largest U.S. plant bonuses of $6,000 to $8,000, boosting the average pay at the Georgetown, KY, plant to the equivalent of $30 an hour. That compares with a $27 hourly average for UAW workers, most of whom did not receive profit-sharing checks last year. Toyota would not provide a U.S. average, but said its 7,000-worker Georgetown plant is representative of its U.S. operations.

Honda Motor Co. and Nissan Motor Co. are not far behind Toyota and UAW pay levels. Comparable wages have long been one way foreign companies fight off UAW organizing efforts.

February 1, 2007.

If you *do not* have a compelling need to change after completing the checklist, then you may as well put the book down now and file it for future reference until you are ready. If the answer is yes, then, by all means, please read on!

Homework

Review your check marks and make a list of where the gaps exist between the Lean culture and the traditional culture characteristics and behaviors. Make a list of actions to offset the gaps and put together a timeline to implement it. An excellent book for this is the **Harada** *Method by Norman Bodek.*

HIGH-LEVEL STEPS TO IMPLEMENTING A LEAN CULTURE

STEP 1: UTILIZE SKIP LEVELS TO SEE WHAT YOUR EMPLOYEES ARE THINKING

Use skip level meetings to meet with two levels below you without their manager or supervisor. Ask the manager or supervisor what you will hear from their employees and see how close it is. Then meet with the manager or supervisor to discuss what was heard and implement improvements based on same. There must be no retribution by the manager or supervisor for this process to work.

STEP 2: EDUCATION AND TRAINING

Train your board of directors in Lean and get their support. Consider assigning a group to monitor your Lean activities. Consider creating a benchmarking group. Toyota has various committees at the board level to facilitate and support its continuous improvement efforts.

Train your senior leaders. Have each set individual and company goals and expectations related to improvements and have each area create its plan to improve, monitor these plans and help to remove barriers. Create an executive team of Lean role models. Consider having "lunch and learns" to discuss Lean books or implement other teach-back techniques. Train everyone in the organization in Total Quality, Lean, and Six Sigma tools. Lead through example, make the training mandatory and make executives attend the training without their smartphones. If you are the CEO, once you have learned Lean, lead some of the training or participate on an implementation team.

STEP 3: CREATE A PULL FOR LEAN

As a CEO, put together your vision and values and Lean implementation plan. Then have every leader develop and report their process cycle times and overall throughput times.

Create a pull for Lean by telling your senior team they have to cut cycle times by 50% over the next year. Make sure your strategic plan contains a continuous improvement strategy. Make sure at every meeting that you emphasize Lean and fact based A3 (PDCA) problem solving.

The only way to truly sustain a Lean organization, especially if you have dedicated Lean resources, is to drive Lean goals, i.e., goals that can only be met by Leaning out the process. These goals have to be driven from the CEO level to create the pull for Lean initiatives. Without this pull, your dedicated continuous improvement folks have to "push" Lean. The more you "push" Lean, the more resistance you will meet. One can get good results initially by putting the ownership on the Lean resources, but they alone cannot sustain it because they don't have authority over the people in the department.

STEP 4: CREATE A LEAN IMPLEMENTATION PLAN

Create an organization-wide implementation plan, including your Lean vision, values, training, and communication plans with deliverable milestones. Make sure all functional area and value stream managers have a say in the plan. Communicate your vision, values, and guiding principles.

Put it on wallet-sized cards and distribute them to everyone in the organization. Communicate, Communicate, Communicate! Remove the "blanks" and make sure everyone is communicating a similar message. If their are voids in communication, employees will fill them in and in many cases it will be with messages that you have not intended to deliver. Utilize a variety of techniques to get the message out as not everyone responds to the same communication methods. Know that not everyone is going to be able to make the journey and be prepared to deal with them quickly.

Seek and receive approval from the board and the physicians on the Lean system implementation plan. Consider having each person sign a "contract for change or physician compact,"[16] outlining the vision and approach to be utilized. Don't be afraid to amend the contract as you incorporate improvements to your strategy; however, every signer must agree to live by the contract or seek employment elsewhere.

Review your organizational chart. Drive accountability and discipline throughout the organization. Do you have the right people on the bus and in the right seats to get you to the next level of your plan? Every 6 months to a year, review your plan, your metrics, and your organization.

STEP 5: CREATE A LEAN STEERING COMMITTEE

Convert your senior leadership team into your Lean steering committee. Make sure there are employee representatives and union leadership on the team if applicable. Remember, Lean becomes the culture, the way you do business from now on.

Homework

Determine the big Y (i.e., your most desired output or goal for your hospital or department delivery system). Then list all the inputs (Xs) that are required to meet the big Y. Then check to see if you have metrics in place that support each of the Xs. You will be surprised how often you don't!

STEP 6: BASELINE METRICS

Baseline your current performance metrics. Establish "process-focused" cycle time and throughput time metrics and goals for every process in every department. This means your leadership team will have to become familiar with every process and sub-process in each department. Create process-centered metrics to support the results-oriented metrics you currently have and understand the linkage between them. Have each department conduct the Big Y exercise.[17] Map the line of site from the frontline worker through the executive leaders making sure that each employee has a clear understanding how their job directly impacts the strategic goals of the organization, and how they can contribute to the organizations success.

Lesson Learned

Process focused metrics will drive results metrics but it does not work the other way around.

Take baseline videos and pictures everywhere. You will be surprised to see how fast things change. It really pays to take pictures so you can create before and after examples for staff.

STEP 7: IMPLEMENT A PILOT—UTILIZE THE BASICS MODEL

Pick a pilot area and implement a Lean project. If you need help, hire a consultant to guide you. It is not unusual to take 6 months to a year to learn the Lean tools. Toyota had its Lean senseis spend 3 years with each U.S. manager at NUMMI to teach and coach them in the system.[18]

---

[16] Harvard Business Review, Virginia Mason, 9-606-044, Richard Bomer, Erika Ferlins, January 11, 2006.
[17] ValuMetrix® Tool, ValuMetrix® Services of Ortho Clinical Diagnostics.
[18] Gary Convis talk to MWCMC, April 16, 2008.

Lean cannot be learned just in the classroom or from online training. One has to learn the principles and then go practice/implement them. We have found 1- and 5-day or more sessions very helpful as a supporting tool for creating a Lean culture and have many testimonials to back it up. But implementation must follow the training in order for employee retention to be maximized.

One can implement Five S with Lean projects, kaizens and point kaizen events or launch Five S cleanups, i.e., some organizations have "dumpster days." Five S can be a lot of fun. But it is important to plan Five S ahead of time. We are not fans of "if in doubt, throw it out." We have seen millions of dollars of equipment thrown out this way. Instead create a disposition and discard process.

Again, once Lean training is conducted, the CEO and his/her staff should become the trainers. This is the Leader as Teacher concept. Continue to implement improvements and continue to hit projects/areas already implemented to continuously drive them toward world class.

STEP 8: GEMBA WALKS

Lead by example. Walk the walk. Get out of your office! Walk around! Conduct audits, talk to employees. Get out of your ivory tower, encourage suggestions, and ask employees how you can help. Eliminate all the reports and create visual metric boards in each area. Remember, if you improve your in-process metrics, the results will follow. This is a big leap of faith but necessary to succeed in creating a Lean culture. Eat lunch with your employees. Encourage them to think; don't give them the answers. Ask them what their metrics are. Quiz them on Lean concepts.

STEP 9: SUSTAIN—HOSHIN AND SUGGESTION SYSTEM

Implement and formalize *Hoshin* planning, which is a combination of top down and bottom-up goal deployment. Then establish a formal, Lean-type suggestion process—not a suggestion box! Toyota's suggestion system is described in the book, *20 Million Ideas in 40 Years*. Recognize, reward, and publicize successes. Remember, rewards do not have to be monetary. Consider having yearly events to recognize best improvements.

STEP 10: CONTINUOUS IMPROVEMENT

Take your Lean culture quiz every 6 months and report the findings to the board-level Lean committee. Update your roadmap or "plan" of continuous improvement to continue to narrow the gaps. Update your VSMs on an annual bases for every department.

Our every day employee goals for a Lean culture can best be embodied by the words of Joel Barker, *"When you combine the paradigm pioneering concept with Kaizen or continuous improvement, the speed of your paradigm curve is increased."* But to do this we all have to improve our jobs every day. As Joel Barker goes on to say, *"1/10th of 1 percent is just fine but you have to do it every day"*.[19]

Initially, it doesn't sound like much, but imagine the power of one-tenth of 1% every day by every employee:

One-tenth of 1% × 100 employees × 100 days = 100% improvement

Company X, which had been around for approximately 125 years, was complaining about the problems it continued to experience. We wanted company X to really think about serious improvement, so we took a chance and honestly inquired, "You've been in business for more than 100 years; shouldn't you have it just about right by now?" Fortunately, despite our candid questioning,

---

[19] Video: "Paradigm Pioneers," Joel Barker, president, Infinity Limited, distributed by Chart House International © 1993.

we were invited back and worked with them to make huge improvements. Sometimes you have to provoke companies a little bit to get that "compelling need to change."

BARRIERS TO CONTINUOUS IMPROVEMENT

There are three main types of barriers: technical, technological, and cultural.

1. Technical barriers examples
   - Lack of communication
   - Lack of data
   - Process changes

   These can be overcome by team empowerment, clear project charters, change management, and communication plans.

2. Technological barrier examples
   - Information systems
   - Equipment/infrastructure costs
   - New technology, i.e., RFID systems, etc.
   - Centralized vs. decentralized equipment decisions

   These may be more difficult to overcome; however, understanding upfront that there may be challenges is important. If the organization's infrastructure is composed of many IT systems which don't communicate with each other, then engaging technology teams or identifying IT personnel to be part time or full time on the Lean implementation teams may be an answer.

   In some cases, there may need to be an openness to revert temporarily to a manual process while changes are being made to the IT software or systems. It may be necessary to implement a temporary freeze on rolling out new technologies until the areas can be "Leaned," i.e., waste is eliminated and the process is streamlined.

   Capital and operation funds should be set aside pre-project to address challenges that may already be known by the area or IT department so, as recommendations surface, the funds are available.

3. Cultural barriers examples
   - Sacred cows—paradigms—not invented here, "We've always done it this way"
   - Organizational barriers—department/silo-focused, lack of IIR support
   - Lack of leadership buy-in, resulting in management stall tactics
   - Financially, results-oriented, driven, short-term thinking resulting in sliding back to results-focused and shoot-from-the-hip behaviors
   - Putting everything on a computer
   - No time for training or training costs too much
   - Laying off your black belt or dedicated Lean resources
   - Expecting the Lean dedicated resources to own the changes

   These barriers are the most difficult and typically can only be overcome by the CEO creating:
   - An open-minded culture where any sacred cow is open to questioning
   - A clear implementation road map
   - A "manage by fact" culture
   - Having everyone sign contracts for change
   - Real-time visual controls
   - Leading by example, clear communication

If Lean is "brought in" at the middle management level, they will tell you their biggest barrier is almost always top management. We hear it over and over. Middle managers will state "they (top management) don't understand Lean or what we are trying to do." The next barrier we hear is finance. "Finance still wants ROI results-driven metrics and headcount reductions." It is difficult for financial analysts and managers to understand the impact of results-focused metrics and that it may take 6 months to a year to achieve visible bottom-line results. Finance often tells middle managers, "We don't care about Lean accounting because we still have to answer to auditors and regulators."

The next department barrier is human resources. For example, during a Lean initiative there is a charge nurse who doesn't want to engage in Lean. Human resources' solution is to place the nurse on a 6-month development plan and, thus, the Lean program in that department grinds to a halt and stalls for 6 months or more.

EFFORT TO OVERCOME EACH BARRIER TYPES

The rule of thumb is technical barriers take 1X effort to overcome, technological take 10X effort to overcome, and cultural take 100X to overcome. Only the CEO and their leadership team can truly overcome the cultural barriers. Why? Because the CEO is the only one who has the authority over everyone and every department in the organization.

WORK TO SUSTAIN AND IMPROVE WITH LEAN

As we have discussed, in order for Lean to be truly embraced and strategically entrenched within an organization, a cultural transformation needs to occur. We have seen Lean sustained in "pockets" in many organizations by management and staff who believe in Lean and have seen the results; however, if Lean has not been embedded as the way the organization does business, ultimately the improvements will turn into what we call "Lean lite," or a watered-down version. The organization will not attain what they could nor will it be able to sustain once the area staff or "believers" move on, and more than likely the area will go back to doing things the way they did before. Therefore, it is important that an organization begins to gain an understanding of how it operates from a leadership and cultural perspective to recognize what challenges it may face in adopting Lean philosophies. This is why the overall success rate with Lean is so small.

HOW DO YOU GET THE CEO ON BOARD?

In order to sustain Lean, the CEO must be on board. Getting them on board will depend on the CEO's exposure to Lean. Encourage them to read, benchmark, and attend executive Lean seminars.

It can be difficult if you are trying to create a Lean culture within a traditional organization. In traditional organizations, the CEOs and financial officers are looking for short-term, quick, and large ROIs. If the organization is traditional, they will respond best if they are shown quick results on one or a series project(s). Many times, Lean goes on for a couple of years, and the CEOs still have not totally bought in. This is mainly due to pressure from the CFO. We normally end up having very candid discussions with the CEO and CFO over their investment in the effort and whether or not they are serious about implementing Lean and embedding it into their culture.

Story...Lean in County Government

Erie County Executive, Chris Collins, who came to politics from business, has made Six Sigma a focal point of his administration. Through his high profile position, he has brought attention to the system... His Six Sigma director, Bill Carey, said the first wave of projects have generated $4.9 million in savings. Additional projects are under way or being planned.[20]

---

[20]"Six Sigma backers say commitment is key," *The Buffalo News. Business Today,* December 22, 2009, by Matt Glyn, update October 11, 2009.

COMMITTING THE RIGHT RESOURCES TO SUSTAIN

When rolling out Lean, many organizations bring in an outside resource or consultant to act as a sensei helping to lead and train management staff in Lean concepts and tools. Leaders of organizations need to make sure there is clarity of the consultant role. The consultant's job should be to make sure the organization becomes self-sufficient in being able to propagate Lean internally.

It is the consultant's job to do the improvement *with* management and the team, not *to them*. To be successful, the ownership must stay with the frontline staff process owners or Lean will not sustain. The operational process owners need to be told up front that they own the projects, timeline, control, and sustain the plan as well as the overall success of the projects. The consultant, internal or external, is there to help and support them. There must be an exit strategy for the internal or external consultants to transition the area back to the process owner. The process owner needs to continue ongoing cycles of improvement once the team has disassembled.

Dedicated Lean organizational resources are necessary to get the changes started. It is important to have dedicated process improvement resources or Lean practitioners within clinical areas dedicated to drive continuous cycles of improvement. Over time, these resources must be folded back into the organization in management and frontline roles. Because most healthcare organizations don't have staff in roles that are initially equipped to handle this accountability, discipline, and responsibility, this skill set will need to be developed.

Care must be taken to protect these dedicated Lean positions, as these tend to be viewed as "easy to cut" positions, since they are not perceived to be dedicated to frontline patient care. The organization should place future potential leaders in the Lean specialist roles to develop them for future roles and incorporate them into their succession planning. When Lean specialists transition back into the line organization, they will reinforce Lean concepts and help drive cultural change across the organization as future leaders. We have witnessed time after time, if there are not good development plans in place or leadership does not buy in, the Lean specialists will leave the organization.

Lesson Learned #1

We need to put development plans in place for all our middle managers and supervisors which provide adequate training to successfully manage in a Lean culture environment.

Lesson Learned #2

If you are going to invest in highly skilled training and Lean-dedicated resources, you must provide structure and challenging development plans for them along with a vision for their futures. Anyone who is dedicated to improvement activities initially worries about their job future, since they are not tied to a department or value stream.

HUMAN RESOURCES AND LEAN

Human resources should help facilitate, support, and drive the Lean culture. Most healthcare organizations are still utilizing the old style, very subjective employee evaluation systems. It is not unusual for the subjectivity to be based on personalities. In the new evaluation system, employees should have a subjective and objective component with a 3- to 5-year development plan. The subjective component should be based on how they are living each of the company values. The objective component should be based on their overall performance to the goals mutually developed with employee and supervisor to meet the strategic plan. Some organizations are eliminating traditional evaluations in favor of real time coaching and feedback.

Toyota uses a system for this, called *Hoshin* planning. *Hoshin* planning provides a mechanism so that every employee can understand how his/her personal goals directly relate and impact the strategic planning goals of the organization.

In order to drive the correct behaviors, employees need to be evaluated on how they are living the new company values and guiding principles. If employees don't live and role model the company values, even if they have exceeded their objective goals, there needs to be a process to correct the behavior. The values (people piece) must carry equal weight with the tools (objective) piece. Failure to do this will result in a non-Lean culture.

Every leader should be evaluated on how well they develop their people. The evaluation should include a professional growth plan outlining the employee's aspirations and what position he/she might be seeking in the next 1–5 years. The manager and employee should each fill out a copy of the evaluation, meet to assess where they agree and disagree, and then together explore the gaps. Once the gaps are discussed and agreed on, the employee should jot down actions they plan on implementing over the next year to overcome the gaps. This becomes their development plan.

The development plan should include an ongoing training plan that leverages books, formal school classes, webinars, seminars, movies, benchmarking, etc. The 360-degree evaluation technique between employee, supervisor, and peers can become a very powerful tool for objective feedback.

SUSTAINING THE CONTINUOUS IMPROVEMENT CULTURE

As we stated earlier, the goal is to sustain the continuous improvement culture. Sustaining is the most difficult part of any Lean journey. One can lose the culture very easily and quickly. The new system is fragile and vulnerable until both the tools and "people piece" are cemented into the organization at all levels and built into company certifications by recognized auditing bodies.

We have seen companies lose the culture they worked so hard to build with the change of a president/CEO or CFO. We have seen companies lose it because the CEO and CFO never totally understood the new system. We have seen companies lose it because they lost the "tools piece" and stopped videotaping, stopped acting on fact, and reverted back to the "shoot-from-the-hip" culture. It gets even more difficult in challenging financial times with declining reimbursements. Of course, this is when it is most critical and important.

Toyota has continually worked at the model. They have created a learning organization. They constantly focus on building "cars that sell." They don't lose sight of the customer. They constantly retrain management in the fundamentals of the system. They have totally changed their systems and organization to support the Lean philosophy. Their CEOs don't monitor the stock price daily and don't make millions of dollars a year. They value their employees, but there is still a rigid command and control discipline in place.[21] The glue that seems to hold it all together is the "standard work paradox." The paradox is standard work is rigid in that everyone must follow it, yet flexible in that everyone is constantly trying to improve every operation every day and then updating the standard work. If you were to ask Toyota, however, I bet they would tell you that they are still working on the system and know that they have not discovered all of its secrets.[22] If they feel they have a long way to go, what does that say for the rest of us? However, it takes a continual pursuit toward excellence and even great companies stray, look at what challenges Toyota has experienced in the past with previously unheard-of recalls. Will investigative research reveal that there was a fundamental change in the way they were doing business that caused their quality to be questioned? One can only speculate at this junction and understand that this journey requires diligence and perseverance to stay course from the executive leaders.

---

[21] E-mail from Russ Scaffede, owner, Lean Manufacturing Systems Group, LLC and management consulting consultant, vice president of manufacturing at Toyota Boshoku America, past senior vice president of global manufacturing at Donnelly Corporation, past vice president of Toyota Motor Manufacturing Power Train, co-author of *The Leadership Roadmap: People, Lean & Innovation*, with Dwane Baumgardner and Russ Scaffede (Great Barrington, MA: North River Press) 2008.

[22] Many of their secrets are in Jidoka, which is mistake proofing and safety built into all their machines that cannot be seen.

Section II

11 Leveraging Lean in Surgical Services

PART 1 - OVERVIEW

The core chapters of this book provided detailed information on the concepts, principles and implementation of Lean in the healthcare environment. It was critical to provide the reader with a broad foundation on the application of Lean in healthcare so one can see the how it can be applied throughout the continuum of care from the emergency room to surgery to the laboratory. Lean concepts and tools can begin in any clinical or non-clinical support area within the integrated delivery system and be universally applied. To yield the full benefits there must be a plan to disseminate the identification of waste in order to strive for zero defects, and successfully achieve the goal of triple aim:

1. improving the health of the population,
2. enhancing the experience of care (quality, satisfaction and value), and
3. reducing the per capita cost.

Since the perioperative services is such a large value stream we have broken the chapter into an overview section with lessons learned, Lean solutions and then a detailed section. The detail section drills down to a level of 'how-to-implement' along with many calculations and formulas. It should be noted the Lean solutions discussed were successfully implemented and sustained but may not necessarily be the best solution for every hospital since each hospital is unique. They are shared here to give the reader an idea of how Lean was successfully applied and will hopefully provide the foundation for how Lean could be applied in other areas and situations. We have however been successful transferring these solutions to other hospitals and clinics with some minor deviations based on their IT systems and corporate cultures etc.

TRADITIONALLY WHAT WE FIND IN MOST OPERATING ROOMS

Lean initiatives are generally recommended by hospital administrators for several reasons. Surgery has always been a main driver of hospital revenue, but now it is under a huge burden. Surgical reimbursements are dropping, surgeon malpractice insurance is increasing, and there is increasing pressure to provide value based healthcare. Profitable heart surgeries have been replaced by minimally invasive technological breakthroughs (i.e., stents) and advancements in medical treatments.

The implementation of HCAHPS (Hospital Consumer Assessment of Healthcare Providers and Systems) survey by CMS implemented in October 2006, with the first public reporting in March 2008 has caused hospitals to look more closely at the drivers of patient satisfaction. Patients now have a venue to view comparative information on hospitals which could be utilized to help them determine where to seek elective and non-emergent care.

Surgical and procedural services in most hospitals or IDNs (integrated delivery networks) represent a significant portion of the revenue and expense. In order to maintain financial viability, it is extremely critical to be an optimally performing entity providing these services. Managing the patient, i.e., customer, who is receiving a procedure, is becoming a greater focus for most organizations because the movement of risk and sharing arrangements now has become more prevalent.

These arrangements offer a unique opportunity to collaborate with providers to optimize care, drive up or maintain quality and identify areas to reduce cost.

When the determination is made that a patient requires a procedure, it immediately disconnects the patient from his or her medical care primary care provider. This means "handing-off" the patient to a surgical provider with whom the patient has not had a prior relationship. The transition of care from the "medical home" or primary care provider to the surgical arena is often fragmented and inconsistent. There are often lapses in care history and sometimes duplication of testing in an effort to get them prepared for surgery; especially if the original tests are not readily available to the providers for review. Additionally, having an urgent surgical or procedural diagnosis may be the first time a patient has sought medical care. This means other medical issues may be identified which need to be addressed as part of the "surgical clearance process". Every transition and hand-off during the process, of which there are many are opportunities for defects and create waste. These wastes can be seen as:

- Customer Expectations – i.e., patient outcomes – if the patient is not optimized for the procedure or properly medically managed throughout the surgical/procedural stay which is part of the overall perioperative stay (value stream).
- The number one waste of over production, i.e., batching, producing more than we should, just in case, or before we need it
- Waste of over processing – i.e., duplication of efforts
- Downstream delays, i.e., delays in pre-op if lab results are abnormal leading to cancellations or delays

We have found, over many years, these wastes are systemic in nature and drive up healthcare costs. Today, conversations around "managing the value stream" of surgical services as pilots of the "perioperative surgical home" are emerging throughout the country and organizations are readily applying Lean concepts and principles to all facets of the surgical and procedural areas.

Organizations have seen the value of Lean and the benefits standardization brings to many processes. Standardization leads to best practices which help eliminate confusion in care delivery and ultimately reduces errors. In this new Lean environment, hospital leadership welcome audits as opportunities to highlight and correct waste in the process.

GLOBAL IMPACT OF OPERATING ROOM FLOW—ORGANIZATIONAL CONFLICTS—COMPETITION FOR BEDS

Designing the optimal patient surgical value stream is dependent on your hospital processes. We begin with the well known challenge of "managing capacity" within the hospital (i.e., beds availability). We find in every hospital, and it should be no surprise, that surgery and emergency departments (EDs) compete for the same hospital beds. This has become even more prevalent with the focus on measuring admit time from the emergency department delivery to the nursing floors. Bed availability is extremely dependent on highly efficient processes within the hospital such as:

- Daily huddles around centralized discharge boards with the providers and nursing staff.
- Discharge forecasted at time of admission.
- Implementation of a "unit based model" for providers.
- Having providers discharge patients in a timely manner – preferably early but level loaded throughout the day.
- Patients who are "ready for discharge should be prepped with their ride home available, home health ordered, medications provided, education preformed, and any DME and appointments made, etc.
- Environmental services should be ready to clean as soon as the patients vacate with a standardized cleaning method.

Bed availability, or lack thereof becomes extremely evident when surgery demand (i.e., proce-dures) increases which tend to occur on Tuesday, Wednesday and Thursday. If the processes are not optimally managed then floor units back up, inpatient holds increase in the ED (sometimes forcing diversions), or where patients are held in the post-anesthesia care unit (PACU) which sometimes even leads to holding patients in the OR suites.

Management typically responds with reactive-type counter measures, which can be costly. Normally, they want to add more rooms (patient, ED, Pre-Op, ORs, etc.) to fix the problems. However, we have found adding rooms is typically a "shoot from the hip", short-term, and often short-sighted solution. Adding capacity may alleviate the challenges for six months or a year, if that, but once we fill those rooms up, what happens? We end up with all the same problems as before, but now on a larger scale because the root causes of the original processes were never identified or fixed. In addition, the rooms are typically added under the stress of meeting a deadline or budget.

Architects attempting to please their customers and meet budgetary constraints tend to design rooms and support services based on wherever they seem to fit the best vs. where they should be placed to improve overall patient flow. Although architects are just now beginning to leverage Lean concepts, they typically, do not analyze process data. If they rely on a multiplier of square footage, i.e., today's square footage multiplied by 50% projected growth then this yields a 50% larger footprint which is much more costly than what we find is needed based on using the Lean analysis tools. Architects often rely on staff to advise them on space needs. Since managers and staff do not use data or process flow mapping techniques or feel there is no time, the majority of staff and managers, when asked, always believe more space is required. Architects sometimes look at process flows, but most often default to what the staff want, which is to base the new layout on their current batch-based processes. Architectural firms almost never challenge managers when it is related to desired administrative space. Designs are produced based on past experience or what other hospitals designed vs. the Lean concepts. Generally, one ends up with adhoc layouts without any type of overall flow or capacity analysis.

More often than not, even when flow is considered, rooms and equipment get "squeezed in" to "available" areas thus disrupting any type of product flow or minimizing travel distance. In the layout example shown (see Figure 11.1), storage, equipment, and a pharmacy were placed between PACU, Pre-Op, and the ORs.

In reality, the best Lean layout is often not feasible owing to constraints within an aging build-ing, existing building that is available, when existing structures and finding are cost prohibitive to remodel.

Lesson Learned

LAYOUTS and BATCHING are the single biggest drivers of the eight wastes. Adding rooms is always a very costly solution. Adding rooms essentially create excess inventory (rooms) which hide the root causes of the hospital's problems. It is an easy way out. If we improve our processes and reduce throughput time, we generally don't need the additional rooms (unless there is a significant growth plan to add volume). In the event we need to add rooms, we must consider an ideal Lean lay-out first (no constraints) and then adjust it to meet the constraints inherent in the existing building.

Hospitals need to ensure revenue streams are maintained amid the changing healthcare environ-ment. They need to retain and attract physicians by creating an efficient environment where surgeons are proud to be affiliated and desire to bring their patients (our primary external or "end" customers).

Implementing the BASICS MODEL - BASELINING

Often, we hear complaints from our physicians "our primary internal customers" because they are "unhappy" or dissatisfied. Our first step is to survey the surgeons, anesthesiologists and hospital staff to identify their issues. For a sample VOC Survey see Table 11.1. At most hospitals we categorize the issues by patient flow; however, we have chosen to view the issues from the Customer Point of View.

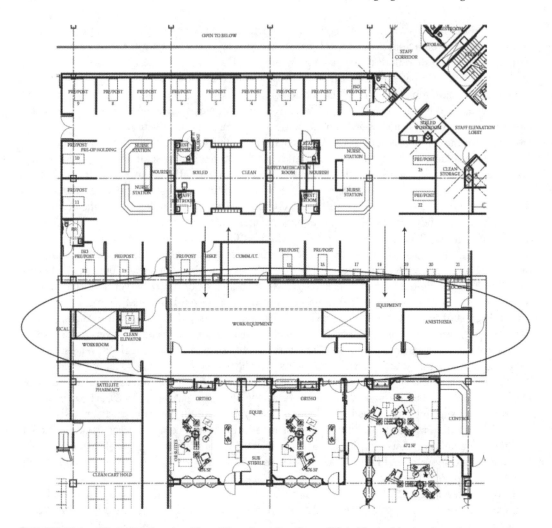

FIGURE 11.1   OR design drawing Note: Flow from Pre-Op to OR is blocked by work equipment, storage rooms and mechanic equipment.

While ultimately the patient is the "end" customer in the hospital business model, the surgeon and anesthesiologists should also be viewed as customers. The staff and administrators represent internal customers as they are linked to one another throughout the process i.e., Pre-Op is a customer of Admitting, OR is a customer of Pre-Op, PACU is a customer of the OR and the floors are customers of PACU. To elucidate, in most hospital models, the surgeons bring the end customer, "the patients", "with them" to the hospital. Without the surgeons, with the exception of the ED or medical admissions who may require surgery, the hospital would have few, very few surgery patients.

Surgeons generate the primary billings for the hospital as well as revenue for ancillary services such as radiology and lab, rehab, consults and inpatient unit hospital stays. Some surgeons prefer to only perform surgeries and let the hospitalists take care of the admitting and attending or the "follow up" portion of care. This model is evolving as episodic payment models develop with payment bundled for the episode. This payment could include pre-op, intra-op and post-operative care. The post-operative care in some models can encompass 30 to 90 days post-procedure. This could include re-admissions in that time period in many cases as well.

This evolution is somewhat of a unique case in Lean because we have several customers: which could be employer groups or ACOs (Accountable Care Organizations), hospitals, the surgeon,

TABLE 11.1

VOC (Voice of the Customer) Survey Results

Voice of the Customer – VOC

Feedback From Survey Only Items With Multiple Responses "What Is Your Main Frustration"

Key Common Concerns point to Efficiency, Staff Resources

Surgeon Team	Anesthesiology Team	OR Surgical Team
Issues	Issues	Issues
Prioritized	Prioritized	Not Prioritized
38 Responses	38 Responses	66 Responses
1. *Turnover*	1. *Lack of Staff*	*Lack of Staff*
2. *Lack of Staff*	2. *Turnover Time*	Education of Staff
3. *On Time Starts*	3. *Waiting in OR for PACU Bed*	Incomplete and Poor access to Supplies
4. Training of Current Staff	4. Incomplete Pre-Op Preparedness	HIS Time Consuming and not Real Time
5. Block Time	5. *Delays*	Poor Evaluation Process and Reward System
6. Loss of Information	6. *Inefficiency*	Poor Scheduling Process
7. No Designated OR for Emergent Cases	7. *PACU Holds*	Accountability, Cooperation, *late Arrival* and Treatment by Physicians
8. Equipment	8. Equipment	Communication & Team building
9. Scheduling		Management Enforcement of Key
10. Labs		Operational and Safety Policies
11. # Of OR Rooms		
12. *OR Throughput*		

and or individual patient. With the changing healthcare environment and patients becoming more savvy related to pricing, due to increasing co-pays and co-insurance, and the payors who are doing cost comparisons of procedures, episodes of care and evaluating outcomes; there is a shift in the perspective payment system to begin to reimburse for outcomes and move to "value based" care.

There are now more customer perspectives than ever to consider. We must be able to satisfy the surgeon and take care of our ultimate end customer "the patient" as they progress through our hospital processes before, during, and after surgery. The basic assumption is if we can satisfy the surgeons, anesthesiologists, staff and administrative issues, the patient will have a good experience. The exception to this issue would be where the patient is undergoing a procedure they really don't need or is being over processed in some fashion. We have categorized the major issues we find in our surgery assessments below:

I. Surgical related Physician Satisfaction Issues
   - Poor surgeon utilization – (i.e., surgeons have to wait between cases)
   - Patient Readiness
   - Pre-Testing Clinic bottlenecks and flow
   - Lack of Standard Orders
   - Late Starts
   - Turnover Time
   - Lack of Bed Availability
   - Staffing (number and competent)
   - OR Scheduling
   - Lack of standardization
   - Instruments and equipment (maintained and available when needed)
   - Available OR time

II. OR Surgical Team (Staff and Administrative) Issues
- Organizational Silos - centralized departments i.e., Transport, Bed Management
- Reactive Management
- Non Standardized, Incomplete, or Undocumented Processes
- Lack of Measurement
- Accountability
- Poor Data Availability
- Non-integrated system
- Data validity
- Appropriate staffing
- Instruments (maintained and available)

Let's briefly explore some of these issues.

I. Surgical Related Physician Satisfaction Issues

When we implement in surgical services we recommend starting with a Gemba walk and a physician and staff satisfaction survey. A sample of survey results can be found in Table 11.1. In many instances, the physicians' complaints are well founded. We find significant waste and workarounds every day by each staff member in order to get the patient through the system. When analyzing the "value stream of the surgical patient" as defined from pre-admission to post-operative (Post-Op) bed placement (in actuality, one might start the value stream at recommendation for surgery and end after patient discharge at payment received). It is difficult to find many staff or managers who have a full understanding of all the activities which take place across the entire value stream. One has to engage participants from every area to gain a true picture of what the "patient customer" encounters as they navigate the surgical value stream.

Poor surgeon utilization – We find surgeons spend a significant amount of their time "waiting". They wait before and between their cases. We define surgeon utilization as the cycle time from "surgeon in to surgeon out" divided by the cycle time of "patient in to next patient in" or total surgery case time. We find surgeon efficiency according to this definition is generally 40% to 50% (while noting that the surgeon's perception is less – if for example, their first assistant closes or there is not a second team standing by to start the next case).

We find it is the anesthesiologist group's availability and many times availability of the hospital's surgical team which influence the schedule. Poor hospital processes impact the ability to provide physician block time, or flexibility in adding cases; all which impact potential revenue and surgeon satisfaction.

The physicians often view themselves as the victims due to inadequate staffing or unsupportive anesthesia teams. Surgeons often don't consider that their utilization within the OR directly impacts the hospital's global budget related to staffing, supplies/instruments, and capital equipment. In typical cost accounting approaches, staff are "earned" through performing surgical cases. When surgeons go on vacation or to meetings, then staffing has to be adjusted. Staff may be reassigned across the OR department or sent home either with or without pay. Anesthesia staff rely on consistent surgical case volumes to keep productive. Most of the issues we discuss throughout the chapter impact surgeon utilization at some level. In reality, there are competing challenges between:

- the optimal utilization of the operating room
- determining the ideal workflow
- productivity and utilization of staff
- room utilization
- the anesthesia's group impact on surgeon workflow and productivity

We find what leads to surgeon satisfaction is providing solutions which alleviate surgeon idle time.

FLIP ROOMS

Flip rooms are one example of what many hospitals attempt to use to decrease surgeon idle time. This solution can be problematic because flip rooms only work when there is an additional (new) team, which includes staff and anesthesiologist, ready to start the next case at the "right" time. However this can impact optimized room utilization as well as staff and anesthesia productivity. Sometimes, making surgeons more productive can result in the OR staff and anesthesia providers being less productive. Flip rooms tend to work best if the surgeon has a physician partner, resident or mid-level provider who can get the "next" case going while the surgeon completes the prior case (surgeon out) to minimize idle time of the anesthesiologist, team and room.

Flip rooms can create a challenge for the hospital if too much anesthesia or room and staff idle time is created, as it may have to hold OR suites "vacant" for a period of time (which now impacts OR room utilization) until the surgeon completes his prior case in order to "flip" to the next room. This can impact the satisfaction of anesthesiologists who want to optimize their day (by generating revenue) performing back to back cases so they do not sit idle waiting for the surgeon to finish the prior case. In addition, this may require additional surgical teams, who when the timing is off, will wait along with anesthesia for the surgeon to complete the prior case. This burns FTE dollars which are not generating revenue for the hospital. In essence there are opposing views of what determines physician satisfaction, between the surgeons, anesthesiologists, hospital administration, and surgical services staff which need to be balanced.

Patient readiness really comes down to two major components:

1. Does the patient have medical clearance for the procedure?
2. Is the patient properly prepared for surgery? (This would include consenting, marking and preparation?, timely antibiotic administration etc.)

One of our most important discoveries we found, during Lean implementations, across many surgery departments, is the following:

The tests for medical clearance are generally ordered by the surgeon. However, it is not the surgeon who really decides if the patient goes ahead with the procedure. That decision is ultimately that of the anesthesiologist.

Therefore the patient must be prepped for surgery based on a combination of surgeon and anesthesiologist orders. We have found this is normally the "weak link" in the chain, the day of surgery.

The patient may arrive in surgery with all the surgeon's orders carried out only to find the anesthesiologist needs another test or piece of information to approve the move to the OR. The surgeon ends up being delayed but normally is unaware of the newly imposed requirements and assumes a staff member is the problem or that the Pre-Op or Pre-Testing process is flawed. In summary we need to concentrate, in parallel, on improving both the pre-testing process and surgical order sets.

Lean Solutions

As the healthcare models evolve and there is more focus on outcomes, LOS, and episodic payment of care, there are many opportunities to use Lean concepts and tools to improve our care pathways. There is a greater awareness of the impact of patient and clinical optimization prior to surgery or procedure; for example pilots underway include glucose, fluid and anemia optimization (to name a few) with hopes that these will improve outcomes and LOS. Pre-procedural education related to post-surgical expectations to proactively streamline the discharge process and in some cases ready patients for post-op rehab needs. These are examples of opportunities which impact surgical outcomes, and costs identified as organizations begin to deconstruct the surgical patient value stream. There are many more to come and to be tested as Lean tools help highlight opportunities.

Standard Orders

We recommend meeting with the Surgery Operations Oversight committee (which should include physician representatives from each subspecialty along with anesthesia and administrative representatives) or a cross specialty adhoc committee which includes the lead anesthesiologist (if there is not an existing committee structure) to work together to develop or revise an existing "standard" order set which clearly defines the expectations for overall surgery clearance. The order set is generally in the form of a grid (with checkboxes of orders) to guide surgeons through best practice recommended orders. See Figure 11.8 in the detailed section. The format and content may vary for each hospital depending on the case mix and acuity level of the patients treated. This is generally at least a one year initiative but typically spanning multiple years but has a significant impact on patient readiness, which reduces delays and cancellations while greatly improving surgeon satisfaction.

Pre-Testing Clinic

We work on streamlining the Hospital's Surgical Pre-testing (or Pre-Admission Testing) Unit. We create standard work and level load the schedule. We develop process focused metrics around cycle times and real time customer satisfaction. We give control of their schedule to the unit vs. having the OR or central scheduling handle the appointments. We develop quality metrics (see Figure 11.2) and real-time Pre-Op (internal customer) feedback to make sure all the orders are carried out properly. We engage physician offices to educate them on the new order-set, pre-testing processes, facilitate communication and emphasize the importance and impact of following "standard work" related to surgical orders and accessing pre-testing.

Late starts frustrate both physicians and staff. These can be measured and root causes (or defects in the process) should be defined and addressed.

Lean Solutions

The two most common root causes we have seen for Late Starts are:

1. *patients aren't ready for surgery*
2. *The surgeon is late.*

We find most of the time the surgeon is late because based on their experience their patients are never ready so this becomes a "catch 22" type problem. When implementing Lean baseline analysis

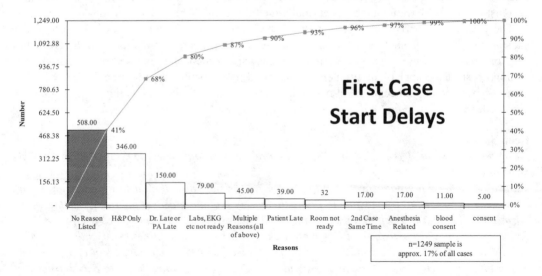

FIGURE 11.2 First Case Delays. Source: BIG Files.

Note: The number one reason is "no reason listed" We find this lack of data to be normal at most hospitals.

tools, we pareto the reasons for late starts (defects) and set the surgeon lateness issue on the back burner. (We use the motto – take care of your own house first.) This is because if our patients were are always ready to go - on schedule - the surgeon would have the confidence in the staff, our processes and schedule to show up on time. We generally find the most common root causes for lateness tie back to patient readiness issues and lack of a clear definition of what a "patient ready for surgery" looks like. As stated above, we create a standard checklists and a standard physician order set to create a ready patient and then create visual controls to sustain our results.

Turnover time drives capacity and surgeon "wait times" and is generally a surgeon and anesthesiologist dissatisfier at every hospital and many surgical outpatient centers. Organizations may not have agreed to what the right metrics are for turnover and more importantly, the definition of turnover time being utilized. It also may not have been clearly communicated, so physicians and staff, when reviewing it, may be interpreting it differently. For example, we find when reviewing the metrics surrounding turnover time that hospitals may report any of the following:

- 'Patient out to patient in'
- 'Surgeon out to surgeon in'
- 'Surgeon close to cut'
- Or some other definition

To really understand what is occurring operationally, however, one may have to break down the process to a more granular level. Figure 11.3 represents the surgery turnover sequence of activities. One could potentially collect and measure any of these data points related to processes within the operative time frame. For example, one could measure the following cycle times:

- 'Patient out' to 'ready for patient' or 'room ready'
- 'Ready for patient' or 'room ready' to 'patient in room' or 'wheels in'
- 'Patient out' or 'wheels out' until 'surgeon cut'
- 'Patient in room' or 'wheels in' to 'patient out of room' or 'wheels out'

It is important that each process data point is clearly defined and communicated so the data is accurately understood and captured. It is important to note that each measure encompasses benefits and drawbacks and therefore may drive different levels and types of improvement suggestions.

Many organizations only utilize 'patient out to patient in' to gauge turnover efficiency; however, there are conflicting goals in efficiency between surgeons, administration, staff, and anesthesiology related to OR utilization and efficiency. One may not want to routinely measure and report each data

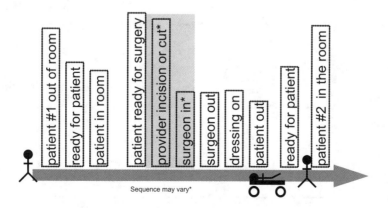

FIGURE 11.3   Turnover Time Sequence. Source: BIG Files.

point on each sub-process; however, being able to identify waste and opportunities that need to be improved at the sub-processes level can be extremely valuable and the only way of determining the root cause of any problems at hand.

Because surgeons want to minimize their "idle time" their definition of turnover is really related to their perceived turnover time 'surgeon out to surgeon in,' which would equate to the time they exit the OR room to the time they make the surgical incision or in some cases begin the next procedure (if they have resident or midlevel provider who started the procedure) on the next case.

The appropriate metric should be determined by where you would most likely identify the wastes.

- The turnover metric could be the "close" time (of the first patient) to the "cut" time (on the next patient), which is more of an operational metric vs. a surgeon efficiency metric.
- 'Patient out' to 'patient in' is routinely measured and reported by most ORs, which gauge only the physical room cleaning, and maybe some patient preparation activity but does not include all the anesthesia or surgery related activity.
- If you look at 'surgeon out to surgeon in,' it will capture inefficiencies within the overall system related to turnover, setting up the room, availability of anesthesia, and timeliness of surgeon. It will even capture inefficiencies related to whoever is left to close the patient (resident, assistant) and steps required prior to moving the patient out of the room, which is not captured in the metric 'patient out to patient in'. It will not capture downtime of the room and the inefficiencies the OR faces or anesthesia encounters while they are waiting for the surgeon to move from room to room (Figure 11.4).

Thus, surgeons are most efficient if they have 2 ORs, and 2 teams (which would include 2 anesthesiologists), so they could complete one case and go directly into the next case to minimize their "idle time." From the room and resource utilization perspective, the hospital or anesthesiologists would rather have cases booked sequentially to prevent "gaps" within the surgical schedule, which are created while a room, team, and anesthesiologist remain available in a "wait state" for the surgeon to complete the preceding case. This creates conflicting measures, makes the OR potentially underutilized, and drives additional staffing resources and more surgical suites.

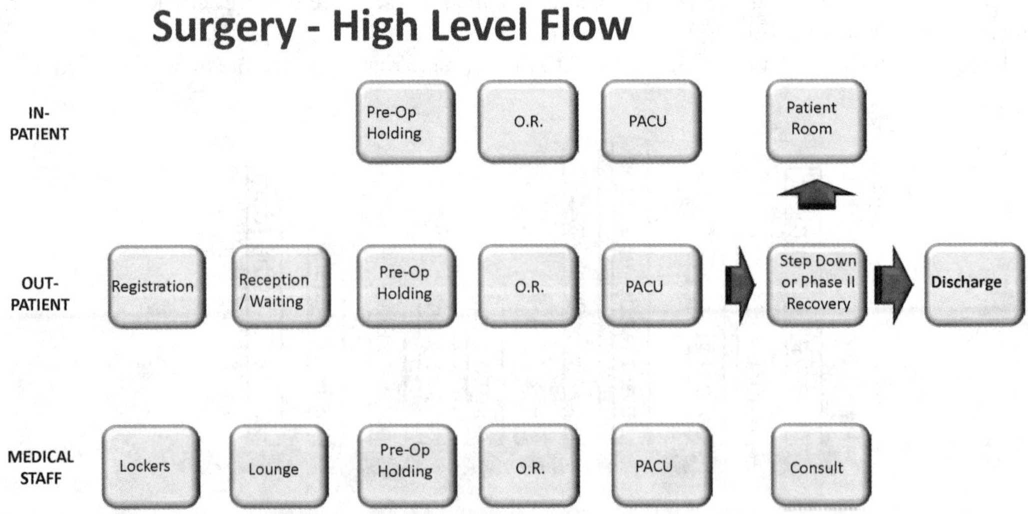

Surgery - High Level Flow

FIGURE 11.4 Surgery High Level Flow. Source: BIG Files.

Lean Solutions

We videotape the process and standardize the room turnover to work much like that of a "pit crew" in a NASCAR race. We can generally reduce turnover times by 50% or more during the first pilot. We identify other defects that contribute to turnover time such as pick sheet accuracy, case picking, supply availability, and standard work related to understanding room ready for the next patient.

Room turnover metrics at most institutions have been historically reported in averages. Optimizing process tends to get "lost in these averages". There are some surgical cases which are very complex with more time consuming set-ups (trays) versus shorter cases, for example an access port set-up VS an abdominal anerysm or large Orthopedic set-up (with ten trays).

Just simply reporting averages can cause significant surgeon dissatisfaction; because, we have found, depending on the type of cases they perform, surgeons do not "feel" that shorter turnover time reported on "paper". Some options to consider might include having a target of percent met (of goal), including standard deviation, or dividing turnover goals into categories based upon complexity of set-up.

A term commonly used in six sigma circles is the function $Y = f(x)$. The big Y is the result or customer expectation where x represents the drivers or root causes of the function impacting the big Y. Listed below are some of the drivers we have identified during our analysis:

"X" Drivers to turnover:

Right tools, right place, maintained

- Accurate preference cards
- Accurate trays (The overall Picking process)

Resources

- Staffing (potentially fractional labor for parallel processing during the turnover i.e., the pit crew "race car model"
- Anesthesia and staff availability

Process

- Patient ready (process to include consent, marking others as identified and medical clearance optimized)
- Standardized and clearly defined, communicated, working and followed "Room Ready" definition by all staff (so no delays in bringing patient back into OR)
- Standard work for "room cleaning" roles and responsibilities
- Target goal that is communicated measured and debriefed daily (to identify opportunities to improve)
- Accountability and culture!!

Bed Availability - We find bed availability is a function of the overall process flow, centralized transport, how physicians round and discharge patients, and the efficiency of support services such as the Laboratory and radiology.

Lean Solution

Start by fixing the inpatient and overall hospital patient flow prior or at least in parallel to working on surgery or the emergency department, as cycle times for ancillary support services can derail process improvements made in the surgery and emergency department. For example, if inpatients are ready for surgery but transport is late in moving them to surgery it delays the case start and will negatively impact the process flow in the operating room.

Staffing generally has three components.

1. The first is that surgeons prefer to have the same staff for every operation. This represents an ongoing struggle between the surgery directors who need to keep their staff skills up and providing cross training so they can staff their surgery schedule during the week and on weekends.
2. The second component is having enough 'competent' (from the physicians perspective) staff available. Travelers and agency staff add a level of uncertainty and sometimes complexity to the mix. Some travelers are very good and some are not as good but all of them have to get used to the new environment, culture and policies within the OR to which they are assigned.
3. The third component of staffing is cost. There is always pressure on the surgery director to meet budget so there is a constant struggle to maintain the "work-life balance" of the staff with a surgery schedule which is typically not "nailed down" until the morning of surgery and requires constant reshuffling of rooms and staff by the charge nurses to meet the schedule, handle emergent cases and while trying to adhere to the budget.

Lean Solutions

In conjunction with level loading the surgery schedules we develop a skills (cross) training matrix which outlines staff trained by service, technology and level to help in guiding appropriate staff skill mix for a case. A "Group Tech" matrix is also developed which helps to further refine geographically which rooms each service line is assigned and then adjust the instruments and supplies close to point of use (POU) accordingly. We videotape the staff and physicians and create standard work which leads to a new staffing model. One can start to see Lean solutions begin to overlap across each area as all of surgery is ultimately an integrated system which is dependent on the overall hospital flow.

Scheduling: The last item we will discuss is level loading of surgical schedules. There are three components to level loading the schedule.

1. The first component is the leveling of the surgeries by day of week.
2. The second is leveling the schedule during the day.
3. The third is leveling by specialty.

We find the first component is impacted by hospitals batching patients on certain days of the week, normally Tuesday through Thursday which bottlenecks the entire system and can lead to holding patients in the ORs because there is no room in PACU. Some floor units backup as well because all the patients are competing for beds. Meanwhile the other days of the week are left with a low census and many times over staffing in these units. The lack of level loading can impact the ability to manage "bed availability", FTE resources, patient (customer) expectations, and capacity throughout the organization thus increasing the overall costs of the hospital.

Batching – by starting a large number of surgical cases at the exact same time in the morning (i.e., 7:30 a.m. starts) drives crazy behaviors throughout the rest of the hospital as all hospital resources are required at the same time. For example, all transporters are needed for an hour period to bring patients from the floors to the OR. All the OR staff are needed at the same time to prepare for the 7:30 a.m. cases creating a tremendous amount of pull for resources at the same time. Registration has to have their maximum people staff at 5:30 a.m. but then later realizes a significant drop in demand so staff are idle.

This batching creates problems which are generally hidden within the overall system. This lack of level loading creates non-reported or tracked peaks and valleys in demand drive excess staffing costs and ultimately result in delays of patients and services throughout the hospital.

The third component is level loading by specialty. One wouldn't want all their neurosurgeons to operate on Mondays and Tuesdays as this would create a demand for all Neuro ICU beds on Monday and Tuesdays as well as creating a competition for services needed by those patients. Because the need is now batched; the majority of patients are "pulling for the same case affiliated resources" around the same times throughout their hospital stay. This leads to shortages in Neuro equipment sets, Neuro OR rooms, and "Neuro trained" staff and materials. The "issues" created by these three components are again generally concealed but directly drive a significant amount of patient, physician and staff dissatisfaction.

Lean Solutions

We work with surgeons, anesthesiologists and administrators to assess each service line to level load both the weekly and daily schedules and show them the benefits which can be gained. It involves some sacrificing on everyone's part but in the long run the surgeons (and hospitals) benefit because we increase the surgeons cases performed (sometimes by one to two more) "within the same amount of time each day". The surgeons must be willing to be open minded and flexible to adjust their office hours, and the administrators and surgeons have to be willing to change the overall approach to scheduling and staffing. The goal is to achieve a work-life balance for everyone involved while maintaining quality, achieving lower costs and increasing patient satisfaction.

Lesson Learned

The only way to fix systemic problems are by implementing system based solutions.

Lack of standardization—drives:

- excess costs for equipment sets
- shortages of equipment sets
- increases in demand for flash sterilization
- increased maintenance costs
- significant hidden waste in terms of wasted time spent hunting and gathering equipment and supplies etc.
- can result in surgeon dissatisfaction when staff become inefficient using non-standardize instrumentation and equipment as they move from surgeon to surgeon (i.e., learning curve)

We find physicians generally do not like to compromise when selecting instrumentation or agree on a "standard" at the service line level. When this is attempted, organizations are often faced with surgeons pushing back on administration, and a CEO who realistically, because of the "SYSTEM[1]" at work, has to "give in" so the non-standardization continues. This practice is very costly as hospitals are unable to control their equipment and capital budgets with the continued "one-off" purchases.

At Hospital X, the "systems thinking principle" is apparent when a perceived "profitable" surgeon desires new or additional instruments just for his or her own use. The instruments are non-standard and costly. The surgery director explains there is no money in the budget this year, which sets off a chain of events. The surgeon goes directly to the COO or CEO and complains. The CEO/COO typically overrides the surgery director, who is then told to purchase the instruments and is now over budget. At budget time, the surgery director is then chastised by the COO or CEO for being over budget.

Lean Solutions

As part of Lean implementations we always take a step back to first identify the "systems" at work behind the scenes. We then strive to standardize anywhere and everywhere possible. We work with physicians to first educate and then standardize instrument sets and supplies, we work to standardize staff supplies and stock them at "point of use" and with physicians and administrators on capital

---

[1] System here is used in the context and is looking at the overall process based on "systems thinking" principles.

equipment purchases. We create standard work to the extent possible and work standards not just for staff jobs but for administrators (such as creating leader standard work) and for how off-line tasks are performed i.e., developing the weekly schedule and updating the group tech matrix or staffing models. Engaging physicians and making them part of the improvement process (contract for change) is critical to help standardize where it makes sense and reduce costs throughout the system. It also helps if this effort is sanctioned and led by a member of the Board of Directors.

Lesson Learned

*Get your house in order first, i.e., work to get your processes under control and stable and standardized first, before you address the physician arrival issues. The problems mentioned above are just a few of an overall list that could be mentioned here. I'm sure you can think of many others. Why do we have these problems? We must consider Systems Thinking Principles! It is important to understand these problems are part of an overall system and represent symptoms of the root causes and cannot necessarily be fixed or sustained by attacking them individually. They come with and are part of the **overall system**. While some hospitals are better than others, most have similar problems and there is always room for improvement. The only way to fix these problems is to **change the system**.*

Story: Changing the Culture

At hospital X, they were having challenges with surgeon dissatisfaction and eroding volumes, the senior leadership team engaged Lean and internal consultants to assess the surgical services area. From the assessment it was discovered that there was no mechanism to engage and collaborate with surgeon leaders to update on findings, prioritize improvement opportunities and drive key decisions. A surgical steering committee was created which was led by a chief surgeon and included surgeons representing key specialties, anesthesiologist leader, and a member from hospital administration. The administrator's key role was to update the committee on Lean activities, hospital initiatives and to facilitate and engage surgery committee to collaborate to address issues and help make decisions that would impact the group, such as creating block booking rules, etc. Part of this new committee's job was to be accountable for the surgical budget as it pertained to equipment and supplies. This empowerment resulted in the forced awareness of the need to create guiding rules, standardize processes, supplies and equipment by the entire committee. This process sounds easy but took many weekly meetings over several months with some very heated arguments to become reality. One of the greatest challenges was the appointment of a Surgeon Leader as head of the committee, as this was a huge cultural change and new role for him. Historically the interactions between surgeons and administration had been reactive. In his first meeting as the Surgeon Leader the who was used to arguing as a member of the committee reverted back to his old ways of complaining with the group, creating a "feeding frenzy" as controversial issues arose. In his new role, he was supposed to be creating an environment of collaboration, consensus building and problem solving. The first several monthly meetings occurred with the surgeon committee leader reverting back to his historical interactions, derailing opportunities to create a collaborative, sharing environment and the meetings often ended in controversy. Then after about the third meeting, negativity erupted from the group as he was speaking on a potential challenge and once again he started to chime in with the others. Then all of a sudden he paused, we all watched as we could see him realize what he had been doing and finally recognized that he was the leader and it was his responsibility to get the group back on track. As he did this, we watched as the group slowly turned, followed his lead and now culturally were on their way to begin working as a group collaborating to make decisions together with the hospital administration.

Lesson learned

There is a saying "culture eats strategy every day" and the best strategies (such as deploying Lean) cannot occur without a cultural change.

There is significant opportunity as hospitals begin to partner more closely with physicians to collaborate on standardization. Some of the less recognized benefits of standardization can be in handling capital equipment. Delays occur and potential user errors are related to staff having to use multiple types of equipment with differing user interfaces as they go from room to room.

Leveraging standardization of supplies and vendors can have significant impact on overall negotiating power in the movement toward achieving the triple aim "reducing the cost of care" and can greatly reduce the learning curve necessary for cross training staff.

II. OR Surgical Team (Staff and Administrative) Issues

OR Surgical Team (Staff and Administrative) Issues—Centralized departments drive batching and delays throughout the hospital. They are created with good intentions, to develop economies of scale and to fully utilize staff but in reality they are many times the root cause for bottlenecks and delays throughout the hospital.

Hospital X decided to centralize Sterile Processing (SPD) and move it from the surgery floor to the basement. They purchased new big "batch" washers with all sorts of conveyors and added transportation which created a new SPD process that now takes three to four times longer than the old process. They even took on sterile processing needs from other hospitals in their system. While on the surface this may seem to make a lot of sense, due to economies of scale, the significantly increased cycle time to clean and sterilize instruments drove significant unplanned costs and delays (for example the need for three to four times more instrument sets) which were obviously not part of the initial ROI for the project. It also created much staff and physician dissatisfaction but since so much money was spent on the new centralized basement system the decision could not be reversed. In some cases, centralizing is done to create space for new ORs on the surgery floor, but if we had "Leaned out the process", decreased turnover times, and level loaded the schedules would we have needed the new ORs? It is important to use the 5 Why tools whenever making these types of centralizing decisions. Remember, centralizing is another word for batching. Do we really need to centralize?

Lean Solution

Decentralize staff functions wherever possible. This means the "value stream" department will have to educate and cross train their staff to ensure efficiency and staff utilization. For example, consider decentralizing transport and lab or work to eliminate the need or necessity for some departments. In some cases we decentralize most of a department while keeping a small centralized portion where it makes sense. We also will install "point of use" testing, for example "mini-labs" where it makes sense that can meet 80% of the diagnostic needs for the area or department.

Lesson Learned

We understand the ageless and ongoing arguments and discussions which exist around centralization. However, keep in mind centralization is ultimately "batching" and one should approach the pro-centralization "economies of scale" arguments very skeptically as the waste encountered by having to schedule and manage the new "centralized" department generally outweigh the benefits resulting in patient and staff dissatisfaction.

Reactive Management—is the antithesis of managing by fact – this issue was difficult to categorize as it generally affects the subsequent decision making for all of the hospital. Our hospital systems are generally difficult to "data mine" and the validity of the resulting data is normally questionable. Most of the data we need for Lean does not exist. i.e., the cycle times for each step in a process. Each of the department silos has their own perceptions of the challenges which their "patient/customer encounters" upon which "reactive" or "shoot from the hip" type decisions are made. For example:

- When interviewed, one may find that surgeons normally complain about turnover, start times, and the fact that the patients aren't ready for surgery.
- In Pre-Op, anesthesiologists often complain of inefficiencies related to patients not having the right tests ordered and that the necessary paperwork is incomplete or unavailable.

Surgeons are mostly insulated from this directly, but experience it through case cancellations, increases in turnover time and "surgeon wait time" resulting in a decrease of their overall utilization. Most of this blame is placed on the nurses in pre-testing, Pre-Op or the ORs yet many times the root causes for the delays can be traced back to the physicians themselves i.e., illegible orders, new anesthesia requirements, or patients not informed or confused by the physician's office pre-testing clinic as to whether or not they should take their medicines or how many hours to fast, along with what does the word "fast" really mean, prior to surgery.

Lean Solution

Identify service line value streams to develop a continuous improvement roadmap to facilitate throughput, and identify drivers of defects in order to improve service, quality and cost across the system.

Non standardized, Incomplete, or Undocumented Processes—represents a lack of standard work. We find this inherent in many hospital processes and is a main failure mode of state and other regulatory audits which can also surface as issues in quality. Lack of standardized processes become obvious as we film different staff or physician members doing the same jobs. Root causes go back to the lack of documentation and the fact everyone is trained differently depending on who they learned from and "how they have always done it before".

Lean Solution

Develop, implement and educate using videos and standard work where applicable from frontline staff to executive leaders throughout the hospital or clinic environment.

Measurement/Accountability—Employees tend not to have hard measures to which they are held accountable. If they do exist, employees are not readily aware of the metrics or how the metrics align with those of the overall organization. When we asked employees on what and how they are measured, they respond with:

- They are not sure how they are measured.
- Their measures are based on whatever their boss communicates at evaluation time.
- They think they are measured on customer satisfaction, number of complaints, or physician satisfaction.
- Even if they can come up with a measure, we find they cannot normally tell us how they are performing against the metric or explain to us exactly what the measures are, their goals for the year, or how the measures are calculated.
- In most cases they do not have a full understanding of how their day-to-day tasks impact the departmental metrics or how their day-to-day activities align to the overall organizational goals.

Lean Solution

The goal with Lean is to adopt and manage using "process focused" metrics which are directly tied to the overall organization's goals for the year and are supported and attained in conjunction with complying and living the organization's value system. In Lean, this system is called Hoshin

Planning. Examples of process focused metrics are Takt time, cycle time, throughput time, first pass yield (FPY) at every step, rolled throughput yield, customer demand by hour, planned vs. unplanned downtime, and OR turnover times. Process-driven metrics require visual controls and an immediate explanation along with countermeasures when an abnormality occurs, followed by a root cause determination of how to fix it so that it never comes back.

Poor Data Availability and Non-Integrated Data Systems—We have found obtaining accurate data, "data mining" or trying to drill down into data extremely challenging at every hospital, some worse than others. At some hospitals, IT system disconnects drive the need for surgical services to invest in its own IT personnel to write reports which can be exported to Microsoft Excel or Microsoft Access and distributed to management. Accurate operational or process based data is not available or difficult to obtain and normally requires manual collection. It is surprising how much data we have obtained from nurses who keep their own manual logs. Many times since chart data has to be input, after the fact, we don't have access to simple things like number of admitted Pre-Op patients by hour or by day until 2–3 days later after the charts have been coded and completed.

IT systems which don't talk to each other create rework by imposing redundant duplication of data entry in different systems or keying in missing data due to "one way" interfaces (communication) from one system to another. An example is where we found pre-testing software which did not talk to the lab information system so the same data was entered into both systems. There is still much manual paperwork, faxes and phone calls which are very prone to legibility issues and human error.

We have found in many cases the surgeons' offices have the errors in or simply even the wrong patient names, and other critical information like DOB, so the wrong charts get pulled or can't be found due to the limited "search capabilities" of the existing software or lack of training of user personnel. Other examples are "screens" which do not update each other causing the same information to be typed over and over again. We witness "system timing out" messages while the nurses are still entering data causing them frustration as they have to re-log in and start the data entry over again. We find IT likes to centralize printers, faxes (and sometimes even computers) because it is easier "for them" rather than giving each nurse a fax/printer or their own computer. So the nurses have to stop during their patient interviews to go get the print out from the IT designated secure centralized printer (normally not the closest to them) and bring it back in order to review it with the patient.

Data Validity—Most of the time there is little or no documentation surrounding the definitions of the data and where there are they are not followed. Additionally there is little data integrity with respect to the data collection methods to ensure data reproducibility and repeatability. Data entry is a very low priority for surgical nurses whose main focus is always on the patient. Many times we get into in-depth discussions over what a "to-follow-on" case means and in virtually no circumstances is detailed data kept on cycle times within each department i.e., registration time, registration to check-in, check-in time, check in to Pre-Op entry, Pre-Op time, Pre-Op to surgery, etc. Sometimes it is tracked on electronic boards but they are on a different system than the surgical system and not everyone enters their times in a timely manner or using the same definition. Real-time data are almost non-existent unless there is an electronic tracking board in place.

Financial data are abundant but may require manipulation to understand, and are generally not timely. When data is available, the definitions must be confirmed, as well as the validity and formulas. For example, at one hospital their inpatient data was suspect. They would classify a patient as an "observation" patient (less than 24 hrs stay) but the patient would end up being admitted. We found they never went back and changed the status of the patient. At another hospital they recovered millions of dollars in charges for patients which were not categorized properly in the surgical system and found more money because Pre-Op didn't realize they had to charge the patients for certain supplies. They thought they were bundled charges. And the list goes on and on.

Lean Solutions

Here are some limited examples of what we find when we implement Lean. First we call everyone together so we can standardize all of the definitions throughout the area. We identify opportunities where redundancies in data collection and input occur and work with IT on implementing software solutions that interface between systems. We create manual time collection systems until we can implement bar coded or other more automated collection systems. We create Microsoft Excel® based spreadsheets and pivot tables until the surgical IT personnel can generate the reports. We train the supervisors, managers and charge nurses in their existing standards and reporting mechanisms and teach them how to do Lean Staffing Models. We look at RIFD or other tracking systems for materials where needed. We add simple things like pick locations to surgical pick lists used for case picking and order them so only one pass is needed to collect supplies for surgical cases.

Lesson Learned

Question all data received prior to utilizing for analysis and decision making. When data doesn't exist put in a manual collection system until it can be automated. This will be met with much resistance but we can't improve the processes, or validate improvements if we have no data on which to base our decisions or to be able to ascertain if the solutions implemented fixed the problems and is sustaining.

Conclusion – Do You Consider the Operating Room a Cost Center or a Profit Center?

Many operating rooms (ORs) are treated and function as cost centers instead of revenue or profit centers. Managers are primarily measured on cost accounting standards and variances to determine how well they met their budget. This puts the main focus on reducing full-time employees (FTEs), (or sometimes driving more FTEs than are really needed) vs. servicing the customer or growth in volume. Many managers do not understand how their accounting standards were developed. We often uncover mistakes in the labor standards and how fixed and variable resources are assigned.

Lean Solution

The OR should be treated as a profit center with a focus on growing the business; however, one needs to be able to develop the data to understand which service lines are profitable.

PART II - SURGICAL SERVICES: DETAIL

INTRODUCTION—WHAT WE FIND

Surgery is a system intertwined and integrated within the hospital. Our findings include (Figure 11.5):

- Unbalanced surgical schedules
- Multiple delays throughout the day
- Poor data with unclear definitions related to turnover time,
- Lack of understanding of "what is really" causing delays—root cause of the issues.
- Workarounds are accepted and rewarded when staff "saves the day".
- Staffing is to desire, not demand.
- No standard work or role clarity (and normally no written procedures or work instructions) exist.
- OR utilization and true OR capacity based on existing data is initially difficult to quantify.
- Low surgeon utilization efficiency (does not mean surgeons are not efficient but that surgeons spend 50% or more of their time waiting).

Architectural Point Of View – Inter-Relationships

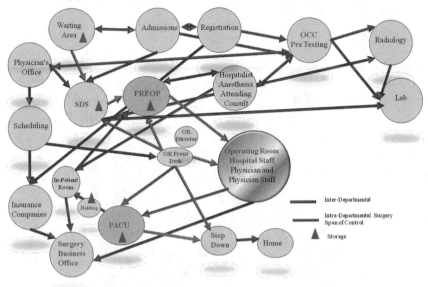

**How Much Control Does The OR Director Have Over The System?
How Do We Compete With Stand Alone Surgical Centers?**

FIGURE 11.5   Surgery Inter-relationship diagram. Source: BIG Files.

- Lack of standardization of supplies and instrumentation.
- Metrics and targets do not measure what is important to the customer and are not communicated to the frontline staff.

TYPICAL SURGERY PROJECTS

Each one of the activities in Table 11.2 could be Lean initiatives an organization may choose to undertake in its quest to improve surgical services.

HOW CAN LEAN IMPROVE OPERATING ROOMS? USING THE BASICS MODEL - BASELINING

Most Lean initiatives start with a value stream map (VSM). This enables the clinical area to begin to understand what occurs across the entire surgical process, from the time the recommendation for surgery is made to the time the patient exits the Post-Op recovery unit (Figure 11.6). The VSM can

---

TABLE 11.2
OR Potential Projects

Assessment (Overall Throughput)	Pre-Op Flow	OR Turnover	Block time rules and utilization
Group Tech Matrix (capacity)	Pre-testing on floors	Billing/Revenue Capture	Sterile Processing
Physician Standard Orders	OR Flow	Forecasting/Marketing	Physician's offices
Pre-testing Flow	PACU Flow	Standardization of instruments	Patient tracking system
Scheduling	Case picking & Materials	IS System related projects	OR Layout

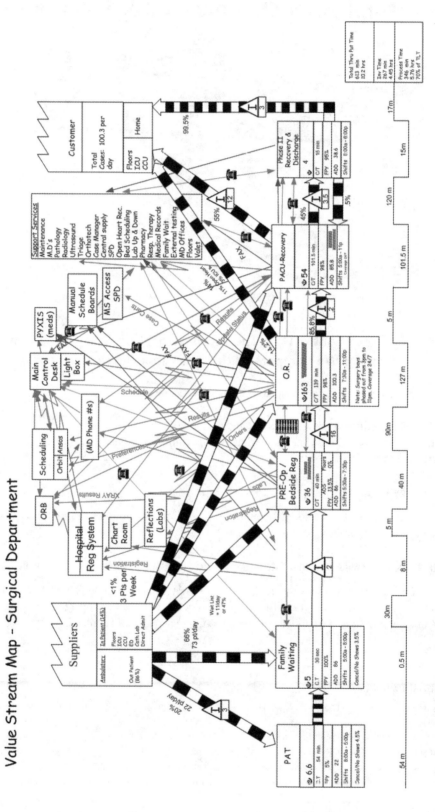

FIGURE 11.6   Surgical System Current State Value Stream Map. Source: BIG Files.

even be taken further downstream to the time the patient is discharged from the hospital. The beginning and endpoint of the VSM depends on the level of detail desired and the goal the organization is trying to achieve. This is outlined in the Team Charter Document.

Once the VSM is completed, it is followed by a process flow analysis (PFA) (Table 11.3) (i.e., following the patient, or test tube), point-to-point diagram, work flow (operator) analysis (WFA, where we follow the staff, including nurses, surgeons, and others), and creating spaghetti diagrams (Figure 11.7). It is surprising how much time a patient can spend waiting and how far a patient is required to walk during the pre-testing process. One organization found that a patient scheduled for *cardiovascular* surgery was required to walk almost one mile in order to complete all their tests.

These tools can help you understand what surgeons desire as well. From the surgeon's point of view, it is often, "I need what I need when I need it!" This ties in with Lean's principle of Just in Time (JIT). Most truly efficient surgeons take the comment "you and your team work as a well-oiled machine" as a compliment. Standard work plays a significant role in applying Lean within the surgical clinical areas. Many really good surgeons already practice Lean techniques, which is exactly how highly skilled surgical teams work. One can go into many ORs and find teams that work together know the standard routine; the surgical technician anticipates each step of the surgeon (through applying standard work for that procedure) and hands the surgeon the right tool that is needed at the right time it is needed.

The goal is to become so standardized that operations go smoothly and safely with extremely high quality. What better tool is there than videoing a resident or young surgeon and reviewing the video together to look for improvement opportunities? When we have filmed surgeons, they are surprised that they identify so many opportunities where they could improve. Occasionally even new ideas for instrumentation or supplies emerge.

Even though there is a "feel" component which can only be gained through experience with many operations, if the best surgeons are videoed, training videos can be created and standardized work which can be used as a teaching tool for residents and medical schools. The Lean principles of flexibility, flow, mistake proofing, JIT, standardized work, etc., integrate perfectly with surgeons in the OR. These tools can also be applied physicians/surgeons' offices to improve their infrastructure and patient experience. Lean has been successfully applied in all areas of healthcare including assisted living, vet clinics, pharmacies and other medical equipment retail stores.

TABLE 11.3
PPF (Product Process Flow) Cardiac Patient

Summary	Baseline	Post Lean Projected	Reduction	Reduction %
Total Steps	82.0	36.0	46.00	56%
Orig Sec:	13,266.0	10,387.0	2,879.00	22%
Min:	221.1	173.1	47.98	22%
Hours:	3.7	2.9	0.80	22%
Days	0.5	0.4	0.10	22%
Distance	4,326.0	1,239.0	3,087.00	71%
VA %	31.61%	40.37%	−8.76%	−28%
NVA %	32.75%	33.52%	−0.77%	−2%
Storage	26.38%	19.14%	7.24%	27%
Inspect	0.00%	0.00%	0.00%	NA
Transport	9.26%	6.97%	2.29%	25%

Note: Patient travels almost a mile to receive pre-testing for medical clearance.

Pre-Testing – Point to Point - Cardiac Patient

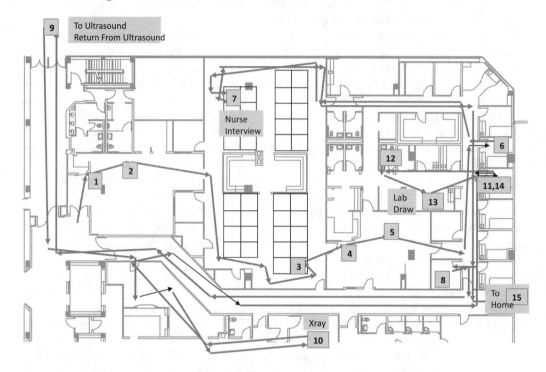

FIGURE 11.7   Point to Point Diagram. Source: Authors – BIG Files.

We have divided this surgical services Detail Part into the flow represented by the ten sections outlined below:

   I. Everything Starts With Demand
  II. Pre-Testing—the Path to Patient Readiness
 III. Pre-Op
 IV. Group Tech Matrix
  V. OR Layout/Capacity
 VI. OR Room Turnover
VII. Surgical Services Materials Readiness
VIII. Post-Anesthesia Care Unit (PACU)
 IX. Lean Leadership and Staff Readiness in the OR
  X. Overarching Results.

Section I - Everything Starts with Demand

At Hospital X,

- surgical case demand was 60 surgeries per day.
- Pre-Op had 10 beds
- Pre-Op had a staff of 5 nurses.
- PACU had 14 beds.
- At Hospital X, surgical case demand was 60 surgeries per day. Pre-Op had 10 beds and PACU had 14 beds. The first "batch" of 17 patients was told to arrive in the Pre-Op area

TABLE 11.4

Nurse Cycle Time Example

# Nurses	Avg TLT/PT Minutes	PTs/Hr	Total Per Hr
1	40	1.5	1.5
2	40	1.5	3.0
3	40	1.5	4.5
4	40	1.5	6.0
5	40	1.5	7.5
6	40	1.5	9.0
7	40	1.5	10.5

between 5:30 a.m. and 6:00 a.m. for 7:30 a.m. starts. Therefore, peak demand was 17 patients over 2 hrs, Takt time was calculated at:

$$2 \text{ hrs or } 120 \text{ min} \div 17 \text{ cases} = 7.05 \text{ min.}$$

- Each morning, the 10 Pre-Op beds were filled, and overflow went to some of the 14 Post-Op care unit beds.
- Pre-Op had a staff of 5 nurses. How can we determine if that is adequate staff? Through video analysis, it was determined the total labor time (TLT) for Pre-Op nurses averaged 40 min. Therefore,

$$\text{Number of nurses required} = 40 \text{ min} \div 7.05 \text{ TT} = 5.67 \text{ Pre-Op staff,}$$

or, in actuality, 6 nurses are needed each day at peak demand to perform the clinical tasks (Table 11.4).

What happens when one is sick? In general, the other nurses or the supervisor may pick up the tasks, but if not, we can predict (since 5 nurses can only see 15 patients in 2 hrs) that 2 patients will not be ready for surgery in time and case delays will occur.

The average length of stay (LOS) for surgery is 108 min. PACU is 145 min and Pre-Op is, by default, paced by surgery. Once the patients are moved to the OR, the 10 Pre-Op and 7 of the Post-Op care unit rooms free up as patients move through the process and the next "batch" of 10 patients arrives to begin the process again. The Takt time is now 10.8 min (108 min ÷10 patients).

$$\text{Number of operators required is } 40 \text{ min} \div 10.8 = 3.7 \text{ nurses.}$$

Because the number of patients are reduced, we now have an extra nurse. With 5 nurses, the patients are ready in 80 min and all the patients wait for an average of 28 min. What happens if a surgeon finishes early and needs a patient who is not in Pre-Op? There is no more room in Pre-Op and the surgeon will have to wait.

Lesson Learned

When you're working on something (someone) you don't need, you can't be working on something (someone) you do need.

Since PACU averages 145 min LOS (patient in to patient ready for discharge), what is going to happen when the second round of surgeries come out? We can't answer the question, as we are missing an element of the total time. We have 'patient in to patient out' for surgery given as 108 min.

We don't have 'patient out to patient in', or room turnover time. If room turnover is 40 min we can predict PACU will have the time (145 min vs. total OR time of 148 min), but we can assume there may be delays as the times are so close. If transport from PACU averages more than 3 min we will have delays because PACU technicians will be busy transporting to the floor.

What happens if our Post-Op care unit is holding six inpatients at 5:30 a.m. in the morning and no floor beds are available until 10:00 a.m.? The Post-Op care unit now has to care for the 6 inpatients (which is probably not in their budget) in addition to getting the seven Pre-Op patients ready for the OR or to go back into Pre-Op. But once the seven Pre-Op patients go to surgery; we still only have eight beds available in PACU because the six others are still filled with inpatients. Fourteen (14) patients will be arriving from the OR in the 8:00 a.m. to 9:30 a.m. range. The Post-Op care unit now has to plead with bed management to find unit or ICU beds for 6 patients as soon as possible or the OR will go into a hold mode.

With the OR time average of 108 min plus turnover of 40 min, our 'patient in to patient in' time is 148 min. What if PACU averages 165 min, what's going to happen next?

$$165 \text{ min} - 148 \text{ min} = 17 \text{ min}.$$

Surgical procedures are being completed at a faster rate than the patients can exit the Post-Op care unit; therefore, a bottleneck is created and the result is holding patients in the ORs.

Our options to address the bottleneck are:

1. Add more Post-Op care unit rooms
2. Add more Post-Op care unit nurses
3. Eliminate inpatient boarders (who are waiting for beds within the hospital)
4. Reduce LOS in Post-Op care unit

One must be aware that Lean is an ongoing problem-solving methodology and approach. This is the linkage Lean shares with Joel Barker's video called "The Business of Paradigms". The first three solutions are all normal reactive solutions to a problem when one doesn't follow a problem-solving methodology. Solutions 1, 2, and 3 are based on the symptoms or current paradigms; however, what needs to be asked is "what is the root cause of the problem?" The root cause is "the system's" batching the arrival and surgeries of our patients. Imagine the stress placed on the overall system by 17 patients arriving at one time. They all hit admitting at once! So at 5:15 a.m. the admitting area is backed up, but doesn't open until 5:30 a.m. Now a large admitting area and several registration personnel are required to meet peak demand. Next, the 17 patients descend on the surgical waiting room and Pre-Op area. Now it appears more Pre-Op beds and staffing are needed because everyone's rushing each morning to Pre-Op these patients who are prioritized based on their surgeon (if they are a high producer or very vocal) or anesthesia (if a "block" is required) or in some cases no priority system is in place. Patients arrive in varying states of "readiness" for their surgical procedure depending on the pre-testing already completed and resulted, so every morning the following problems occur:

- Incomplete charts.
- Inaccurate or incomplete consents.
- Surgeon orders are either not done or are incomplete.
- History and physical examinations (H&Ps) were not provided by the office, or were provided the night before to pre-testing (which does not open until 7:00 a.m.) but needed in Pre-Op or the faxes were lost somewhere along the way.
- Surgeons are late.
- Blood work is not complete, i.e., type and cross, etc. or additional testing is required based on patient and chart examination by anesthesia.
- Inpatients co-morbid medical conditions have not been addressed medically clearing them for the surgical procedure.

Nurses scamper to get the ORs ready and backfill missing personnel. Nurses then try to find missing supplies and equipment either because they were missing, cases were not "picked" (process of gathering routine supplies and equipment for a case) accurately, they were used on a previous case and have to be cleaned, or the preference card was wrong inaccurate or incomplete. Now 17 patients are rolled in procession into the OR, and once surgery is completed, 17 patients are moved into the PACU/Post-Op care unit. Then the second "batch" rush starts.

Surgery Is Like a Repair Shop

Surgery in its simplest form is like an auto repair shop. Clinicians may have difficulty with this analogy, but there are some similarities. Obviously, surgeons and clinicians are highly educated, trained and skilled, and people are not cars, but parallels do exist. As consumers, we take our car to the auto shop (which could be the surgeon's or physician's office or hospital), because there is a problem which needs to be "diagnosed", determine what needs to be done, and repair the issue.

Patients go to surgeons offices so the surgeons can diagnose the situation, and determine a course of action (repairs needed or medical treatment or recommend surgical intervention). Auto shops (hospitals) have highly trained and skilled technicians (physicians and ancillary personel) that carry out the repairs (surgical intervention). Sometimes, certain parts are back ordered (such as a specialized instruments, implants or screws) which delays the repair. Each repair (surgical case) is different and requires different equipment and supplies. One question we always ask of our teams is: If you were the owner of the repair shop (hospital), what processes would you set up to deliver your service in a low cost, high quality, and efficient manner in order to generate revenue?

1. Scheduling—If this was your shop (surgery department), how would you setup the schedule? In reality, in most car shops, some people may call ahead while others drop off their cars without warning (thus add-ons). Most people drop off their cars in the morning on their way to work, therefore the majority of cars or peak demand occurs first thing in the morning. In addition, Mondays and Fridays tend to be the busiest with pent up demand for service on Monday and the desire on Friday for service prior to the weekend. Operating rooms have the same challenges with unleveled work load. Cases are not level loaded throughout the week and peak demand occurs in the morning as physicians ask all their patients to show up at the same time in the morning for fear if the first patient doesn't show or has an issue they will sit idle waiting for the next case or even be bumped. What is the impact when all cars come in for service at the same time? What would be the added costs of heavier schedules on certain days? Would the shop need more tools and supplies, and more labor on those days? Does it have enough bays (OR suites) or will cars get behind schedule? Does the shop know how long an oil change will take, as well as any other repair? Again, if you owned the shop, would you standardize your equipment, tools, and supplies or would you buy different equipment, tools, and supplies for each mechanic?

In many cases, hospital surgical services management teams may recognize the challenges they face internally when cases are not level loaded throughout the week. When they have 20 cases to staff one day and 10 the next day, there are challenges in anesthesia coverage and extra instrument sets needed to meet the peak demand. They may not have enough specialty OR rooms, and Post-Op beds creating delays. Most managers do not recognize the impact they have on the entire hospital when assigning block time (scheduling cases).

Illustration

There is one six-surgeon, neurosurgical group practicing at Hospital X, scheduling all their cases on Mondays, Wednesdays, and Thursdays. This causes peaks and troughs in staffing and rooms/ beds in both the OR and in the neurosurgical intensive care units, transportation, and other ancillary services such as pharmacy, radiology, and laboratory. The system becomes stressed on Mondays, Wednesdays, and Thursdays owing to the non-leveling of cases. Cases need to be scheduled so there are no equipment conflicts which can negatively impact the same surgeons. This then creates a need for more equipment sets and the resulting work to clean, sterilize, store, pick, and maintain them which stresses the sterile processing department and also the floor units that receive the patients.

Lean Solution

Work with the neurosurgical group to see if some of the surgeons in that group could adjust their office hours and perform cases on Tuesdays and Fridays. This would level capacity in the OR, reduce peak demand for instrument sets, ICU and medical surgical beds, FTE labor, etc. This simple example illustrates the organizational and cost reduction impact that leveling surgical cases in the OR can have.

2. What if each mechanic wanted his/her own tools? This is not uncommon practice, but who pays for them? The mechanic does. The problem with having employee-owned tools is that they can interfere with creating standard work. Another problem occurs when the mechanics customize them and no one else has access to that particular tool. When the mechanic leaves no one can figure out how the mechanic performed the job.

Surgeons and physicians typically do not see standardizing supplies and instruments as important. Why? One reason is because they are not paying for them. In addition, they may find it intrusive to their practice, as in general, they want to use the tools/instruments with which they have become trained and comfortable, and therefore any change is met with resistance. How does this impact hospital staff who have to stay proficient with the varying pieces of equipment. Do physicians standardize equipment and supplies in their offices? Do they level load their office schedules? Do they maximize their time in their offices?

The auto repair shop and surgery have synonymous goals:

- Level loading
- Standardize parts and supplies
- Flexible (cross trained) labor
- Optimizing throughput in and out as quickly as possible, providing high quality with zero defects

What do we do if we only have one oil change person or one front-end alignment person? How would that impact the overall operations or goals? What if they were out sick or have a doctor's appointment?

What would happen in the hospital environment with only one specially trained surgeon, surgical technician, housekeeper, transporter, etc.?

There has been a slow migration of physicians leaving private practice to become hospital-employed, and we are beginning to see a shift in willingness by some physician groups to break down barriers and work more toward common goals.

Lesson Learned

Level loading, standardizing on supplies and equipment, flexible labor, and optimizing throughput are important to creating and sustaining a Lean environment.

SECTION II PRE-TESTING—THE PATH TO PATIENT READINESS

The surgical processes, in its most simplistic form, can be divided into several steps: Pre-Op testing, which could take place anytime from the day of surgery to several days prior; registration Pre-Op; surgery (OR); and Post-Op (PACU) period. These areas in combination form the overall OR process flow. In order to flow, four key process focused areas must be addressed:

- Patient readiness
- Materials and equipment readiness
- OR turnover
- Staff readiness (includes surgeon and anesthesia)

We met with the surgery director and asked her to explain the problems they were having, and then proceeded to walk through their process. The main problem was they couldn't get patients through the surgery process efficiently, and everyone in the system was blaming everyone else. The surgeons were blaming the nurses. The nurses were blaming anesthesia and transport. Everyone was blaming management, and it was a very unhappy and unprofessional environment.

We asked to see if they had any data related to their processes. They had limited data from their system and what they were able to produce for us wasn't accurate. (We have experience this problem at many other hospitals.) We explained that with Lean they may be looking at making some significant "out of the box" changes to their overall system. They said they knew that and that they were ready to "break plates" and never look back. The next 6 weeks was spent talking to frontline staff and stakeholders, collecting and sifting through the data, value stream mapping and assessing where the problems were. What we learned was that no one person or group was to blame. Blame only hides problems. We ultimately found the problem was the overall perioperative services system.

While cycle times are important, it turns out that the first pass yield (FPY– or percent of "right the first time" units of work) in the VSM held the key to the problems. *Their biggest problem was that patients were not ready when it was time for surgery.* As a result, cases were not started on time, schedules backed up, patients waited, and surgeons lost faith in the system and experienced lots of idle or wasted time. Surgeons decided it didn't make sense to arrive on time for a 7:30 a.m. case since patients were never ready to go until 8:00 a.m. Additionally, when patients are consistently not ready on time, surgeons tend to tell all their patients to come in even earlier for surgery, all at the same time in the morning around 5:00 a.m., so that they can adjust their schedule to accommodate whichever of their patients are ready first. This just adds even more of a peak workload on registration, surgery waiting and Pre-Op and adds to the confusion and frustration of nurses, case picking, sterile processing, anesthesiologists and surgeons. Many surgeons thought the problem was long turnovers and blamed the nurses, when all along the problem was actually that their patients just weren't ready to go into the room for their surgical procedure. The next step was to root cause the problem. The FPY in Pre-Op was less than 30%, which was caused by patients not being sent by the surgeons to pre-testing, thus arriving to the Pre-Op area the day of surgery without everything they needed to go through with surgery. It is also a problem with Pre-Op in that they do not have the resources or support services available to totally process (work up) the patient the same day of surgery within the required cycle time, hence the need for a separate pre-testing visit prior to the day of surgery. (There are some other benefits to pre-testing early with the ability to collect additional revenue and prevent certain cancellations day of surgery for complex patients.) We found if the patient arrives totally prepared for surgery, the surgery process starts out efficiently. However if the patient arrives the day of surgery and needs re-evaluation or is delayed because the preparations are not complete, perhaps the patient ate, needs additional testing or x-rays, or took prohibited medications, the process starts behind and will seldom catch up. So the real area we first needed to focus on was getting patients ready for surgery.

We focused on the surgical information flow processes first and then the pre-testing department. When we first walked into pre-testing, we noticed a crowded lobby. Only about 20% of patients were being pre-tested. The pre-testing office was like walking into a chaotic town center. Papers were everywhere. The copy machine and fax machines were all centralized in another room and the manual schedule was difficult to read. Six to eight nurses were doing nothing but clerical work; receiving faxes, filing, and calling offices instead of seeing patients. What a waste of talent! During our analysis of pre-testing we discovered several of the problems had root causes that originated in surgeon's offices and related to anesthesiology requirements for medical clearance.

Patient readiness (quality) should be one of the number one Lean measures in surgical services, followed by turnover time which includes cleaning, setup, materials, case picking, preference cards which all impact throughput time.

If patients are ready, surgeries are quick and smooth. But why aren't patients ready? Patients may not be required by their surgeon to go to pre-testing prior to the day of surgery, or if they do go, the pre-testing process may be inadequate to provide the intended result. If the pre-testing process was good, i.e., FPY reached 100%, it would indicate that everything performed was accurate and right the first time and the intended results were achieved. What would the impact be of having a patient show up on the day of surgery with all the testing and documentation complete? How long would it take to get the patient ready? Would the patient still have to come in as early? Just consider how positively this could impact the patients, physicians and hospital staff, i.e., fewer Pre-Op beds needed and labor savings as patients will not need to be prepped or monitored for as long while "waiting" for surgery.

When analyzing patient readiness, we have identified several key tasks directly related to pre-testing which will ensure patient readiness:

1. Create a Standard Order Set for Surgical Clearance: A standard set of physician orders needs to be jointly developed by the surgeons and anesthesiologists, which guarantee not only medical clearance by the physician/surgeon, but also anesthesia clearance as anesthesia ultimately makes the decision if the surgery goes ahead or not.
2. Adoption of Standard Orders and Need for Pre-testing: The physicians and their offices need to adopt a standardized pre-testing process that would include supplying standard orders prior to the patient's arrival at the pre-testing facility. The other option is for the physician's office to perform the required pre-testing.
3. Mandate Pre-testing (at a minimum for first case starts and for key patient populations): Develop a mandate that pre-testing is important and required as it plays a major role in patient readiness and impacts first case on-time starts. The pre-testing area needs the ability to have any abnormal results reviewed by the surgeon and the anesthesiologist and immediately acted on.
4. Efficient Pre-testing Clinic: The pre-testing clinic needs to have a formalized review process, streamlined, standardized work flow, and level loading of patients.

Typical Pre-Testing "Patient Readiness for Surgery" Projects

1. Patient readiness project assessment (overall)
2. Define and standardize what it means to be "ready for surgery" on the day of surgery (outpatients or same day admits)
3. Define the term for inpatient "ready for surgery"
4. Develop surgery Pre-Op standard order form driven by surgeons and anesthesia which outlines the necessary tests for medical clearance
5. Surgeon office education and communication of the new process
6. Patient flow—pre-testing to OR
7. Information flow—pre-testing to OR
8. Pre-testing infrastructure
9. Pre-Op area assessment
10. Standardize Pre-Op checklist
11. Standardize inpatient Pre-Op checklist
12. Standardize timing of completion of inpatient readiness
13. Communicate definition of "ready for surgery"

THE PRE-TESTING MODEL

Each hospital we visit seems to have different models for pre-testing. These will be discussed later in this chapter. Which one is best? From a Lean and systems view, pre-testing is an "inspection" process. The ideal would be not to have to do it at all. The next best solution would be to do it on the day of surgery, and there are a few hospitals doing this. But most hospitals cannot do it on the day of surgery because their processes are not robust enough to support the "testing result" turnaround times (TAT) necessary. This means waiting until the day of surgery to perform "readiness checks on all patients" could result in an increased number of last-minute cancellations and impact patient and family satisfaction.

TRADITIONAL PRE-TESTING PROCESS

The ultimate goal is to create a "robust" pre-testing process by surfacing any problems that may cause the surgery to be cancelled or delayed and help improve the surgical outcome. When the patient arrives on the day of surgery, we want them to be "defect" free with all the forms and tests that can be completed prior to that day documented, and reviewed for necessary actions to medically clear the patient. New models are taking optimization further upstream to the time that the procedure is recommended, NOT scheduled and identifying "medical clearance issues" to optimize outcomes earlier so weeks ahead glucose, anemia can be identified and optimized prior to the procedure, this is truly the ideal state to optimize outcomes in the pre, intra and post op stay. The only activities left the day of surgery are those that must be completed within the perioperative time frame, i.e., diabetics or patients on blood thinners may need repeat blood tests.

Let's look at where the opportunities are to streamline the process. We have to start with the initial patient visit to the surgeon. What is the surgeon's job? The surgeon determines if the patient may benefit from surgical intervention, discusses the options with their patient, the benefits and risks of surgery, and the right to a second opinion. They see their job initially as explaining the surgery to the patient and answering any questions. They may or may not decide what orders are required, but the orders written for surgical preparation are from their (the surgeon's) perspective and may not meet the same needs of the anesthesiologists or hospital to "clear" the patient for surgery. The patient is then "handed off" to the office staff. The office staff pulls the order sheet (protocols) for the designated surgery and then calls the hospital to schedule the pre-testing visit along with their assigned OR scheduled time or refers the patient to a physician to do the pre-testing work.

There are several ways a patient may be "prepared or receive medical clearance" to become "ready for surgery." From the hospital perspective, this process results in "paper" (laboratory and x-ray results, various consents, orders, H&Ps all arriving by fax or e-mail) from multiple sources for next-day surgeries to surgeries several months out. Gathering and sorting this in the pre-testing clinic requires a vast number of personnel and most hospitals utilize nurses to handle all this paperwork. We have found that this incoming "paperwork" is often received in multiple places within or outside the pre-testing department, making coordination and consolidation virtually impossible. Test results, consents, and other paper-work can be lost, causing frustration and rework for the surgeons and their offices, and for the pre-testing clinic. The surgeons and their staff then have to chase down, secure, and resubmit to pre-testing or Pre-Op on the day of surgery, the appropriate documents for medical clearance. In addition, in many organizations there has not been an agreed upon "standard for medical clearance" between all the anesthesiologists and surgeons requiring more testing and rework for nurses and patients, creating more confusion and delays. In many cases, even obtaining agreement from one anesthesiologist to another is extremely difficult.

Most hospitals have a screening or interview process referred to as "medical clearance" and have "forms" such as consents which need to be completed by the patient prior to surgery. Who evaluates the patient varies across the organization. It may be a hospitalist, anesthesiologist, nurse anesthetist, or a pre-testing nurse in the "pre-testing process." On the day of surgery, the final review is carried out by a nurse anesthetist and/or anesthesiologist.

NEED FOR STANDARD ORDERS

The need for standard orders arose as we reviewed the faxed orders sent to the pre-testing department. Typical problems we encountered are the following:

- The orders are illegible.
- Patient names are spelled wrong (birth dates are normally correct, but the computer system doesn't search by birth dates).
- Every office order form is different and some are different from within each office.
- Many times, patients arrive with no orders, forcing expedited calls to offices.
- Variability from surgeon to surgeon on their pre-testing orders and procedures.

These manual processes and paperwork deciphering create a ripe environment for errors and ongoing work for both the pre-testing department and the surgeon's offices. It is no wonder this all-important relationship is sometimes so strained. Some pre-testing departments actually have a "do not call list" where surgeons have refused to allow them to call their offices. As a result, we have found that surgeons can unintentionally be their own worst enemies. Whose responsibility should it be to make sure the patient is ready? One would assume it has to start with the surgeon. But we find that this is not the case. Ultimately, the anesthesiologist decides what is required and determines if the surgery "goes according to schedule if at all."

In many cases, pre-orders written by the surgeon do not agree or do not contain everything the anesthesiologist requires to assure that the patient is medically ready and cleared for safe surgeries, i.e., sleep apnea, etc. The surgeon and anesthesiologist each are coming from different patient care perspectives. The anesthesiologist must ensure the patient is healthy enough to administer anesthesia, can make it through the operations, and then be able to wake up.

One of the challenges we have encountered is the lack of clarity in definition of medical clearance, i.e., an agreement across all parties (surgeons and anesthesia) of what medical surgery clearance ultimately entails. Some anesthesiologists have told us that surgeons simply don't have the knowledge necessary to screen their patients according to the criteria required by anesthesia. While surgeons and anesthesiologists believe they are in agreement, we have found when you dive into the details, there is not an "agreed" on standard tests, results, and reports needed to "clear a patient" for surgical intervention. Thus, depending on the anesthesiologist reviewing the case on the day of surgery, the expectations of what needs to be done vs. what has been done may not match what needs to be done in their opinion and so the delay begins.

We also have found that even among anesthesiologists and/or nurse anesthetists there are disagreements as to what criteria or expectations are required and what constitutes "medical clearance" for surgery. We witness this in every hospital when one anesthesiologist takes over another's patient.

STANDARD PRE-TESTING AND PRE-OP ORDER SETS

Lean Solution

In order to eliminate the patient readiness problem, it is necessary to create a standard order set for pre-testing and Pre-Op. This order set (see Figure 11.8) contains both the surgeon criteria and an agreed-upon anesthesia clearance criteria in the form of a grid based on patient condition and what anesthesia tests are required. We have found it typically takes a year or more, once a serious effort is expended to undertake the initiative. The end result is an astounding increase in patient readiness, reduction or elimination of early morning surgeon calls, improved office/pre-testing and Pre-Op relationship, reduced cancellations, and happier patients.

The first step to creating standard orders is to get all the anesthesiologists to agree on what is necessary by patient demographics and surgery type and develop medical clearance criteria. This in

DATE	TIME WRITTEN	

PRE-OPERATIVE ORDERS

DOCTOR - PLEASE USE BALL POINT - PRESS FIRMLY

NOTE: ORDERS MUST BE REVIEWED AND AUTHENTICATED BY RESPONSIBLE PHYSICIAN.

Patient Name: Diagnosis.

Physician:

Surgery/Procedure Date: **Admit to:** ☐ Inpatient Services   **Place in:** ☐ Outpatient Services

Surgery/Procedure Name:

1. **Shave and Prep:**

2. **Pre-op tests:** ☐ Done prior to admission ☐ On admission ☐ Obtain results from:

3. **Preoperative testing guidelines:**

   If patient has:

CHF:	☐ H&H	☐ BUN ☐ Creat	☐ EKG if not done in last 6 months
Cardiovascular Disease:	☐ H&H	☐ EKG if not done in last 6 month	
Pulmonary Disease:	☐ H&H	☐ EKG if not done in last 6 months	☐ CXR
Liver disease, hepatitis or jaundice	☐ H&H	☐ PT/ INR ☐ aPTT	☐ AST ☐ ALT
Renal impairment	☐ H&H	☐ potassium ☐ BUN	☐ Creat
Blood/Bleeding Disorder	☐ H&H	☐ PT, INR ☐ aPTT	☐ Platelet Count

   Diabetes: ☐ BUN   ☐ Creatinine   ☐ Glucose   ☐ EKG if not done in last 6 months

   If patient is on:

   Antihypertensives: ☐ EKG if not done in last 6 months

   ACE Inhibitors   ☐ BUN   ☐ Creatinine   ☐ EKG if not done in last 6 months

   Diuretics: ☐ potassium

   Digoxin: ☐ potassium   ☐ EKG if not done in last 6 months

   Steroids: ☐ potassium   ☐ Glucose

   Coumadin: ☐ H&H   ☐ PT, INR

   Heparin: ☐ H&H   ☐ aPTT ☐ Platelet Count

   If patient has childbearing capacity   ☐ Pregnancy Test

   If patient greater than 50 years old: ☐ EKG if not done in last 6 months

4. **Other preoperative tests:**

   ☐ H&H **OR** ☐ Hemogram OR ☐ Hemogram with platelets OR ☐ Hemogram with platelets, differential

   ☐ PT,INR ☐ aPTT ☐ platelet function analysis ☐ Urinalysis ☐ Urine culture and sensitivity

   ☐ ELECT **OR** ☐ basic metabolic panel ☐ comprehensive metabolic panel

   ☐ hepatic function panel ☐ Lipid profile ☐ potassium ☐ BUN ☐ creatinine ☐ AST ☐ALT

   ☐ Type and Screen **OR**

   ☐ _____ units Red Blood Cells (T&C), leuko- reduced   ☐ Autologous

   ☐ CXR   ☐ EKG   ☐ ABGs   PFTS ☐ Screen ☐ Complete

5. ☐ **Old charts:** All charts within one year to floor ASAP and send to OR with patient

6. **Diet:**   ☐ Nothing by mouth   ☐ Nothing by mouth except meds with sip of H20

7. **Consult:** Dr. _____ for _____

8. **Medical clearance:** Obtain from Dr. _____

9. ☐ Incentive Spirometer

10. ☐ Antiembolic Hose - Thigh high   **OR**   ☐ Sequential Compression Hose

11. **Antibiotic:**

   All antibiotics will be given within one hour prior to skin incision: except Vancomycin (Vancocin) or otherwise ordered.

   Physician's Signature: _____   Date/Time _____

ALLERGIES:	Patient Diagnosis:	Height:	Weight:

FIGURE 11.8 Physician Standard Orders. Source: BIG Archives.

and of itself is a challenge! The next step is to develop the standard order set, which incorporates the "anesthesia" medical clearance criteria. Then we need the organization, including surgeons, trained in and agreeing to adopt the standard orders as part of their processes. The surgeon then completes, signs, and dates the orders for each patient. The surgeon's offices have to complete the forms and schedule the patient's surgery and pre-testing visit before they leave.

HOW TO: THE PROCEDURE TO CREATE STANDARD ORDERS FOR "MEDICAL CLEARANCE FOR SURGERY"

1. Meet with chief of anesthesia/designated leader of the anesthesia practice and surgical medical directors, identify and include key stakeholders. Meet with any other policy or procedure committee necessary that will be involved in the approval process for the forms. Include the legal department, if necessary.

2. Propose standard orders and answer the "change" questions:
   a. What is the change?
   b. Why is it necessary?
   c. What is in it for all parties involved (this will be different for different stakeholders)?
3. Solicit thoughts and/or objections. We view objections as good. Once the objections are overcome, we can move forward.
4. Have chief of anesthesia/designated leader of anesthesia practice and appointees create standard anesthesia requirements.
5. Have the chief of anesthesia/designated leader of anesthesia practice get consensus for all anesthesiologists to agree.
6. Approve final draft and standard orders for piloting and put on Internet.
7. Pick first and second round pilot surgeons.
8. Meet with pilot surgeons and explain the new system, expectations, and what will be shared with their offices.
9. Meet with their offices and educate them on the new form and process.
10. Implement first round pilot for 2 weeks, and monitor system. Call offices 2 or 3 times a week to see how it is going, and if they have any improvement ideas. Check with anesthesia medical director 2 or 3 times per week to see if any patient was not ready due to missing anesthesia requirements and change form as required.
11. Roll out second round of pilots (same as first).
12. Roll out the rest of the system. This must be done individually; it does not work with "lunch and learns."

The surgeon should have an area on the form to add any additional orders as necessary to the standard order form (see standard order form). Since many surgeon specialties already have Pre-Op standard orders by surgery type, an alternative would be allowing them to use their standard forms in conjunction with the new "standard order form for medical clearance." The standard order forms need to be readily accessible to all surgeons and their offices, along with other forms outlined by the organization (such as surgical consent, blood consent, etc.) that need to be completed before the patient enters the OR. We normally provide this form on the Internet so any updates are real time to the surgeon's offices.

Each surgeon's office may need to be educated on the new forms and the necessary process steps to streamline readiness. Education should include standards related to how to:

1. Call to schedule patients for surgery
2. During the same call to schedule the surgery, transfer to pre-testing to schedule the pre-testing appointment
3. Streamline where the documentation needs to be sent. Options for sending: scan, fax, or e-mail order form or consent to one pre-testing location

Take caution

Before mandatory pre-testing is fully implemented, one may want, in parallel, to streamline operations in the pre-testing area. Consider a Lean initiative looking at the pre-testing operations and infrastructure to make sure that it is easy to do business with (ETDBW). Pre-testing must be able to provide a high quality service level to their patients. If not, patients will complain to the surgeon's office, and then the surgeons will no longer want to participate in the new pre-testing process as outlined.

Key Considerations

If there is not adequate space or staff to meet the projected demand within the pre-testing department, the manager may determine that they slow down or "pace" the physician office training of the new process and "rollout." This will enable the clinic to slowly adjust to meet the demand of their customers (physician offices). The team should work closely with ancillary support services that are needed during clinic operating times to ensure that laboratory and radiology etc., can meet the new customer demand.

STANDARD ORDERS ROLLOUT—GENERAL LEAN PROJECT SYSTEM IMPLEMENTATION CONSIDERATIONS

PHYSICIAN ACCEPTANCE AND ADOPTION

In general, if one is considering a Lean initiative in surgical services, it is important to engage physician leaders to steer the initiative. This gives them "ownership" and creates "buy-in" for the new process. This group could be a committee that already exists within the organization or a new one developed to oversee operations within surgical services. It is recommended that whether considering an existing committee or developing a new one, the members include representatives from each large surgical subspecialty, administration, anesthesia, and surgeon leaders. The committee should determine what projects should be engaged, assess the progress, remove barriers and make "surgeon" decisions related to the projects. As an example, the committee should review the new standard orders that incorporate medical clearance. We have found this helps in physician change management and to remove physician-related barriers to facilitate compliance. In addition, it provides a mechanism for the Lean team to get feedback on what is important from the customer's viewpoint.

HOW TO IMPLEMENT THE PHYSICIAN OFFICE COMPONENT

Physician Office Education

Key activities

- Selecting pilot surgeon offices
- Training and coaching offices on the process
- Results and full implementation

Selection of Pilot Offices

When implementing standard orders, it is best to identify 2—maybe 3—surgeons to pilot the implementation. The requirement for the first pilot is simply finding a surgeon(s) who is willing to try the new process and activities, be open-minded, provide feedback, and make it successful. In addition, it is helpful to identify an informal leader within the surgical arena, a surgeon who is respected and will be able to drive the adoption of others once the pilot phase is complete.

Once the surgeon(s) agrees to the pilot, it is necessary to meet with the involved physicians, the director of surgery, and director or group leader of anesthesia (and other stakeholders, as identified) to explain the new process and desired behaviors and outcomes.

We create an education packet which explains to the offices the new process with a practical runthrough of the new standard order form(s), where they are located, how to download it or complete the form(s) on the Internet, and the procedure for furnishing it to pre-testing.

Necessity for Pre-Testing

It is necessary to explain to the office staff the challenges and current statistics relating to patient readiness for their surgeon. In addition, it is important to explain why patient readiness is so critical to starting surgery on time and what is in it for them (patient and surgeon satisfaction, and, in addition, they may receive fewer phone calls and rework in trying to obtain last-minute results that may have been lost).

Necessity to Schedule Pre-Testing at least 3–10 days (or more as indicated whenever possible) Prior to the Surgery Date. As we move toward understanding and re-defining "readiness for surgery" related to glucose, anemia management and standardization of other pre-op pathways/guidelines, timelines may need to increase to optimize patients to achieve the best outcomes. Other obstacles to same-day testing is the timeliness or TATs for laboratory results and x-rays; in addition, some organizations have expressed challenges related to reimbursement for tests performed the same day of surgery. The argument for three plus days prior is that it provides a buffer that allows time for processing tests (laboratory and radiology), review of the results, and implementation of corrective actions, or additional testing that may be required. Having pre-testing performed prior to the day of surgery provides a relaxed atmosphere to interview the patient and ascertain if any other complications could arise prior to the day of surgery. It is not unusual to find patients who aren't sure of their surgeons' names or don't even fully understand the surgery they are contemplating.

Pre-testing can alleviate potential problems that, if not identified and addressed, may cause delays or cancellations on the day of surgery. Cancellations the same day of surgery can be very disruptive to both the patients and their families who have emotionally and logistically prepared for surgery. In addition, same-day cancellations also disrupt the surgical schedule and impact, staffing, anesthesiologists, and other patients.

General Considerations in working with surgeon's offices:

- Consents need to be signed in surgeon's office
- Provide contact numbers for faxing, email, and feedback
- Agreement that the offices send their patients to pre-testing and pre-testing will take care of everything for them (with a defined process)
- If the offices send them to an outside provider, i.e., internist or family practitioner, separate laboratory, or radiology center, etc., then the doctor's office is responsible to convey all the reports and furnish them "as a package" to a designated contact in pre-testing
- Explain the process for how "any abnormals" will be handled

LEAN PRE-TESTING MODEL

The pre-testing Lean initiative should utilize the following tools: VSM, base-line metrics and photos, five why's, PFA (TIPS) analysis, operator full work analysis (WFA), layout review, capacity and staffing analysis and scheduling. In most cases, we have found that a new layout is required, deploying standard work and a staffing plan ("staff to demand"), which would include forecasting and level loading demand. We have found that once standard orders are implemented, demand for pre-testing grows. It should be noted that pre-testing is, in fact, inspection and, therefore, a non-value-adding activity. Eventually, the goal should be to eliminate the need for or minimize the amount of pre-testing criteria and time necessary.

PRE-TESTING INFRASTRUCTURE

When we work with pre-testing, our goal is to work two parallel projects. One is to implement the standard orders initiative, including the development of the form, physician education, and pilots, and the other is to improve the flow and efficiency of the pre-testing clinic.

Pre-testing clinic infrastructure must be streamlined before one considers mandated pre-testing. Takt time will tell us how many rooms will be needed to see patients. PFAs and point-to-point diagramming are beneficial in determining the layout and new work flow through the unit. PFAs will help identify where and when phlebotomy and electrocardiograms (EKGs) are performed. full work analysis will aid in determining value-added steps, workstation design, where to place printers, faxes, and other equipment. WFA will reveal TLT, that, when divided by Takt time, will help in determining how many staff will be required. One must remember that today, volume may be low, but on adoption of standard orders and mandated pre-testing, demand will grow. Forecasting growth related to rooms required and staff is extremely critical to meet customer needs and must be considered in the new layout. Customer surveys may be needed to determine the optimal times (hours and days) to operate the clinic to maximize patient satisfaction.

We have discovered many models for pre-testing. Each has pros and cons and can be influenced by many variables. We have identified the following different pre-testing models to date:

1. Surgeon performs some pre-testing in office (patient and sometimes results not sent to pre-testing area).
2. Family physician or internist performs pre-testing (referred by surgeon not sent to hospital pre-testing clinic).
3. Patient drives the process (patient provided orders by surgeon and patient determines where to go).
4. Pre-testing performed by pre-testing clinic nurse phone call only (no visit) to determine which patients should come in to be seen by an anesthesiologist and schedules appointments for others.
5. All patients are sent by surgeons' offices to the hospital pre-testing clinic where the process is:
   • Nurse in pre-testing performs pre-testing interview, carries out standard orders, follows up on results, and communicates with surgeons or physicians, as needed.
   • Phone call by pre-testing nurse, followed by a visit to pre-testing clinic (nurses).
   • Combination of nurse interview and anesthetist nurse screening.
   • Anesthesia (physician) screens patient in pre-testing (or their office) and nurse in pre-testing does interview.
   • Hospitalist screens patient in pre-testing clinic and nurse does interview. Hospitals using this model, will tell you a nurse is not a doctor and the hospitalist can complete the H&P and consents needed for surgery.
   • Physician's assistant (PA) or advanced registered nurse practitioner (ARNP) in pre-testing area screens patient and nurse does interview.
6. Some hybrid combination of all the above.

We have found that pre-testing clinics with standardized processes are the most successful. In addition, depending on the contracts with the anesthesia groups and hospitalists, models that include physicians in pre-testing may be cost prohibitive for many organizations. There can also be complications where hospitals have more than one hospitalist group. Pre-testing models are influenced by the ability to charge for services rendered by physicians in the clinics (anesthesia, hospitalist, etc.). Depending on the surgeon's relationships with the local family practitioners, and internists, there may be some reluctance to refer patients to physician hospitalist groups in the pre-testing clinic. Other concerns result as to who is the "attending" or admitting physician. In some cases, the hospitalist model is very effective if the hospitalist becomes the "attending" physician. They are then responsible and reimbursed for the care of the patient, which frees up the surgeon to do more surgeries. As discussed, the ultimate goal with standard orders and pre-testing is to make sure that the patient is ready the day of surgery and the case does not get cancelled or rescheduled. New models of ownership options are continually evolving as there is movement to align physicians and hospitals and payment methodologies change.

TRADITIONAL PROCESS FLOW AND ISSUES OF THE "READINESS FOR SURGERY PROCESS"

The process starts with the patient consenting to surgery. The surgeon begins by writing orders and then, in most cases, the office staff will normally provide the patient with a packet of information that includes what the patient can expect. The office may tell the patient at that time or inform the patient that they will be notified of the surgery date and time. They may tell the patient to call for a pre-testing appointment, or schedule it for the patient, or have pre-testing done that day (depending on the timing of surgery and pre-testing models and process in place).

Pre-Testing Phone Call Process

Some pre-testing models only make phone calls first, but most combine pre-screening phone calls with visits. Once the pre-testing nurse is able to contact the patient, she/he will go through the routine assessment and enter the patient information into a computer. This facilitates a reduction of patient time spent in the clinic, and provides insight into medical history. If it is determined the patient has complicated medical risks and the case could be delayed or cancelled, the patient is instructed to come in for the pre-testing process and medical clearance. Most pre-testing managers want all their patients to visit to ensure they are properly prepared. Most can be quoted as saying "A phone call is not the same as "hands-on."

Pre-Testing Patient Interview

During the interview, the nurse enters the patient's information into the surgical information system. Some hospitals simply collect the information to have on hand and use for decision making. Other hospitals utilize this tool to trigger consults during Post-Op care. This is both good for the patient and good for the hospital.

THE PRE-TESTING MODEL—PATIENT VISIT

When patients go to pre-testing, they are normally checked in by a person who will ask the patient to sign in and, complete any forms that may be missing

At some point, the patient is called by registration to verify insurance information and co-payment collection. The patient is then directed back to the waiting room to wait for the nurse. The nurse takes the patient's vitals, fills out a nursing assessment (if they have them), completes orders for any other test results and x-rays (as needed), and provides instructions for the day of surgery. At some point, a phlebotomist comes into the room to draw blood and/or do an EKG. The nurse then completes the process and makes sure the consents are proper and signed. After this, depending on the model, the patient may see a nurse anesthetist, physician, or whoever is responsible for reviewing the patient's information. They may examine the patient and determine if they meet all the criteria. If rendered necessary, he or she may then order an additional laboratory test (blood draw or EKG) or contact the surgeon (Figure 11.9).

Problems Typically Encountered

- Nurse productivity is low.
- Management thinks they need more rooms.
- Forms are everywhere.
- Chart making is batched in sections.
- Wait times for patients are long.
- There is a long LOS for the process.
- Matching up paperwork from different sources is often difficult. I have seen processes where 6 to 8 nurses were needed to match up paperwork which was coming from doctor's offices, independent laboratories, physician offices, etc., for surgeries days to months out.
- Chart completion percentage at Pre-Op is low.
- Orders may or may not be in the chart when patient arrives.

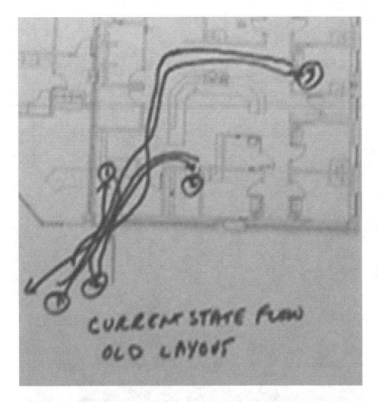

FIGURE 11.9   PreTesting - Patient Flow Diagram. Source: BIG Archives.

- FPY at Pre-Op is low.
- There are no standard orders to follow (across all surgeons).

HOSPITAL X LEAN RESULTS IN PRE-TESTING ARE PROVEN

A financial-based decision was made to close a small pre-testing department at a day surgery site adjacent to the main hospital campus. The department had 3 nurses with an average of 13–17 patients per day. The main campus pre-testing clinic was able to absorb the additional volume with no increase in staff. The 3 nurses were re-deployed elsewhere in the hospital. In addition, the clinic has increased volume by 38%, increased patients per nurse by 19.4%, and improved on-time chart completion from 36% to 70% while even implementing more stringent criteria. When this was conveyed to the unit secretaries, their faces lit up and they said, "We are going to keep raising it!" The clinic has been able to eliminate virtually all overtime. In addition, by changing the information flow and how charts were assembled, they were able to work on completing charts up to 2 weeks or more in advance, when just getting the next day's charts used to be a struggle. Everyone prefers the new system.

Level Loading the Schedule

Hospital X was having difficulty staffing the unit and patients were experiencing long wait times. When analyzed, it was determined that staffing did not match the demand nor the wide variation in the times that patients arrived. The schedule was controlled by the OR, not the pre-testing unit. We transferred control of the schedule to the pre-testing unit, thereby giving them control over their own destiny. The first thing we did was to level load the appointments. This is called Heijunka (Figure 11.10). The software had to be "fooled" to accomplish this, as the software scheduled by

FIGURE 11.10 Simple Heijunka Box schedule by the half hour. If a patient is late or doesn't show it is immediately visible. This is known as a visual control. Source: BIG Archives.

room, not by the hour. Once we implemented the Heijunka system, the demand averaged out per hour and the nurses could easily manage the demand. The nurses were much happier and less frustrated.

We then implemented visual controls for registration (Figure 11.11) so the pre-testing department always knew who was at which registration desk, next door. We then implemented Heijunka cards (Table 11.5) where we captured the cycle times for each part of the process and logged them into a spreadsheet each day real time. A day-by-the-hour sheet (Figure 11.12) was created and each room had an in and out envelope in which the Heijunka card would go. Now we knew who was in what room all the time. The charge nurse now had simple visual tools to manage the department and continually improve the system (Table 11.6).

HOSPITAL B—STANDARD WORK—THOUGHTS AND DISCUSSIONS SURROUNDING THE INTRODUCTION OF STANDARD WORK TO STAFF IN A PRE-TESTING CLINIC

As part of a Lean initiative, the nurses were videoed as they performed their daily activities within the pre-testing area. Each step the nurses performed was documented and a WFA sheet was created. Two acting charge nurses (who were on the Lean team) met in private to review each of their

FIGURE 11.11 Registration queue stationed at the clinic reception. Since Registration was next door and out of site they lost track of their patients. This simple box with each registration desk number noted allowed anyone to see not only which patients were in registration but which at which desk they were located. Source: BIG Archives.

TABLE 11.5
Heijunka Cycle Time (CT) Card

Pre Testing Stats

Patient Label

Appt. Time:				Date:	
Circle Type: K	M	DS	RR	GI	OB

Lab EKG CXR UA

Check In:	
Reg In:	Out:
Ord. Start:	End:
Room In:	
Nurse start:	End:
Anes In:	Out:
BD/EKG In:	Out:
Nurse Name:	
Comments.	

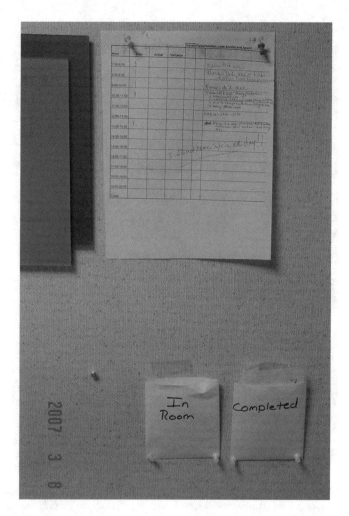

FIGURE 11.12   PreTesting - Day by Hour Chart and Temporary Patient in Room and Completed holders for Heijunka Cards. Source: BIG Archives.

steps from their video on the WFA and came to agreement on how they would set up new standard work and sequence of operations. A job breakdown sheet (JBS) was created. When asked what they thought of the process, they were surprised how differently they each performed the patient interview. They did things in different order, asked different questions and, in some cases, certain questions were not asked at all.

We used their analysis as a strawman (model) to develop a new standardized process.

The standard work concept was introduced to the entire department during an afternoon huddle meeting after we reviewed the "idea board." The meeting was held each week as part of our Lean initiative with a goal to get it to a 10-min "standup" meeting. We explained the advantages of standard work along with how it would help ensure the quality of patient care. As one might imagine, we were met with some resistance and comments such as:

- "We were trained to do nursing independently and now you want to tell us what to do!"
- "Our licenses are at stake and, since you are not a nurse, you don't understand that."
- "If you make us do everything the same, we will forget and quality will be compromised!"
- "You don't care about the patients; you just want us to be robots."
- "Nursing is an art form learned over years of experience. It is not a science."

TABLE 11.6

Heijunka Cycle Times

						Data						
Date	Average of Reg CT	Average of Reg Wait Time	Average of orders CT	Average of Order Entry Delay Time	Average of Exam Room Wait Time	Average of Patient Exam Room CT	Average of Nurse CT	Average of anesthesia CT	Average of anesthesia Wait Time	Average of BD/EKG Wait Time	Average of BD/EKG CT	Average of LOS/Throughput Time
19 March	0:04	0:03	0:02	0:06	0:16	0:28	0:32	0:05	0:03	0:04	0:09	1:10
20 March	0:04	0:09	0:01	0:04	0:17	0:28	0:32	0:05	0:04	0:04	0:10	1:18
24 March	0:04	0:06	0:01	0:02	0:15	0:31	0:33	0:04	0:03	0:04	0:09	1:17
25 March	0:04	0:03	0:03	0:04	0:15	0:32	0:35	0:05	0:04	0:06	0:07	1:17
26 March	0:03	0:04	0:03	0:05	0:21	0:31	0:33	0:05	0:01	0:20	0:08	1:13
27 March	0:03	0:08	0:02	0:03	0:18	0:32	0:35	0:05	0:06	0:33	0:09	1:23
30 March	0:05	0:05	0:03	0:04	0:22	0:36	0:41	0:05	0:04	0:05	0:08	1:29
Grand total	0:04	0:05	0:02	0:04	0:18	0:31	0:34	0:05	0:04	0:12	0:09	1:19

After the staff vented their concerns, it was explained that many processes in the hospital are broken, which is why hospitals continually fail audits. At risk is the safety and welfare of our patients, which should be put first in our decision making. When everyone does a process differently, what are the chances that each patient is getting the same high-level quality of care? How would you measure it? You couldn't because everyone does it differently. You can't implement an improvement across the board when everyone does it differently. In many cases, most procedures were not written down. Everyone is trained by a different nurse with different tribal knowledge and opinions on how things should be done. How can quality be better in this environment?

We explained when everyone does tasks differently it is actually dangerous and is supported by a recent example where a nurse bypassed protocol (bed management) and a patient was literally lost in the system.

The goal is not to change what the nurses do, but to structure it so every patient gets the same necessary standard and high quality of care. We must document the process and improvements to the process (no longer person-dependent) in order to:

- Train new hires
- Have the ability to audit the process
- Pass audits and incorporate changes as a result of audits
- Create a video for new hires (on standard processes)
- Obtain consistent times and expectations for the process across all nurses
- Know how far a patient is through the process with any nurse at any time
- Make their job easier
- Highlight variation in the process to encourage ongoing continuous improvement

We told them we had done this many times before. We then passed out the "straw man" of the job breakdown sheets (Figure 11.13) of their daily tasks that the our two charge nurses had created.

All the nurses were given the opportunity to review it for a week and to see what changes, if any, they wanted to make. The department grumbling and rumor mill continued throughout the week, and we were told that morale was way down. This is typical of what will occur through a Lean initiative, as there is normal resistance to change. We walked the nurses through the change that was recommended, discussed why it was being made, how it would affect them, and if they changed what was in it for them.

We also explained that standard work would not be set in stone, and the expectation would be to continually improve it. A week later, the "big" night came. We met with the staff after the clinic was closed. We showed the nurses a movie about taking time out of processes. After the movie, the manager of the area debriefed the movie and told everyone that Lean was about giving our patients the best care and making sure the patient chart and patients were ready for surgery.

We handed the meeting over to the two charge nurses who reviewed the activities step-by-step, in the standard work. Listed below is how the review started. The charge nurse said:

Step 1—Grab the Charts

"Does everyone agree?" asked the charge nurse, who was dreading this exercise. All eleven present agreed! Ok, Only 39 more to go.

Step 2—Introduce Yourself to the Patient

Does everyone agree? Rules were set prior to the meeting that one person would talk at a time. Well, it didn't last long. One nurse asked about preparing the chart. "We have to sign the signature sheet, fill out consents..." Another nurse said, "I just tell the patient what I'm doing and it is not a problem." The first nurse said, "When I do it, the patients think I am ignoring them and make comments."

Nurse Standard Work

Area	Total Labor Time	Available Time Minutes	Daily Demand	Takt Time Mins
Pre Testing	2,842	700	42	17

	HEAD COUNT:	1	3	4	5	6
	CYCLE TIME:	2842	947	710	568	474
	HOURLY OUTPUT:	1	4	5	6	8
	DAILY OUTPUT:	15	44	59	74	89

Layout Area and Walk Patterns

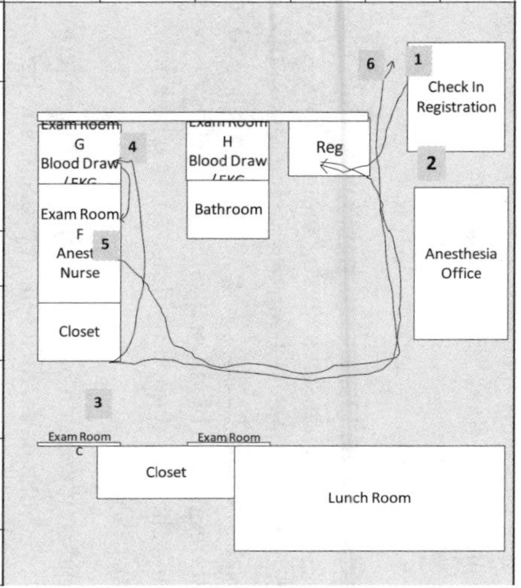

Standard Work Area: Surgery Pre Testing Clinic

Job Step #	Nurse Description (what they do)	Key Points and Quality Notes (how they do it)	Reasons for Key Points	Min Time (secs)	Max Time (secs)	Avg Time Secs	Cumulative Avg Time Mins
1	Pick up chart, and go to room or get patient from lobby	If there is no patient, you should make a phone call. If there is a patient, Reg will put the patient in your room. If you do not have one in there. If all the rooms are full, Reg will put the chart in the file (labeled on the counter) and put the patient in the lobby	Our priority is visiting patients first and then phone calls. However phone calls are very important and have to get done as well.	120	160	140	140
2	Prep the chart outside	checklist, signature sheet, consents, check orders and labs, stickers if needed	We don't watching us prep the chart and they think we are ignoring them	60	120	90	141.5
3	Get the patient if necessary. Flip flags as required. Then introduce yourself to the patient and explain the process.	See script	It is important we follow the script especially in the case of dealing with more difficult patients	60	80	70	142.7
4	Log into PICIS and HOM. Locate the patient in the computer but go to HOM first	see procedure for logging in o PICIS and repeat some of the information Reg just asked you.	Let Patient Know We are going to HOM	60	60	60	143.7
5	Begin Charting	Verify correct DOB and DOC and review orders. Have patients sign consents, Check bib? sheets and armbands if applicable and review spelling of sticker		300	300	300	148.7
6	Look for med list in chart, then chart meds, in HOM. Allergies, height, weight, advance directives and print			300	300	300	153.7

FIGURE 11.13 Nurse job breakdown sheet/standard work. Source: BIG Files.

I then asked what other nurses thought and they all started sharing their thoughts and feelings, some more passionately than others. When we were done, we added a new Step 2, prepare the chart prior to entering the room with the patient.

Step 3—Take Vitals

One nurse stated she takes vitals right away while the computer is loading the programs. Another nurse does it about ten steps down, another does it toward the end, and yet another does it at the end. As facilitator, I had each nurse give the reason they did vitals when they did them. One said she did it toward the end because she found when she did it right away, some patients were so nervous she had to retake the blood pressure later. So by doing it later in the process, the patient was more relaxed and they got a good reading. After much discussion, we decided to move it toward the end of the process.

Note - And so it went on and on, with everyone discovering how differently they each did the same job, how everyone had a different approach, and how many left important questions out and others asked questions that weren't necessary.

In one case, a nurse felt her job and license were on the line if she didn't mention every single drop-down box regardless of how the patient answered the questions. The system is designed so that if a patient answers "no" to a question, one moves on to the next question vs. continuing to ask the patient if they have any of the ten items in the drop-down box that they already answered "no" to. It instantly became clear why this nurse had the longest interview times, sometimes taking more than an hour and a half for a process that should average 25–30 min. This nurse felt we were lowering our standards and not being thorough. The rest of the nurses very nicely explained to her how the system was designed to work and that, as long as they properly documented the patient's responses, we still maintain the same high level of quality and it would never jeopardize her license. Over an hour later, we were halfway through the document and adjourned for the evening. We would schedule another "movie" night to conclude the exercise.

LESSONS LEARNED AND IDEAS IMPLEMENTED FROM VARIOUS LEAN PRE-TESTING INITIATIVES

- Deployed standard work which was agreed on by consensus
- Standard work must incorporate the motto "quality first, the speed will come"
- Created visual cues to track patient visits outside each room
- Nurses do not have to continually log in and out of different computers
- Created a new chart flow so the nurses could follow up and complete their patient

Before, moving from room to room between every patient, nurses had to give the charts to the charge nurse to keep them centralized and so as not to get lost. So, the "system" created a process where the charge nurse had to follow-up and complete every chart. There was no time to supervise or watch the flow. The new process, below, freed up the supervisor to work on ongoing improvements.

We assigned a nurse to a specific room each day—benefits:

- Each nurse had a place for personal items.
- By creating separate rooms for lab, EKG, and vitals, we were able to replace six "unfriendly" examination beds in each room with recliners. We also eliminated the interview rooms as a bottleneck and saw more patients. This freed up several computers and eliminated a lot of gathering (and socializing) at the nurse's station.
- Standardized the rooms—designate a leader for this effort and require everyone's participation. Results: each nurse got an individual printer, saved money in wasted steps per day and per year, and were able to follow up orders and complete charts easier.

- Spreading phone calls across all the nurses, in addition to having a phone call nurse.
- Create standard orders: as one physician said, "Now I don't get calls at home or on the way into the hospital at 5:30 a.m."
- Explain how the standard order form works and that the goal is to eliminate mistakes prior to anesthesia screening.
- Standardize Pre-Op order form for medical clearance. The form needs to be designed to be simple check boxes that then dictate the necessary screening. The form also provides room for additional consults, which the surgeon or office staff can fill in or complete. There is room for the surgeon to add tests, orders, or consults they deem necessary. Again, it can replace, in some cases, dozens of existing surgeon forms or be used in conjunction with them.

In the physician's office, the following was identified:

- There is a need to have consent forms signed in the surgeon's office.
- Establish and provide contact numbers for faxing and feedback.
- There should be an agreement by offices that, if they send their patient to pre-testing, pre-testing will take care of everything for them.
- If they send the patient to a family practitioner, separate laboratory, or radiology center, etc., then the doctor's office will be responsible to convey all the reports and furnish as a package to the pre-testing area.
- There should be an explanation of how any "abnormals" will be handled.
- During the office visit, provide the opportunity for any questions and a frequently asked questions (FAQ) sheet.

Results

Hospital X[2] was profiled in an article for their implementation of Lean principles while hospitals Y and Z utilized the Lean System Implementation method we propose in this book (Table 11.7). It can be clearly seen the BASICS approach resulted in greater productivity. Quality has maintained or improved with every implementation to date.

Pre-Testing Model Calculations

Figure 11.14 is an example of sample value stream process boxes from a pre-testing area. Owing to the business model of this department, we had to implement in phases. We started with an Average Daily Demand (ADD) of 45 patients.

Available time = 12 hrs or 720 min (5:00 a.m. to 5:00 p.m. clinic)

Customer average daily demand = 45 patients.

To calculate our Takt time, we take the available time (12 hrs) and the customer demand at 45 patients per day. Our average Takt time is:

$$720 \div 45 = 16 \text{ min per patient.}$$

This means we have to devise a system that can get a patient in and out every 16 min on average. Utilizing the example box Step #3 of the process nurse review, we can calculate how many rooms and how much labor we need.

---

[2] "Streamlining Care (Pre-testing)," *Advance For Nurse* (Vol. 10 No. 13, June 8, 2009, 8).

TABLE 11.7

Pre-Testing Clinic Results From Three Different Hospitals Implementing Lean Pre-Testing Departments

	Hall Patients	Phone Calls	Total Patients and Calls	# Nurses	# Clerical	# Techs	Total Persons	Working Days'	Working Hours (assumes 40 hrs per week)	Nursing Hours Per Patient Visit	Total Labor Hours Per Patient	Patients Seen Per Person Per Day	# Total FTEs	Hours Per FTE	Notes
Hospital #1	UK	UK	13,000	22	2	6	30	250	45,760	3.52	4.80	1.73	UK	UK	No data on change nurses
Hospital #2	10,534	3962	14,496	11	3	2	16	250	22,880	1.58	2.30	3.62	UK	UK	Secretaries also do scheduling
Hospital #3	12,314	6376	18,690	9.9	3	2	14.9	250	20,592	1.10	1.66	5.02	14.80	1.65	Does not include change nurse. 11 nurses but 9.9 FTEs. Actual productivity running 1.39 or less

Note: Hospital #1 was profiled in a paper as having streamlined their care compared to hospital #2 and #3, which conduced Lean system implementations. UK = unknown.

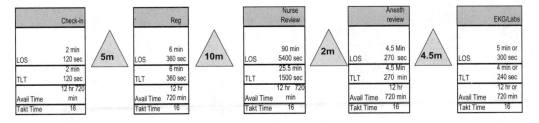

FIGURE 11.14 Pre testing Clinic Value Stream Map Baseline. Source: BIG Files.

TABLE 11.8
Pre-Testing VSM Boxes - Enlarged

Nurse Review

Given	
LOS	90 min 5400 sec
TLT	25.5 min 1530 sec
Available time	12 hrs 720 min
Calculated	
Takt time	16
Rooms	5.6 or 6
FTE(s)	1.59

If we have the Takt time, we use the formula LOS ÷ Takt time = # rooms:

$$90 \text{ min} \div 16 \text{ min} = 5.63 \text{ rooms},$$

and TLT ÷ Takt time = # persons required

$$25.5 \text{ min} \div 16 \text{ min} = 1.59 \text{ FTEs}.$$

assuming one can balance the work evenly across the employees, see Table 11.8.

SECTION III PRE-OP

An opportunity was identified post-VSM to improve the Pre-Op area (Figure 11.15). First, several patients were followed through the process. It was determined that patients would be categorized by the length of time it took to work up a patient. The specialties of orthopedics, general surgery, and cardiovascular were selected. Nurses, technicians, and physicians of each skill type were videotaped. Each video was then analyzed with the individual filmed present and the results were as follows.

The PFA analysis provided the cycle time or LOS for each process step. The WFA analysis showed the Total Labor Time (TLT) equaled 60 min for one patient. Several of the Pre-Op nurses were videoed, caring for patients with different levels of acuity. As the videos were analyzed we asked the staff to document each step, determine if there were any issues, and identify problems and ideas that could lead to improvements (Figure 11.16). Outlined is a list of ideas from reviewing the videotape with the staff.

- Point of use materials and supplies
- Materials located in multiple areas (excessive travel for staff)

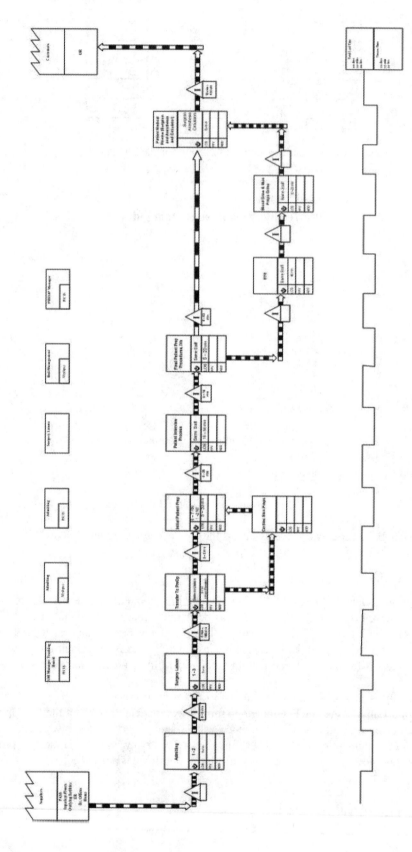

FIGURE 11.15 VSM PreOp Map "In the making". Source: BIG Files.

Idea Board

FIGURE 11.16   PreOp Idea Board. Source: BIG Files.

- Lidocaine not refrigerated
- IV cart needed to be relocated to be more accessible
- Standardize supplies at bedside
- IV bags more accessible
- Flow—consider team approach vs. non-team approach
- Determine appropriate skill level for task
- Need standard work (work standard)
- Trigger Pre-Op pull for next patient from OR charge nurse
- Flip rooms (what is the impact, positive or negative?)
- Free up storage space (5S the area)
- Review charts the night prior to surgery for "abnormals," draw blood, MRI, CT
- Surgeon consult done ahead of time in consult room located near surgery
- Need nerve block room location
- Set up speed dial on phones
- Move Lidocaine and angiocaths to more accessible location
- Pre-testing to write consents
- Add check boxes to belongings sheet
- Make allergy sticker/contact/weight printable
- Combo sticker with standard allergy portion on bottom
- Pre-testing to fill out allergy, weight, contact on front of chart
- Property list filled out in waiting area
- Decrease supplies at bedside, combine supplies in bedside carts, correct supplies with par levels
- Charge Lidocaine at end of day for all patients
- Carts at bedside for all supplies (like PACU)
- Handheld printer scanners for blood draw
- Move ECG machine
- Dress stretcher with gown packet

PRE-OP TIME STUDY

Because there is so much variation in Pre-Op and there were no computerized tools to track cycle times, we manually tracked cycle times for several weeks (Figure 11.17). Over time, we found they averaged out per nurse and per technician. The results of the time study allowed us to create a predictive model (Figure 11.18). The model could perform "what ifs" based on patient and staff arrival times per hour or per morning or per day. If someone was out sick, we could predict our completion time and take the necessary countermeasures.

BENEFITS OF TEAM NURSING IN PRE-OP

The team nursing approach was suggested by several of the Pre-Op nurses who had worked with it before at other hospitals. The manager of the area was initially against the approach. We decided to create the standard work and settled on a "hands on" nurse and a "hands off" nurse. The "hands on" performed all the steps requiring patient contact, such as IV, and the "hands off" nurse took care of the computer system and paperwork, including consents. The system was very successful and reduced the cycle time from 51 to 21 min. While it is only a 9 min saving overall, because the nurses worked in teams, it gave the technicians' time to work with the patients, reducing the cycle time further to 19 min. In the past, the technicians spent much of their time wandering around looking for ways to help out, but since each nurse now took a patient, there was not much for them to do. The benefits of the team nursing were:

- Right skill level for tasks—technicians can see patients, now 100% efficient vs. 50% efficient.
- Patients get completed more quickly vs. many patients being worked on but not completed.
- Team nursing is 20%–25% more efficient than individual nursing.
- 90%–100% of patients completed by 7:15 a.m. most days.
- No longer interrupted by anesthesia, so blocks get done quicker.

LET'S EXAMINE PRE-OP ON THE DAY OF SURGERY

Hospital X has 60 patients scheduled for surgery, 20% come from the floors (admitted) and 80% or 48 of the patients arrive for surgery on the same day in the Pre-Op unit. Historically, the patients were not required to have any pre-testing or medical clearance evaluation for surgery; therefore, often patients had their surgery delayed on the day of surgery while waiting for laboratory results or investigation of potential medical problems. Because of this, the surgeons began requiring the patients to arrive in the Pre-Op area between 5:00 a.m. and 6:00 a.m., no matter what time their surgery was scheduled (Table 11.9). The Pre-Op unit would be inundated with patients, and the result was that many cases were delayed since the nurses had difficulty in preparing the first cases for surgery while simultaneously tending to patients who had surgery scheduled for later in the day. Figure 11.19 is a graph of how the patients arrive in the Pre-Op unit each morning.

The average length of stay (ALOS) in the Pre-Op unit was 150 min; the available time is 8 hrs or 480 min. The TLT to prepare a patient for surgery is 65 min. If we assume that we bring patients in 2.5 hrs early as the first cases begin at 7:30 a.m., we can calculate how many rooms and how much labor we need, given how the patients are currently being "asked to arrive," since patients do not have to be in the OR until 7:30 a.m. and we are asking the first set to arrive at 5:00 a.m. Let's determine the Takt time, which is

Available time from 5:00 a.m. to 7:30 a.m. or 150 min (2.5 hrs) ÷ 32 customers (customer demand for the first 2.5 hrs, 20 + 12), Takt time = 4.7 min per patient.

Date:	Room	Time of Surgery	Patient Down	Tech start Prep	Tech End Prep	Tech In	Tech Out	Tech CT	Nurse 1 start Prep	Nurse 1 end prep	Nurse 1 in	Nurse 1 out	Nurse 1 CT	Nurse 2 start Prep	Nurse 2 end prep	Nurse 2 in	Nurse 2 out	Nurse 2 CT	Overall CT for PT	Total Labor Time	Anesthesia In	Surgeon In	Patient to Surgery	Nursing Team	Tech Name	Comments
Patient #1	B	7:30	5:45	6:01	6:07	6:08	6:12	0:11	5:48	5:48	5:59	6:03	0:15	5:59	5:59	5:59	6:03	0:04	0:20	0:24						
Patient #2	C	7:30	5:45	5:46	5:50	5:46	6:05	0:19	6:05	6:11	6:12	6:17	0:12	6:05	6:12	6:12	6:17	0:12	0:31	0:43						
Patient #3	H	7:30	5:48	6:23	6:23	6:24	6:27	0:04	5:48	5:48	5:48	6:01	0:13	5:48	5:48	5:48	6:01	0:13	0:17	0:30						
Patient #5	PACU 16	7:30	5:54						5:54			7:00	1:06						1:06	1:06						Batch
Patient #4	PACU 21	7:30	5:48						5:48			7:00	1:12						1:12	1:12						Batch
Patient #6	PACU 22	7:30	6:27						6:27			7:00	0:33						0:33	0:33						Batch
Patient #7	D	7:30	6:06	6:08	6:08	6:08	6:23	0:15	6:22	6:22	6:22	6:32	0:10	6:22	6:22	6:22	6:32	0:10	0:25	0:35						
Patient #8	E	7:30	7:13	7:12	7:19	7:19	7:25	0:13	6:08	6:11	6:11	6:26	0:18						0:29	0:29	6:56					
Patient #9	A	7:30	6:10	6:12	6:12	6:12	6:23	0:11	6:19	6:26	6:27	6:43	0:24						0:27	0:51						
Patient #10	G	7:30	6:06	6:24	6:25	6:25	6:27	0:03	6:27	6:32	7:10	7:10	0:43						1:05	1:05						
Patient #11	PACU 17	7:30	6:46	6:50	7:07	7:07	7:12	0:22	6:47	6:53	6:54	6:48	0:13						0:31	0:44						
Patient #12	I	7:30	7:30	6:28	6:31	6:32	6:46	0:18	6:33	6:33	6:33	6:48	0:15						0:21	0:36						
Patient #13	F (floor)			6:33	6:33	6:33	6:33	0:06	7:52	7:55	7:56	8:01	0:09						0:17	0:26						
Patient #14	B		6:30	7:35	7:35	7:35	7:43	0:08	8:05	8:05	8:05	8:21	0:16						0:33	0:33						
Patient #15	D		7:35	7:57	8:00	8:00	8:14	0:17	8:18	8:25	8:35	8:43	0:25						0:31	0:56						
Patient #16	J		7:56		8:19	8:19	8:25	0:06	8:02	8:04	8:04	8:13	0:11						0:22	0:33						patient in shower 10
Patient #17	I		7:35	7:56	7:56	7:56	8:07	0:11	7:50	7:57	7:58	8:27	0:37						0:54	1:31						
Patient #18	G		7:43	7:48	7:48	7:48	8:05	0:17															9:56			
Patient #19	H		8:17	8:30	8:33	8:47	8:47	0:17	8:30	8:53	8:54	9:09	0:39						0:56	0:56						"x" on break

FIGURE 11.17 Pre-Op Time Study (Note: Names have been removed). Source: BIG Files.

PREOP Model 7:30 Starts

	Tech	CT	Minutes Per Shift	# of Hours per shift	Patients Per Shift	Nurse 1	CT	Minutes Per Shift	# 60 min shifts	Patients Per Shift	Nurse 2	CT	Minutes Per Shift	# 60 min shifts	Patients Per Shift	Overall CT	Total (minutes converted to decimal)	PTs / Hour	factor	# 60 min shifts	Patients Per Shift	Total Labor Time / pt	Total Labor Time
team 1	1	0.14	60	1.00	4.29	1	0.19	75	1.25	3.95	1	0.19	75	1.25	3.95	0.33	33.00	3.16	2.50	1.25	3.95	0.53	3.31
Team 2	1	0.14	75	1.25	5.36	1	0.19	75	1.25	3.95	1	0.19	75	1.25	3.95	0.33	33.00	3.16	2.50	1.25	3.95	0.53	3.31
Team 3	0	0.00	60	-	-	1	0.21	75	1.25	3.57	1	0.21	45	0.75	2.14	0.21	21.00	2.86	2.00	1.00	2.86	0.42	2.02
Veronica	0	0.00	60	-	-	1	0.45	90	1.50	2.00	0	0.00	90	-	-	0.45	45.00	1.33	1.50	1.50	2.00	0.45	1.30
																		10.51	2.13	1.25	12.75		10.34

4.375	Team 1	33.00	min avg CT / pt
8.75	Team 2	33.00	min avg ct for both teams with tech
2	Team 3	21.00	min avg ct / pt for veronica
2.25	Team 4	45.00	min avg ct /pt for team without tech
		410.526	weighted avg clock minutes
11.00 Total pts per 7:30 start with all 3 teams		32.19	min weighted avg cycle time per pt
13 Total pts per 7:30 start with all 3 teams and Veronica		5.88	min weighted avg CT per patient per Team (d
		6.54	min weighted avg CT per Team w/o veronica
810	7:15 AM	10	58.81
		11	64.70
		12	70.58
		13	76.46 total clock minutes required
		14	82.34 total clock minutes required w/o veronica
		15	88.22 total clock minutes required w/o veronica
		16	94.10 total clock minutes required w/o veronica
		17	99.99 total clock minutes required w/o veronica
		18	105.87 total clock minutes required w/o veronica
	2nd case starts		
	10 cases *		10.20 cases per hour possible

Right-side values: 75.00 available Time / 75.00 / 19 / 0.45 / 0.91 / 0.71429 / 30 Takt Time; 6.842105 / 5.47; 5.77 Takt Time; 1.46

FIGURE 11.18 PreOp Predictive Staffing Model. Source: BIG Files.

TABLE 11.9

Pre-Op Patients by Hour

Hour (a.m.)	# of Patients
5:00	20
6:00	12
7:00	8
8:00	5
9:00	3

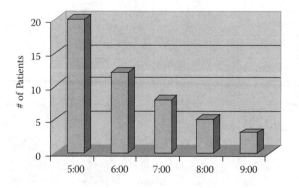

FIGURE 11.19 Pre-Op patients per hour graph

We use the formula LOS ÷ Takt time = # rooms

$$150 \text{ min} \div 4.7 \text{ min} = 32 \text{ rooms,}$$

and TLT ÷ Takt time = # persons required

$$65 \text{ min} \div 4.7 \text{ min} = 13.8 \text{ FTEs,}$$

this assumes one can balance the work evenly across the employees. The surgical services department performed a VSM and determined that surgeries were canceled owing to issues stemming from "patients not ready" for surgery when they arrived. A Lean initiative was undertaken, as described above, and a dramatic improvement was seen in patients arriving "gift-wrapped" the day of surgery. If we assume we now bring down just the first 20 patients, since we only have 20 ORs, what will be the impact?

2.5 hrs ÷ 20 customers = 7.5 min per patient.

We use the formula LOS ÷ Takt time = # rooms

$$150 \text{ min} \div 7.5 \text{ min} = 20 \text{ rooms,}$$

and TLT ÷ Takt time = # persons required

$$65 \text{ min} \div 7.5 \text{ min} = 8.7 \text{ FTE.}$$

There was a significant decrease in the number of rooms needed from 32 to 20 and the number of FTEs was reduced from 13.8 to 8.7. If the average nurse wage was $28/hr or $58,000 per year, the reduction of approximately five FTEs would yield $290,000.

The TLT in the Pre-Op unit was reduced from 65 to 40 min. The surgeons agreed to bring their first cases in 90 min prior to surgery instead of the 150 min that they historically required. The Takt time calculation was performed again using the available time, 90 min:

1.5 hrs ÷ 20 customers = 4.5 min per patient. We use the formula LOS ÷ Takt time = # rooms

$$90 \text{ min} \div 4.5 \text{ min} = 20 \text{ rooms,}$$

and TLT ÷ Takt time = # persons required

$$40 \text{ min} \div 4.5 \text{ min} = 8.9 \text{ FTE.}$$

The number of rooms would still be 20, and the number of FTEs needed would be nine staff. Sixty (60) minutes of "in-room monitoring" time was saved per FTE because now the patients arrived at 6:00 a.m. instead of 5:00 a.m. This also meant registration personnel started an hour later.

Once same-day patient readiness is completed, in order to achieve on time starts, inpatient readiness would need to be addressed. If only the same day patients were ready, the OR may not feel the entire impact if patients from the floor that were "not ready" were mixed throughout the schedule with patients who came "gift wrapped" from pre-testing.

Hospital X Pre-Op Lean Improvements

Once Pre-Testing and Pre-Op implemented the Lean initiatives, the "waste" was eliminated, clarity in "definition of patient readiness" was determined and standardized, and standard work was deployed. The next phase was to determine what it meant to be "ready for surgery" from the inpatient perspective. Several of the causes for delays to surgery on the inpatients included orders that were not completed when surgery called for the patient. The units were not always aware of when the patient was scheduled for surgery and there was no standard Pre-Op checklist. Some of the improvements made included creating standardized Pre-Op checklist for all surgery floor units, expectations related to "timing" on when to have the patient ready to go to surgery and a standardized distribution of the surgical schedule, including location and owner on the units, and streamlined handoff communication.

Adjustments in process resulted in "on-time first-case starts" improving from 50% to 78%. To get to 90%–100% required interaction and collaboration between surgeon desires and scheduling. The goal was to "clean our house" first, meaning the internal hospital processes, and then address the surgeon and anesthesia-related opportunities.

SECTION IV GROUP TECH MATRIX

The goal of the group tech matrix (Figure 11.20) is to identify at what capacity the ORs are being utilized. It requires continually collecting data, which includes volume data (number of cases) by service line, by month, and average case time in hours by service line, see Figure 11.21. The average case time should be represented by "patient in to next patient in" times (if possible). The capacity of an OR is dictated by how long the room is tied up or unavailable for use, with or without a patient. Obviously, the room is tied up during the surgery, but it is also unavailable during a room turnover, as a patient cannot be moved into the room until it has been mopped and cleaned. So, capacity includes turnover time, hence we use the metric "patient in to next patient in".

It was discussed earlier that there are bottlenecks in the Post-Op recovery units owing to inpatient beds not being available for patients to move into; so what is the root cause? The root cause is that we are not level loading our schedules. Why are we not level loading?

- We've always done it this way.
- Surgeons all want 7:30 a.m. case starts and we have to keep them happy.
- That's how our block time is set up.
- The data have not been analyzed to optimize flow; therefore, the impact is not understood.

So, what would level loading look like? The operating hours for a routine scheduled case in surgery is from 7:00 a.m. to 5:00 p.m. If peak patient demand is 60 patients per day and a 108 min LOS (patient in to patient in), how many rooms are required?

Available time = 600 min or 10 hrs/day

60 patients with LOS of 108 min which equals a total of 6,480 min.

6,480 ÷ 600 min (available time per day per room) = 10.8 surgery rooms needed (not taking into account flip rooms or any other issues such as equipment failures, etc.)

Once the global number of rooms has been established to truly level load and have impact downstream (unit), the number of surgical rooms needed should be calculated by service line, the next step is to understand the number and type (if specialized equipment or use) of surgery rooms and hours of operation by service line. In addition, demand by service line should be calculated by day of week (which will can drive block times or scheduling). Typical service lines include: cardiac, vascular, thoracic, cardiothoracic or cardiovascular and thoracic (CVT), orthopedics, neurosurgery, general surgery, gynecology, urology, plastics, podiatry, ENT, ophthalmology, etc. Once the data are obtained, the average case time by service line and trends can be calculated.

Figure 11.22 is an example of a group tech matrix, in which one can adjust the number of rooms and available times determine utilization scenarios.

MUH - DEPARTMENT OF SURGERY

Available Time Hours	141.5									Data Issues (Patient Out to Patient In) From File:		Patient in - Patient
		1st floor rooms	2nd floor rooms	# Rooms	Room Hours	Avg Hours / Room	Total Hours	Percent	wt avg rooms / day			Patient In to Patient
Available Time Per Room hours	12.4555	13		13	7:30a - 3P	7.5	97.5	69%	8.96	Xtra patient in room		Patient out to patie
Available Time Per Room min	747.331	9		9	3p - 7p	4	36	25%	2.29	schedule wrong		
Avg number of rooms scheduled (staffed)	11.3604	2		2	7p - 11p	4	8	6%	0.11	scheduled >55		
Working Days Per Month	21			20	Total Rooms		141.5	100%	11.36	Total Issues		
Capacity based on Rooms Scheduled (staffed)	61.9%			Capacity based on overall # rooms					35.18%			

Notes: ORMIS Download File:

1ST AND 2ND FLOOR

OR CASE SUMMARY - TOTAL HOURS PER CASE BY SERVICE LINE PER MONTH (Patient In to Patient In - Total Room Time)

Jul 2005 - Jun 2006

SERVICE	Oct-06	Nov-06	Dec-06	Jan-07	Feb-07	Mar-07	Apr-07	May-07	Jun-07	Jul-07	Aug-07	Sep-07	Totals	Average Hours per Month per Service Line	Std Dev	Daily Demand Hours Per Service Line	Avg hours / Case Patient In - Patient In	Avg Minutes Patient In - Patient In	No of Rooms per day Required based on time (avail time above)	No of Rooms per day Required based on time (9.5 hrs / day) Play with this column to figure out capacity by adjusting hours to get to total rooms	% of hours per case	Check Number (LOS /TT)
Anesthesia	1.53	2.12	0.42	0.72	0.00	0.38	0.42	2.02	0.00	0.45	1.60	1.27	11	0.9	0.8	0.04	0.52	31.2	0.02	0.005	0.05%	0.0035
Cardio-Thoracic	387.88	332.20	350.28	344.65	349.85	351.28	338.03	321.98	276.48	302.50	396.63	398.57	4150	345.9	36.6	16.47	3.23	194.1	1.32	1.734	20.41%	1.3223
ENT	64.53	106.07	99.38	102.97	102.38	82.80	76.35	119.15	130.23	73.22	101.12	128.90	1187	98.9	21.3	4.71	2.15	129.0	0.38	0.496	5.84%	0.3782
General Surgery	483.80	494.37	372.13	461.30	476.07	464.45	500.60	491.20	420.55	460.73	486.95	431.32	5543	461.9	37.4	22.00	2.07	123.9	1.77	2.316	27.26%	1.7661
Urology	99.75	62.05	90.52	73.23	111.67	93.95	84.62	88.5*	86.05	86.13	88.43	58.75	1024	85.3	14.8	4.06	1.61	96.7	0.33	0.428	5.03%	0.3262
Gynecology	60.62	48.35	39.47	57.95	39.73	64.53	51.60	43.2*	54.12	75.27	60.77	20.18	616	51.3	14.4	2.44	1.74	104.4	0.20	0.257	3.03%	0.1962
Neurosurgery	431.98	395.15	405.92	388.68	396.93	493.58	443.10	456.02	456.02	535.63	467.67	355.70	5236	436.3	50.8	20.78	3.39	203.3	1.67	2.187	25.74%	1.6681
Orthopedics	99.95	65.78	55.80	84.70	70.38	100.92	71.35	80.17	73.12	97.20	101.93	87.90	992	82.7	15.0	3.94	1.10	66.0	0.32	0.414	4.88%	0.3161
Ophthalmology	0.00	25.48	38.60	16.88	0.00	12.70	0.00	14.87	3.70	0.00	3.73	0.00	118	9.9	12.3	0.47	5.38	323.1	0.04	0.049	0.58%	0.0377
Oral Surgery	181.47	116.20	112.93	111.08	130.78	131.82	122.90	141.53	165.73	119.63	222.32	151.85	1707	142.3	33.4	6.78	2.56	153.4	0.54	0.713	8.40%	0.5440
Plastic Surgery	17.72	11.63	6.18	17.03	39.52	60.68	8.57	36.22	16.10	29.78	40.48	48.88	333	27.7	17.5	1.32	2.50	150.1	0.11	0.139	1.64%	0.1060
Transplant	97.37	86.73	100.68	94.62	76.43	114.68	110.65	83.00	104.22	124.15	95.37	79.03	1167	97.2	14.6	4.63	4.84	290.5	0.37	0.487	5.74%	0.3718
GRAND TOTALS	1927	1746	1675	1754	1794	1972	1808	1878	1795	1908	2067	1762	22085	1840.4	111.7	87.64	2.44	146.6	7.04	9.2	257	7.0362

Notes: ORMIS Download (File Alldataver(2) - count of cases per month by specialty - not filtered and does not include outpatient surgery center

OR CASE VOLUME SUMMARY- CASES BY SERVICE

Jul 2005 - Jun 2006

SERVICE	Jul-05	Aug-05	Sep-05	Oct-05	Nov-05	Dec-05	Jan-06	Feb-06	Mar-06	Apr-06	May-06	Jun-06	Totals	Average Cases Per Month	Std Dev	Weekday Demand (24 working days)	Takt Time Min	Takt Time Based on 26 Ors (min)	Takt Time Based on 13.5 Ors (min)	Takt Time Based on 13.5 Ors (min)	Takt Time Based on 13.5 Ors (min)
Anesthesia	3	5	0	5	0	0	1	2	0	0	3	1	1.8	1.5	0.08	8968.0	121,247	233,167.4		
Cardio-Thoracic	115	104	107	101	96	117	103	103	92	93	122	120	106.9	10.4	5.09	146.8	1,985	3,816.5		
ENT	37	47	43	45	48	38	36	54	58	37	51	58	46.0	8.1	2.19	341.2	4,613	8,870.5		
General Surgery	238	245	208	219	227	230	204	245	198	224	202	223.7	15.3	10.65	70.2	949	1,824.3		
Urology	58	45	55	48	54	51	64	52	50	42	52.9	6.3	2.52	296.6	4,010	7,711.0		
Gynecology	28	30	26	34	23	33	35	27	30	41	14	29.5	6.8	1.40	532.0	7,193	13,832.0		
Neurosurgery	126	117	109	124	114	151	123	145	151	146	131	108	128.8	15.9	6.13	121.9	1,648	3,169.3		
Orthopedics	97	64	61	81	69	88	88	81	64	81	80	67	75.2	11.1	3.58	208.8	2,823	5,428.5		
Ophthalmology	0	4	6	3	0	2	0	4	1	0	1.8	1.3	0.09	8560.3	115,736	222,568.8		
Oral Surgery	73	46	42	52	49	49	19	58	60	46	88	56	55.1	13.1	2.65	281.9	3,812	7,330.1		
Plastic Surgery	9	5	9	8	14	27	4	15	10	16	16	11.1	6.9	0.53	1416.0	19,144	36,815.9		
Transplant	22	17	17	19	18	28	21	18	22	24	15	20.1	3.6	0.96	781.4	10,565	20,317.5		
GRAND TOTALS	806	729	681	735	719	818	728	817	733	754	821	699	9,040	753.3	49.5	35.873	20.8	282	541.6		

FIGURE 11.20 OR Group Tech Matrix Example. Source: BIG Files.

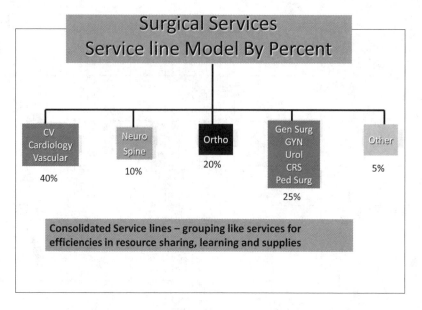

FIGURE 11.21   OR service line model. Source: BIG Files.

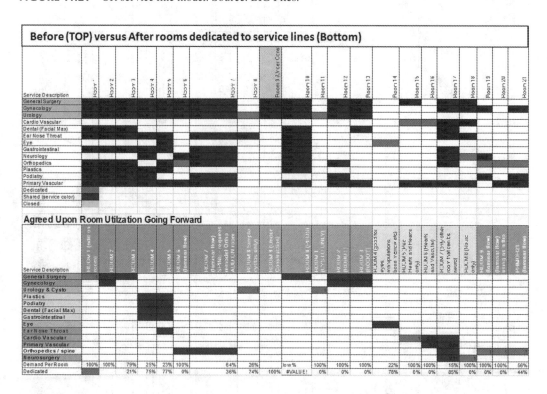

FIGURE 11.22   OR room allocation model.

GROUP MATRIX BENEFITS

- Provides insight to case length by category
- Number of rooms needed by service line
- Utilization of ORs overall and by service line

- Assists in determining appropriate OR layout
- Materials strategy related to rooms, i.e., where to locate shared equipment

Once we determine the number of surgeries per service line/per room/per day, we create a spreadsheet template comparing how the rooms are currently utilized vs. dedicating certain rooms to certain surgeries based on geographic location (Figure 11.22).

For instance, if we know we use 3 rooms every day for heart cases, then we would pick 3 adjacent rooms and relocate our supplies and equipment for the heart cases in or near those rooms. Some hospitals do this already by "feel" or intuition, but we find in most cases, there is a still a lot of opportunity to further dedicate and standardize rooms and then develop materials and equipment strategies to support the rooms. The big objection we hear is "what if we need that room for another case?" In the event you have to use the room for a different type of surgery, it is no problem. It just means the supplies and equipment for that surgery may be located in a different area.

Once the group tech matrix is created, it is critical to have someone maintain it, as the surgery mix and, therefore, dedicated rooms will change over time.

Section V OR Layout/Capacity

How do we determine the capacity and what the new layout should look like? In most hospitals, there are limited data and, in many cases, the data are not accurate. In addition, experience has shown that accuracy and reliability of data, especially turnover time, is questionable, and assumptions may have to be made that may impact the final outcome. Generally, historical data are available to evaluate demand, but they are not always accurate. In many cases, future demand is only an estimate based on current demand, and sometimes we find marketing growth projections and planned business development initiatives are available. We also have to consider surgical case times and turnover times to determine if potential increases are needed in capacity (Table 11.10).

Other challenges lay in the unknown of what new technological advances will take place as surgery moves from open to minimally invasive or less invasive procedures migrating out of OR suites. When determining capacity:

- Does one count on an improvement or reduction in cycle time to calculate turnover time in the future?

TABLE 11.10
OR Group Tech Capacity Analysis

Available Time Hours	141.5	1st floor Rooms	2nd floor Rooms	# Rooms	Room Hours	Avg Hours/Room	Total Hours	Percent	wt avg Rooms/day
Available Time Per Room hours	12.4555	13		13	7:30a - 3P	7.5	97.5	69%	8.96
Available Time Per Room min	747.331	9		9	3p - 7p	4	36	25%	2.29
Avg number of rooms scheduled (staffed)	11.3604	2		2	7p - 11p	4	8	6%	0.11
Working Days Per Month	21			19	Total Rooms		141.5	100%	11.36
Capacity based on Rooms Scheduled (staffed)		**61.9%**			Capacity based on overall # rooms				**29.8%**

- What is the percentage of time flip rooms will be utilized?
- When building for the future, will the case lengths remain the same, get longer or shorter?

These are all inherent challenges when determining capacity and layouts.

Just because we are faced with these challenges does not mean that we should not try to make the best possible estimate of the rooms needed based on the information at hand, even if it is not complete. The goal would be to try to provide a sound analysis that provides a buffer for the best possible plan. In addition, Lean tools, such as process flow, point-to-point diagrams, and spaghetti diagramming, should be used to determine flow.

Lean Solution

Leveraging PFAs, WFAs, Takt time, customer demand and the group tech matrix will assist in providing the future capacity and new layout details. Remember that the decisions made today will impact the organization from a cost perspective and the lives of staff operationally in the future.

OPERATING ROOM CALCULATIONS

When analyzing the utilization of data, one should look at types of surgeries done by day of week and opportunities to level load cases throughout the week. For example, if 20 orthopedic cases (each lasting 170 min, patient in to patient out) were performed on the same 2 days of the week, the average number of orthopedic cases per day is 10, total operating minutes per day

$$170 \text{ min/case} = X \text{ 10 cases} = 1700 \text{ min or 28.3 hrs.}$$

If the operational hours of the OR were 7:30 a.m. to 3:30 p.m. = 8 hrs or 480 min of available time per room. The total rooms needed are $1700 \div 480$ min = 3.5 rooms per day.

This would mean that the OR would have to supply four orthopedic surgical teams in order to meet the demand for the two operating days. What happens to the staff the remaining 3 days? How many extra pieces of equipment would be needed to run 4 rooms simultaneously? What is the impact to the Post-Op recovery unit, intensive care units, and surgical floors, as all the patients demand the same level of service on the same days? What if we level loaded the 20 orthopedic cases over 4 days?

$$20 \text{ cases} \div 4 \text{ days} = 5 \text{ cases per day}$$

$$170 \text{ min/case} \times 5 \text{ cases} = 850 \text{ min or 14.2 hrs.}$$

The available time for each room is 480 min; therefore, the total rooms needed each day are $850 \div 480$ min = 1.8 rooms. Less equipment sets would be needed as only 2 rooms would be operating and "pulling" on equipment, two surgical teams would be needed and the likelihood that the surgeons could work with the same teams would increase. This would result in downstream leveling of demand in the Post-Op units and on the floors.

Although a group tech matrix can assist in determining the number of rooms, helping to level load cases in the ORs and assessing utilization, administration and area management must take into account customer preference and the use of flip rooms under certain conditions, which may reduce surgeon idle time between cases. This will be discussed in further detail in section VI. Remember, the primary customers of surgery (after patients) are surgeons and, as we often hear, "surgeons don't want more block time; they want more cases per day."

Lesson Learned

Be careful with averages when using the group tech matrix. Until schedules can be level loaded, one must look at peak times by service line when apportioning rooms to service lines as well as future forecasted demand. In addition, someone must own and now maintain this matrix as hospitals live in a dynamic environment where technology and surgeon changes can greatly impact existing demand and room allocation. Recognize that changes in case mix and new technologies can provide challenges when predicting OR demand.

SECTION VI OR ROOM TURNOVER

Traditional OR turnovers start when the patient leaves the room, i.e., "patient out or wheels out." It may be initiated by a staff member notifying a charge nurse station who communicates that the patient has exited the room and the room needs to be "turned over." This means that the room must be cleaned and prepared for the next patient.

All hospitals tend to vary as to what occurs at this point. The scrub nurse may start or have already started tearing down the case, as the patient is exiting the room accompanied by the circulating nurse and anesthesia doctor. Housekeeping or the OR technical staff may be paged; whether it is centralized or decentralized determines when they show up to assist.

Once the case is "broken down," the "dirty" items are taken to the "dirty" area where they are cleaned and then "flash" sterilized. If taken to the dirty elevator, they proceed to the sterile processing department where the instruments are cleaned and sterilized. The room is mopped or vacuumed and sanitized and a new "case cart" containing the surgical instrumentation and supplies for the next case is rolled into the room. The ideal scenario would be that all the items (supplies and instrumentation) on the surgeon's preference list (which lists all supplies and special instruments by case type) are "pulled" accurately, and the right instruments and supplies are at the right room, at the right time for the next case. In the event something is missing, the nurse or other staff member has to search and travel to get the needed supplies, either in the "core," hallway, or down in central supply. If the surgeon and team members are lucky, this is identified as the case is being set up. Yet, we have followed nurses searching for certain pieces of equipment and supplies for 20 min or more, delaying the start of the case. During this time, the anesthesiologists and the surgeon and, more importantly, the patient are left waiting! This waste all costs money in time (labor time of staff), excess anesthesia charges for the patient, potential delays to the next case, and physician dissatisfaction.

Yet most of this cost is hidden, as these costs are not tracked. Cases are delayed, cancelled, or rescheduled, and room utilization is not optimized.

Turnover is "midstream" in the surgical process; if one's goal is to improve turnover which is a big "Y" in Six Sigma terms for most OR metrics, then all the "x's" or causes that impact a successful turnover must be understood in order to achieve the desired turnover time.

Room turnovers do not occur in silos; thus many upstream processes, defects, and delays will impact one's goal. Reducing turnover times is important as they directly impact one of the internal/external customers in the surgical services area, the surgeon. For example, one can streamline the turnover, but if the patient is not ready at the time the case is scheduled and/or the anesthesiologist and surgeon hold up the patient to do necessary tasks such as have the consent signed or have the H&P ready, then the turnover time will still not decrease.

Figure 11.23 outlines "x's" or variables that impact turnover, which would be times collected for patient in to patient in.

- Inaccurate or missing supplies and equipment ready to set the case up (case picking or equipment availability—materials flow)
- Anesthesiology availability
- Support staff availability (transportation or anesthesia technicians)
- "Patient readiness" or medical clearance for surgical procedures
- Nurse/surgical technician team availability
- Level loading

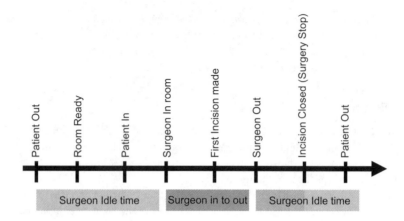

FIGURE 11.23   Surgeon Idle Time Analysis. Source: BIG Files.

Extended turnovers affect surgeon idle time and frustration. Surgeons provide services that are time dependent, thus creating revenue for both the hospital and themselves based on the time they can work, which is limited to the minutes and hours in a day (Table 11.11). If the surgeon's time is idle, then generally they are wasting money, as the only way surgery generates revenue is if the patients are in the ORs. This holds true for both surgeon and anesthesiologists. This is how the surgeons perceive turnover: Surgeons are only concerned with 'surgeon out to surgeon in,' which comprises their idle time.

How Do We Improve Turnover?

Our goal, like in manufacturing, is to obtain "single minute" turnovers. This means 9 min 59 sec or less for internal time (the time the room is down or does not have a patient utilizing it). At first glance, one may think this is impossible. Outpatient surgery centers can routinely hit these times, but it is much tougher in a hospital setting, although it has been achieved. This is accomplished by putting together a multiple disciplinary team to analyze the tasks that are required to "turn a room over." Each individual involved in the turnover is videoed at the same time. The videos are reviewed with each person present and opportunities for improvement are identified.

We categorize time into two components; internal and external time. In car racing, internal times are things that can only be done when the car is in the pitstop, and external times are things that can be done in the pit while the car is going around the track.

Like car racing, the goal in healthcare is to improve the process using a "pit crew" approach. Each step is broken down into its components and determined whether the step is internal or external. In this case, internal work is work that can only be done when the OR is down, or being changed over. External work can be done while the patient is in the room (and parallel to other processes that may be occurring). The goal is to convert as much internal work to external work as possible. Internal work vs. external work can't be defined until you define the input and output boundaries of the setup.

It is not unusual to think that all work can't start until the patient leaves the room or after the patient enters the room, but this is not the case. Shingo's setup reduction process was called SMED (single minute exchange of dies) (Table 11.12). In hospitals, we call it SMER (single minute exchange of rooms) or SMEP (single minute exchange of patients). Prior to the start of the turnover, the pit crew (turnover dedicated staff) reviews the schedule to plan their attack. The charge nurse gives them 15 to 30 min advanced notice. Everyone from nurses to doctors chip in to get the room turned over. A team was put together made up of a Lean specialist, surgical technician, circulating nurse, surgical assistant (role is to transport patients to, within, and from surgery, and room cleaning) and service line coordinator. Understanding that different service lines have varying

TABLE 11.11

Surgeon Efficiency Model

Comparison of Surgeon Times

Year	(All)
WeekType	Weekday
Valid Close-Cut	(All)
Valid Out-In	(All)
Surgeon	(All)
Procedure	(All)
Data	

Service Description	Sum of Surgery Close-Cut (Minutes)	Sum of Patient Out-In (Minutes)	Notice difference between patient vs. surgeon perspective % of patient	Sum of CT1 (Patient In-Out) Minutes	Sum of CT3 (Procedure Start-Stop) Minutes	Sum of Count (# cases)	Total Patient in to out + patient out to in	Efficiency close to cut/Total
Cardio Vascular	30,506	14,005	46%	164,579	115,628	680	178,584	82.9%
Dental (Facial Max)	4,413	2,803	64%	12,498	9,992	115	15,301	71.2%
Ear Nose Throat	26,571	14,763	56%	52,858	33,894	587	67,621	60.7%
Eye	11,114	8,077	73%	24,642	16,927	295	32,719	66.0%
Gastrointestinal	4,842	3,587	74%	4,713	3,533	162	8,300	41.7%
General Surgery	179,968	116,330	65%	319,067	212,731	3,340	435,397	58.7%
Gynecology	81,186	54,867	68%	202,875	148,948	1,752	257,742	68.5%
Neurology	55,892	32,238	58%	139,109	96,651	924	171,347	67.4%
Orthopedics	180,816	120,379	67%	360,723	247,491	3,193	481,102	62.4%
Plastics	8,683	6,022	69%	28,303	20,581	179	34,325	74.7%
Podiatry	3,367	2,585	77%	10,130	7,094	120	12,715	73.5%
Primary Vascular	23,610	12,944	55%	54,972	36,297	458	67,916	65.2%
Urology	86,776	64,523	74%	133,729	95,596	1,685	198,252	56.2%
#N/A	84	53	63%	209	52	4	262	67.9%
Grand Total	697,828	453,176	65%	1,508,407	1,045,415	13,494	1,961,583	64.4%

TABLE 11.12
Die Explanation

A die in manufacturing is a tool that is changed over on a press. An analogy would be to think
 of play dough when you were a kid. You squeezed the play dough through a square form
 (die) and then changed the die over to a circle (die) and the squeezed it through the circle.

setups, this organization opted to address turnover one service line at a time. The team started
with general surgery.

Step 1: Videoing each staff member as they performed the turnover at the same time. Findings were:

- No standard work.
- No specific standard work to tear down cases while the patient is still in the room.
- No role clarity (who is responsible for which task); some were not done and other tasks
  were duplicated.
- Surgeons were as much as 30 min late to surgery.
- Larger patients were hard to transfer and took longer.
- Some patients took longer to intubate than others or had difficult line placement.
- Cases not picked correctly (inaccurate or missing supplies and equipment).
- Not a lot of parallel setup processing to patient entering room.
- Communication issues related to surgical assistance.
- Surgical assistants did not show up timely, when needed.
- Necessary room related equipment was missing from the room.
- Pre-Op delays related to patient communication.
- No clear definition of "room ready" and when to call for patient and variability of break-
  down a case post procedure.

Step 2: Operator analysis of each member was performed to determine the value-added vs. non-
value-added activities, the skill required to do each task, and what extended the turnover. In addition the rate limiting sequential step or tasks should be identified. These sequential tasks will drive
the minimum turnover time. What was identified was that the circulating nurse was the rate limiting
step he/she was responsible for

- Documenting the case
- Accompanying the patient to the Post-Op recovery unit
- Going to the Pre-Op unit to obtain information on the next patient scheduled
- Accompanying the patient to the room
- Assisting in counting the instrumentation

Lesson Learned

*Identify the critical tasks that need to be performed and who should perform them, and when they
should be performed in a prioritized order to minimize "internal time."*

The circulator was performing most of the tasks sequentially during the turnover while no patient
was in the room. The circulator nurse's assigned tasks were in the critical path of reducing room
turnover. Each task that was critical was identified. Each task was analyzed to determine if it had to
be internal or external, and who should do each task, and was there a need for them to be sequential.
For instance, the surgical assistants spent time searching for a stretcher or bed, leaving everyone in
the room waiting (including the patient).

Step 3: A surgical assistant checklist was created defining external work to be performed (while the case was still going on). It listed what needed to be ready outside each room, such as a bed with IV pole and cleaning cart. Since this happened when the team was in the room, there was no waiting for beds or IV poles, etc. All tasks were realigned across the team members.

Step 4: Standard work was created for each staff member so there was role clarity and responsibility for tasks. This alleviated tasks not getting performed or duplicated by the staff. In addition, since there was heavy circulating nurse activities required, the service line coordinator was assigned the responsibility to step in during critical components as fractional labor to aid as a "facilitating nurse in the turnover" to complete steps in parallel while the circulator was going to PACU and Pre-Op. The facilitator took on some of the sequential tasks that the circulator was doing, converting them to parallel tasks.

Example

As the circulator was accompanying the patient to the PACU, the facilitator could help unpack the next case with the surgical technician (which previously would have been the responsibility of the circulating nurse); this task could not be converted to external work (as one cannot unpack or setup the next case while the patient is still in the room). In some cases, anesthesiologists take the patient to PACU and also have the anesthesiologist and surgeon bring the patient from Pre-Op. This frees up the circulator for the room changeover. The anesthesiologist then gives a report to the PACU nurse.

Below is a sample of key process steps that occur in room turnover (these steps do not need to be in sequential order and many can and should be performed in parallel):

- Patient dressing on
- OR table breakdown
- Patient out of room
- Room cleaning and mopping
- Linen and trash removal
- Next case cart (supplies and equipment) in OR
- Linen on bed
- Next patient interview occurs
- Case documentation complete
- Patient called for—room is "ready for patient"
- Patient in room
- Patient on OR table
- Case supplies begin to be opened
- Case supplies complete
- Counting complete
- Patient induced
- Patient draped
- Pause for cause
- Incision made surgery start
- Having clean supplies and bed, IV poles, etc., ready

Step 5 Creating Standard Definitions, Expectations, and Role Clarity:

One key finding was that there was no standard across the OR of "what constituted room ready" or the standard agreed-on time to bring the next patient in to the OR. There was great variability from circulating nurse to circulating nurse on timing and expectation of what needed to be accomplished prior to bringing the next patient into the room. This contributed to wide variability in turnover times.

This hospital determined that, owing to the culture within the OR and where they were on the Lean journey, it was best to work on activities that the hospital could control first, such as critical tasks, timing of tasks internal vs. external, standard work for staff, availability of supplies, and accuracy of case picking, thereby making improvements that impacted primarily patient out to patient in. They determined that they would address issues that related to physicians and anesthesia in subsequent initiatives.

LEAN RESULTS IMPACT OF TURNOVER PROJECTS

Our goal and typical result is to maximize the number of cases the surgeon can perform within the same amount of time. We find through turnover time reduction that we can normally get each surgeon 1 or 2 more cases per day; however, turnover time is impacted by many other hospital processes, i.e., SPD, case picking, materials, suppliers, transport, housekeeping, etc. It is important to decentralize transport, registration, and housekeeping and have the staff report both to surgery operationally and, in the case of registration, have them matrix to the head of registration or billing.

TURNOVER EXAMPLE

If the current average turnover time is 50 min and our average surgery time is 120 min (this assumes the turnover and surgery times are tracked; the average surgery time should be surgery start to surgery stop), turnover time can be expressed as patient out to patient in or can also be defined as surgery close to surgery cut. The latter definition will force more steps to come under scrutiny for improvement related to surgeon and team activities. If we can save 40 min of turnover time (patient out to patient in), then for every three surgeries, we pick up approximately one extra surgery case in capacity:

If we do 60 surgeries per day and have additional demand then this would translate into 18.5 extra cases per day in the same amount of time. This translates into millions of dollars of potential revenue and extremely happy surgeons. Most surgeons want to be able to do more cases per day in the same amount of time and eliminate all the waiting around.

Before implementing turnover improvements, one needs to make sure that Pre-Op can continue to supply patients at the new rate and that the Post-Op recovery unit can recover more patients with the number of beds they have, otherwise the turnover effort will fail.

Lesson Learned

If we can introduce significantly more revenue per day, wouldn't this pay for additional people to support the dedicated turnover teams? The answer is an unequivocal "yes," but we have to get over the issue of finance wanting to cut our indirect FTEs and the issue of centralized transport, etc. We need to staff for growth and treat surgery as a profit center, not a cost center.

Our experience is that surgeons have a built-in expectation of 30 min or less for turnaround time for medium to large cases and less than 15 min for short cases. But to a surgeon, this definition is based on their time, which is 'surgeon out to surgeon in'. This is drastically different from patient out to patient in.

As one analyzes turnover data, we have found that the data are inconsistent, organizations tend to categorize turnovers either globally such as 30 min for large cases and 10 min for small cases, or by service line grouping. The challenge is that there is wide variability in the tasks performed when viewing data globally as setup of equipment and amount of supplies can vary. Like cases don't necessarily follow one another. One surgeon may leave a room and he or she may have completed a large case (with significant cleanup); the following case may be with a different surgeon with a simple case, requiring fewer set-ups. This creates challenges in expectations of surgeons and scheduling times for cases following one another.

OTHER TURNOVER/SETUP STRATEGIES

INDUCTION ROOMS

We first encountered induction rooms in the HBR video series Competing Against Time* with Tom Hout and George Stalk as they profiled Karolinska Hospital in Sweden. Karolinska utilizes induction rooms with added anesthesiologists in order to decrease turnover times. The patient was induced and in some cases positioned prior to surgery and rolled in when the OR was cleaned and set up. In many older hospitals, you will find induction rooms that are no longer utilized. After an Internet search, it was found that this is very common in European hospitals but not in the United States. It does seem to be used in some U.S. pediatric hospitals.

PROS FOR INDUCTION ROOM

The induction room addresses the internal time utilized by anesthesia that cannot be compensated by nursing, housekeeping, etc. We can decrease turnover time significantly to the point where the anesthesiologist puts the patient under and the patient is prepped. This is especially true for heart cases and orthopedic cases where there can be up to 45 min turnovers while the patient is being prepped. Meanwhile, the surgeon is waiting (idle). Our experience is that 40%–60% or more surgeons spend their time waiting. We can't increase surgeries without increasing surgeon efficiency.

CONS FOR INDUCTION ROOMS

In order to support induction rooms, layouts may have to be changed and additional anesthesiologists, who may or may not be available, may be required. So the change can involve construction costs and anesthesiologists' costs. A cost benefit analysis has to be performed to see if it makes sense. One has to determine how many extra cases a day would offset the cost to hire an additional anesthesiologist. One should also consider what this would do for surgeon morale and the opportunity to grow the business with no need for expensive construction of additional ORs.

FLIP ROOMS

A flip room is providing 2 rooms for a surgeon who has cases that follow one after another with 2 staffs and 2 anesthesiologists. One would have a delayed start, ready and waiting so that the surgeon can literally go from the end of one case (while the resident, fellow, or PA finishes the first case) to begin on the next or to follow the case where a second team composed of another anesthesiologist and a second surgical team (which might again include resident, fellow, or PA) has the patient prepped and ready to go. This is desired by many surgeons because their idle time is essentially eliminated. This makes sense in cases where the surgeon has a full team that surrounds him/her that can complete one case and start another. From the hospital perspective, this can reduce the time a room remains unused. If flip rooms were provided for every surgeon, it would be very costly for an organization, as the number of rooms, anesthesiologists, and staff resources would increase.

PROS FOR FLIP ROOMS

- Reduced surgeon turnover time to essentially zero.
- Increased surgeon satisfaction.
- Surgeons can do more cases in 1 day or end their day early as their day is compressed.
- Reduced overtime for staff
- Reduction in extended days (if rooms available/capacity)

CONS FOR FLIP ROOMS

- Staff can be idle if the first case has a delay or complication.
- Anesthesiologist idle time (costly or requires robust anesthesiology scheduling practice).
- Could cause the organization to need additional space and rooms.
- Potential for additional teams

NEW ROOM FOR A "TO FOLLOW" CASE REFERRED TO AS "MOVE"

This approach includes staggering rooms and schedule times. When a surgeon has a "to follow case" (sequential cases) and completes the first case, a 'move' would be having the next case set up and ready to go in a new room. The anesthesiologist, surgeon, and staff would all move to the new room. The perception from the surgeon's view is a decrease in turnover time.

PROS FOR MOVE ROOMS

- Move rooms minimize turnover time; however, in our experience this is sometimes only perceived, depending on the location of the available room and the availability of the anesthesiologist and staff.
- The same staff may still have to set up the new room, get the patient, etc., which can be done in less than 10 min.
- The old room can be changed over on "external time" and be ready for the next case. It is good for two or more "to follow" cases.

CONS FOR MOVE ROOMS

- Ties up an extra OR (which is only bad if there is no demand for them).
- OR/cases can change rooms, which then impacts the case cart, supplies, etc. (and supplies may not always end up at the right place and at the right time, eliminating any time savings).
- Cases can be cancelled, resulting in cost of opened items or re-sterilizing instruments, when communication fails.

Lessons Learned:
- *Room turnover improvements don't sustain unless driven by senior management.*
- *Much of room setup can occur while the patient is in the room.*
- *If we can get a changeover down to less than 10 min, do we still need flip rooms or move rooms?*

Family Waiting

Traditionally, surgeons have to walk to the surgery waiting area to consult with patients' family members. We can't tell you how many times we see surgeons hunting or searching for family members after long walks (sometimes upstairs and down) to the waiting room; families may not be aware that the surgery is near completion, and that they should be in the waiting room. More often than not, it is the one time they left the room, Murphy's Law. How might we improve this? Some organizations are creating an area near the OR where the surgeon can meet with family members, separate from the waiting room, similar to a "consult room." The room staff communicates with the waiting area to bring the family member to the surgeon in the "consult room." We have never found this to be a dissatisfier for patient families (i.e., having to walk to the consult room). This approach makes surgeons happy and saves them time and frustration.

SECTION VII SURGICAL SERVICES MATERIALS READINESS

Preference Cards

Preference cards or lists are a documented accounting, generally by a surgeon, by case type of the instruments and supplies required to perform a case (Figure 11.24). This helps to ensure that the right instruments and supplies are gathered for a surgeon ("his or her preference") for a scheduled procedure.

This has been a challenge for most organizations, as preference cards end up being a Lean project at every hospital. They can reach 10,000–20,000 or more, as they are made for each surgeon for each case performed. In many cases, the preference cards are the foundation for billing supplies used in the OR for each surgical procedure.

They are difficult to keep updated or complete (unless a surgeon assigns one of his/her staff to be responsible). The root causes of inaccuracies normally center on the lack of ownership and accountability for the updating process. This can cause major opportunity costs in terms of billing costs, if there is not a good accounting of what has been "pulled" to setup the case.

The sheer number of preference cards and the difficulty in updating them emphasizes the problems most ORs face related to the lack of standardization by surgeons for supplies and instruments. We have found the most efficient surgeons standardize on materials and supplies. Historically, most healthcare organizations have had difficulty trying to get surgeons to standardize on supplies and equipment. Having non-standard supplies is costly as it creates increased inventory to order, track, and monitor, but does not enable the hospital to obtain volume discounts. More importantly, depending on the equipment, there may be safety issues surrounding the staff needed to keep up proficiencies on multiple types of equipment.

Standardization in the OR is a challenge for organizations as surgeons who come from different training institutions have established comfort with particular types of instruments, and they do not want to be forced to conform to other less familiar instruments. In addition, they may have alliances with companies for example relationships that provide incentives that are may influence their choice in product selection i.e., training or consulting, perform research or have collaborative development arrangements etc. What if we could reduce preference cards to only "A" or high inventory or high dollar items? This would mean:

- Expensing "B" and "C" items (low dollar items) and incorporating them into the overhead cost per case.

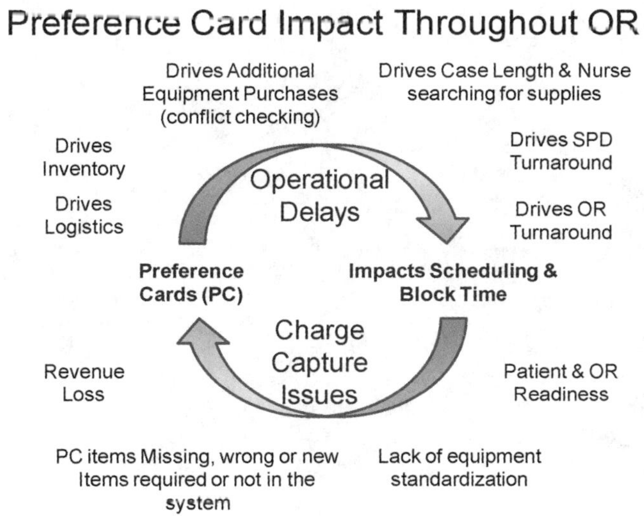

Preference Card Impact Throughout OR

FIGURE 11.24   Surgery preference card analysis. Source: BIG Files.

- This would decrease the number of picked items, assuming the B and C items were located in or adjacent to the ORs.
- This would alleviate defects or inaccuracies in the "picking process."

What if we could standardize and create more custom packs? While custom packs are kits (preassembled groups of supplies) and not truly Lean, it is difficult in many OR cores and halls to have enough room to pick cases with the number of supplies that are required for the different case types and variety in surgeon preferences. The cons of custom packs are how to treat items not used and how to handle ongoing maintenance of the packs. They also tend to be more costly than stocking materials separately. The pros are that they are easy to unpack and eliminate searching when setting up the sterile field. They also eliminate waste in the current "green" environment.

CASE PICKING

Case picking is the process of gathering supplies, instruments, and specialized equipment so that it is ready for the "surgical team" to setup for the case, by what is documented on the preference cards (Figure 11.25). Traditional case picking involves knowledgeable workers who know where everything is located. When they pick a case, they place their cart in a centralized area and then make trips like "Supermarket Sweeps" back and forth, carrying as much as they can (Figure 11.26).

At Hospital X, we created a new process working with one of the case pickers. She liked the new process that was more than 50% faster and better. Yet, we could not get anyone else to follow the new process, and our operator was chastised by her co-workers. To facilitate adoption and resistance to change, we opted to make the charge nurse responsible for the new picking process and re-laying out of the supply core area, ignoring the conventional wisdom in which we would have changed it all over a weekend.

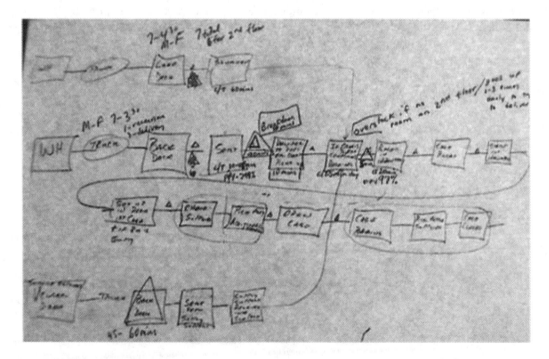

FIGURE 11.25 Case picking materials value stream map from receiving dock to OR including returns after initial walkthrough. Source: BIG Files.

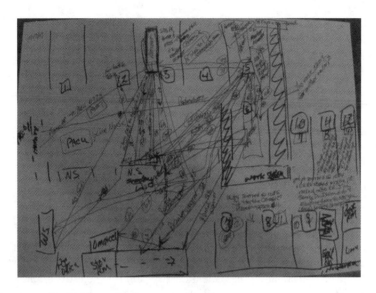

FIGURE 11.26   Case Picking Spaghetti Map. Source: BIG Files.

Note - It did not matter to us how the area was laid out since we could set up the preference cards to "pick by location."

The charge nurse was instructed to have a staff meeting to determine their optimal layout. After a couple of very heated arguments, the staff reached a consensus. The entire materials core was moved around during the next week throughout the day and night shifts. While there was some chaos and confusion, the new configuration was set up bin by bin with the nurses (constantly rotating) by our sides guiding the order and location of supplies and assisting in the implementation. Everyone participated in the change (see Figure 11.27).

Once this was complete, the charge nurse insisted that the new case-picking process be utilized. The original team member now became the training coach for the others and was no longer chastised but respected for her participation.

Note - In many cases when re-organizing the supplies within the surgical cores, one will realize savings in inventory as supplies that historically might have been located throughout the OR will

FIGURE 11.27   New Configuration of surgical material bins.

be consolidated, saving on redundant inventory; however, we have seen significant soft benefits in staff satisfaction as they are empowered to make changes that ultimately improve accessibility of supplies and in their environment, which make their daily life easier.

Lean Results
Case Picking

- 44% reduction in case picking time (32 min to 18 min) and 65% total walking distance reduction (928 ft. to 323 ft.)

Section VIII Post-Anesthesia Care Unit (PACU)

When we did the VSM, we discovered that the Post-Op recovery unit process cycle time is driven by the recovery time of the patient, which is directly influenced by the anesthesiologist caring for the patient (Figure 11.28). It was discovered through video analysis that the nurse's job was broken into pieces, including steps to be performed when the patient arrived and steps performed in what we termed "cycling" or re-evaluating the patient every 15 min, which was required at a minimum by the Association of Perioperative Registered Nurses (AORN)[3] standard and stipulates the nurse-to-patient ratio based on patient recovery criteria outlined in the AORN guidelines.

What We Find

The first hour in PACU is the most critical and can require 1:1 nursing. In this case, the nurse is tied to the patient (Table 11.13). Some patients are more critical than others, yet we apply 1:1 or 2:1 standard to all patients, just in case. If we had better monitoring technology, maybe nurses would be able to watch more patients safely. When reviewing the WFA of the operator, we found the following problems:

- A lot of reaching for supplies.
- A lot of walking around beds.
- Computers take up too much space.
- Duplication of documentation.
- Too many pages for documentation.
- Trash can and linen containers are not readily accessible.
- Walking to the front desk to get the patient's printouts.
- Need hand washing between patients.
- Warm blankets were put on twice.
- It took 17 min after giving report to the floor nurse and yet no transporters responded to the PACU transport request, and the PACU technician had to take the patient to the floor.
- The layout is poor. The nurse station is in the south end of the area so the charge nurse cannot see all the patients. The area is not user-friendly or ergonomically correct. The head wall is set back due to the counter. You can't completely hook up a patient without walking from side to side.
- Can't get to the cabinet storage when there is a patient in the bay, and we don't need most of what is in storage.
- Nursing carts aren't standardized. Each nurse has their own cart.
- Nurses are doing work technicians could do (because they are transporting).
- When transport does not show up on time, patients may have to be given more pain medication. This can change their status from being ready to discharge from PACU to additional

---

[3] http://www.aorn.org/PracticeResources/AORNStandardsAnd RecommendedPractices/

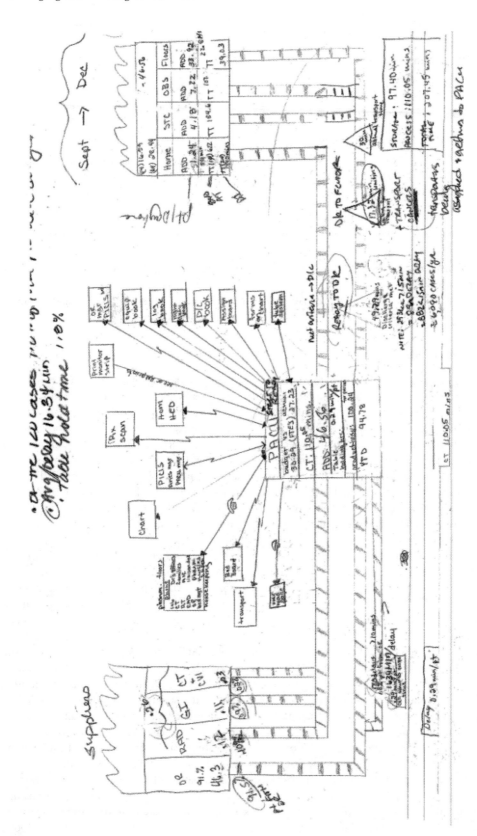

FIGURE 11.28 VSM (value stream map) hand-drawn PACU- copy.

TABLE 11.13
PACU Nurse Job Breakdown

Criteria Scale

0 to 7	Patient Arrival Tasks 15–20 min
	Take Report, Hook up monitors and IV's Check dressings, SCD's, assess patient, review history, document, blankets etc.
	Patient Monitoring Tasks
4–7	Cycle every 15 min of which 3 to 5 min is checking vitals and charting, call liaison
	Other tasks – meds, ice chips, Check Bed status etc.
	Patient Discharge D/C Tasks
8–10	5 to 15 min (average 5.6 min)
	Average Nurse had 2 patients

monitoring needed prior to transfer. So when the transporter finally shows up, the patient is no longer ready to leave.

- We normally hear we need more PACU beds, but this is almost never the root cause of the problem.

PACU Opportunities

The biggest opportunity in PACU is to reduce LOS while maintaining safety. What is driving our LOS in PACU? The answer should be recovery time, but this is not always the case. Many times, something as simple as lack of patient transportation can tie rooms up for hours. When all the rooms are tied up, we shut down the ORs, causing surgeons and staff to wait until the bottleneck is removed. This is extremely costly to the system and to physician satisfaction. The driver of recovery time is the anesthesia given to the patient. Sometimes, the patient is given a second "bump" due to a problem in surgery or a slow surgeon. This creates longer recovery times in PACU. There is quick-recovering anesthesia available, but it doesn't make sense to use them until such time as we can move the patients out of PACU. Lack of floor beds also creates PACU holds. We have found that 57% of the time we were delayed by lack of bed availability on the floors.

Other opportunities include 5S, point of use materials, standard work, workstation design, and overall layout. The 5S test: any nurse should be able to use any cart or find and reach everything at bedside setup within 3 seconds. Due to the critical nature of the patients, the Post-Op recovery units require nurse to patient ratios of 1:1 to 1:2 and that nurses are "tied" to patients in a similar manner to manufacturing, where operators are "tied" to machines (nurses don't like this comparison but the analogy is real). If we had better monitoring technology, nurses would not have to "watch" each patient.

Most hospitals have installed some type of fast track PACU process geared toward specific patients. The fast track includes a "step down" or "Phase II" recovery area with recliners and a nurse until the patient's family arrives. This area frees up PACU beds. The only problem with this type of system is that it can "mask" the real problem—we can't seem to get patients out of PACU. The organization had a centralized transportation service and the Post-Op recovery unit was listed seventh within the transport priority listing. Therefore, the Post-Op recovery unit nurses and technicians had to take the patients to the floor. In addition, this resulted in "boarding time" for the remaining patients and, at times, would back up cases and force patients to wait in the ORs for a Post-Op recovery bed. The VSM findings revealed that once patients had met the criteria to exit the Post-Op recovery unit, 99% of those patients were delayed by "waiting" for centralized transport. This represented the time it took from when transport received the call until a transporter was assigned, but it took another 30 min before transporters showed up and took patients to the floor.

Because this area was given a low level of priority, transporters sometimes were not assigned for more than an hour. When the Post-Op recovery unit couldn't wait for transport to show up, the request would be cancelled, and the recovery unit staff would transport the patients to the floor. Interestingly enough, transport did not keep track of the number of cancellations and, when a request was cancelled, they totally removed the elapsed time from their database; therefore, the data reported were skewed and under-reported to management. Because of the bottlenecks that were created, management thought more capacity was needed. Capacity was determined by looking at the overall average time that patients spent in the Post-Op recovery unit, which was about 3 hrs (which we were told is all the hospital is reimbursed).

The next step was to calculate available bed hours. There were 21 Post-Op recovery unit beds (one was isolation); however, only 16 beds were available based on staffing. The unit ran 12 hrs shifts, 9:00 a.m. to 9:00 p.m. This resulted in 12 hrs (of available time) × 16 (staff beds) = 192 bed hours of available time. This is then divided by a 3 hrs ALOS (which includes all the delays), yielding the ability to handle 64 patients in that 12 hrs period. They currently processed an average of 51 patients a day. If all the beds were utilized (staffed), the overall capacity would be 12 hrs × 20 beds = 240 bed hours, divided by 3 hrs (ALOS), yielding the ability to handle 80 patients in a 12 hrs shift. Once 64 patients is reached or if LOS rose above 3 hrs, then the Post-Op recovery unit would back up and result in a bottleneck for the OR and surgery would grind to a halt. To prevent this; either more staff would need to be brought in, Post-Op recovery beds opened, or more beds would need to be available on the units.

Result

The answer was not to build another unit; they just needed to staff the beds they currently had and move patients to the floors in a more timely fashion.

PACU Initial First Month Lean Results

- OR table hold hours per month reduced from 4.5 to 4.07
- Transport average delays 21 min to zero
- Productivity increased 4.66 to 4.41 worked hours per patient

Note: PACU holds are impacted by the available beds and the ability to manage capacity throughout the organization. Often organizations have not "worked" to understand inpatient flow and rely on PACU to hold patients or increase PACU beds as a release valve to inefficiencies in inpatient flow and does not address the root cause of the problem. Often ICU level nurses in PACU are left caring for patients who have already "met criteria" who could potentially be moved lower level of care and to an environment where their family members could readily visit.

Lesson Learned

When areas like surgery are managed in silos, each silo works on what is best for them, not the overall system and seldom is the patient even considered. The head of transport in the case discussed earlier was proud of his transport react times and was never evaluated otherwise by management. What is lacking is someone in charge of looking and improving the overall system and held accountable for the overall metrics. Even though most hospitals have a surgery director they seldom have authority or accountability over the entire stream.

Section IX Lean Leadership and Staff Readiness in the OR

Staff readiness is the last component of a successful surgical system. Staff must arrive on time and be scheduled to demand. One can tell when the surgical schedule is not level loaded, as the "easy way out" is to schedule a full complement of staff every day and then "census manage" people home early. It makes it "easy" for the manager, but very frustrating for employees. Traditional ORs operate with an anesthesiologist, surgeon(s), PA (RNFA or first assistant), nurse circulator, and surgical technician/nurse scrub.

Most surgeons want dedicated teams. Dedicated teams get to know the surgeon and the operations. For more on this, see the book, Complications.[4] The ability to have "specialized teams" is dependent on a variety of factors which include complexity and volume to support having that team, it is often difficult to allow surgeons to have the same team. There are pros and cons to this. The pros are that the surgeon's cases will go much faster with the same team and surgeries are probably safer and more efficient. The con is cross-training and keeping staff competencies, as staff will want to flex to other areas in times of low volume when they "need hours". The surgery director must make sure people can flex so they can fill their schedules properly, support add-on/emergencies, time-off coverage and weekend cases. Staff also needs ongoing Lean training in order to continue the pursuit of ongoing improvements. We have found that both of these wishes can live together, if scheduled properly.

When you are managing in the old OR batch environment, you probably spend most of your time fighting fires. In a Lean environment, the supervisor's role morphs into that of a coach or mentor. Most of the firefighting goes away and the leader's job is now to do the following: become a leader, explain, and teach and coach. The leader must understand Lean principles, be willing to apply Lean, and practice as a Lean leader. Gemba walks are critical in the OR environment to go and see what is actually occurring in order to understand what waste can be eliminated and to identify opportunities to improve. The leader must have standard work and set the standard for acceptable behaviors and eliminate undesirable behaviors (Table 11.14). The leader must continue to video and analyze, do continuous process improvement activities ("Kaizen"), and create ways to generate ideas for continuous improvement from all employees. The leader must cross-train the employees so they can be flexible. An example of a Lean initiative in one hospital's Operating Room who wanted to ensure that patients are consistently ready when surgeons wish to begin a procedure, reduce patient wait and walking time during the OR preparation process, and reduce inventory carrying costs.

CULTURE

We would be remiss if we did not at least mention that culture plays a critical role in being able to implement any Lean initiatives across the surgical continuum. In order to achieve success it takes senior level executives to lead the charge, remove the barriers and provide support as the resistance to change surfaces. This means the senior executives have to understand Lean Principles, unwaivering belief in the Lean System and have a compelling need to change. It is imperative executives play a visible role in the process improvement initiative and have a clear understanding of the challenges as they surface and the progress being made. Ensuring that area management and staff stay the course and maintain open lines of communication with physicians and frontline staff is critical as challenges within surgical services can play a significant role in the overall viability of the organization.

CONCLUSION

The surgical value stream creates some unique opportunities. Other areas that Lean has been applied to is the Sterile Processing Department (which is very similar to the manufacturing environment) there are many examples of these found across the internet. Applying Kanban principles within the surgical core, to set inventory levels, buffers, apply Just in Time, to gain space, flow and supply savings, etc. Additionally Lean has application in the case picking process to optimize flow and case accuracy. Although we have not covered every opportunity to eliminate waste and streamline the processes, we hope that providing some examples as to what others have uncovered on their quests to improve the surgical experience for surgeons, staff, and patients helped you gain insight into the possibilities.

---

[4] Atul Gawande, *Complications: A surgeon's Notes on an Imperfect Science* (New York: Metropolitan Books) 2003.

TABLE 11.14
Leader Standard Work—Pre-Op—PACU—PASS Manager

Job Step #	Manager Description (what they do)	Hours	Items to Look For:
	Daily		
	Labor reports		
	HR issues		
	Gemba walking × 3 departments		
	Attending to daily issues		
	Assist with AM starts in Pre-Op		
	Bi-Weekly		
	Ordering supplies biweekly		
	Weekly		
	Lean team meeting (entire day)		
	Lean weekly checkout		
	6 S audits in each department		
	Weekly meeting with OR director		
	Lean weekly		
	Meeting with clinical leader		
	Sit in on weekly huddles in each dept		
	Update Five Ups for each department		
	Review metrics for each department		
	Make sure huddle boards are up to date		
	Review and update control plan		
	Review Leader Standard Work		
	Make sure action items are updated for each department		
	Follow up on standard order rollout		
	Bi-Monthly		
	Penimer data verification bimonthly × 3 departments		
	Managers meeting		
	Monthly		
	Monthly variance reports		
	Monthly licenses verification		
	Monthly anesthesia meeting		
	Monthly joint meeting		
	Monthly charge nurse meeting		
	monthly tollgate		
	Staff meeting		
	surgical services council meeting monthly		
	Quarterly		
	Quarterly LDI		
	Totals seconds		
	Totals minutes		

Section X Overarching Results[5]

- Average patient wait time dropped from 126 min to 75 min – a 40% improvement.
- The average distance walked by patients fell from 1,646 ft. to 326 ft. – an 80% reduction.
- Better inventory management saved $182,000 and eliminated a restocking procedure that was consuming 600 nursing hours a year.

Other Hospital Results—Surgery

- $2 million in cost savings.
- 7.8% decrease in labor expense per case.
- Improved pre-admission testing first pass yield from 5% to 80%.
- 48% reduction patient in to cut.
- 27% reduction – patient out to patient cut.
- Increased nurse satisfaction; improved flow of materials from SPD to OR room.
- Core Stock: Freed up over $100,000 of stock in multiple locations by standardizing each area and use of group tech matrix.
- CVT Service: Increased number of cases done each week by over 10%.
- Improved ordering process (simplified) for cultures taken during surgery to be sent for testing.
- Heart services videotaped. Opportunities identified.
- Identified opportunity to reduce inventory by over 80% and convert it to VMI.
- Reduced ED diversions from 26 hrs to 6 hrs (now 0 hr).
- Reduced surgery holds from 6 hrs per month to zero.
- Reduced PACU holds from 624 hrs to 157 hrs per month.

Pre-Testing Results

- Volume total visits 63.51 to 87.7
- # Completed charts 41% to 90%
- % Patients to pre-testing 46% to% 80%
- Productivity 1.80 to 1.35 hrs per patient
- Pre-testing FTE's only increased from 15.8 to 15.96
- Days ahead on telephone interviews from 0 to 5.5

Pre-Op

- % Charts completed with orders 80.3%
- Hours patients arrive prior to OR schedule 151 min to 120 min
- Pre-Op TLT Time/PT from 83 min to 45 min
- On time case starts (no buffer) 44.3% to 75%
- Productivity through from 1.58 to 1.49 hrs/patient
- Arrival in Pre-Op prior to OR schedule 79.8 min to 60 min
- OR Table hold hours per month 4.5 to 4.07

Other Misc. Results

- Transport average Delays decreased 21 min to zero
- Productivity 4.66 to 4.41
- Implemented a process to reduce the number of lost OR Instruments
- Standardized operating room supply design and set-up
- Standardized supply par levels for operating room

---

[5] These actual results are from various hospitals whose names are not mentioned because they were not written up in approved case studies. This is the reason some results appear duplicated with different result numbers.

- New instrument and supply location blueprint and process complete
- Visual management plan applied to operating room supply and equipment rooms
- Lean ease picking process completed and implemented
- 5S the supply room with new shelving material, bin labels, min - max quantities

CONCLUSION

STEPS FOR YOUR SURGICAL/PROCEDURAL LEAN PROJECT CHECKLIST

1. Define Business Problem you are trying to solve
2. Develop the preliminary scope - Input and Output boundaries
   Note: Are you looking for quick wins i.e., 5s; or large change - multi-week to several month initiative that will encompass "many Kaizens" for systematic transformational change
3. Determine the preliminary metrics
   Note: try to avoid global metrics such as "improve patient experience as these have too many "x's" that impact the big "Y" and will be difficult to show results
4. Set the Timeline (It will vary with scope depth and breadth of initiative)
5. Identify Stakeholders
6. Create the Shared Vision - driven by executive sponsor
7. Compile the Team
   - Executive Sponsor (barrier removal and executive owner)
   - Operational Owner (barrier removal, learning, sustain)
8. Recommendations of team members (it can depend on the scope/area defined – example if you focus on OR you may want SPD staff engaged so they can see your process and remove barriers as all the departments have interdependencies and can gain empathy for barrier removal etc.)
   - Lean Practitioner
   - Nursing staff: OR, Pre-test, PreOp and PACU(1-4) (remove barriers and propagate learnings and empathy)
   - Surgical Technician (remove barriers and propagate learnings and empathy)
   - Sterile Processing Staff (remove barriers and propagate learnings and empathy)
   - Case Picking Staff (remove barriers and propagate learnings and empathy)
   - Physician Surgeon and Anesthesia (advisory and review)
   - Materials (remove barriers and propagate learnings and empathy)
   - Unit Nursing/ED (remove barriers and propagate learnings and empathy)
   - Other Surgical in system if available (to transfer learning)

   Other extended team members
   - Finance (advisory for reviewing data and saving)
   - HR (advisory) - if you change roles and responsibilities or staffing model
   - Marketing (advisory if planning to leverage data to do marketing)
   - Analyst (access if the team needs helps analyzing data - to manage by fact)
   - Construction or capital dollars to purchase items for visual management or aligning resources to work (moving faxes, computers, desks etc) (depending on the initiative)
9. Outline Training methodology
   - Team, leader training, and extended team training (helpful for barrier removal so they understand what you are trying to do)
   - Basic Lean Concepts
   - Tool application
10. Make a simple project plan (roadmap) - can be done formally in project or in excel or word, this will keep you on track make sure it has tasks with defined owners, target dates, deliverables and status with milestones for go-no-go

11. Determine tools (refer to BASICS Model) - include activities in plan
12. Develop Communication Plan
13. Determine what you are going to Value stream map (high level and next level down if necessary)

    For example:

    - You may want a high level map that maps the patient from initial decision to have surgery through delivery to ICU/Unit to identify your greatest areas of opportunity
    - This will lead you to other VSM examples:
      - Surgical Decision to Pre-Op (this would cover scheduling, pre-testing and pre-op ready to surgery) – you may need to break this up into Inpatient and Outpatient as they may look very different
      - Arrival in Pre-Op to Wheels In (Surgery) or to Cut-time (On-Time Starts and other case delays) – In and Outpatient
      - Wheels in to Cut Time (for all patients)
      - Inpatient Decision to Wheels In – to review the readiness from floor/Unit all the way to surgery room – to uncover delays for ON-TIME starts
    - Map a surgical tray from end of case (in OR) to reassembly (SPD)
    - Value stream mapping will provide the opportunity to determine
    - "Quick wins" - things you can do immediately to improve process (eliminate waste)
    - Narrow scope of area with greatest opportunity

14. Develop roadmap for improvements
15. Set the Team up to work

    - Set-up a work area for team (preferably close to area frontline)
    - Supplies to include access to camera - stills and video, computer, printer etc
    - Provide access to 'data" and reports (may have to work with information technology department)

16. Formally kick-off the initiative

    - Executive sponsor to define expectations and provide role clarity
    - Establish check points - for barrier removal, milestones and work the "plan" to stay on track and focused

17. Revise scope if needed once opportunities are identified through Value Stream Mapping
18. Finalize metrics
19. Remember to re-visit stake-holders analysis
20. Work the communication plan
21. Celebrate the quick wins
22. Pilot, the change, it's ok to fail, as long as you learn from your failures
23. Re-pilot!!
24. Create sustain plan - Operation owner needs to own this! - include a review team and establish cycles of improvement to propagate learnings and achieve desired results

    Keys to success:

    - Executive participation; you get what you expect
    - Address barriers
    - Manage by fact!
    - Communicate often !!
    - Share lessons learned!
    - Celebrate with the team
    - Monitor Sustain plan
    - Ongoing cycles of improvement – embed "waste removal" as part of daily work – "it's the way we do business"!!!

For details please review to the core book chapters, reference BASICS model.

Index